Star

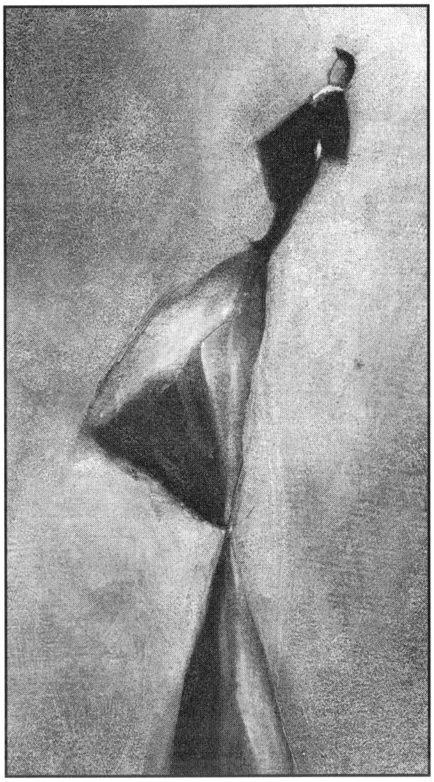

Crime and Criminology

Contending Ideas and Opinions

Academic Editor
Steven H. Cooper, M.S.
University of California, Irvine

Coursewise publishing inc.

Bellevue • Boulder • Dubuque • Madison • St. Paul

Our mission at **Coursewise** is to help students make connections—linking theory to practice and the classroom to the outside world. Learners are motivated to synthesize ideas when course materials are placed in a context they recognize. By providing gateways to contemporary and enduring issues, **Coursewise** publications will expand students' awareness of and context for the course subject.

For more information on **Coursewise,** visit us at our web site: http://www.coursewise.com

To order an examination copy, contact Houghton Mifflin Sixth Floor Media: 800–565–6247 (voice); 800–565–6236 (fax).

Coursewise Publishing Editorial Staff

Thomas Doran, ceo/publisher: Environmental Science/Geography/Journalism/Marketing/Speech
Edgar Laube, publisher: Geography/Political Science/Psychology/Sociology
Linda Meehan Avenarius, publisher: **Courselinks**™
Sue Pulvermacher-Alt, publisher: Education/Health/Gender Studies
Victoria Putman, publisher: Anthropology/Philosophy/Religion
Tom Romaniak, publisher: Business/Criminal Justice/Economics
Kathleen Schmitt, publishing assistant
Gail Hodge, executive producer

Coursewise Production Staff

Lori A. Blosch, permissions coordinator
Mary Monner, production coordinator
Victoria Putman, production manager

Note: Readings in this book appear exactly as they were published. Thus, inconsistencies in style and usage among the different readings are likely.

Cover photo: Ian Lawrence/1998/nonstock

Interior design and cover design by Jeff Storm

Library of Congress Catalog Card Number: 99-067976

ISBN 0-395-97373–2

Printed in the United States of America by Coursewise Publishing, Inc.
7 North Pinckney Street, Suite 346, Madison, WI 53703

10 9 8 7 6 5 4 3 2 1

from the **Publisher**

Tom Romaniak
Coursewise Publishing

Crime. You hear about it all the time. The media constantly inform us about the latest sensational crime and whether the crime rate is rising or falling. And virtually all politicians appear to be tough on crime. Have you ever heard a politician state that prison sentences should be reduced or that more prisoners should be granted parole? I didn't think so.

But have you ever analyzed the issues surrounding crime and criminology? Are politicians reducing crime with the legislation they pass? For example, have tougher sentences on illegal drug possession reduced the number of drug-related crimes, or has our political stance on illegal drugs actually caused the crime rate to increase? There has been much debate about the illegal drug issue and whether current laws are causing our prisons and jails to grow out of control. Are we targeting the right offenders? Are we putting people in prison who don't belong there? Should we instead focus our efforts on prevention, or should we simply throw in the towel and legalize drugs?

This is just one of the many crime and criminology issues that you will find in *Stand! Crime and Criminology.* This reader presents the many sides of various criminological issues involving behavior, law enforcement, and the rights and treatment of criminals.

Steven Cooper has done a tremendous job of selecting issues and readings that will be of interest to you. He worked closely with the members of his Editorial Board to make sure that the readings were not only interesting, but also thought provoking and balanced. I want to thank Steven and every member of the Editorial Board for their conscientious efforts. I think they have done a great job.

But my opinion isn't the only one that counts. Let us know what *you* think of this volume and the corresponding **Courselinks**™ site for Crime and Criminology. How did we do? Are the issues appropriate? What about the reading selection? At Coursewise, we want to continually improve the quality of the learning materials we provide. We can't do this without input from you. So please, take the time to drop us a line. My email address is tomr@coursewise.com

Tom Romaniak
Publisher

STAND!

Steven H. Cooper is an adjunct professor at California State University, Fullerton, and is completing his Ph.D. in criminology, law, and society from the University of California, Irvine. He just finished his tenth year of service in the United States Army. He served on active duty for four years as an infantryman and military police officer, and currently is a reservist in the military police corps.

Cooper's bachelor's degree is in criminal justice from California State University, Sacramento. As an undergraduate, Cooper was active in numerous organizations and served as the national vice-president of Alpha Phi Sigma (The National Criminal Justice Honor Society). After completing his master's in criminology at Florida State University, Cooper transferred to the University of California, Irvine, where he is completing his Ph.D.

Cooper also edited Perspectives: Criminology (Coursewise, 2000), and he is currently co-editing a book on policing. His next goals include a book on racial profiling, an edited volume on ethics, and a textbook on criminology and criminal justice. He continually writes and presents papers for both the American Society of Criminology and the Academy of Criminal Justice Sciences, and reviews manuscripts for the Journal of Criminal Justice Education. Cooper also serves as advisory board member for the Criminal Justice Distance Learning Consortium and has recently created two CD-ROM supplements for Frank Schmalleger's textbooks (Criminal Justice Today and Criminal Law Today, both published by Prentice-Hall).

Cooper's research interests involve technology, education, police, and disparities in the criminal justice system. He teaches courses in research methods and criminological theory, and enjoys incorporating new technologies, such as the Internet, email, and web-based presentations, into his class.

from the Academic Editor

Steven H. Cooper, M.S.
University of California, Irvine

Why Study Crime and Criminology?

Criminology and criminal justice are the fastest growing academic disciplines in the country. Everybody's talking about crime, a lot of people are criminals, and each day, the number of people working in the criminal justice system increases. The bottom line is that these fields are downright exciting, dynamic, and emerging!

To facilitate a meaningful forum for you to learn, I offer some guidelines that you may find helpful as you explore the fascinating, yet highly controversial issues presented in this reader:

1. There are no right or wrong answers in criminology and criminal justice.
2. In many cases, the challenges are very difficult.
3. Viewpoints of criminologists and the public often differ.
4. We need to constantly critique existing ideologies.
5. We must understand and accept the varying perspectives of our friends, families, and colleagues because of guideline 1.

A growing body of research demonstrates that many Americans hold several misconceptions about crime. For example, even though crime has generally been decreasing for the last several years, studies consistently show that the public's fear of crime is increasing.

A tough challenge lies ahead if we are to successfully address the issue of crime and public policy. First and foremost, criminologists must conduct challenging and labor-intensive research. But, as some would argue, they must also ensure that the criminal justice system responds effectively to crime and criminals. This is problematic because many academics believe that research should be objective and free from public policy. Moreover, they contend that the findings should "speak for themselves" and not require interpretation. The bottom line is that highly regarded criminological work often is not presented in a manner that lends itself to practical application by practitioners (police officers, attorneys, correctional officials, etc.).

There are only a handful of criminologists (defined as those holding a Ph.D. in criminology or a closely related field who conduct criminological research). However, the people working in the criminal justice system—who deal with public policy, crime legislation, budgets, and crime prevention programs every single day—number in the thousands! It's this group—the practitioners—who are charged with applying the research knowledge acquired by criminologists to current social issues. To that end, I suggest that we find a way to assist practitioners with the contributions of criminologists.

Although many of the readings in this volume are academic pieces grounded in research, they will help you to understand the various perspectives that certain groups assert. This background will allow you to make more informed decisions when, as a member of the criminal justice system, you are faced with a challenge.

The real challenge is not deciding *what* we should do about crime and criminals, but determining *how* to effectively organize ourselves to better respond to crime. This requires the development of strategies for confronting crime. Collaboration, information dissemination, and leadership may be just as important in the criminal justice system as the actual criminological research that we use to respond to the current crime phenomenon.

Thinking about These Issues in a Larger Context

The growth of the criminal justice system results in controversy, and ultimately, disparities. The number of controversial issues we will face in the future will most likely increase, rather than decrease, and no single issue is all important. What is significant is that we find practical mechanisms for addressing pressing social issues. If we can do that, then we may be able to efficiently and fairly handle controversial issues as they arise.

In one way or another, most of you have already been exposed to the controversial issues that this reader addresses. As you read, keep in mind that the readings do not "solve" these issues. In fact, because they often highlight the grave contradictory assertions of their authors, they may lead you to thinking about new questions.

Authors on both sides of each issue have compelling arguments, but no particular issue is the nexus of our system of justice. Our criminal justice system exists because of the contending ideologies that various groups and individuals in society share.

I Look Forward to Hearing from You!

I hope that you enjoy the readings in *Stand! Crime and Criminology* and that they inspire spirited discussions with professors, colleagues, friends, and family. Please feel free to drop me a note and let me know what worked for you, what could be improved, or any other suggestions that you may have for the second edition. My email address is coopers@uci.edu. I look forward to hearing from you!

Acknowledgments

First and foremost, I want to thank Tom Romaniak of Coursewise Publishing, who provided strong leadership and superb guidance. If it were not for Tom's tenacity and clear goal setting, this edited volume probably would not have gone to press before my retirement! Moreover, I benefited immensely from Tom's working knowledge of the academic field of criminology and of contemporary and controversial issues inundating our discipline. I now sit here and wonder why Tom is not listed as a co-editor. Thank you, Tom!

Next, I would like to thank the Editorial Board members for their professional and critical guidance, feedback, and mentoring. I also appreciate Joan Petersilia's extensive feedback and direction. Finally, my friends and family have been wonderful (!), understanding that my preoccupation with this project was not an avoidance of our relationship but, rather, a dedication to something I hope is beneficial to you. Thanks, everyone!

Finally, I would like to dedicate this book to a cause: advancing criminology and criminal justice. I hope that criminologists can continue to produce work that helps us to establish criminology and criminal justice as autonomous academic disciplines with their own independent body of knowledge.

Editorial Board

We wish to thank the following instructors for their assistance. Their many suggestions not only contributed to the construction of this volume, but also to the ongoing development of our Crime and Criminology web site.

Alejandro del Carmen

University of Texas at Arlington

Alejandro del Carmen received his bachelor's degree from Florida International University, and his master's and doctoral degrees from Florida State University. He is an assistant professor of criminology and criminal justice and director of the Center for Criminal Justice Research and Training at the University of Texas at Arlington. He has taught several courses in the areas of criminal justice, criminology, corrections, law, and victimology. Outside academic work, he enjoys listening to Frank Sinatra.

Cecil Greek

Florida State University

Cecil Greek attended Eastern College and the New School for Social Research, earning a Ph.D. in sociology in 1983. His doctoral dissertation, "The Religious Roots of American Sociology," was later published by Garland Press. He has written on antipornography crusading, the use of forfeiture penalties, and juvenile justice. He is currently an associate professor of criminology at Florida State University, and is in charge of Internet-based distance education initiatives. Over the past five years, he has been using the Internet as a teaching/research tool in his classes and for personal research. He developed the Criminal Justice Page, a web site with links to criminal justice research information worldwide at: http://www.criminology.fsu.edu/cj.html.

John C. Harris

University of Wisconsin, Oshkosh

John C. Harris is a former prosecutor, with experience in child abuse and other criminal cases. He has also been a defense attorney and civil litigator. He received his J.D. from the University of California's Hastings College of Law in San Francisco and his Ph.D. in social ecology (criminology specialty) from the University of California, Irvine. His research interests include the implementation of criminal sentencing reforms, medical-legal issues, and white-collar crime. He currently teaches in the Department of Public Affairs at the University of Wisconsin in Oshkosh.

Tom Kando

California State University, Sacramento

Tom Kando received a master's degree (1967) and a Ph.D. (1969) in sociology from the University of Minnesota. He has published six books and numerous articles. His books include *The Achievement of Gender Identity* (1973), *Leisure and Popular Culture* (1975,1980), *Social Interaction* (1977), *Sexual Behavior and Family Life* (1978), and *Readings in Criminology* (1995). Kando was an assistant professor at the University of California, Riverside (1972–1973), and an associate professor at Penn State (1977–1979). Since 1979, he has been a professor of sociology at California State University, Sacramento. He has published articles in refereed journals, as well as in popular media, such as *The Wall Street Journal, Sacramento Bee,* and *LA Examiner.*

William A. "Tony" Lavelle

Private Consultant

William A. "Tony" Lavelle received his bachelor's degree in communications studies and his master's degree in criminal justice from California State University, Sacramento. From 1984 through 1996, Lavelle served as a U.S. Air Force Officer in the Security Police, specializing the last two years in counterterrorism. From 1996 through 1998, Lavelle was a lecturer in the Criminal Justice Division at California State University, Sacramento, and he currently works in the private sector under contract with the Department of Defense.

Tom O'Connor

North Carolina Wesleyan College

Tom O'Connor is an assistant professor of justice studies at North Carolina Wesleyan College. He holds a doctorate in criminology from the Indiana University of Pennsylvania, a master's in criminal justice from the University of Illinois, and a bachelor's in sociology from Knox College. His interests are in theoretical and applied criminology and the computerization of law enforcement. He contributes to journals such as *Security Administration,* and to books such as *Criminal Psychology and Forensic Technology.* He is the webmaster for MegaLinks in Criminal Justice (http://faculty.ncwc.edu/toconnor).

Matthew Robinson

Appalachian State University

Matthew Robinson earned his Ph.D. in August 1997 from Florida State University and is an assistant professor of criminal justice at Appalachian State University in North Carolina. His research focuses primarily on criminological theory, criminal victimization, crime prevention, and criminal justice education. His most recent publications appear in the *British Journal of Criminology; Journal of Crime and Justice;* the *Advances in Criminological Theory* series; *Journal of Security Administration; International Journal of Risk, Security, and Crime Prevention; Environment and Behavior; Howard Journal of Criminal Justice;* and *Journal of Criminal Justice Education.*

Frank Schmalleger

The Justice Research Association

Frank Schmalleger is director of The Justice Research Association, a private consulting firm and "think-tank" focusing on issues of crime and justice. Schmalleger holds degrees from the University of Notre Dame and The Ohio State University. From 1976 to 1994, he taught criminal justice courses at the University of North Carolina at Pembroke, where he chaired the university's Department of Sociology, Social Work, and Criminal Justice for 16 years. Schmalleger is the author of numerous articles and many books, including the widely used *Criminal Justice Today, Criminal Law Today, Criminology Today,* and *Criminal Justice: A Brief Introduction.*

Brion Sever

Monmouth University

Brion Sever is currently an assistant professor in the Criminal Justice Department at Monmouth University and a consultant for the Asbury Park Police Department, New Jersey. He received his Ph.D. in criminology and criminal justice from Florida State University and is currently working on several research projects on the topic areas of deterrence, corrections, race and policing, and academic integrity. He has recently published articles in *Corrections Management Quarterly* and *Dialogue* and received funded grants from the Culpepper Foundation and Florida State University.

WiseGuide Introduction

Critical Thinking and Bumper Stickers

Question Authority

The bumper sticker said: Question Authority. This is a simple directive that goes straight to the heart of critical thinking. The issue is not whether the authority is right or wrong; it's the questioning process that's important. Questioning helps you develop awareness and a clearer sense of what you think. That's critical thinking.

Critical thinking is a new label for an old approach to learning—that of challenging all ideas, hypotheses, and assumptions. In the physical and life sciences, systematic questioning and testing methods (known as the scientific method) help verify information, and objectivity is the benchmark on which all knowledge is pursued. In the social sciences, however, where the goal is to study people and their behavior, things get fuzzy. It's one thing for the chemistry experiment to work out as predicted, or for the petri dish to yield a certain result. It's quite another matter, however, in the social sciences, where the subject is ourselves. Objectivity is harder to achieve.

Although you'll hear critical thinking defined in many different ways, it really boils down to analyzing the ideas and messages that you receive. What are you being asked to think or believe? Does it make sense, objectively? Using the same facts and considerations, could you reasonably come up with a different conclusion? And, why does this matter in the first place? As the bumper sticker urged, question authority. Authority can be a textbook, a politician, a boss, a big sister, or an ad on television. Whatever the message, learning to question it appropriately is a habit that will serve you well for a lifetime. And in the meantime, thinking critically will certainly help you be course wise.

Getting Connected

This reader is a tool for connected learning. This means that the readings and other learning aids explained here will help you to link classroom theory to real-world issues. They will help you to think critically and to make long-lasting learning connections. Feedback from both instructors and students has helped us to develop some suggestions on how you can wisely use this connected learning tool.

WiseGuide Pedagogy

A wise reader is better able to be a critical reader. Therefore, we want to help you get wise about the articles in this reader. Each section of a *Stand!* reader has three tools to help you: the WiseGuide Intro, the WiseGuide Wrap-Up, and the Frame the Debate review form.

WiseGuide Intro

WiseGuide Intro

In the "Introduction" to each section, the Academic Editor gives you an overview of the issues covered in that section. In the "WiseGuide Intro" for each issue, the Academic Editor explains why particular articles were selected and what's important about them. You'll also find questions designed to stimulate critical thinking. Wise students will keep these questions in mind as they read the articles for each issue. When you finish reading the articles for an issue, check your understanding. Can you answer the questions? If not, go back and reread the articles. The Academic Editor has written sample responses for many of the questions, and you'll find these online at the **Courselinks**™ site for this book. More about **Courselinks** in a minute. . . .

WiseGuide Wrap-Up

Be course wise and develop a thorough understanding of the topics covered in this course. The WiseGuide Wrap-Up at the end of each issue will help you do just that with concluding comments or summary points that repeat what's most important to understand from the articles you just read.

In addition, we try to get you wired up by providing a list of select Internet resources—what we call R.E.A.L. web sites because they're **R**elevant, **E**nhanced, **A**pproved, and **L**inked. The information at R.E.A.L. sites will enhance your understanding of a topic. (Remember to use your Passport and start at http://www.courselinks.com so that if any of these sites have changed, you'll have the latest link.)

Frame the Debate Review Form

At the end of the book is the Frame the Debate review form. Your instructor may ask you to complete this form as an assignment or for extra credit. If nothing else, consider doing it on your own to help you critically think about the readings for each issue.

Prompts at the end of each article encourage you to complete this review form. Feel free to copy the form and use it as needed.

The Courselinks™ Site

The **Courselinks** site for your course area is a wonderful world of integrated web resources designed to help you with your course work. This is where the readings in this book and the key topics of your course are linked to an exciting array of online learning tools. Here you will find carefully selected readings, web links, quizzes, worksheets, and more, tailored to your course and approved as connected learning tools. The ever-changing, always interesting **Courselinks** site features a number of carefully integrated resources designed to help you be course wise. These include:

http://www.courselinks.com

- **R.E.A.L. Sites** At the core of a **Courselinks** site is the list of R.E.A.L. sites. This is a select group of web sites for studying, not surfing. Like the readings in this book, these sites have been selected, reviewed, and approved by the Academic Editor and the Editorial Board. The R.E.A.L. sites are arranged by topic and are annotated with short descriptions and key words to make them easier for you to use for reference or research. With R.E.A.L. sites, you're studying approved resources within seconds—and not wasting precious time surfing unproven sites.
- **Editor's Choice** Here you'll find updates on news related to your course, with links to the actual online sources. This is also where we'll tell you about changes to the site and about online events.

- **Course Overview** This is a general description of the typical course in this area of study. While your instructor will provide specific course objectives, this overview helps you place the course in a generic context and offers you an additional reference point.
- **Take a Stand!** Register your opinion about the issues presented in your *Stand!* reader online. You can see what students and faculty members across the country are thinking about the controversial issues presented in your text. Then add your own vote.
- **www.orksheet** Focus your trip to a R.E.A.L. site with the www.orksheet. Each of the 10 to 15 questions will prompt you to take in the best that site has to offer. Use this tool for self-study, or if required, email it to your instructor.
- **Course Quiz** The questions on this self-scoring quiz are related to articles in the reader, information at R.E.A.L. sites, and other course topics, and will help you pinpoint areas you need to study. Only you will know your score—it's an easy, risk-free way to keep pace!
- **Topic Key** The online Topic Key is a listing of the main topics in your course, and it correlates with the Topic Key that appears in this reader. This handy reference tool also links directly to those R.E.A.L. sites that are especially appropriate to each topic, bringing you integrated online resources within seconds!
- **Message Center** Share your ideas with fellow students and instructors, in your class or in classes around the world, by using the Message Center. There are links to both a real-time chat room and a message forum, which are accessible all day, every day. Watch for scheduled CourseChat events throughout the semester.
- **Student Lounge** Drop by the Student Lounge, a virtual "hangout" with links to professional associations in your course area, online article review forms, and site feedback forms. Take a look around and give us your feedback. We're open to remodeling the Lounge per your suggestions.

Building Better Stand! Readers

Please tell us what you think of this *Stand!* volume so we can improve the next one. Here's how you can help:

1. Visit our **Coursewise** site at: http://www.coursewise.com
2. Click on *Stand!* Then select the Building Better *Stand!* Readers Form for your book.
3. Forms and instructions for submission are available online.

Tell us what you think—did the readings and online materials help you make some learning connections? Were some materials more helpful than others? Thanks in advance for helping us build better *Stand!* readers.

Student Internships

If you enjoy evaluating these articles or would like to help us evaluate the **Courselinks** site for this course, check out the **Coursewise** Student Internship Program. For more information, visit: http://www.coursewise.com/intern.html

Contents

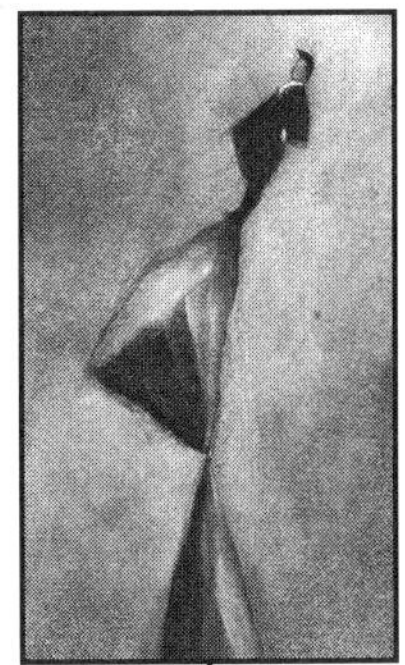

section 1
Causes of Crime

Issue 1: Are Criminals Biologically Predisposed to Committing Crimes?

Diana Fishbein, a prominent criminological researcher in biological causes of deviance, argues in Reading 1 that there is much empirical support for the role of biological factors in antisocial behavior. She reviews much of the literature from the behavioral sciences and posits that a multidisciplinary approach to studying criminality will yield greater results in terms of addressing our crime problem. However, this type of research has been highly controversial. In Reading 2, Lee Ellis claims that mainstream criminology must take note of the advancements in biologically based criminological research if, as an academic discipline, it is to contribute to crime reduction.

Issue 2: What Is the Best Way to Deter Criminals from Offending?

On the right, William Bennett, co-chairman of the National Council on Crime in America, argues in Reading 3 that we need to shut the revolving doors on criminals and "get tough" on crime. Advocating for prison reform on the left, James Bryne and Mary Brewster note that our criminal justice system is less than effective in responding to the needs of both offenders and society. As a result, they call for alternative measures to reduce recidivism and prison overcrowding.

Issue 8: Should We Decriminalize Drugs?

In Reading 15, James Q. Wilson, one of our most prominent social scientists and professor of management and public policy at UCLA, argues from a moral standpoint against the legalization of drugs. In Reading 16, on the other hand, Ethan Nadelmann addresses many of the concerns raised by decriminalization of drugs. He also analyzes the history of drug prohibition and parallels this issue with prohibition of alcohol.

Issue 9: Should Drug Pushers Lose Their Property?

In Reading 17, William Schroeder, chief of the Legal Forfeiture Unit of the FBI, examines the technicalities of forfeiture laws and provides law enforcement agencies with moral encouragement to use civil forfeiture as a viable tool against various criminal enterprises. In Reading 18, Eric Jensen (professor of sociology at the University of Idaho) and Jurg Gerber (professor of criminal justice at Sam Houston State University) express philosophical and legal opposition to asset forfeiture.

Issue 10: Does the Death Penalty Deter Crime?

Michael Radelet and Ronald Akers, both professors of sociology at the University of Florida, surveyed former presidents of three professional criminology organizations to determine their views on the death penalty. The results of that study, presented in Reading 19, show that most of these experts feel that the death penalty is not a deterrent to crime. In Reading 20, Walter Berns, resident scholar at the American Enterprise Institute, and Joseph Bessette, professor of government and ethics at Claremont McKenna College, argue from a utilitarian standpoint that the death penalty is acceptable and warranted.

Issue 14: Does the Harm Outweigh the Good with Public Notification of Sex Offenders?

In Reading 27, Police Chief John Turner discusses how well public notification has worked in his community and how he went about notifying the community of the presence of a sexual offender in his neighborhood. In Reading 28, Bonnie Steinbock explains the challenges associated with community notification laws. According to Steinbock, community notification laws have proven ineffective, have placed innocent people in harm's way, and are misdirected.

At **Coursewise,** we're publishing connected learning tools. That means that the book you are holding is only a part of this publication. You'll also want to harness the integrated resources that **Coursewise** has developed at the fun and highly useful **Courselinks™** web site for *Stand! Crime and Criminology.* Visit http://www.coursewise.com.

Topic Key

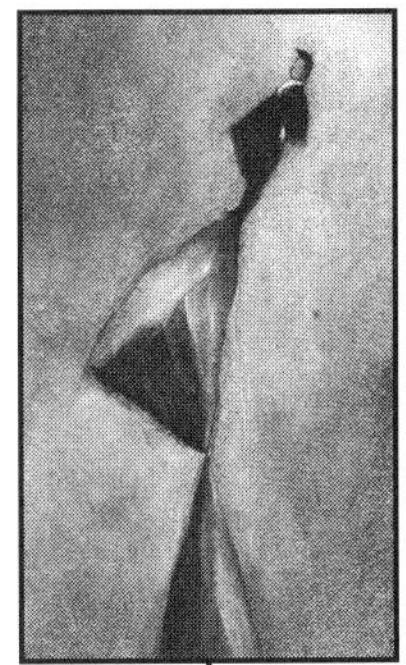

This Topic Key is an important tool for learning. It will help you integrate this reader into your course studies. Listed below, in alphabetical order, are important topics covered in this volume. Below each topic you'll find the reading numbers and titles, and R.E.A.L. web site addresses, relating to that topic. Note that the Topic Key might not include every topic your instructor chooses to emphasize. If you don't find the topic you're looking for in the Topic Key, check the index or the online topic key at the **Courselinks™** site.

Discrimination

Drugs

Office of National Drug Control Policy (ONDCP)
http://www.whitehousedrugpolicy.gov/

Drug Enforcement Agency
http://www.usdoj.gov/dea/index.htm

National Clearinghouse for Alcohol and Drug Information
http://www.health.org/

Due Process

Forfeiture Endangers American Rights
http://www.fear.org/

Economic Impact

Ethics

Human Rights

Human Rights Watch
http://www.hrw.org/reports98/police/index.htm

Police

Police Complaint Center
http://www.policeabuse.com/

Police Officer's Internet Directory
http://www.officer.com/

The Police Executive Research Forum
http://www.policeforum.org/

Punishment

Death Penalty Information Center
http://www.essential.org/dpic/

Recidivism

Rehabilitation

STAND! **section 1**

Causes of Crime

Introduction

All we know about crime is that it is committed mostly by young people, most of whom are male. Everything else is open for debate. Central to the study of crime and criminology is the concept of correlation. A criminologist studies why people commit crime and tries to determine the degree of association between two or more variables. For example, a criminologist might ask, "What, if any, is the association (or correlation) between people who use drugs and people who commit crimes?"

While criminologists are gradually adding to the growing body of criminological literature, we still don't know why people commit crimes. Numerous theories attempt to explain deviance, but no single explanation can account for all crime. In fact, the best theories only help us to understand a tiny portion of the question. However, that doesn't mean that we stop searching for clues.

This section begins with an exploration of a major area of criminological theory: biological causes of deviance. Readings 1 and 2 review the classical debate of nature versus nurture and examine the relationship, if any, that genetic structure plays in violence and aggression.

Another way of studying the cause of crime is to look at it from a deterrence perspective, as discussed in Readings 3 and 4. People who have benefited from programs and techniques that have been successful at reducing crime can be compared with people who did not benefit from these efforts. Such comparisons may offer clues as to why certain offenders are deterred from recidivating. This, in turn, may help identify some of the underlying causes or correlates of crime.

This section concludes with an analysis of the crime rate in Readings 5 and 6. Rates of offending have a profound impact on the study of crime and provide one more piece of the puzzle regarding the causes of crime.

When criminological research is conducted in a proper manner, its purpose is to understand the criminal event, the victim, and the perpetrator. Criminologists do not study crime so that they can excuse the actions of the wrongdoer, but so that the knowledge can be used to create a safer community and to help those requiring assistance. Criminologists do not seek to excuse or condone criminal behavior. The criminal offender should not be the focus of their efforts. The greater duty is to protect and assist law-abiding citizens, and this is best accomplished through extensive and rigorous criminological research.

As you read the articles in this section, ask yourself which ideas make sense and which don't. Think about your experience with criminals, if any, and begin to analyze how criminals are different from (and similar to!) law-abiding people. Then consider the best way to prevent crime, given what we know and our current resources.

Are Criminals Biologically Predisposed to Committing Crimes?

ISSUE 1

Take a Closer Look

1. What are the implications raised by biological research in criminology?
2. If genetics contributes to delinquency, then how can people who commit crimes cease on their own without medical intervention?
3. Is there evidence to support the notion of a "crime gene"?
4. If genetics is at least partially responsible for criminal behavior, what does this mean for the future of our criminal justice system?
5. According to Ellis, what are the major obstacles that criminologists need to overcome?

WiseGuide Intro

Numerous theories attempt to explain why people commit crimes. For the most part, the theories are intricate, theoretical, and grounded in criminological research. However, no theoretical assertion is as controversial as the one that suggests a biological basis for criminality. In modern times, we make two broad distinctions concerning deviance: Either something about our society forces people to commit crimes, or the individuals who commit crimes are flawed in some way.

Generally speaking, most criminologists are trained in sociology programs. As a result, they teach and write that the social factors that come to bear upon an individual explain most criminality. On the other hand, researchers who have been trained in the biological or medical sciences feel that other factors, such as the genetic makeup or the psychological state of the offender, are primary contributors to criminal behavior.

To study how genetics contributes to deviance, the National Institute of Health (NIH) scheduled a conference entitled "Genetic Factors in Crime" for October 1992. Due to the moral outrage of public interest groups and researchers, the NIH withdrew financial support for the meeting. Those opposed to the conference were concerned about the racial implications of such research and asserted that social factors are responsible for crime and deviance, not genetic predisposition.

Around the same time that the proposed conference was to take place, the National Research Council (NRC) issued a report, called "Understanding and Preventing Violence," that summarized what is known about the social, psychological, and biological causes of violent behavior. Concerning the role of genetics and crime, the NRC concluded:

- Only general statements can be made about the biological causes of aggression.
- Aggressive acts cannot be attributed to just one gene.
- The research regarding biological factors of criminality is complicated and spans numerous disciplines.
- Much more needs to be studied about the biology of violence and its relation to psychology, sociology, and the physical environment.

In her definitive article "Biological Perspectives in Criminology," Diana Fishbein examines the vast amount of empirical support for the role of biological factors in antisocial behavior. After reviewing much of the literature from the behavioral sciences, Fishbein posits that a multidisciplinary approach to studying criminality will yield greater results.

In "A Discipline in Peril: Sociology's Future Hinges on Curing Its Biophobia," Lee Ellis claims that mainstream criminology must take note of the advancements in biologically based criminological research if, as an academic discipline, it is to contribute to the reduction of crime.

R E A D I N G 1

Issue 1: Are criminals biologically predisposed to committing crimes?

Biological Perspectives in Criminology

Diana H. Fishbein

Diana Fishbein has a doctorate in psychobiological criminology from Florida State University and is a faculty member of the Criminal Justice Department, University of Baltimore. She received a fellowship from the National Institute of Health to conduct research at the University of Maryland School of Medicine and has since been on the staff of the Addiction Research Center, National Institute on Drug Abuse.

Wilson and Herrnstein (1985) recently published a massive evaluation of the implications of biological data for topics of interest to criminologists. Their message is that insufficient consideration has been given to biological and social interactions in criminological studies. Consistent observations that a small percentage of offenders are responsible for a preponderance of serious crime (Hamparin et al., 1978; Moffitt et al., 1989; Wolfgang, 1972) suggest that particular forces produce antisocial behavior in particular individuals. Further, much research shows that violent criminals have an early history of crime and aggression (Loeber and Dishion, 1983; Moffitt et al., 1989). The possibility that biological conditions may play a role in the development of antisocial and criminal behavior is accentuated by these reports and has spurred a search for biological markers in "vulnerable" subgroups (Mednick et al., 1987).

In the past, theories of the biological aspects of criminal behavior were marked by a general lack of knowledge regarding the human brain and by serious methodological shortcomings (see, e.g., Glueck and Glueck, 1956; Goddard, 1921; Hooten, 1939; Jacobs et al., 1965; Lombroso, 1918; Sheldon, 1949). Indeed, "biological criminology" was eventually discredited because its findings were largely unscientific, simplistic, and unicausal. Biological factors were globally rejected due to the inability of theorists to posit a rational explanation for the development of criminal behavior.

More recently, biological aspects of criminal behavior have been investigated by numerous behavioral scientists employing a multidisciplinary approach that promises to enhance substantially the rigor of the findings. Scientists in such fields as genetics, biochemistry, endocrinology, neuroscience, immunology, and psychophysiology have been intensively studying aspects of human behavior that are relevant to the criminologist and the criminal justice practitioner. Due to the highly technical and field-specific language of much of this research, findings generated from these works are not usually included in the literature reviews of criminologists. The relative lack of interdisciplinary communication has resulted in a lack of awareness of data pertinent to the study of crime and criminal behavior. This paper is a small step toward filling that gap.

The primary purpose of this paper is to present an overview of biological perspectives on the study of crime. Once acquainted with the parameters and findings of biological research, criminologists may begin to incorporate reliable biological aspects of criminal behavior into their theoretical and applied frameworks. Specific findings in biology are presented for criminologists to consider. Although the paper provides only an initial, condensed introduction to the vast amount of work accomplished in the behavioral sciences, it may help develop a sound, scientific, and pragmatic framework for future criminological research with a multidisciplinary orientation.

Theoretical and Methodological Parameters

Several critical issues must be addressed in order to (1) establish the relevancy of biology to the study of crime, (2) develop the groundwork for including biological data in criminological theories, (3) design research projects using compatible measurement instruments, data sets, and statistical techniques, and (4) determine the boundaries of practical applications of biological findings. These four requirements for multidisciplinary investigation in criminology are contingent on the assumptions and paradigm of the researcher, which

"Biological Perspectives in Criminology" by Diana H. Fishbein from *Criminology*, Vol. 28, No. 1, 1990, pp. 27–72. Reprinted by permission of the American Society of Criminology.

have yet to be set forth adequately in the criminological literature. Pertinent issues include nature versus nurture, free will versus determinism, identifying relevant behavioral disorders and subject populations, assumptions and conceptual framework, and finally, methodological considerations. The discussion of these issues that follows may be opposed or modified by other criminologists with a biological orientation. This discussion is not intended as the last word, but rather as one of the first.

Nature or Nurture?

The first issue that must be addressed before the parameters of biological research in criminology can be established is the age-old question of whether human behavior is a product of nature or nurture. Theoreticians of the past generally espoused one or the other viewpoint. Those who claim that nature contributes predominantly to an individual's behavior have been affiliated in the past with conservative political ideologies and were known as "hereditarians." In this circle, behavior was primarily attributed to inherited predispositions, and genetic influences were considered responsible for most of the variance in complex human behaviors.

The argument that nurture is the impetus for behavior was advocated by the "environmentalists," who were generally associated with a liberal ideology. Watson's (1925) interpretation of John Locke's *tabula rasa* (blank slate), for example, maintained that humans are born without predispositions to behave in any predetermined or predictable manner. Environmental inputs were considered primarily responsible for the final behavioral product, and manipulations of external inputs were thought to modify behavior.

These opposing views are reflected in past political and social movements, such as *radical behaviorism* and *social Darwinism,* many of which have had devastating social and scientific consequences. The concept of *predatory ethics,* couched in the possibility of the state's punitive sanctioning of "unacceptable" or merely predicted future behaviors, eventually contributed to a complete rejection of biological perspectives by many scientists and their sponsors. The threat of "control and oppression by science" was realized and feared.

Few behavioral scientists today adhere to either of these extreme views. A consensus has been emerging over the past 10 to 15 years that the "truth" lies somewhere in between—a "nature plus nurture" perspective (see Plomin, 1989). Although the nurture perspective has dominated fields such as criminology for the past few decades, substantial biological findings can no longer be ignored. Several studies on alcoholism, temperament, criminality, depression, and mental illness have established a solid role for genetic and biological influences (selected recent examples are detailed below). Even though behavioral scientists have yet to determine precisely the separate, relative contributions of biology and social learning to behavior, their findings are particularly relevant to the criminologist, who should play an instrumental role in their evaluation given the potential impact on policy.

Evidence for an interaction between nature and nurture comes from both animal and clinical studies, which demonstrates the strength and importance of the dynamic link between biological and acquired traits. One example of this interaction is that aggressive behavior in monkeys can be elicited by stimulating certain areas of the brain with implanted intracerebral electrodes (see Carlson, 1977:442–449). The final behavioral result depends on the hierarchical structure of the monkey colony. Dominant monkeys will exhibit aggressive behavior with electrical stimulation of the brain in the presence of a submissive monkey. The same monkeys will suppress aggressive behavior, on the other hand, if another dominant monkey is present. An example of this interaction in humans is illustrated by recent reports that gender differences in cognitive ability are decreasing (see Geary, 1989). Cognition, however, is fundamentally influenced by neural processes that operate during an individual's development (ontogeny). In an effort to explain changing trends in a seemingly immutable biological process, researchers are discovering that cultural and experiential conditions directly influence the developing pattern of cognitive abilities. For example, activity patterns (e.g., frequency of rough and tumble play) may alter cognitive ability (e.g., spatial skills) by modifying processes of brain development.

These illustrations remind us that as evidence for a substantial genetic influence grows we must be cautious not to replace environmental explanations with biological deterministic views. Instead, a more accommodating, balanced approach will carry more empirical weight.

Free Will or Determinism?

The acceptance of biological explanations for human behavior has been thought by many to preclude the possibility of free will. This fundamental fear has resulted in a pervasive rejection of biological contributions to behavior. Although some behavioral scientists are deterministic in their views, attributing behavior to everything from socioeconomic conditions to neurochemical events, most individuals prefer to credit their own free will for their behavior. A compromise reflecting a more accurate position on the forces behind human behavior is widely accepted, however—the theory of "conditional free will" (see Denno, 1988, for discussion of "degree determinism," a related view).

In probabilistic or stochastic theories, numerous causes or alternatives are presented to explain an effect. Each cause has a certain probability of resulting in that outcome, in some cases a measurable probability. Because it is rarely the case that an effect can be associated with only one cause, some dynamic interaction of causes, working in concert, is frequently responsible for the final result. In the assessment of human behavior, a most complex phenomenon, it is particularly difficult to separate those causes to assess their relative contributions.

In accordance with probability theory, social human behavior is contingent on a countless number of possible decisions from among which the individual may choose. Not all of those decisions are feasible, however, nor are the resources available that are required to act on them. Choosing a course of action, therefore, is limited by preset boundaries, which narrows the range of possibilities substantially. Decision-limiting factors include current circumstances and opportunities, learning experiences, physiological abilities, and genetic predispositions. Each one of these conditions collaborates internally (physically) and externally (environmentally) to produce a final action. The behavioral result is thus restricted to options available within these guidelines, yet it is "indeterminable" and cannot be precisely predicted. Stable individuals generally behave with some degree of expectability, however. In other words, certain patterns of behavior are a common individual characteristic, and some patterns are more probable than others in a given situation in a given individual.

The principle of conditional free will does not demand a deterministic view of human behavior. Rather, it postulates that individuals choose a course of action within a preset, yet to some degree changeable, range of possibilities and that, assuming the conditions are suitable for rational thought, we are accountable for our actions. Given "rational" thought processes, calculation of risks versus the benefits, and the ability to judge the realities that exist, the result is likely to be an adaptive response, that is, the behavior will be beneficial for the individual and the surrounding environment.

This theory of conditional free will predicts that if one or more conditions to which the individual is exposed are disturbed or irregular, the individual is more likely to choose a disturbed or irregular course of action. Thus, the risk of such a response increases as a function of the number of deleterious conditions. For example, a child with a learning disability may function well in society. With the addition of family instability, lack of appropriate educational programs, and a delinquent peer group, however, the learning-disabled child may be more prone to maladaptive behavior, which may, in turn, result in actions society has defined as criminal. The child's range of possible decisions has, in other words, been altered.

Selected Studies of the Biology of Maladaptive Behavior

Evolutionary Dictates

Human instinctual drives (e.g., eating, reproduction, and defensive behavior) ensure our survival and are essentially stable over time. The mechanisms for acting on these drives, however, especially the brain, continuously evolve to enhance our survival capabilities and have improved substantially. With the advent of human consciousness, psychological forces and cultural values interact and sometimes compete with biological drives dictated by evolutionary trends (Thiessen, 1976). Thus, human behavior is a product of the profound and complex interaction of biological and social conditions. Due to the intricacy of this interaction and the elusiveness of evolutionary directions, the nature and outcome of this process are difficult to identify and to study.

Most behaviors have some adaptive significance (i.e., they reflect an attempt to adapt to environmental conditions) and, thus, can be studied in an evolutionary context. Aggression is one form of behavior that has been extensively studied with respect to its adaptive significance. For example, "abnormal" environmental conditions have been associated with a display of extreme, overt aggression because they are perceived as threats to survival. The administration of an electrical shock or painful stimulus, loud noises, extreme heat, ESB, starvation, crowding, and other conditions elicit or exacerbate fighting behaviors in many primate species, including humans (Carlson, 1977; Thiessen, 1976; Valzelli, 1981). Abnormal environmental conditions characterize prisons and may contribute to the incidence of overt aggressive behavior among inmates; they may also partially explain the relationship between contacts with the criminal justice system (e.g., amount of time incarcerated) and recidivism rates. Also, the prevalence of abnormal environmental conditions has increased with the ever-increasing breakdown of the family structure, community disorganization, disparity between public policy and biological needs, crowding, learned helplessness, and other frequently cited characteristics of U.S. urbanization (Archer and Gartner, 1984:98–117; Larson, 1984:116–141). Investigation of how these deleterious conditions exacerbate maladaptive behavioral mechanisms may eventually lead to socioenvironmental programs to enhance, rather than detract from, adaptive capabilities.

Unfortunately, aggression has been inconsistently defined, and most studies of its evolution and adaptive significance have examined nonhuman animals, probably because of the complexity of human social systems that contribute to the manifestation of aggressive behavior. Due to space limitations and the relative lack of well-supported research in this area, a discussion of evolutionary dictates and aggressive behavior is not included here. The interested reader may refer to Thiessen (1976) and Valzelli (1981) for such discussion.

Genetic Contributions

Research on the genetic components of human behavior suffers in general from numerous methodological and interpretive flaws (Blehar et al., 1988; Clerget-Darpoux et al., 1986; DeFries and Plomin, 1978; Ghodsian-Carpey and Baker, 1987). It is difficult to isolate genetic factors from ontogenetic (developmental) events, cultural influences, early experiences, and housing conditions. As a result, most studies of human behavior have examined the transmission of socioenvironmental factors that can be more empirically observed and manipulated.

Genetic studies of criminal behavior specifically have been even more severely criticized (Mednick et al., 1987; Plomin et al., 1990; Rowe and Osgood, 1984; Walters and White, 1989; Wilson and Herrnstein, 1985). This research suffers from a high level of abstraction because "criminal behavior" is a legalistic label, not descriptive of actual behavior. This weakness is not unique to genetic research, however. Criminal behavior, as a single phenomenon, is far too variable and subject to individual and cultural judgments to be defined for reliable and valid investigation. Instead, research should be predicated on disaggregated behaviors that are reflective of actual acts that can be consistently and accurately measured and examined. Accordingly, genetic studies that focus on criminal behavior per se may be inherently flawed; as criminal behavior is heterogeneous, genetic effects may be more directly associated with particular traits that place individuals at risk for criminal labeling. Mednick et al. (1984) took a first step toward this goal by differentiating violent from property offenders. Concepts such as violent behavior, depression, alcoholism, and psychopathy more aptly reflect an actual behavioral pattern to which specific criteria for their identification can be applied (Plomin et al., 1990). Researchers need only agree on the criteria and measuring instruments.

As a rule, what is inherited is not a behavior; rather, it is the way in which an individual responds to the environment. It provides an orientation, predisposition, or tendency to behave in a certain fashion. Also, genetic influences on human behavior are polygenic—no single gene effect can be identified for most behavior.

Intellectual deficits, which are closely tied to delinquent and criminal lifestyles (Hirschi and Hindelang, 1977), are understood to be largely heritable (Bouchard and McGue, 1981; Cattell, 1982). Temperamental traits and personality types, possible precursors of maladaptive or criminal behavior, have also been shown to have heritable components in humans, for example, extraversion, depression, alcoholism, dominance, neuroticism, mania, impulsivity, hyperactivity, conduct disorder, sensation seeking, and hyperemotionality (Biederman et al., 1986; Cadoret et al., 1985; DeFries and Plomin, 1978; Ghodsian-Carpey and Baker, 1987; Plomin et al., 1990; Rushton et al., 1986). Individuals with such personality dispositions, compared with those without, have an increased familial incidence of similar behavioral problems and show differences, along with their family members, in certain biochemical, neuropsychological, and physiological parameters (Biederman et al., 1986; Cadoret et al., 1975; DeFries and Plomin, 1978; Hare and Schalling, 1978; Plomin et al., 1990; Rushton et al., 1986; Tarter et al., 1985; Zuckerman, 1983). The behavioral outcome is contingent on various stressors in the environment, life experiences, and current opportunities. A withdrawn and shy child, for instance, can alter his or her introverted temperament through the self-awareness and training required to become a more, outgoing adult, given the availability of necessary personal and external resources.

Numerous studies have attempted to estimate the genetic contribution to the development of criminality, delinquency, aggression, and antisocial behavior. Each has used one of three methods designed to assess the relative contributions of environment and heredity to various aspects of human behavior: family, twin, and adoption studies. Overall, many of these behavioral genetic studies suffer from one or more of the methodological weaknesses discussed earlier. Genetic research designs and selected seminal studies are briefly described below. (Only a few researchers have comprehensively and critically reviewed the bulk of these studies; see Mednick et al., 1987; Plomin et al., 1990; Walters and White, 1989; Wilson and Herrnstein, 1985.)

Family Studies

The family study seeks to identify genetic influences on behavioral traits by evaluating similarities among family members. Cross-generational linkages have been reported for personality and behavioral attributes related to criminal behavior, including temper outbursts (Mattes and Fink, 1987), sociopathy (Cloninger et al., 1975, 1978; Guze et al., 1967), delinquency (Robins et al., 1975; Rowe, 1986), hyperactivity and attention deficit disorder (Cantwell, 1979), conduct disorder, aggression, violence, and psychopathy (Bach-y-Rita et al., 1971; Stewart et al., 1980; Stewart and DeBlois, 1983; Stewart and Leone, 1978; Twito and Stewart, 1982).

Despite conclusions from many of these studies that genetic effects are largely responsible for criminal behavior, this method of study does not directly assess genetic contributions. Environmental influences on measures of behavior may be common to parents and offspring, and thus, large environmental correlations among relatives cannot be accounted for. Diet, environmental toxins, neighborhood conditions, and television-viewing habits are only a few examples of environmental factors that similarly influence family members. Family studies also suffer from many of the weaknesses listed above. At this point, one may only conclude that the incidence of criminal and related behaviors appears to have a familial basis. The relative influences of genetics and environmental conditions cannot, however, be estimated.

Twin Studies

The classic twin design involves the testing of identical (monozygotic or MZ) and fraternal (dizygotic or DZ) twins. MZ twins share genetic material from the biologic parents and are thus considered genetically identical. DZ twins are approximately 50% genetically alike, as are regular siblings. The extent to which MZ resemblances with respect to a characteristic are greater than DZ resemblances provides evidence for a genetic influence on the variable. To the extent that there is still some degree of DZ resemblance after genetic influences have been accounted for, there is evidence for the influence of common family environment on the variable. For example, if a sample of MZ twins is 60% similar for IQ and a matched sample of DZ twins is 25% similar for IQ, one can conclude that IQ is largely a function of heredity.

Christiansen (1977b) reviewed nine twin studies on criminal behavior, including his own exemplary study (Christiansen, 1977a). Overall, the studies provide evidence for a genetics-environment interaction (see discussion in Wilson and Herrnstein, 1985). Dalgard and Kringler's (1976) findings were the exception. Although they found a trend, they did not find statistical significance for differences between MZ and DZ criminality. More current twin studies have found significant genetic effects for both self-report and official rates of delinquent or criminal behavior (Rowe, 1983; Rowe and Osgood, 1984) and personality or temperamental traits related to criminal behavior, for example, aggression (Ghodsian-Carpey and Baker, 1987; Rowe, 1986; Rushton et al., 1986, Tellegen et al., 1988). Two additional studies did not find significant MZ-DZ differences in concordance rates for childhood aggression (Owen and Sines, 1970; Plomin et al., 1981). Plomin et al. (1990) examined numerous twin studies of criminal/delinquent behavior and aggression and noted that the results were highly inconsistent, possibly because no uniform measure of self-reported aggression and its constructs has been applied.

Twin studies commonly suffer from a number of unique methodological weaknesses (Plomin et al., 1980). First, MZ twins are selected more frequently due to their visibility, and study group sizes thus become disproportionate. Second, sampling techniques may favor the selection of MZ pairs that are similar in relevant behavioral traits, which biases the results. Third, MZ twins tend to share more similar environments than do DZ twins because of their similar appearance (DZ twins look no more alike than regular siblings). Because environmental assessments are not commonly conducted, such similarities cannot be estimated to determine their relative influence. In favor of the validity of the twin method, however, is evidence that physical and environmental similarities among MZ twins do not bias studies of personality (see DeFries and Plomin, 1978:480; Plomin and Daniels, 1987). Fourth, only recently have researchers employed biochemical tests to verify the zygosity of the twins. The bulk of genetic studies were performed prior to the ready availability of such tests, and thus, the genetic influence may have been underestimated. Fifth, measurement errors may further increase the tendency to underestimate genetic influences. On the other side of the coin, the twin method can only examine the level of genetic contribution over and above environmental influence. Thus, there is contamination from an unknown amount of environmental contribution and the influence of heredity may be overestimated.

No definitive conclusions can be drawn from twin studies of aggressiveness or criminal behavior because no consistent pattern of genetic influence emerges. Nevertheless, twin studies of criminal and related behaviors fairly consistently provide some intriguing evidence for a genetic effect, and genetic influences warrant continued, but more rigorous, study.

Adoption Studies

Adoption studies examine individuals who were raised from infancy by nonrelated adoptive parents rather than biological relatives. To the extent that subjects resemble the biological relatives and not the nonbiologic relatives, heredity is thought to play a contributory role. The adoption study method promises to provide unambiguous evidence for the relative contribution of heredity as a cause for behavioral traits and for genetics-environment interactions. Nevertheless, the method has some weaknesses (see Walters and White, 1989, for examples). First, due to difficulties in locating subjects, sample sizes tend to be small, which reduces the power of the results. Second, selection bias may be introduced in the adoption process because assignment to adoptive parents may not be random with respect to biological parent characteristics. Third, a primary criticism of a majority of adoption studies on criminality is the inadequacy and inconsistency of the methods used to operationalize and measure the dependent variable (see Plomin et al., 1990; Walters and White, 1989). Fourth, researchers should ensure that the duration and type of biological parenting, similar among all subjects to avoid contamination. Ideally, infants should have been adopted within a few weeks of birth so that the age of adoption does not relate to subsequent criminal behavior (see Mednick et al., 1984).

Several adoption studies indicate noteworthy genetic effects on criminal or delinquent behavior and related psychopathology (i.e., psychopathy).[6] For the most part, these studies suggest that biological relatives of criminal or antisocial probands have a greater history of criminal convictions or antisocial behavior than the biological relatives of noncriminal control adoptees. In general, family environment, including such indices as social class, rearing styles, and parental attitudes, played a smaller role than did purported genetic effects.

Bohman et al. (1982) further argue that genetic influences on criminality may differ from those who are also alcoholic. Specifically, when the biological parents are both criminal and alcoholic, crimes of adoptees tend to be more violent. There is no direct evidence, however, that criminality/antisocial personality and alcoholism are genetically linked to the same antecedent conditions. Nevertheless, the link between the two behaviors has been widely documented (see Cadoret et al., 1985).

Adoption studies highlight the importance of gene-environment interactional models (Rowe and Osgood, 1984). Mednick et al. (1984) proposed that having a criminal adoptive parent most profoundly affects those with a genetic propensity for criminality. In other words, those who inherited certain antisocial personality and temperamental traits are more likely to manifest criminal behaviors in the presence of deleterious environmental conditions (e.g., criminal parents). Even though these conditions interact to produce antisocial behavior, many researchers attest that environmental and genetic factors differentially influence behavior and that their relative contributions may be measurable (see Plomin et al., 1990).[7]

Biological Contributions

Genetic foundations for behavioral disorders are manifested in a phenotype, which is the resulting, visible expression of a genetic trait. For example, one may have the genetic blueprint (or genotype) for brown and blue eyes, but the final, observable eye color (the phenotype) is brown. Although researchers can rarely trace a behavioral disorder to a specific gene, they can more aptly measure the manifestation of a genetic blueprint in nervous system features. Other biological traits associated with behavioral problems are not directly genetic in origin; they may be due to mutations in a genetic constitution, biochemical exposures, or a deleterious social environment. All of these conditions, from the genetic to the environmentally precipitated, exert their influence on the nervous system and, thus, can be measured and manipulated. The following correlates of behavioral disorders illustrate selected ways in which genetic and environmental factors impact on the nervous system to alter behavior.

Biochemical Correlates

A number of biochemical differences have been found between controls and individuals with psychopathy, antisocial personality, violent behavior, conduct disorder, and other behaviors associated with criminal behavior. These groups have been discriminated on the basis of levels of certain hormones, neurotransmitters, peptides, toxins, and metabolic processes (Brown et al., 1979; Davis et al., 1983; Eichelman and Thoa, 1972; Mednick et al., 1987; Rogeness et al., 1987; Roy et al., 1986; Valzelli, 1981; Virkkunen and Narvanen, 1987).

Current investigations of biochemical mechanisms of aggressiveness focus on the study of central neurotransmitter systems. Observations from animal and human studies, for example, indicate that serotonin, a neurotransmitter, globally inhibits behavioral responses to emotional stimuli and modulates aggression (Muhlbauer, 1985; Soubrie, 1986; van Praag et al., 1987). Several indicators of lower levels of serotonin activity in individuals characterized as violent or impulsive, in comparison with those who are not, have been reported (Brown et al., 1979; Fishbein et al., 1989; Linnoila et al., 1983; Virkkunen et al., 1987, 1989). These studies indicate that serotonin functioning is altered in some types of human aggressiveness and violent suicidal behavior. Thus, a decrease in serotonergic activity may produce disinhibition in both brain mechanisms and behavior and result in increased aggressiveness or impulsivity.

Findings of reduced serotonergic activity among individuals with impulsivity and aggressivity are well supported by behavioral and personality studies of animals and humans. Nevertheless, this research is relatively new to the area of antisocial behavior and frequently suffers from theoretical and methodological inadequacies (see Soubrie, 1986). First, categorizing subjects according to their behavioral attributes has been inconsistent across studies, and group assignment within studies is, in some cases, controversial. Second, because aggression is not a unitary phenomenon it is important to determine whether serotonergic activity levels are specific to types of aggression or whether they globally regulate aggression. Third, psychopathy or antisocial personality is frequently used to describe subjects without respect to the presence of trait anxiety (see above), which is known to involve serotonergic systems (Soubrie, 1986). This confusion may produce findings that are inconsistent and lack functional significance (van Praag et al., 1987). And fourth, serotonergic activity is all too often studied in isolation of other interacting biological systems. Thus, these studies have not been able to identify precisely the neural mechanisms for regulating aggression. They do, nevertheless, bring us closer to identifying neurobiological mechanisms for aggression, impulsivity, and antisocial behavior.

There is a noticeable absence of research on female criminality in general, and reports that do exist are largely sociological or anecdotal. Widom (1978) wrote that biological factors contributing to individual differences in temperament, arousal, or vulnerability to stress may be important in the etiology of female criminal behavior. Different socioenvironmental influences may differentially interact with biological sex differences to produce variations in male and female criminality (see, e.g., L. Ellis and Ames, 1987).

There is evidence that high levels of the male sex hormone testosterone may influence aggressive behavior in males (Kreuz and Rose, 1971; Olweus et al., 1988; Reda et al., 1983; Schiavi et al., 1984), although discrepant studies exist (Coe and Levine, 1983). It has been further suggested that sex hormones may also contribute to antisocial behavior in some women. The premenstrual period in particular has been associated with elevated levels of aggressivity and irritability. This phase of the hormonal cycle is marked by an imbalance in the estrogen-progesterone ratio, which may trigger both physical and psychological impairments in a subgroup of women. Sharp changes in mood, depression, irritability, aggression, difficulty in concentration, and substance abuse are only a few behavioral disturbances that typify premenstruation in affected women (Haskett, 1987; Trunnell and Turner, 1988).

A significant number of females imprisoned for aggressive criminal acts were found to have committed their crimes during the premenstrual phase, and female offenders were found to be more irritable and aggressive during this period (Cooke, 1945; Dalton, 1964, 1966; D. Ellis and Austin, 1971; Morton et al., 1953; see D'Orban and Dalton, 1980, and Epps, 1962, for negative findings). Overall, most of these studies have been criticized for serious methodological shortcomings (see Harry and Balcer, 1987). Nevertheless, there remains a general impression among investigators and clinicians that a small number of women appear to be vulnerable to cyclical changes in hormonal levels, which causes them to be more prone to increased levels of anxiety and hostility during the premenstrual phase (Carroll and Steiner, 1987; Clare, 1985). Ginsburg and Carter (1987) provide a thorough discussion of the controversy about premenstrual syndrome, including evidence for its existence, its association with behavioral disorders, and the legal, social, and biomedical implications. Because premenstrual syndrome is difficult to diagnose and its etiology is still under investigation, an association between the menstrual cycle and female criminal behavior is too remote and indirect to be conclusive at this time.

Exposure to toxic trace elements is yet another factor that has been shown to interfere with brain function and behavior. Chronic or acute exposure to lead, for example, has a deleterious effect on brain function by damaging organ systems, impairing intellectual development, and subsequently interfering with the regulation of behavior. Sources of lead include our diet and environment (e.g., paint chips and house dust), and contamination among children may be serious and grossly underestimated (Bryce-Smith and Waldron, 1974; Moore and Fleischman, 1975). Resulting impairments may be manifested as learning disabilities and cognitive deficits, particularly in measures of school achievement, verbal and performance IQ, and mental dullness (see Benignus et al., 1981; Lester and Fishbein, 1987; Pihl and Parkes, 1977). Because of the high correlation among school failure, learning disabilities, and delinquency, lead intoxication is a relevant criminological issue.

A growing body of research has further demonstrated that lead intoxication is significantly associated with hyperactivity and impulsivity (David et al., 1972; Needleman et al., 1979), putative precursors to delinquency, and criminal behavior (Denno, 1988). Following chelation (removal) of lead from the body, David et al. (1976) found behavioral improvements among hyperactive children. Pihl et al. (1982) reported that violent subjects had significantly elevated concentrations of lead compared with nonviolent criminals. They further suggest that subtoxic levels of lead have a potential effect on behavior and that lead detection can be an important diagnostic procedure. Children who are at risk for exposure to lead also tend to have poor diets, that is, diets low in calcium and iron, which help to protect the body from lead's effects. Many of these studies lack proper control groups and double blind procedures, yet accumulating evidence strongly suggests that, given other deleterious socioenvironmental conditions, an individual exposed to lead is more likely to manifest maladaptive behavior (see Rimland and Larson, 1983, for a review of studies).

Psychophysiological Correlates

Psychophysiological variables, for example, heart rate, blood pressure, attention and arousal levels, skin conductance, brain waves, and hormone levels, are quantifiable indices of nervous system function. These measurable conditions directly reflect emotional responses and can be experimentally manipulated in human populations.

Studies of criminal behavior, aggression, and psychopathy have repeatedly found psychophysiological evidence for mental abnormality and central nervous system disturbances as putative markers for criminal behavior. For example, psychopaths have been found to differ from nonpsychopathic controls in several physiological parameters. These indices include (a) electroencephalogram (EEG) differences, (b) cognitive and neuropsychological impairment, and (c) electrodermal, cardiovascular, and other nervous system measures.[8]

In particular, psychopathic individuals have been found to show relatively more slow wave activity in their spontaneous (that is, when resting with no provocation) EEG compared with controls, which may be related to differences in cognitive abilities (Hare, 1970; Howard, 1984; Pincus and Tucker, 1974; Syndulko, 1978). Some investigators have suggested that relatively high levels of EEG slowing in psychopathic subjects reflect a maturational lag in brain function (Kiloh et al., 1972; Pontius and Ruttiger, 1976). Thus, EEG slowing among individuals who also demonstrate immature behavior and an inability to learn from experience supports a maturational lag hypothesis. It may be suggested that EEG slowing among some psychopaths is consistent with findings of hypoaroused autonomic function (see above) and other differences in psychophysiologic parameters. Their need for external stimulation may be higher and more difficult to satisfy than in other populations due to a lower level of internal stimulation.

Psychopharmacological Inducements

Psychopharmacology is the study of the psychological and behavioral aspects of drug effects on brain metabolism and activity. Aggression, for example, can be elicited or extinguished by the administration of a pharmacologic agent. In fact, the pharmacologic treatment of aggressive and violent behavior has become increasingly popular and its efficacy in many cases has been demonstrated (Kuperman and Stewart, 1987; Lion, 1974, 1979; Yudofsky et al., 1987). Certain drugs, particularly many of the illicit drugs, are reported to increase aggressive responses, for example, amphetamines, cocaine, alcohol, and phencyclidine (PCP). The actual expression of aggressive behavior depends on the dose, route of administration, genetic factors, and type of aggression.

Several biological mechanisms have been proposed as explanations for alcohol-induced aggression: (1) pathological intoxication, sometimes involving psychomotor epilepsy or temporal lobe disturbance (Bach-y-Rita et al., 1970; Maletsky, 1976; Marinacci, 1963); (2) hypoglycemic reactions (low blood sugar; Cohen, 1980; Coid, 1979; Wallgren and Barry, 1970); and (3) alterations in neurotransmitter activity (Weingartner et al., 1983). These explanations do not completely account for the relationship, however, because most drinkers do not become aggressive. Indications are that alcohol either changes the psychological state or the psychological state has an effect on the behavioral outcome of alcohol consumption. In the second scenario, alcohol would stimulate an existing psychiatric condition or psychological predisposition to aggress or misbehave (Pihl and Ross, 1987). Hence, alcohol does not appear to "cause" aggression, but rather permits its expression under specific circumstances and biological conditions.

Chronic use of PCP, an illicit drug that is commonly used in combination with marijuana, has been repeatedly associated with extreme violence to self and others in individuals both with and without histories of violent behavior (Aronow et al., 1980; Fauman and Fauman, 1980; Linder et al., 1981; Schuckit and Morrissey, 1978; Seigal, 1978; Smith and Wesson, 1980). Violent reactions appear, according to some anecdotal reports, to be an extension of PCP toxic psychosis, which affects some users (Fauman and Fauman, 1980). Because only a subpopulation of users manifest violent behavior and some studies (e.g., Khajawall et al., 1982) did not find a relationship between PCP use and violence, additional research is needed to (1) determine whether PCP reliably elicits aggressive behavior among vulnerable users, (2) identify underlying mechanisms in PCP-induced aggression, and (3) determine the nature of the vulnerability that causes certain individuals to be particularly susceptible to that behavioral effect.

Investigators recognize that PCP effects result from a complex interaction among physical, psychological, and sociocultural variables (Smith and Wesson, 1980). PCP-related aggression may be due to influences on hormonal and neurotransmitter activity (Domino, 1978, 1980; Marrs-Simon et al., 1988). Also, neuropsychological impairments have been observed that minimally reflect a temporary organic brain syndrome (Cohen, 1977; Smith and Wesson, 1980). Additional studies of PCP users indicate that specific factors in the user's background, personality, and drug history are important determinants of the drug-related experience (Fauman and Fauman, 1980; McCardle and Fishbein, 1989). As a whole, these observations suggest that the consequences of PCP use, independent of the drug's purity and varying strengths, are determined by a number of factors, including pharmacological, psychological, and situational.

"Vulnerability" studies suggest that certain personality types may be more at risk for drug abuse than other types (Brook et al., 1985; Deykin et al., 1986; Kellam et al., 1980; McCardle and Fishbein, 1989). This does not mean, however, that these individuals will inevitably become drug abusers due to a natural predisposition. More recent studies provide evidence for the substantial contribution of family support systems in the final determination of whether an individual with a vulnerable personality type will, in fact, abuse drugs (Tarter et al., 1985;346–347). The dynamic interaction between natural and acquired traits in a given environment must always be considered inseparable in the evaluation of such complex phenomenon as human behavior.

Implications for Criminal Justice Practices

In order to determine the relevance and significance of biological perspectives for criminology, researchers must estimate the incidence of biological disorders among maladaptive populations, identify etiologic mechanisms, assess the dynamic interaction among biological and socioenvironmental factors, and determine whether improvements in behavior follow large-scale therapeutic manipulations.

At this stage of scientific inquiry in the biological sciences, researchers have yet to determine the significance of biological disorders in criminal populations. Nor are they able to speak of a causal link between biological abnormalities and specific behavioral disorders. They are beginning to identify putative correlates or markers of antisocial behavior using biological tests (e.g., EEG slowing, body lead burden, neurotransmitter imbalance). Some of those correlations may prove to be spurious, but at present, which ones cannot be identified. Seen in this light, it would be premature to apply biological findings routinely to criminal justice procedures. Demands for evaluation of causal relationships are made in decisions regarding the granting of bail, release on personal recognizance, competency, guilty pleas, sentencing options, probation and parole, and proclivity to recidivate. Conclusions and prognoses regarding the role of biological factors in an offender's behavior, however, are not definitive at this time, regardless of the informational source.

To further establish the relevance of biology to criminology, researchers must demonstrate the ability to predict antisocial behavior reliably using a combination of biological and social variables. The central question thus becomes, can more of the variance in the incidence of antisocial behavior be explained with an integrated approach than with a unidisciplinary perspective? Many mental health professionals and researchers have reached a tentative consensus that predicting antisocial behavior with social or legal variables is inherently unreliable (Cocozza and Steadman, 1974; Gottfredson, 1986; Monahan, 1981; Wenk et al., 1972). Is it possible that prediction studies incorporating biological measures into sociological data bases will facilitate the isolation of significant predictors of antisocial behavior and enhance explanatory power?

In the introduction of Brizer and Crowner's recent text (1989) on the prediction of violence, Brizer aptly notes that the actual study of predictive ability suffers from methodological limitations, and thus, one cannot conclude that valid prediction is impossible. Studies reviewed in their text indicate that the inclusion of biological variables (e.g., integrity of central nervous system function) may, indeed, enhance predictive ability if dispositional (temperament and other features considered "innate") and situational factors are considered as interacting forces. In a separate study illustrative of this approach, Virkkunen et al. (1989) examined a selected set of behavioral and psychobiological variables to identify predictors of recidivism in a sample of violent offenders and arsonists. Their results suggested that recidivism is best predicted using a combination of behavioral and psychological variables, rather than with behavioral variables alone.

Denno (1988) conducted a fairly comprehensive study of the effects of numerous environmental and biological variables on criminal behavior, juvenile delinquency, and disciplinary problems. The model was able to predict 25% of future adult criminality among males and 19% of future adult criminality among females. Denno drew the following conclusions:

> Biological and environmental variables exert strong and independent influences on juvenile crime. . . [and] crime appears to be directly related to familial instability and, most important, a lack of behavioral control associated with neurological and central nervous system disorders (p. 659).

She cautions, however, that behavior should be predicted in terms of a series of probabilities of expected behavior, not in terms of cause and effect. Perhaps an approach that neither neglects nor places undue emphasis on socioenvironmental or biological features of behavior provides considerable promise as the direction of future research into practical problems in criminology.

The final stage of scientific inquiry requires that researchers be able to manipulate and control antisocial behavior, in this context with biological variables. Reliable behavioral changes attributable to biological treatments have yet to be demonstrated in this field, however. Biological intervention studies and programs render mixed and controvertible results, which indicate that the biology of antisocial behavior is under preliminary stages of investigation and requires further study before it can be applied to criminal justice practices. One particularly visible example of the controversial application of biological data is the pharmacologic treatment of sex offenders.

Antiandrogen agents (e.g., Depo-Provera), which compete with male hormones believed to be responsible for sexual deviance, are administered in some clinics to suppress sex drive and, consequently, sex offending. Some research indicates that this approach has been moderately successful (Berlin, 1983; Berlin and Meinecke, 1981; Bradford, 1983; Cordoba and Chapel, 1983; Murray, 1987; Spodak et al., 1978). Others, however, criticize the approach because of (1) the equivocal findings that provide empirical support, (2) the fact that the behaviors resurface when the drug is discontinued, (3) its strictly experimental nature, (4) the issue of forced compliance, and (5) evidence that only nonviolent sex offenders respond to antiandrogen treatment (see Demsky, 1984). Such biological management techniques require further scientific support and, even more important, time for the legal system to become acquainted with their premises in order to establish appropriate guidelines.

It is perhaps unreasonable to expect dramatic behavioral improvements following a biological treatment, even when a disorder has been properly diagnosed. One of the central tenets of this paper is that behavior is a result of a dynamic interaction among many diverse social and biological conditions. The appropriate administration of a medication or other treatment may certainly be warranted for some individuals with identifiable pathology. However, this approach undermines the proposal that multiple factors are responsible for behavior. One cannot manipulate biological variables and expect behavior to change without attending to other interacting contributions. Once an individual has entered the criminal justice system, behavioral problems are substantially compounded and the treatment of only one condition does not yield adequate therapeutic results.

Findings of biological involvement in antisocial behavior have, in a few studies (e.g., Lewis et al., 1979, 1981, 1985, 1986, 1988), disclosed measurable abnormalities, but in a number of studies, measurements do not reach pathologic levels. In other words, many studies show group differences between violent and nonviolent subjects, but the biological values do not necessarily exceed normal limits and would not alarm a practicing physician. Findings of this type do not have intrinsic clinical significance, and they indicate that individual intervention programs should not be globally implemented based on current information.

Nevertheless, at the very least, the inclusion of biological measures holds promise of explaining individual variation within a social context. Why is it, for example, that not all children exposed to child abuse become violent as adults? Research into individual differences may be interpreted to suggest that whether child abuse contributes to violent behavior partially depends on the presence of brain damage or other central nervous system disorder (Lewis et al., 1979). Perhaps abused children without concomitant or resultant brain damage would be less aggressive and more in control of their impulses. Research yet to be conducted may also show that individuals with biological "disadvantages" respond with more violent or criminal behavior in a criminogenic environment than those equipped with biological "insulators," for example, high intelligence or adequate serotonergic activity.

Statistically significant findings generated to date show biological involvement in antisocial behavior only with respect to populations. Thus, society is closer to enacting prevention programs aimed at populations who are at risk for exposure to biological and socioenvironmental hazards that are known to increase the incidence of behavioral problems. Factors that may prove to be important contributors to relevant behavioral disorders (e.g., toxic element concentrations, child abuse/neglect, poor prenatal care, neurological impairments, substance abuse, and learning disabilities) could subsequently be manipulated on a wide scale to prevent the onset of behavioral or forensic disorders in the general population. Early detection programs could be implemented by school systems, and parents could be educated to recognize signs of an impairment. Screening clinics, regulating environmental toxins, school programs, prenatal care facilities, and public educational programs are only a few of the preventative measures possible. The number of "risk" factors could, in essence, be reduced or minimized.

An excellent example of this strategy was suggested by Moffitt et al. (1989) in their review of minor physical anomalies (MPAs), that is, observable minor malformations that result from a disturbance in fetal development. MPAs are thought to be indicators of other hidden anomalies, such as central nervous system impairment, that may result from some perinatal trauma (e.g., illness, poor diet, drug use, stress). Further, a relatively large number of MPAs have been observed among hyperactive and criminally violent populations. Obviously, there is no acceptable mode of individual remediation in such cases, particulary because of the remote association of MPAs with behavior. These consistent observations, however, emphasize the need for a global effort to provide proper prenatal care. Consequently, society can hope to reduce the incidence of developmental deficits related to the onset of behavioral disorders by recognizing their possible influence.

Closing Comments

How biological variables interact with social and psychological factors to produce human behavior generally and antisocial behavior specifically is unknown. The bulk of biological studies, both those described herein and others not included, have examined only a few isolated variables and have generally failed to evaluate dynamic interrelationships among biological and socioenvironmental conditions (see Denno, 1988, and Wilson and Herrnstein, 1985, for detailed critiques). In order to evaluate the relative significance of biological contributions to antisocial behavior, sophisticated, statistical techniques (i.e., structural equation models) must be applied to multivariate designs that use rigorous measurement instruments. Studies of biological influence would benefit greatly from adopting the methodological and statistical techniques of sociologists to increase the rigor and relevance of the findings.

Caution against the premature application of biological findings is clearly called for. The weaknesses in design, sampling techniques, and statistical procedures delineated above preclude drawing definitive conclusions, and results are frequently contested and unreliable. Policies and programs based on equivocal and controversial findings waste time and money and potentially compromise individual rights and community safety. A number of legal, ethical, and political obstacles to the acceptance and application of biological and medical information by the criminal justice system are covered extensively elsewhere (Fishbein and Thatcher, in press; Jeffery, 1985; Marsh and Katz, 1985). At the very least, care must be taken not to stigmatize or otherwise traumatize individuals or groups that are, as yet, innocent of a criminal or civil violation. As researchers, we must avoid applying labels to behaviors we do not understand. In the event that biological measures are shown to be reliable and valid predictors of behavior and mental status, several serious civil rights and constitutional issues related to early identification and intervention in the absence of a proven violation of law would demand careful consideration. In cases in which a conviction is upheld, for example, forced compliance with a "therapeutic regimen" might result from findings that a biological abnormality played a role in an individual's antisocial behavior. One must recognize the numerous legal and ethical concerns generated by such a strategy. To avoid these transgressions, a collaborative, multidisciplinary approach might be forged strictly to identify the underlying sources of antisocial behaviors and minimize their occurrence in the population.

Overall, evidence to suggest that biological conditions have a profound impact on the adaptive, cognitive, and emotional abilities of the individual is compelling. Investigation of the discriminants for behavioral dysfunctions indicates that the impact of these factors is substantial. When a biological disadvantage is present due to genetic influences or when a physical trauma occurs during developmental stages of childhood, the resultant deficit may be compounded over time and drastically interfere with behavioral functions throughout life. Such conditions appear to place an individual at high risk for persistent problematic behavior. Disturbances associated with poor environmental and social conditions coupled with impaired brain function may eventually be amenable to intervention. The unfortunate reality for those who come into contact with the courts by virtue of their dysfunction, however, is that the underlying causes of their disorder are inaccurately evaluated or simply unattended. The capability to identify and predict the factors responsible for maladaptivity may eventually enable society to employ innovative methods of early detection, prevention, remediation, and evaluation.

Criminal justice policies must be based on well-founded theories and findings that survive scientific scrutiny. The application of scientific principles or findings to criminal justice programs that are well recognized and accepted by the discipline have more value than trial-and-error approaches in preventing or minimizing the onset of criminal behavior. Although biological techniques in the assessment of human behavior are still under the microscope and definitive answers have yet to surface, the foregoing description of biological foundations for behavior provides evidence of their applicability and value. The study of biological drives may also help to explain the development of specific social structures and control mechanisms (Jeffery, 1977; Pugh, 1977; Thiessen, 1976). Biological perspectives, for example, may enhance understanding of how certain control techniques employed throughout the criminal justice system, particularly in corrections, operate to further criminal activities through prisonization, crowding, dehumanization, and so forth. Use of this information in court or in policymaking can still be contested. Nevertheless, by undertaking a collaborative strategy, researchers can hope to develop more effective programs to reduce the incidence of antisocial behaviors (e.g., violence) and develop a legal system that reflects public consensus, meets human needs, and maintains an ethical and organized social structure.

Notes

Footnotes 1–5 are not included in this publication.

6. For the former see Cloninger et al. (1982), Crowe (1972), Hutchings and Mednick (1975), Mednick et al. (1984), Sigvardsson et al. (1982); for the latter see Cadoret (1978), Cadoret et al. (1985), Crowe (1974), Schulsinger (1985).
7. Plomin and Daniels (1987) provide convincing evidence that genetic influences may explain within-family resemblances and that environmental influences more aptly explain within-family differences.
8. For (a), see Hill and Watterson (1942), Howard (1984), Mednick et al. (1981), Syndulko et al. (1975), Volavka (1987), Yeudall et al. (1985); for (b), see Bryant et al. (1984), Hurwitz et al. (1972), Jutai and Hare (1983), Lewis et al. (1985, 1986, 1988), Pontius and Yudowitz (1980), Raine and Venables (1987), Sutker and Allain (1987); and for (c), see Allen et al. (1971), Hare (1978), House and Milligan (1976), Lykken (1957), Mednick et al. (1982), Waid et al. (1979).

References

Allen, H., L. Lewis, H. Goldman, and S. Dinitz. 1971. Hostile and simple sociopaths: An empirical typology. *Criminology* 9(1)27–47.

Archer, D., and R. Gartner. 1984. *Violence and Crime in Cross-National Perspective.* New Haven: Yale University Press.

Aronow, R., J.N. Miceli, and A.K. Done. 1980. A therapeutic approach to the acutely overdosed patient. *Journal of Psychedelic Drugs* 12:259–268.

Bach-y-Rita, G., J.R. Lion, and F.R. Ervin. 1970. Pathological intoxication. Clinical and electroencephalographic studies. *American Journal of Psychiatry* 127:698–703.

Bach-y-Rita, G., J.R. Lion, C.E. Climent, and F.R. Ervin. 1971. Episodic dyscontrol: A study of 130 violent patients. *American Journal of Psychiatry* 127:1473–1478.

Benignus, V.A., D.A. Otto, K.E. Muller, and K.J. Seiple. 1981. Effects of age and body lead burden on CNS function in young children. II: EEG spectra. *Electroencephalography and Clinical Neurophysiology* 52:240–248.

Berlin, F.S. 1983. Sex offenders: A biomedical perspective and a status report on biomedical treatment. In J.G. Greer and I.R. Stuart (eds.), *The Sexual Aggressor: Current Perspectives on Treatment.* New York: Van Nostrand Reinhold.

Berlin, F.S., and C.F. Meinecke. 1981. Treatment of sex offenders with antiandrogenic medication: Conceptualization, review of treatment modalities, and preliminary findings. *American Journal of Psychiatry* 138:601–607.

Biederman, J., K. Munir, D. Knee, W. Habelow, M. Armentano, S. Autor, S.K. Hoge, and C. Waternaux. 1986. A family study of patients with attention deficit disorder and normal controls. *Journal of Psychiatric Research* 20(4):263–274.

Blehar, M.C., M.M. Weissman, E.S. Gershon, and R.M.A. Hirschfeld. 1988. Family and genetic studies of affective disorders. *Archives of General Psychiatry* 45:289–292.

Bohman, M., C.R. Cloninger, S. Sigvardsson, and A–L. von Knorring. 1982. Predisposition to petty criminality in Swedish adoptees: I. Genetic and environmental heterogeneity. *Archives of General Psychiatry* 41:872–878.

Bouchard, T.J., Jr., and M. McGue. 1981. Familial studies of intelligence: A review. *Science* 212:1055–1059.

Bradford, J. 1983. Research on sex offenders. *Psychiatric Clinics of North America* 6:713–715.

Brizer, D.A., and M. Crowner. 1989. *Current Approaches to the Prediction of Violence.* Washington, D.C.: American Psychiatric Press.

Brook, J.S., S. Gordon, and M. Whiteman. 1985. Stability of personality during adolescence and its relationship to stage of drug use. *Genetic, Social and General Psychology Monographs* 111(3):317–330.

Brown, G.L., F.K. Goodwin, J.C. Ballenger, P.F. Goyer, and L.F. Major. 1979. Aggression in humans correlates with cerebrospinal fluid amine metabolites. *Psychiatry Research* 1(2):131–139.

Bryant, E.T., M.L. Scott, C.J. Golden, and D.C. Tori. 1984. Neuropsychological deficits, learning disability, and violent behavior. *Journal of Consulting and Clinical Psychology* 52:323–324.

Bryce-Smith, D., and H.A. Waldron. 1974. Lead, behavior, and criminality. *The Ecologist* 4:367–377.

Cadoret, R.J. 1978. Psychopathology in adopted away offspring of biologic parents with antisocial behavior. *Archives of General Psychiatry* 35:176–184.

Cadoret, R.J., L. Cunningham, R. Loftus, and J. Edwards. 1975. Studies of adoptees from psychiatrically disturbed biologic parents. II. Temperament, hyperactive, antisocial and developmental variables. *Journal of Pediatrics* 87:301–306.

Cadoret, R.J., T.W. O'Gorman, E. Troughton, and E. Heywood. 1985. Alcoholism and antisocial personality: Interrelationships, genetic and environmental factors. *Archives of General Psychiatry* 42:161–167.

Cantwell, D.P. 1979. Minimal brain dysfunction in adults: Evidence from studies of psychiatric illness in the families of hyperactive children. In L. Bellak (ed.), *Psychiatric Aspects of Minimal Brain Dysfunction in Adults.* New York: Grune and Stratton.

Carlson, N.R. 1977. *Physiology of Behavior.* Boston: Allyn & Bacon.

Carroll, B.J., and M. Steiner. 1987. The psychobiology of premenstrual dysphoria: The role of prolactin. *Psychoneuroendocrinology* 3:171–180.

Cattell, R.B. 1982. *The Inheritance of Personality and Ability: Research Methods and Findings.* New York: Academic Press.

Christiansen, K.O. 1977a. A preliminary study of criminality among twins. In S.A. Mednick and K.O. Christiansen (eds.), *Biosocial Bases of Criminal Behavior.* New York: Gardner Press.

Clare, A.W. 1985. Hormones, behaviour and the menstrual cycle. *Journal of Psychosomatic Research* 29(3):225–233.

Clerget-Darpoux, F., L.R. Goldin, and E.S. Fershon. 1986. Clinical methods in psychiatric genetics. III. Environmental stratification may simulate a genetic effect in adoption studies. *Acta Psychiatric Scandanavia* 74:305–311.

Cloninger, C.R., T. Reich, and S.B. Guze. 1975. The multifactorial model of disease transmission: II. Sex differences in the familial transmission of sociopathy (antisocial personality). *British Journal of Psychiatry* 127:11–22.

Cloninger, C.R., K.O. Christiansen, R. Reich, and I.I. Gottesman. 1978. Implications of sex differences in the prevalences of antisocial personality, alcoholism, and criminality for familial transmission. *Archives of General Psychiatry* 35:941–951.

Cloninger, C.R., S. Sigvardsson, M. Bohman, and A–L., von Knorring. 1982. Predisposition to petty criminality in Swedish adoptees: II. Cross-fostering analysis of gene-environment interaction. *Archives of General Psychiatry* 39:1242–1247.

Cocozza, J.J., and H.J. Steadman. 1974. Some refinements in the measurement and prediction of dangerous behavior. *American Journal of Psychiatry* 131:1012–1014.

Coe, C.L., and S. Levine. 1983. Biology of aggression. *Bulletin of the American Academy of Psychiatry Law* 11:131–148.

Cohen, S. 1977. Angel dust. *Journal of the American Medical Association* 238:515–516.

———. 1980. Alcoholic hypoglycemia. *Drug Abuse and Alcoholism Newsletter* 9(2):1–4.

Coid, J. 1979. Mania a potu: A critical review of pathological intoxication. *Psychological Medicine* 9:709–719.

Cooke, W.R. 1945. The differential psychology of the American woman. *American Journal of Obstetrics and Gynecology* 49:457–472.

Cordoba, O.A., and J.L. Chapel. 1983. Medroxyprogesterone acetate antiandrogen treatment of hypersexuality in a pedophiliac sex offender. *American Journal of Psychiatry* 140:1036–1039.

Critchley, E.M.R. 1968. Reading retardation, dyslexia, and delinquency. *British Journal of Psychiatry* 115:1537–1547.

Crowe, R.R. 1972. The adopted offspring of women criminal offenders: A study of their arrest records. *Archives of General Psychiatry* 27:600–603.

———. 1974. An adoption study of antisocial personality. *Archives of General Psychiatry* 31:785–791.

Dalgard, O.S., and E. Kringler. 1976. A Norwegian twin study of criminality. *British Journal of Criminology* 16:213–232.

Dalton, K. 1964. *The Premenstrual Syndrome.* Springfield, Ill.: Charles C. Thomas.

———. 1966. The influence of mother's menstruation on her child. *Proceedings of the Royal Society of Medicine* 59:1014–1016.

David, O.J., J. Clark, and K. Voeller. 1972. Lead and hyperactivity. *Lancet* 2:900.

David, O.J., S.P. Hoffman, J. Sverd, J. Clark, and K. Voeller. 1976. Lead and hyperactivity: Behavioral response to chelation—A pilot study. *American Journal of Psychiatry* 133:1155.

Davis, B.A., P.H. Yu, A.A. Boulton, J.S. Wormith, and D. Addington. 1983. Correlative relationship between biochemical activity and aggressive behavior. *Progress in Neuro-Psychopharmacology and Biological Psychiatry* 7:529–535.

DeFries, J.C., and R. Plomin. 1978. Behavioral genetics. *Annual Reviews in Psychology* 29:473–515.

Demsky, L.S. 1984. The use of Depo-Provera in the treatment of sex offenders. *The Journal of Legal Medicine* 5:295–322.

Denno, D.W. 1988. Human biology and criminal responsibility: Free will or free ride? *University of Pennsylvania Law Review* 137(2):615–671.

Deykin, E.Y., J.C. Levy, and V. Wells. 1986. Adolescent depression, alcohol and drug abuse. *American Journal of Public Health* 76:178–182.

Domino, E.F. 1978. Neurobiology of phencyclidine—An update. In R.C. Peterson and R.C. Stillman (eds.), *Phencyclidine (PCP) Abuse: An Appraisal.* NIDA Research Monograph 21. Rockville, Md.: National Institute on Drug Abuse.

———. 1980. History and pharmacology of PCP and PCP-related analogs. *Journal of Psychedelic Drugs* 12:223–227.

D'Orban, P.T., and J. Dalton. 1980. Violent crime and the menstrual cycle. *Psychological Medicine* 10:353–359.

Eichelman, B.S., and N.B. Thoa. 1972. The aggressive monoamines. *Biological Psychiatry* 6(2):143–163.

Ellis, L., and M.A. Ames. 1987. Neurohormonal functioning and sexual orientation: A theory of homosexuality-heterosexuality. *Psychological Bulletin* 101:233–258.

Ellis, D., and P. Austin. 1971. Menstruation and aggressive behavior in a correctional center for women. *Journal of Criminal Law, Criminology and Police Science* 62:388–395.

Epps, P. 1962. Women shoplifters in Holloway Prison. In T.C.N. Gibbens and J. Prince (eds.), *Shoplifting.* London: The Institute for the Study and Treatment of Delinquency.

Fauman, M.A., and B.J. Fauman. 1980. Chronic Phencyclidine (PCP) abuse: A psychiatric perspective. *Journal of Psychedelic Drugs* 12:307–314.

Fishbein, D.H., and R. Thatcher. In press. Legal applications of electrophysiological assessments. In J. Dywan, R. Kaplan, and F. Pirozzolo (eds.), *Neuropsychology and the Law.* New York: Springer-Verlag.

Fishbein, D.H., D. Lozovsky, and J.H. Jaffe. 1989. Impulsivity, aggression and neuroendocrine responses to serotonergic stimulation in substance abusers. *Biological Psychiatry* 25:1049–1066.

Geary, D.C. 1989. A model for representing gender differences in the pattern of cognitive abilities. *American Psychologist* 44:1155–1156.

Ghodsian-Carpey, J., and L.A. Baker. 1987. Genetic and environmental influences on aggression in 4 to 7 year old twins. *Aggressive Behavior* 13:173–186.

Ginsburg, B.E., and B.F. Carter. 1987. *Premenstrual Syndrome: Ethical and Legal Implications in a Biomedical Perspective.* New York: Plenum.

Glueck, S., and E.T. Glueck. 1956. *Physique and Delinquency.* New York: Harper & Row.

Goddard, H.H. 1921. *Juvenile Delinquency.* New York: Dodd, Mead.

Gottfredson, S. 1986. Statistical and actual considerations. In F. Dutile and C. Foust (eds.), *The Prediction of Criminal Violence.* Springfield, Ill.: Charles C Thomas.

Gove, W.R., and C. Wilmoth. In press. Risk, crime and physiological highs: A consideration of neurological processes which may act as positive reinforcers. In L. Ellis and H. Hoffman (eds.), *Evolution, The Brain and Criminal Behavior: A Reader in Biosocial Criminology.* New York: Praeger.

Guze, S.B., E.D., Wolfgram, J.K. McKinney, and D.P. Cantwell. 1967. Psychiatric illness in the families of convicted criminals: A study of 519 first-degree relatives. *Diseases of the Nervous System* 28:651–659.

Hamparin, D.M., R. Schuster, S. Dinitz, and J.P. Conrad. 1978. *The Violent Few: A Study of Dangerous Juvenile Offenders.* Lexington, Mass.: Lexington Books.

Hare, R.D. 1970. *Psychopathy: Theory and Research.* New York: John Wiley & Sons.

———. 1978. Electrodermal and cardiovascular correlates of psychopathy. In R.D. Hare and D. Schalling (eds.), *Psychopathic Behavior.* New York: John Wiley & Sons.

Hare, R.D., and D. Schalling. 1978. *Psychopathic Behavior.* New York: John Wiley & Sons.

Harry, B., and C. Blacer. 1987. Menstruation and crime: A critical review of the literature from the clinical criminology perspective. *Behavioral Sciences and the Law* 5(3)307–322.

Haskett, R.F. 1987. Premenstrual dysphoric disorder: Evaluation, pathophysiology and treatment. *Progress in Neuro-Psychopharmacology and Biological Psychiatry* 11:129–135.

Hill, D., and D. Watterson. 1942. Electroencephalographic studies of the psychopathic personality. *Journal of Neurological Psychiatry* 5:47–64.

Hirschi, T., and M.J. Hindelang. 1977. Intelligence and delinquency: A revisionist review. *Science* 196:1393–1409.

Hooten, E.A. 1939. *The American Criminal: An Anthropological Study.* Cambridge, Mass.: Harvard University Press.

Howard, R.C. 1984. The clinical EEG and personality in mentally abnormal offenders. *Psychological Medicine* 14:569–580.

Hurwitz, I., R.M. Bibace, P.H. Wolff, and B.M. Rowbotham. 1972. Neuropsychological function of normal boys, delinquent boys, and boys with learning problems. *Perceptual and Motor Skills* 35(2):387–394.

Hutchings, B., and S.A. Mednick. 1975. Registered criminality in the adoptive and biological parents of registered male criminal adoptees. In R.R. Fieve, D. Rosenthal, and H. Brill (eds.), *Genetic Research in Psychiatry.* Baltimore: John Hopkins University Press.

Jacobs, P.A., M. Brunton, M.M. Melville, R.P. Brittain, and W. McClemont. 1965. Aggressive behaviour, mental sub-normality, and the XYY male. *Nature* 108:1351–1352.

Jeffery, C.R. 1977. *Crime Prevention through Environmental Design.* Beverly Hills, Calif.: Sage.

———. 1985. *Attacks on the Insanity Defense: Biological Psychiatry and New Perspectives on Criminal Behavior.* Springfield, Ill.: Charles C Thomas.

Jutai, J.W., and R.D. Hare. 1983. Psychopathy and selective attention during performance of a complex perceptual-motor task. *Psychophysiology* 20:146–151.

Kellam, S.G., M.E. Ensminger, and M.B. Simon. 1980. Mental health in first grade and teenage drug, alcohol, and cigarette use. *Drug and Alcohol Dependence* 5:273–304.

Khajawall, A.M., T.B. Erickson, and G.B. Simpson. 1982. Chronic phencyclidine abuse and physical assault. *American Journal of Psychiatry* 139:1604–1606.

Kiloh, L.G., A.J. McComas, and J.W. Osselton. 1972. *Clinical Electroencephalography.* 3rd ed. London: Butterworths.

Kreuz, L.E., and R.M. Rose. 1971. Assessment of aggressive behavior and plasma testosterone in a young criminal population. *Psychomatic Medicine* 34:321–332.

Kuperman, S., and M. Stewart. 1987. Use of propranolol to decrease aggressive outbursts in younger patients. *Psychosomatics* 28:315–319.

Larson, C.J. 1984. *Crime, Justice and Society.* New York: General Hall.

Lester, M.L., and D.H. Fishbein. 1987. Nutrition and neuropsychological development in children. In R. Tarter, D.H. Van Thiel, and K. Edwards (eds.), *Medical Neuropsychology: The Impact of Disease on Behavior.* New York: Plenum.

Lewis, D.O., S.S. Shanok, and D.A. Balla. 1979. Perinatal difficulties, head and face trauma and child abuse in the medical histories of serious youthful offenders. *American Journal of Psychiatry* 136:419–423.

Lewis, D.O., S.S. Shanok, and J.N. Pincus. 1981. The neuropsychiatric status of violent male delinquents. In D.O. Lewis (ed.), *Vulnerabilities to Delinquency.* New York: Spectrum.

Lewis, D.O., E. Moy, L.D. Jackson, R. Aaronson, N. Restifo, S. Serra, and A. Simos. 1985. Biopsychosocial characteristics of children who later murder: A prospective study. *American Journal of Psychiatry* 142:1161–1167.

Lewis, D.O., J.H. Pincus, M. Feldman, L. Jackson, and B. Bard. 1986. Psychiatric, neurological, and psychoeducational characteristics of 15 death row inmates in the United States. *American Journal of Psychiatry* 143:838–845.

Lewis, D.O., J.H. Pincus, B. Bard, E. Richardson, L.S. Prichep, M. Feldman, and C. Yeager. 1988. Neuropsychiatric, psychoeducational, and family characteristics of 14 juveniles condemned to death in the United States. *American Journal of Psychiatry* 145:584–589.

Linder, R.L., S.E. Lerner, and R.S. Burns. 1981. The experience and effects of PCP abuse. In *The Devil's Dust: Recognition, Management, and Prevention of Phencyclidine Abuse.* Belmont, Calif.: Wardsworth.

Linnoila, M., M. Virkkunen, M. Scheinin, A. Nuutila, R. Rimon, and F.K. Goodwin. 1983. Low cerebrospinal fluid 5-hydroxyindoleacetic acid concentration differentiates impulsive from nonimpulsive violent behavior. *Life Sciences* 33:2609–2614.

Lion, J.R. 1974. Diagnosis and treatment of personality disorders. In J.R. Lion (ed.), *Personality Disorders: Diagnosis and Treatment.* Baltimore: Williams and Wilkins.

———. 1979. Benzodiazepines in the treatment of aggressive patients. *Journal of Clinical Psychiatry* 40:70–71.

Loeber, R., and T. Dishion. 1983. Early predictors of male delinquency: A review. *Psychological Bulletin* 94:68–99.

Lombroso, C. 1918. *Crimes, Its Causes and Remedies.* Boston: Little, Brown.

Maletsky, B.M. 1976. The diagnosis of pathological intoxication. *Journal of Studies on Alcohol* 37:1215–1228.

Marinacci, A.A. 1963. Special types of temporal lobe seizures following ingestion of alcohol. *Bulletin of the Los Angeles Neurological Society* 28:241–250.

Marrs-Simon, P.A., M. Weiler, M.C. Santangelo, M.T. Perry, and J.B. Leikin. 1988. Analysis of sexual disparity of violent behavior in PCP intoxication. *Veterinary and Human Toxicology* 30(1):53–55.

Marsh, F.H., and J. Katz. 1985. *Biology, Crime and Ethics: A Study of Biological Explanations for Criminal Behavior.* Cincinnati: Anderson Publishing.

Mattes, J.A., and M. Fink. 1987. A family study of patients with temper outbursts. *Journal of Psychiatric Research* 21:249–255.

McCardle, L., and D.H. Fishbein. 1989. The self-reported effects of PCP on human aggression. *Addictive Behaviors* 4(4):465–472.

McGee, R., S. Williams, D.L. Share, J. Anderson, and P.A. Silva. 1986. The relationship between specific reading retardation, general reading backwardness and behavioural problems in a large sample of Dunedin boys: A longitudinal study from five to eleven years. *Journal of Child Psychology and Psychiatry* 27:597–610.

McManus, M., A. Brickman, N.E. Alessi, and W.L. Grapentine. 1985. Neurological dysfunction in serious delinquents. *Journal of the American Academy of Child Psychiatry* 24:481–486.

Mednick, S.A., J. Volavka, W.F. Gabrielli, and T.M. Itil. 1981. EEG predicts later delinquency. *Criminology* 19:219–229.

Mednick, S.A., V. Pollock, J. Volavka, and W.F. Gabrielli, Jr. 1982. Biology and violence. In M.E. Wolfgang and N.A. Weiner (eds.), *Criminal Violence.* Beverly Hills, Calif.: Sage.

Mednick, S.A., W.F. Gabrelli, Jr., and B. Hutchings. 1984. Genetic influences in criminal convictions: Evidence from an adoption cohort. *Science* 224:891–894.

Mednick, S.A., T.E. Moffitt, and S.A. Stack. 1987. *The Causes of Crime: New Biological Approaches.* New York: Cambridge University Press.

Moffitt, T.E., S.A. Mednick, W.F. Gabrielli, Jr. 1989. Predicting careers of criminal violence: Descriptive data and predispositional factors. In D.A. Brizer and M. Crowner (eds.), *Current Approaches to the Prediction of Violence.* Washington, D.C.: American Psychiatric Press.

Monahan, J. 1981. *The Clinical Prediction of Violent Behavior.* Rockville, Md.: U.S. Department of Health and Human Services.

Moore, L.S., and A.I. Fleischman. 1975. Subclinical lead toxicity. *Orthomolecular Psychiatry* 4:61–70.

Morton, J.H., H. Addition, and R.G. Addison. 1953. A clinical study of premenstrual tension. *American Journal of Obstetrics and Gynecology* 65:1182–1191.

Muhlbauer, H.D. 1985. Human aggression and the role of central serotonin. *Pharmacopsychiatry* 18:218–221.

Murray, J.B. 1987. Psychopharmacological therapy of deviant sexual behavior. *Journal of General Psychology* 115:101–110.

Needleman, H.L., C. Gunnoe, A. Leviton, P. Reed, H. Peresie, C. Maher, and P. Barrett. 1979. Deficits in psychologic and classroom performance of children with elevated dentine lead levels. *New England Journal of Medicine* 300:689–695.

Olweus, D., A. Mattsson, D. Schalling, and H. Low. 1988. Circulating testosterone levels and aggression in adolescent males: A causal analysis. *Psychosomatic Medicine* 50(3):261–272.

Owen, D., and J.O. Sines. 1970. Heritability of personality in children. *Behavior Genetics* 1:235–248.

Perlmutter, B.F. 1987. Delinquency and Learning Disabilities: Evidence for compensatory behaviors and adaptation. *Journal of Youth and Adolescence* 16:89–95.

Pihl, R.O., and M. Parkes. 1977. Hair element content in learning disabled children. *Science* 198:204.

Pihl, R.O., and D. Ross. 1987. Research on alcohol related aggression: A review and implications for understanding aggression. In S.W. Sadava (ed.), *Drug Use and Psychological Theory.* New York: Haworth Press.

Pihl, R.O., F. Ervin, G. Pelletier, W. Diekel, and W. Strain. 1982. Hair element content of violent criminals. *Canadian Journal of Psychiatry* 27:533.

Pincus, J., and G. Tucker. 1974. *Behavioral Neurology.* New York: Oxford University Press.

Plomin, R. 1989. Environment and genes: Determinants of behavior. *American Psychologist* 44:105–111.

Plomin, R., and D. Daniels. 1987. Why are children in the same family so different from one another? *Behavioral and Brain Sciences* 10:1–16.

Plomin, R., J.C. DeFries, and G.E. McClearn. 1980. *Behavioral Genetics: A Primer.* San Francisco: W.H. Freeman.

Plomin, R., T.T. Foch, and D.C. Rowe. 1981. Bobo clown aggression in childhood: Environment, not genes. *Journal of Research in Personality* 15:331–342.

Plomin, R., K. Nitz, and D.C. Rowe. 1990. Behavioral genetics and aggressive behavior in childhood. In M. Lewis and S.M. Miller (eds.), *Handbook of Developmental Psychopathology.* New York: Plenum.

Pontius, A.A., and K.F. Ruttiger. 1976. Frontal lobe system maturational lag in juvenile delinquents shown in narratives test. *Adolescence* XI(44):509–518.

Pontius, A.A., and B.S. Yudowitz. 1980. Frontal lobe system dysfunction in some critical actions as shown in the narratives test. *The Journal of Nervous and Mental Disease* 168:111–117.

Poremba, C. 1975. Learning disabilities, youth and delinquency: Programs for intervention. In H.R. Myklebust (ed.), *Progress in Learning Disabilities.* Vol. III. New York: Grune & Stratton.

Pugh, G.E. 1977. *The Biological Origin of Human Values.* New York: Basic Books.

Rada, R.T., D.R. Laws, R. Kellner, L. Stivastava, and G. Peake. 1983. Plasma androgens in violent and nonviolent sex offenders. *Bulletin of the American Academy of Psychiatry Law* 11:149–158.

Raine, A., and P.H. Venables. 1987. Contingent negative variation, P3 evoked potentials and antisocial behavior. *Psychophysiology* 24(2):191–199.

Richman, N., J. Stevenson, and P.J. Graham. 1982. *Pre-school to School: A Behavioural Study.* London: Academic Press.

Rimland, B., and G.E. Larson. 1983. Hair mineral analysis and behavior: An analysis of 51 studies. *Journal of Learning Disabilities* 16:279–285.

Robins, L.N., P.A. West, and B.L. Herjanic. 1975. Arrests and delinquency in two generations: A study of black urban families and their children. *Journal of Child Psychology and Psychiatry* 16:125–140.

Rogeness, G.A., M.A. Javors, J.W. Maas, C.A. Macedo, and C. Fischer. 1987. Plasma dopamine-B-hydroxylase, HVA, MHPG, and conduct disorder in emotionally disturbed boys. *Biological Psychiatry* 22:1155–1158.

Rowe, D.C. 1983. Biometrical genetic models of self-reported delinquent behavior: A twin study. *Behavior Genetics* 13:473–489.

———. 1986. Genetic and environmental components of antisocial behavior: A study of 265 twin pairs. *Criminology* 24(3):513–532.

Rowe, D.C., and D.W. Osgood. 1984. Heredity and sociological theories of delinquency: A reconsideration. *American Sociological Review* 49:526–540.

Roy, A., M. Virkkunen, S. Guthrie, R. Poland, and M. Linnoila. 1986. Monoamines, glucose metabolism, suicidal and aggressive behaviors. *Psychopharmacology Bulletin* 22(3):661–665.

Rushton, J.P., D.W. Fulker, M.C. Neale, D.K.B. Nias, and H.J. Eysenck. 1986. Altruism and aggression: The heritability of individual differences. *Journal of Personality and Social Psychology* 50(6):1192–1198.

Schiavi, R.C., A. Theilgaard, D.R. Owen, and D. White. 1984. Sex chromosome anomalies, hormones, and aggressivity. *Archives of General Psychiatry* 41:93–99.

Schuckit, M.A., and M.A. Morrissey. 1978. Propoxyphene and phencyclidine (PCP) use in adolescents. *Journal of Clinical Psychiatry* 39:7–13.

Schulsinger, F. 1985. The experience from the adoption method in genetic research. *Progress in Clinical and Biological Research* 177:461–478.

Seigal, R.K. 1978. Phencyclidine, criminal behavior, and the defense of diminished capacity. In R.C. Peterson and R.C. Stillman (eds.), *Phencyclidine (PCP) Abuse: An Appraisal.* NIDA Research Monograph 21. Rockville, MD.: National Institute on Drug Abuse.

Sheldon, W.H. 1949. *Varieties of Delinquent Youth.* New York: Harper & Row.

Sigvardsson, S., C.R. Cloninger, M. Bohman, and A–L. von Knorring. 1982. Predisposition to petty criminality in Swedish adoptees. III. Sex differences and validation of the male typology. *Archives of General Psychiatry* 39:1248–1253.

Smith, D.E., and D.R. Wesson. 1980. PCP abuse: Diagnostic and pharmacological treatment approaches. *Journal of Psychedelic Drugs* 12:293–299.

Soubrie, P. 1986. Reconciling the role of central serotonin neurons in human and animal behavior. *The Behavioral and Brain Sciences* 9:319–364.

Spodak, M.K., Z.A. Falck, and J.R. Rappeport. 1978. The hormonal treatment of paraphiliacs with Depo-Provera. *Criminal Justice and Behavior* 5:304–314.

Stewart, M.A., and C.S. de Blois. 1983. Father-son resemblances in aggressive and antisocial behavior. *British Journal of Psychiatry* 142:78–84.

Stewart, M.A., and L. Leone. 1978. A family study of unsocialized aggressive boys. *Biological Psychiatry* 13:107–117.

Stewart, M.A., C.S. de Blois, and C. Cummings. 1980. Psychiatric disorder in the parents of hyperactive boys and those with conduct disorder. *Journal of Child Psychology and Psychiatry* 21:283–292.

Sutker, P.B., and A.N. Allain. 1987. Cognitive abstraction, shifting, and control: Clinical sample comparisons of psychopaths and nonpsychopaths. *Journal of Abnormal Psychology* 96(1):73–75.

Syndulko, K. 1978. Electrocortical investigations of sociopathy. In R.D. Hare and D. Schalling (eds.), *Psychopathic Behavior: Approaches to Research.* Chichester, England: John Wiley & Sons.

Tarter, R.E., A.I. Alterman, and K.L. Edwards. 1985. Vulnerability to alcoholism in men: A behavior-genetic perspective. *Journal of Studies on Alcoholism* 46(4):329–356.

Tellegen, A., D.T. Lykken, T.J. Bouchard, K. Wilcox, N. Segal, and S. Rich. 1988. Personality similarity in twins reared apart and together. *Journal of Personality and Social Psychology* 54(6):1031–1039.

Thiessen, D.D. 1976. *The Evolution and Chemistry of Aggression.* Springfield, Ill.: Charles C Thomas.

Trunnell, E.P., and C.W. Turner. 1988. A comparison of the psychological and hormonal factors in women with and without premenstrual syndrome. *Journal of Abnormal Psychology* 97:429–436.

Twito, T.J., and M.A. Stewart. 1982. A half-sibling study of aggressive conduct disorder. *Neuropsychobiology* 8:144–150.

Valzelli, L. 1981. *Psychobiology of Aggression and Violence.* New York: Raven Press.

van Praag, H.M., R.S. Kahn, G.M. Asnis, S. Wetzler, S.L. Brown, A. Bleich, and M.L. Korn. 1987. Denosologization of biological psychiatry or the specificity of 5-HT disturbances in psychiatric disorders. *Journal of Affective Disorders* 13:1–8.

Venables, P.H. 1987. Autonomic nervous system factors in criminal behavior. In S.A. Mednick, T.E. Moffitt, and S.A. Stack (eds.), *The Causes of Crime: New Biological Approaches.* New York: Cambridge University Press.

Virkkunen, M., and S. Narvanen. 1987. Plasma insulin, tryptophan and serotonin levels during the glucose tolerance test among habitually violent and impulsive offenders. *Neuropsychobiology* 17:19–23.

Virkkunen, M., A. Nuutila, F.K. Goodwin, and M. Linnoila. 1987. Cerebrospinal fluid monoamine metabolite levels in male arsonists. *Archives of General Psychiatry* 44:241–247.

Virkkunen, M., J. DeJong, J. Bartkko, F.K. Goodwin, and M. Linnoila. 1989. Relationship of psychobiological variables to recidivism in violent offenders and impulsive fire setters. *Archives of General Psychiatry* 46:600–603.

Volavka, J. 1987. Electroencephalogram among criminals. In S.A. Mednick, T.E. Moffitt, and S.A. Stack (eds.), *The Causes of Crime: New Biological Approaches.* New York: Cambridge University Press.

Waid, W.M., M.T. Orne, and S.K. Wilson. 1979. Socialization, awareness and the electrodermal response to deception and self-disclosure. *Journal of Abnormal Psychology* 88:663–666.

Wallgren, H, and H. Barry. 1970. *Action of Alcohol.* Vols. 1 and 2. New York: Elsevier.

Walters, G.D., and T.W. White. 1989. Heredity and crime: Bad genes or bad research? *Criminology* 27:455–486.

Watson, J.B. 1925. *Behaviorism.* New York: W.W. Norton.

Weingartner, H., M.V. Rudorfer, M.S. Buchsbaum, and M. Linnoila. 1983. Effects of serotonin on memory impairments produced by ethanol. *Science* 221:472–474.

Wenk, E.A., J.O., Robison, and G.W. Smith. 1972. Can violence be predicted? *Crime and Delinquency* 18:393–402.
Widom, C.S. 1978. Toward an understanding of female criminality. *Progress in Experimental Personality Research* 8:245–308.
Wilson, J.Q. and R.J. Herrnstein. 1985. *Crime and Human Nature.* New York: Simon & Schuster.
Wolff, P.H., D. Waber, M. Bauermeister, C. Cohen, and R. Ferber. 1982. The neuropsychological status of adolescent delinquent boys. *Journal of Child Psychology and Psychiatry* 23:267–279.
Wolfgang, M.E., R.M. Figlio, and T. Sellin. 1972. *Delinquency in a Birth Cohort.* Chicago: University of Chicago Press.
Yudofsky, S.C., J.M. Silver, and S.E. Schneider. 1987. Pharmacologic treatment of aggression. *Psychiatric Annals* 17:397–406.
Zuckerman, M. 1983. A biological theory of sensation seeking. In Zuckerman, M. (ed.), *Biological Basis of Sensation Seeking, Impulsivity and Anxiety.* Hillsdale, N.J.: Lawrence Erlbaum Associates.

FRAME the DEBATE

Form at end of book

Issue 1: Are criminals biologically predisposed to committing crimes?

A Discipline in Peril: Sociology's Future Hinges on Curing Its Biophobia

Lee Ellis

Lee Ellis is a professor of sociology at Minot State University, Minot, North Dakota 58707. E-mail: ellis@warpb.cs.misu.nodak.edu

Several lines of evidence are reviewed regarding sociology's decline as a college major and as a respected academic discipline in recent decades. The present article attributes most of the decline to biophobia, i.e., *the tendency to avoid considering biological causes of human behavior. Four explanations are offered for sociology's biophobia: semantic factors, lack of training in biology, exclusive focus on humans, and moral/political factors. Ironically, a recent survey indicated that most sociologists are at least mildly receptive to the view that biological factors play some role in several important aspects of human behavior, including academic achievement, sexual orientation, serious adult criminality, and even gender differences in aggression. In addition, many sociologists have proposed biosocial explanations of human behavior, although often having to publish in non-sociology outlets. The article ends by illustrating how biological and social factors can be combined to help explain a well-established relationship between religiosity and criminality.*

Nearly twenty years ago, I wrote a little-noted article entitled "The decline and fall of sociology, 1975–2000" (Ellis, 1977) warning that sociology would suffer a serious decline if sociologists continued to subscribe to the absurd assumption that biology is unimportant for understanding sociological phenomena. Since then, little has changed, and my forecast sadly seems to be materializing. Recently, two sociology journals devoted entire issues to discussing sociology's decline as a respected academic discipline and as a college major—*Sociological Forum* (1994) and *Sociological Spectrum* (1995).

I will show that, even though most sociologists retain extremely environmentalistic perspectives, a substantial minority has broken ranks in recent years. Suggestions are made for ways in which they can shape sociology into a discipline that is no longer antagonistic to a biosocial perspective.

Recent Assessments of the State of Sociology

If the theme of this article seems overly alarming, reflect on a couple of comments recently appearing in *Footnotes*, the official newsletter for the American Sociological Association. First, after reviewing evidence of sociology's theoretical sterility, Porter (1993) suggested that the discipline "may die out by the end of this century." Second, in an article entitled "A discipline in trouble: Why more sociology departments may be closing shortly," Lynch et al. (1993) reviewed information pertaining to the quality of teaching and research in U.S. colleges and universities. The authors concluded that sociology departments across the nation were rated at or near the bottom in both categories.

Elsewhere, Lopreato (1994:318) asserted that sociology seems to be in the process of "being cannibalized by various disciplines," most notably biology, psychology, and anthropology. A few years earlier, van den Berghe (1990:185) blamed sociology's "intellectual bankruptcy" on its "sorry state of theoretical affairs."

There are several other indications that since its heyday in the 1960s, sociology has lost much of the respect afforded it by the academic community and the public at large. As to why this has occurred, I will argue that the underlying cause is not inherently poor teaching, and it is certainly not because the social problems sociologists have sought to ameliorate have retracted. Rather, the main cause is that most sociological theories are absurd, especially those premised on the naive Durkheimian assumption that all social phenomena must have only social causes. This article briefly explores the modern roots of sociology's resistance to biology and closes with an example of how biological concepts can begin to be integrated into sociological theorizing.

"A Discipline in Peril: Sociology's Future Hinges on Curing Its Biophobia" by Lee Ellis. Reprinted by permission of Transaction Publishers from *The American Sociologist*, Summer 1996.

Reasons for Concern

Since 1960, enrollment in United States colleges and universities has nearly tripled. During roughly the same time, the number of students majoring in sociology has dropped by more than half (Das, 1989:356; Kantrowitz, 1992; U.S. Department of Education, 1992:294; Knottnerus & Maguire, 1995:19). While a slight reversal of sociology's declining popularity as a college major took place in the late 1980s (Kelly, 1991), the overall trend is still dramatically downward. Over the past three decades, most of the other social and behavioral sciences have either held steady or substantially increased in their attraction of majors (Das, 1989:356; U.S. Department of Education, 1992:294).

At least as worrisome as the decline in the number of undergraduate majors in sociology is the reduced support being given to sociology departments by American universities. Since 1990, several reports have been published regarding substantial cutbacks in funding for sociology (e.g., Kantrowitz, 1992; Stone, 1992). In fact, three universities have gone so far as to close their sociology departments—Washington University in St. Louis (Heyl, 1989; Pittman & Boden, 1989; Heller, 1990; Fabianic, 1991:35), the University of Rochester (Coughlin, 1992), and San Diego State University (Horowitz, 1993:3). Sociology departments at Duke, Utah, and Southern Methodist have also come close to dismantlement in recent years (Rhoades, 1981; Lipset, 1994:215). While it may be reassuring to know that 2,000 sociology departments remain (Knottnerus & Maguire, 1995:17), the fact that all of those closed so far used to be prominent, thriving departments commands attention.

Also disturbing are public comments by sociologists themselves. In his book, *The Decomposition of Sociology*, Horowitz (1993:16) maintained that sociology's current down-sizing in the academic community reflects the fact that sociology has become "a residue of what it once was." Horowitz criticized the willingness of most sociologists to put more emphasis on political correctness than on innovative thinking:

> Sociology has become a series of demands for correct politics rather than a set of studies of social culture. Theoretical differences are evaporating as gentle intimidation displaces intellectual inquiry, and the result is an advanced form of decay disguised but not removed by the plethora of ideologists who have invaded this once omnibus "science of society." (1993:17)

There are other disturbing signs that sociology is moving toward academic marginality. One is the recent cessation of publication of *Sociology and Social Research*, the second oldest sociology journal in America. The reason given for its termination was simple: "too few readers" (Felson, 1992). Recently, an ASA task force reported that the Sociology Section of the Graduate Record Exam "may be on its last leg" (Hall, 1994). Why? Too few students are signing up to take it (also see Howery, 1994).

The Source of the Problem

What has caused these trends? Has sociology declined because the subject matter is no longer interesting or important? Or, do the causes have more to do with credibility?

Without being overly simplistic, I submit that there is one over-riding reason sociology has declined. That reason is what Daly and Wilson (1988:152) aptly characterized as sociology's biophobia. *Biophobia,* they said, refers to the tendency to give no serious consideration to biological factors when attempting to understand human behavior, especially human social behavior.

Van den Berghe (1986:676) and Nielsen (1994:268) have come to similar conclusions regarding sociologists' almost instinctual tendency to turn a blind eye to all biological influences on human behavior. Van den Berghe went on to note that, unlike what has occurred in psychology and anthropology, and even to some extent in economics, sociology continues to ignore the evidence that biological factors have major influences on human behavior (also see Carey & Lopreato, 1994:407; Udry, 1994; Casterline, 1995; Gove, 1994, 1995; Lauritsen, 1995:90; Walsh, 1995).

Why would biophobia have continued to flourish in sociology while retracting in all of the other major social sciences? As represented in Figure 1, I submit that four factors are primarily responsible. One factor is semantic, a fact that may at first glance seem trivial. It has to do with the unfortunate tendency to equate *sociological causes* with *social causes.* The second factor involves the fact that far too few sociologists are biologically literate. The third factor has been the inattention that sociologists give to research on social animals other than humans. And the fourth factor involves a strong moral/ideological commitment to human equality that prevents many sociologists from considering the possibility of biologically based causes of individual and especially group differences in behavior. Hopefully, by understanding these factors, they can be overcome. With that in mind, each factor is elaborated on below.

Regarding semantics, many sociologists (and other social scientists) have come to think of *biological* and *sociological* as mutually exclusive (e.g., Halpern et al., 1994:217), and they have come to equate *social causes* with *sociological causes* (e.g., Siegel, 1989:219). Both of these

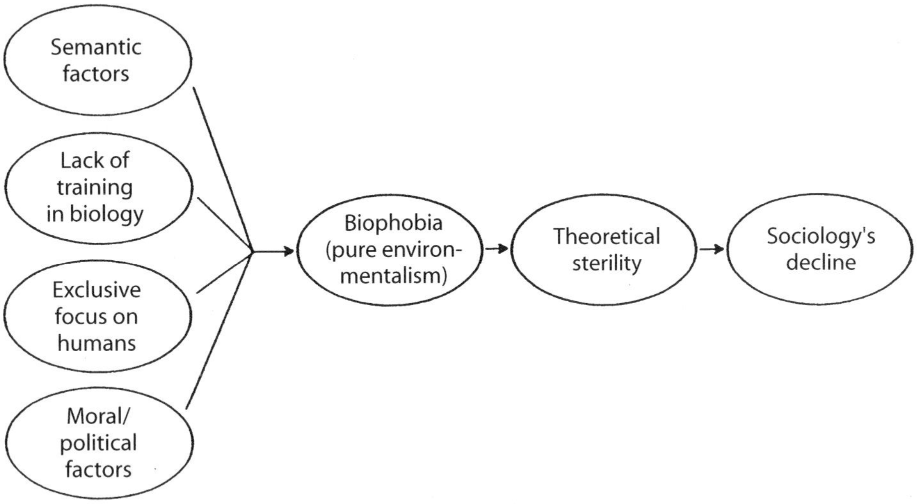

Figure 1. A proposed model for explaining sociology's decline.

conceptualizations imply that sociologists are outside of their realm of expertise, and perhaps even betraying their discipline, whenever they give attention to biological causes of sociocultural phenomena.

Sociologists need to keep in mind that social phenomena are exhibited exclusively by animals, and, as such, social phenomena are in fact biological phenomena (Ellis, 1990:4). I believe that it is very important to define sociology in terms of what sociologists attempt to explain, i.e., sociocultural phenomena, not in terms of the causal variables that they consider when offering explanations. For example, the fact that I have proposed that nonsocial biological factors contribute to human social stratification (Ellis, 1991b, 1993b, 1994c) should not make me less of a sociologist than members of the discipline who offer strictly social explanations for social stratification.

Concerning academic training as a source of biophobia, sociologists take far too few courses in biology; they should at least take as many as do most psychologists and anthropologists. It is incumbent upon those of us already in the discipline to change this "tradition." I still recall a colleague informing me several years ago with a sense of pride and accomplishment that he had earned his Ph.D. in sociology without ever having taken even an undergraduate course in biology. It goes without saying that he continues to encourage advisees not to waste their time in biology classes if their goal is to better understand human behavior. This anti-biological perspective is continuing to erode sociology's credibility, and it is depriving future sociologists of the conceptual tools they need to understand many important aspects of human nature (including our social nature).

As shown in Table 1, many sociologists in recent years actually have begun to incorporate a number of biological concepts into their research and theorizing. Unfortunately, most sociologists are unable to understand, let alone coherently criticize, most of these publications. Without at least basic biological training, along with the dead-wrong Durkheimian assumption that only "social factors cause social phenomena," it is easy to see why the works cited in Table 1 are falling on so many deaf ears within the sociological community.

It is a grave disservice to undergraduates majoring in sociology not to have at least four basic courses in biology. These are introductory biology, and then three more specialized courses in evolutionary theory, genetics, and neurology/neurochemistry. As far as graduate students are concerned, a doctorate degree should never be conferred if a sociologist cannot demonstrate some graduate level proficiency in each of these three areas.

The third cause of sociology's biophobia has to do with the discipline's continued narrow focus on just one species of social animal, the human species. Carey and Lopreato (1994) have called sociologists' failure to investigate the numerous parallels in the social behavior of nonhumans and humans *anthropocentrism.* I would call it *specieism,* and submit that it is as closed minded as *racism* is for those who are seeking to achieve an unbiased appreciation of social phenomena.

Psychologists and anthropologists have enriched their studies of human behavior in recent decades with both naturalistic and experimental investigations of numerous species of nonhuman animals. Sociologists need to do likewise. To encourage this to happen, I recommend that editors of the leading sociology journals set aside a significant proportion (say 20%) of their pages for research reports on the social behavior of nonhuman

Table 1 **Areas of Study by Sociologists Who Have Included Biological Concepts in Their Research and Theorizing Since the Early 1970s**

Primary Focus	Sociologist(s)[1] Involved
Altruism and morality	**Lopreato,** 1981, 1988; **Piliavin** & **Charng,** 1990; **Allison,** 1992
Communication behavior	**Mazur, Rosa,** Fraupel, Heler, Leen, & Thurman, 1980
Criminality, delinquency, and human aggression	**van den Berghe,** 1974; **Robins,** 1975, 1978; **Jeffery,** 1977, 1979; **Burgess,** 1980; **Lightcap, Kurland,** & **Burgess,** 1982; **Burgess** & **Garbarino** 1983; Rowe & **Osgood,** 1984; **Ellis,** 1987a, 1987b, 1987c, 1987d, 1989, 1990a, 1990b, 1990c, 1991b, 1996a; **Walsh,** 1987, 1991a, 1991b; **Burgess** & Draper, 1988; **Burgess,** Kurland, & Pensky, 1988; **Ellis** & **Coontz,** 1990; **Baldwin,** 1990; **Machalek** & **Cohen,** 1991; **Gove** & Wilmoth, 1990; **Rahav** & **Ellis,** 1990; **Udry,** 1990; Drigotas & **Udry,** 1993; **Walsh** 1991b; **Sampson** & Laub, 1992; Halpern, Vila & **Cohen,** 1993; Henry, Moffitt, **Robins,** Silva, 1993; **Cochran, Wood,** Arneklev, 1994; **Wood, Gove,** & **Cochran,** 1994; **Cohen** & **Machalek,** 1994; **Wood, Cochran,** Pfefferbaum, & **Arneklev,** 1995
Demography and fertility	**Lopreato,** 1994a
Drug use/abuse	**Robins** & Mills, 1993; **Wood, Cochran,** & Pfefferbaum, 1995
Ethnicity and race	**van den Berghe,** 1978, 1987, in press; **van den Berghe** & Frost, 1986; **Lopreato,** 1984; **Horowitz,** 1995
Family structure and relations	**van den Berghe** & Barash, 1977; **van den Berghe,** 1979, 1980, 1984, 1988; **Burgess,** 1994; Hsieh & **Burgess,** 1994
Human emotions, motivations, and feelings	**Tiger,** 1979; **Kirsten,** 1981, 1988; Boukydis & **Burgess,** 1982; **Walsh,** 1983; **Kemper,** 1987; **Walsh** & Walsh, 1989; **Ellis** & Peckham, 1991; **Gove** 1994
Human health and longevity	**Ellis,** 1994b; **Lopreato,** 1994b; **Carey** & **Lopreato,** 1995
Incest/incest avoidance	**van den Berghe,** 1980, 1983, 1987; **Shepher,** 1983; **Lopreato,** 1984:

species. If this strikes civil libertarians as too much of a quota system, it could be simply used as a guideline for accepting journal articles. The goal should be to encourage sociologists to explore the fascinating insights into social behavior that can come from a comparative approach in the broadest sense.

Here is an example: I recently compared the formation of hierarchical relationships among humans and other species, and found that human social status and dominance relationships among other animals are fundamentally the same phenomenon (Ellis, 1993). The only important difference that I could identify was that humans express many (but not all) of their hierarchical tendencies in linguistic forms, whereas other animals manifest theirs only in nonlinguistic forms (Ellis, 1993:29; also see Lopreato, 1984:73).

If it is true that social status and dominance are fundamentally the same phenomenon, much of the research on human social stratification should be carefully compared to the social processes underlying hierarchical formations in other species. I did so for two variables—height (or body size in the case of nonhumans) and health/longevity—and found the similarities striking. Overall, high status in humans and high rank in nonhumans were both associated with increased height (in humans) and body size (in nonhumans) (Ellis, 1994a). Likewise, high status in humans and high rank in nonhumans were associated with health and longevity (Ellis, 1994c). This sort of knowledge can lead to a rich array of new cross-species hypotheses. Studies will no doubt find divergencies as well as similarities between human and nonhuman social stratification, but these findings will enhance sociological understanding of the entire phenomenon of social hierarchy formations and unequal access to resources.

I also undertook a recent meta-analysis of research on dominance and reproductive success among nonhuman animals (Ellis, 1995). Doing so revealed interesting patterns that I used to suggest how human social status might be related to fertility rates, both before and after the so-called *demographic transition.*

My hope is that such information will someday be incorporated into basic texts on social stratification. At the present time, however, most social stratification texts do

Table 1 *(continued)*

Primary Focus	Sociologist(s)[1] Involved
Intelligence/academic ability	**Eckberg,** 1979; **Eckland,** 1980; **Gordon,** 1980, 1986, 1987; **Gottfredson,** 1986, 1994; **Gottfredson** & Crouse, 1986; **Retherford** & **Sewell** 1988, 1989
International relations and ecology	**Burgess,** 1978; **Lopreato** & **Green,** 1990
Leisure and play behavior	**Baldwin,** 1986
Personality development	**Udry** & Talbert, 1988
Religion/religiosity	**Tiger,** 1979, 1985; **Crippen** & **Machalek,** 1989; **Walsh,** 1980; **Lopreato** & Houghton, 1981; Halpern, **Udry** et al., 1994; **Ellis,** 1985, 1996a
Sex roles/gender-typical behavior	**Rossi,** 1977, 1978, 1981, 1986, 1984, 1994; **Ellis,** 1986; **Walsh** 1993; **Hooks** & **Green,** 1993; **Udry,** 1994
Sexual and reproductive behavior	**Newcomer & Udry,** 1984; **Shepher** & Reisman, 1985; **Udry** et al., 1985, 1986; **Udry** & Billy, 1987; **Udry,** 1988; **Felson,** 1993
Sexual orientation	**Bell,** Weinberg, & Hammersmith, 1981; **Whitam,** 1983; **Harry,** 1984; **Ellis** & Ames, 1987; **Ellis,** 1996b
Social stratification	**Goldberg,** 1973; **Rosa & Mazur,** 1979; **Kemper,** 1990, 1994; **van den Berghe** & Whitmeyer, 1990; **Ellis,** 1991a, 1993, 1994a, 1994b, 1994c; **Green,** 1994; **Mazur,** 1994; **Machalek,** 1995; **Mueller & Mazur,** 1995, in press; **Mazur & Mueller,** in press
Sociocultural evolution and general biosocial theory	**Mazur** & Robertson, 1972; **Ball,** 1973; **Wilterdink,** 1976; **Boulding,** 1978; **van den Berghe,** 1978, 1990; **Mazur,** 1978; **Blute,** 1979; **Rosa** 1979; **Baldwin** & Baldwin, 1981; **Wallace,** 1983; **Lopreato,** 1984, 1986, 1990; **Kitcher,** 1985; **Gove,** 1987, 1995; **Dietz, Burns,** & **Buttel,** 1990; **Mueller,** 1991, 1992; **Sanderson,** 1991; **Catton,** 1992; **Crippen,** 1992, 1994; **Maryanski & Turner,** 1991, 1992; **Burgess** & Molenaar, 1993; **Carey** & **Lopreato,** 1994; **Freese,** 1994; **Maryanski,** 1987, 1993, 1994; **Nielsen,** 1994; **Walsh,** 1995; **Udry,** 1995

1. In this table, sociologists (in bold type) are persons who teach in sociology departments and/or received Ph.D.s in sociology.

not even mention dominance, let alone explain to readers how similar dominance and social status really are.

Another interesting extension of evidence that human social stratification and nonhuman dominance hierarchies are essentially the same phenomenon has to do with the underlying biochemistry. In several nonhuman species, dominance-related aggression exhibits modest positive associations with testosterone levels in the blood (and presumably in the brain) (Ellis, 1986). Similar associations have also been found in humans (Thiessen, 1990; Dabbs, Carr, Frady, & Raid, 1995). At least in rats, status-related aggression can even be augmented by injecting them with synthetic testosterone (anabolic steroids) (Bonson et al., 1994).

On the other hand, dominance-related aggression tends to decrease whenever serotonin levels in the brain are elevated, even though serotonin is a neurotransmitter that is generally inversely associated with blood levels of testosterone, at least among males (Kostowski et al., 1984; Vergnes et al., 1988; Bonson et al., 1994). Given that nonhuman animal dominance and human social status are essentially the same phenomenon, one should find similar patterns in our species. Accordingly, research among men has linked high testosterone to interpersonal dominance striving (Mazur, 1985), antisocial behavior (Dabbs & Morris, 1990) and aggression (Christiansen & Knussmann, 1987; Dabbs et al., 1987; Thiessen, 1990; Choi, Parrott, & Cowan, 1990). Testosterone also appears to be higher in men who choose more rather than less competitive/confrontational occupations (e.g., lawyer vs. minister) (Dabbs & de La Rue, 1990). In regard to serotonin levels and status, the evidence in humans is still fragmentary, but suggestive of the same inverse relationship documented for rank among nonhuman primates (Brammer, Raleigh, & McGuire, 1994:91).

The fourth factor that appears to perpetuate biophobia among sociologists concerns the political and moral implications of admitting that biology is important for understanding human behavior (Degler, 1991:236). These political/moral implications have been given renewed urgency by the publication of at least three new books which argue that individual and racial/ethnic variations in intelligence are central to explaining individual and racial/ethnic variations in both social status and numerous social

Table 2 **Sociologists' Views about the Importance of Biological Factors in Determining Human Behavior**

Behavior Traits	Average Percentage of Each Behavior Attributed to: Genetics	Prenatal Factors	Postnatal Nonsocial Factors*	Total Biological (Nonsocial)
Academic achievement	16.7%	5.4%	6.1%	28.2%
Sexual orientation	20.5%	3.5%	2.3%	26.3%
Minor criminality and delinquency	4.2%	1.8%	3.2%	9.2%
Serious criminality	6.8%	2.5%	3.8%	13.1%
Marital stability	2.5%	0.7%	1.8%	5.0%
Lifetime earnings	6.8%	2.3%	3.1%	12.2%
Racial and ethnic attitudes	0.8%	0.2%	0.7%	1.7%
Sex differences:				
In aggressive criminality	11.0%	1.0%	3.3%	15.3%
In child nurturing behavior	8.0%	0.7%	2.1%	10.8%
In occupational interests	3.0%	0.5%	1.2%	4.7%
Race differences in academic achievement	4.6%	3.4%	5.3%	13.3%

*E.g., nutritional and health related variables.

problems (Herrnstein & Murray, 1994; Rushton, 1994; Walsh, 1995).

Such possibilities have been skirted by sociologists as though their very consideration is tantamount to resurrecting the Third Reich. Someday historians of social science will be astounded to find the word *intelligence* is usually not even mentioned in late-twentieth-century text books on social stratification (e.g., Kerbo, 1991; Rossides, 1990; Rothman, 1993; Rothenberg, 1995).

In confronting the issues linked to intelligence and social stratification, I am well aware of the inflammatory and divisive effects that their discussion can have. Nonetheless, their association is clearly in the domain of sociology, and a dispassionate consideration even for undergraduates is needed.

What Sociologists Believe in Spite of Their Biophobic Theories

To assess sociologists' receptivity to biologically related issues, Steven Sanderson and I surveyed 168 sociologists in 1990 (Sanderson & Ellis, 1992). We allowed those responding to our questionnaire to answer on a percentage basis (rather than just yes or no) regarding how much influence they felt biological and social environmental factors had on various aspects of human behavior. Much of what we found was interesting.

Despite the absence of biological variables in any prominent sociological theories, the "modal sociologists" actually said they believed that biological factors have at least minor influences on many aspects of human behavior. This even included the possibility that biological factors may underlie individual and racial/ethnic differences in academic ability. Some of the results are summarized in Table 2.

In part of the survey, sociologists were asked to identify the causes of several aspects of behavior in terms of three biological categories (i.e., genetic, prenatal, and nonsocial environmental factors) and three social environmental categories (i.e., family, community, and cultural factors). For all eleven behavior patterns, respondents assigned percentages to each of these six categories. Table 2 shows that large proportions of sociologists realize that their environmental theories are inadequate for completely explaining human behavior (see Sanderson & Ellis, 1992:37 for details).

Notice that for two of the eleven categories of human behavior—academic achievement and sexual orientation—sociologists on average attributed over one-fourth of the variation to biological causes. Notice also that over 10% of the variations in (a) serious criminality, (b) lifetime earnings, (c) sex differences in aggressive criminality, and (d) sex differences in nurturing behavior also were attributed to biological factors. Most controversial of all, sociologists assigned an average of 13% of racial variation in academic achievement to biological factors.

Even though these averages were based on distributions that were sometimes substantially skewed, they reveal a fundamentally important point: despite the fact that today's sociological theories are all exclusively environmentalistic, most sociologists recognize that biological variables have a role to play in human behavior. If biological variables were to become part of most sociological theories, imagine how much richer and more credible those theories would be.

Proposals for Rejuvenating Sociology

A number of suggestions have been made in recent years for reversing sociology's decline (e.g., Gans, 1992; Lipset, 1994; Molotch, 1994). One writer observed that today's sociology teachers and textbooks often come across as "dry, dull, and lacking in much interest or appeal to students" (Fabianic, 1991:27). Other suggestions have included making sociology more attractive to majors by developing more innovative curricula (McMillian & McKinney, 1985), and by better publicizing job opportunities (Das, 1989). Another suggestion was that "Sociology ought to brag about itself more often" (Knottnerus & Maguire, 1995:30).

While these improvements-in-packaging/public relations approaches to revitalizing sociology may help, I submit that the heart of the problem still lies in the content of what sociologists teach. In particular, the intolerance that sociologists have for biological variables in their theories and research is eroding the discipline's credibility to a growing proportion of educated persons.

I disagree strongly with those who argue that sociology should become more focused on enhancing the quality of human life (e.g., Turner & Turner, 1990; Cole, 1994:154; Durant, 1994:9). In my opinion, it is sociology's applied emphasis without a solid theoretical foundation that is primally responsible for its current predicament. At this point in time, activism is hindering, not promoting, sociology's long-term survival prospects. This does not mean that sociologists as individuals should not be politically and socially active. It simply means that sociology is still far too poorly developed to be used to guide any societies out of their major social problems. By pretending otherwise, we do serious damage to sociology's credibility.

If we would have concentrated over the past half century on improving sociology's theoretical understanding of sociocultural phenomena rather than on trying to put the world right (actually left), I doubt that we would now be facing such dire prospects for our discipline. If sociology is to survive in the twenty-first century, its practitioners need to stop twisting "sociological wisdom" into justifications for left-wing political agendas. Perhaps, after we have gone much further in integrating our theories with the growing evidence linking social and biological phenomena, some political action will flow from sociological understanding.

Because I see sociology's long-term survival contingent upon sociologists integrating biological and social learning variables, allow me to illustrate with recent theoretical work I have done in the area of religion and crime. The theory to be described is neither vague nor complex, and therefore it illustrates how a biologically based sociological theory can help to explain a perplexing relationship.

A Biosocial Explanation of Covariation in Criminality and Religiosity

Over fifty studies have examined various possible relationships between criminality and religiosity (Ellis, 1985, 1996a). Out of this research, one relationship has become well established—the inverse relationship between church attendance and criminality. In my 1985 review, I cited thirty-one studies that had specifically investigated whether or not criminality was associated with church attendance. All but five of these studies found a significant inverse correlation (Ellis, 1985:507). The remaining five studies also found inverse correlations, but the relationships were not deemed statistically significant. In the intervening years, nine more studies have been published, and all of them have confirmed that church attendance and criminality are inversely correlated (Sloane & Potvin, 1986:91; Lester, 1988; Bainbridge, 1989; Ellis & Thompson, 1989; Mitchell et al., 1990:492; Nagin & Paternoster, 1991:580; Free, 1992; Chadwick & Top, 1993; Cochran et al., 1994; Evans, Cullen, Dunaway, & Burton, 1995).

Before outlining a biosocial theory to explain this relationship, two qualifying points should be made. First, the inverse relationship between crime and church attendance appears to be stronger than the relationship between crime and any specific religious beliefs (Ellis, 1985; Gartner et al., 1991:9; Joubert, 1994; Evans et al., 1995). In other words, belief in a particular type of god or in immortality seems to have less bearing on criminal behavior than does church attendance or church membership. Second, the church attendance-crime relationship appears to be stronger in the case of victimless offenses, especially drug offenses, than in the case of violent and property crimes (Burkett & White, 1974; Albrecht et al., 1977; Sloane & Potvin, 1986:91; Ellis & Thompson, 1989; Chadwick & Top, 1993:66).

The theory that I have proposed for explaining the religiosity-criminality relationship is arousal theory. Without getting into the underlying neurochemistry (see Ellis, 1996a), the theory maintains that much of what motivates human activities can be understood in terms of people's attempts to maintain a preferred (or optimal) level of arousal. If we experience too much novel and intense stimulation at any point in time, we feel *anxiety* and *stress.* At the other extreme, if too little is happening in our environment, we feel *bored.*

Arousal theory assumes that everyone's brain functions differently with respect to how much novel and intense stimuli is considered "too much" or "too little." Because of variations in how our brains function, some of us "naturally" prefer much more environmental stimulation than do others. These people feel bored frequently unless they can experience a great deal of diverse and intense stimuli. People who are at the extremely high end in terms of the amount of environmental stimulation they prefer have come to be called *sensation seekers* (Zuckerman, 1979; Raine, 1993:179).

According to arousal theory, sensation seekers have brain functioning patterns that elevate their probabilities of committing crimes and other acts that are very irritating to others. This reasoning is supported by evidence from numerous studies showing higher sensation seeking scores (variously measured) among persons with criminal backgrounds than among those without such backgrounds (reviewed by Ellis, 1987d:911). In addition, sensation seekers should have a low probability of voluntarily attending most routine church services. The evidence regarding this second prediction is fairly well supported (Levin & Schalmo, 1974; Pearson & Sheffield, 1975; Zuckerman & Neeb, 1980; Zuckerman & Myers, 1983; but see Pearson, Francis, & Lightbown, 1986).

There is more to arousal theory than can be presented here, including some neurochemical factors that may help explain why males are more criminal and less religious than females (Halpern, 1994; Ellis, 1996a). Nonetheless, the description just presented illustrates how a few biological concepts can help to provide theoretical insight into a well-established connection between two seemingly disparate social behavioral variables. Arousal theory remains to be fully tested, but already has been found to predict the relationship between criminality and religiosity at least as well as Hirschi's (1969) well-known control theory (Cochran et al., 1994).

Are biosocial theories such as arousal theory appropriate for sociologists to consider? I think so. As I stated earlier, Durkheim's misguided view that sociological theorizing must be restricted to the social environment has seriously damaged the discipline. To help purge sociology of this narrow view, I recommend that no theories of behavior be given single disciplinary labels. In other words, there should be no more references to *sociological theories* of anything. This will encourage researchers to evaluate theories of behavior strictly on their merits, not according to the discipline with which they happen to be most closely associated (for whatever reason).

Eventually, I believe that all theories of human behavior will include references to biological, cognitive, and social variables. Thus, categorizing them as strictly "biological," "psychological," or "sociological" is artificial and divisive, and will eventually become outmoded.

Conclusion

The theme of this article has been that sociology is on the proverbial ropes, and that its main adversary continues to be itself. Above all, sociology's loss of majors and its deteriorating image are mainly due to most sociologists still stubbornly insisting, contrary to overwhelming evidence, that biology is not important for understanding human social behavior. Biology is important, and thinking otherwise is a disservice to progress in understanding such behavior. As shown in Tables 1 and 2, many sociologists know this, even though they feel trapped into continuing to advocate biophobic theories because of the discipline's antibiological legacy.

Since the 1960s, psychology and psychiatry have moved far beyond their Freudian roots. It is time for sociology to stop resuscitating the views of Durkheim, Weber, and Marx (except as historical landmarks). This is not because their ideas were not innovative and important for their time. Rather, sociology's niche within the greater scientific community is being undercut by the continued failure of sociologists to incorporate modern evolutionary, genetics, and neurochemical concepts into their theories. Nineteenth-century sociologists can be forgiven for failing to recognize the importance of biology for the study of human behavior; contemporary sociologists cannot be excused.

In commenting on sociology's current predicament, Lenski (1993) offered sound advise, although he could have gone even further than he did. He called attention to how modern communications has made today's college students much more aware than their parents and grandparents were of the topics covered in sociology classes (also see Fabianic, 1991:28). Lenski said that, as a consequence of this greater awareness, much of what is being taught in today's sociology classes boils down to things most students already know enveloped in technical jargon and statistics. To make sociology more informative, Lenski recommended that it stop focusing on contemporary North America (and a few other Western industrial nations), and shift to a cross-cultural and comparative approach.

I support this recommendation, but would add that sociology must go beyond cross-cultural comparisons to comparisons with social animals. By so doing, the absurdity of developing entirely separate explanations for essentially the same behavior in humans and nonhumans becomes exceedingly obvious. As mentioned in the body of this report, the field of social stratification is ripe for merging much of what is now known about humans and nonhuman tendencies to form social hierarchies (Ellis, 1993b, 1994c, 1995).

As Table 1 makes clear, many sociologists are now incorporating biological concepts into their research and theories. This is especially true in the field of criminality. Ironically, it is still common in criminology text books to equate "sociological theories" with theories that explicitly exclude all biological variables (e.g., Siegel 1989:219; Hagan, 1994:165; Beirne & Messerschmidt, 1995:365). In other words, despite the widespread (mis)use of the term *sociological* to mean *anti-biological,* Table 1 shows that since 1970 at least 19 sociologists have proposed that biological factors do contribute to variations in criminal behavior. Criminologists who still believe that sociological theories cannot include biological variables need to confront the fact that some of the best work now being carried out to blend biological and social variables are in fact being done by sociologists.

One can find a similar example in the study of incest. Two of the most prominent theorists on how biological factors appear to affect incestuous relationships are sociologists (Shepher and van den Berghe). Nonetheless, nearly everyone who thinks of sociological theories of incest (and incest avoidance) would consider sociological theories the antithesis of biological theories.

As stated earlier, it is imperative that we stop equating *sociological* with *nonbiological.* This is partly because it is simply not reflective of reality, and otherwise because it does serious damage to sociology's credibility, given that biological variables *are* important for understanding all aspects of social behavior.

My main point may be summarized as follows: Table 1 shows that a substantial number of sociologists have moved toward accommodating growing evidence that biological factors have substantial influences on human social behavior. Table 2 makes a related point. It suggests that although the majority of sociologists still cling to strictly environmentalist theories, many of them in fact realize that biological variables are contributing to variations in sociocultural phenomena.

While I would guess that the tendency of sociologists to accept the importance of biological variables is growing, Table 2 suggests that most still have a long way to go. Unfortunately, the pace of change may be too slow to prevent the discipline from experiencing a major implosion between now and the end of the twentieth century. I believe that *the single most important key to the discipline's long-term survival rests upon our changing sociology's curriculum.* Even at the undergraduate level, sociology students need to have a solid background in biology.

References

Albrecht, S. L., B. A. Charwick, and D. S. Alcorn. 1997. "Religiosity and deviance: Application of an attitude-behavior contingent consistency model." *Journal for the Scientific Study of Religion* 16: 263–274.

Allison, Paul D. 1992. "The cultural evolution of beneficent norms." *Social Forces* 71: 279–301.

Bainbridge, William Sims. 1989. "The religious ecology of deviance." *American Sociological Review* 54: 288–295.

Baldwin, John and Janice Baldwin. 1981. *Beyond Sociobiology.* New York, NY: Elsevier.

Baldwin, John D. 1986. Behavior in infancy: Exploration and play. In G. Mitchell & J. Erwin (Eds.) *Comparative primate biology, vol. 2, part A. Behavior, conservation and ecology.* New York: Alan R. Liss, pp. 295–326.

Baldwin, John D. 1990. The role of sensory stimulation in criminal behavior, with special attention to age peak in crime. In Lee Ellis & Harry Hoffman (Eds.) *Crime in biological, social, and moral contexts.* New York: Praeger, pp. 204–217.

Ball, Donald W. 1973. Biological bases of human society. In Jack D. Douglas (Ed.) *Introduction to sociology: Situations and structures.* New York, NY: Free Press.

Beirne, Piers and James Messerschmidt. 1995. *Criminology, 2nd Edition.* Fort Worth, Texas: Harcourt Brace.

Bell, A.P., M. S. Weinberg, S. K. Hammersmith. 1981. *Sexual preferences: Its development in men and women.* Bloomington, Indiana: Indiana University Press.

Blute, M. 1979. "Sociocultural evolutionism: An untried theory." *Behavioral Sciences* 24, 56–58.

Bonson, Katherine R., Robert G. Johnson, David Fiorella, Richard A. Rabin, J. C. Winter. 1994. "Serotonergic control of androgen-induced dominance." *Pharmacology Biochemistry and Behavior* 49: 313–322.

Boukydis, C. F. Z. and Robert L. Burgess. 1982. "Adult physiological response to infant cries: Effects of temperament of cry, parental status and gender." *Child Development* 53: 1291–1298.

Boulding, Kenneth E. 1978. *Ecodynamics: A new theory of social evolution.* Beverly Hills, California: Sage.

Brammer, Gary L., Michael J. Raleigh, Michael T. McGuire. 1994. Neurotransmitters and social status. In Lee Ellis (Ed.) *Social stratification and socioeconomic inequality, Volume 2: Reproductive and interpersonal aspects of dominance and status.* Westport, CT: Praeger, pp. 75–91.

Burgess, Robert L. 1978. A bio-behavioral approach to the analysis and solution of three environmental problems: Overpopulation, resource use, social conflict. In S. Bijou (Ed.) *Proceedings of the 6th Annual Symposium on Behavioral Modification.* Hillsdale, NJ: Lawrence Erlbaum.

Burgess, Robert L. 1980. Family violence: Some implications from evolutionary biology. In Travis Hirschi and Michael Gottfredson (Eds.) *Theory and fact in contemporary criminology.* Beverly Hills: CA, Sage, pp. 91–101.

Burgess, Robert L. 1980. Implication from evolutionary biology. In T. Hirschi & M. Gottfredson (Eds.) *Understanding Crime.* Beverly Hills, CA: Sage, pp. 91–101.

Burgess, Robert L. 1994. "The family in a changing world: A prolegomenon to an evolutionary analysis." *Human Nature* 5: 203–221.

Burgess, Robert, Jeffery Kurland, Emily Pensky. 1988. "Ultimate and proximate determinants of child maltreatment: Natural selection, ecological instability, and coercive interpersonal contingencies." *Sociobiological Perspectives* 31: 293–319.

Burgess, Robert L. and P. Draper 1988. A biosocial theory of family violence: The role of natural selection, ecological instability, and coercive interpersonal contingencies. In Lloyd Ohlin & Michael H. Tonry (Eds.) *Crime and Justice: An Annual Review of Research.* Chicago: University of Chicago Press, pp. 59–116.

Burgess, Robert L. and J. Garbarino. 1983. Doing what comes naturally? An evolutionary perspective on child abuse. In D. Findelhor, R. J. Gelles, G. T. Hotaling, & M. A. Straus (Eds.) *The Dark Side of Families. Current Family Violence Research.* Beverly Hills, CA: Sage, pp. 88–101.

Burgess, Robert L. and Peter C. M. Molenaar. 1993. "Human behavioral biology: Commentary on Lerner and von Eye's Sociobiology and human development: Arguments and evidence." *Human Development* 36: 45–54.

Burkett, S. R. and White, W. 1974. "Hellfire and delinquency: Another look." *Journal for the Scientific Study of Religion* 13: 455–462.

Carey, Arlen and Lopreato, Joseph. 1994. "Sociobiology and the wayward critic." *Sociological Perspectives* 37: 403–430.

Carey, Arlen D. and Lopreato, Joseph. 1995. "The biocultural evolution of the male-female mortality differential." *Mankind Quarterly,* 36:3–28.

Catton, William, Jr. 1992. Separation versus unification in sociological human ecology. In Lee Freese (Ed.) *Advances in Human Ecology.* Greenwich, CT: JAI Press, pp. 65–99.

Chadwick, Bruce A. and Brent L. Top. 1993. "Religiosity and delinquency among LDS adolescents." *Journal for the Scientific Study of Religion* 32: 51–67.

Choi, P. Y. L., A. C. Parrott, D. Cowan. 1990. "High dose of anabolic steroids in strength athletes: Effects upon hostility and aggression." *Human Psychopharmacology* 5: 349.

Christiansen, K. and R. Knussmann. 1987. "Androgen levels and components of aggressive behavior in men." *Hormones and Behavior* 21: 170–180.

Cochran, John K., Peter B. Wood, Bruce, J. Arneklev. 1994. "Is the religiosity-delinquency relationship spurious? A test of arousal and social control theories." *Journal of Research in Crime and Delinquency* 31: 92–123.

Cohen, Lawrence E. and Richard Machalek. 1994. "The normalcy of crime." *Rationality and Society* 6: 286–308.

Cole, Stephen. 1994. "Why sociology doesn't make progress like the natural sciences." *Sociological Forum* 9: 133–154.

Coughlin, Ellen K. 1992. Sociologists confront questions about field's vitality and direction. *Chronicle of Higher Education*: A6–A8.

Crippen, Timothy. 1992. "An evolutionary critique of cultural analysis in sociology." *Human Nature* 3: 379–412.

Crippen, Timothy. 1994. "Towards new-Darwinian sociology: Its nomological principles and some illustrative applications." *Sociological Perspectives* 37: 309–335.

Crippen, Timothy and Richard Machalek. 1989. "The evolutionary foundation of the religious life." *International Review of Sociology* 3: 61–84.

Dabbs, James M. Jr. and R. Morris. 1990. "Testosterone, social class, and antisocial behavior in a sample of 4,462 men." *Psychological Science* 1: 209–211.

Dabbs, James M. Jr., Timothy S. Carr, Robert L. Frady, Jasmin K. Raid. 1995. "Testosterone, crime, and misbehavior among 692 male prison inmates." *Personality and Individual Differences* 18: 627–633.

Dabbs, James M. Jr., D. de La Rue, P. M. Williams. 1990. "Testosterone and occupational choice: Actors, ministers, and other men." *Journal of Personality and Social Psychology* 59: 1261–1265.

Dabbs, James M. J., R. L. Frady, T. S. Carr, N. F. Besch. 1987. "Saliva testosterone and criminal violence in young adult prison inmates." *Psychosomatic Medicine* 49: 174.

Dabbs, James M. J. and Robin Morris. 1990. "Testosterone and antisocial behavior in a sample of 4,462 men." *Psychological Science* 1: 209–211.

Daly, Martin and Margo Wilson. 1988. *Homicide.* New York, Aldine de Gruyter.

Das, Mitra 1989. "Making sociology attractive." *Teaching Sociology* 17: 356–360.

Degler, Carl N. 1991. *In search of human nature: The decline and revival of Darwinism in American social thought.* New York, NY: Oxford University Press.

Dietz, T., Burns, T. R., & Buttel, F. H. 1990. "Evolutionary theory in sociology: An explanation of current thinking." *Sociological Forum* 5: 155–171.

Drigotas, Stephen M. and J. Richard Udry. 1993. "Biosocial models of adolescent problem behavior: Extension to panel design." *Social Biology* 40: 1–7.

Durant, Thomas J., Jr. 1994. "Sociology in the 21st century: Where there is no vision, the people perish." *Sociological Spectrum* 15: 3–15.

Eckberg, D. L. 1979. *Intelligence and Race.* New York: Praeger.

Eckland, Bruce K. 1980. "Education in the meritocracy." *American Journal of Education* 89: 76–85.

Ellis, Lee. 1977. "The decline and fall of sociology, 1977–2000." *American Sociologist* 12: 56–66.

Ellis, Lee. 1985. "Religiosity and criminality: Evidence and explanations surrounding complex relationships." *Sociological Perspective* 28: 501–520.

Ellis, Lee. 1986a. "Evidence of neuroandrogenic etiology of sex roles from a combined analysis of human, nonhuman primate and nonprimate mammalian studies." *Personality and Individual Differences* 7: 519–552.

Ellis, Lee. 1986b. "Evolution and the nonlegal equivalent of criminal behavior." *Aggressive Behavior* 12: 57–71.
Ellis, Lee. 1987a. Neurohormonal bases of varying tendencies to learn delinquent and criminal behavior. In E. K. Morris & C. J. Braukmann (Eds.) *Behavioral approaches to crime and delinquency.* New York: Plenum, pp. 499–518.
Ellis, Lee. 1987b. "Criminal behavior and r/K selection: An extension of gene-based evolutionary theory." *Deviant Behavior* 8, 149–176.
Ellis, Lee. 1987c. "Religiosity and criminality from the perspective of the arousal theory." *Journal of Research on Crime and Delinquency* 24, 215–232.
Ellis, Lee. 1987d. "Relationships of criminality and psychopathy with eight other apparent behavioral manifestations of sub-optimal arousal." *Personality and Individual Differences* 8:905–925.
Ellis, Lee. 1989. *Theories of rape: Inquiries into the causes of sexual aggression.* New York: Hemisphere.
Ellis, Lee. 1990a. The evolution of violent criminal behavior and its nonlegal equivalent. In L. Ellis & H. Hoffman (Ed.) *Crime in biological, social, and moral contexts.* New York: Praeger, pp. 61–81.
Ellis, Lee. 1990b. The evolution of collective counterstrategies to crime: From the primate control role to the criminal justice system. In L. Ellis & H. Hoffman (Ed.) *Crime in biological, social, and moral contexts.* New York: Praeger, pp. 81–99.
Ellis, Lee. 1990c. Left- and mixed-handedness and criminality: Explanations for a probable relationship. In Stanley Coren (Ed.) *Left-handedness: Behavioral implications and anomalies.* North-Holland: Elsevier Science Publishers, pp. 485–507.
Ellis, Lee. 1991a. "A biosocial theory of social stratification derived from the concepts of pro/antisociality and r/K selection." *Politics and the Life Sciences* 10: 5–22.
Ellis, Lee. 1991b. "Monoamine oxidase and criminality: Identifying an apparent biological marker for antisocial behavior." *Journal of Research on Crime and Delinquency* 28: 227–251.
Ellis, Lee. 1993. A biosocial theory of social stratification: An alternative to functional theory and conflict theory. In Lee Ellis (Ed.) *Social stratification and socioeconomic inequality, Volume 1: A comparative biosocial analysis.* New York: Praeger, pp. 159–174.
Ellis, Lee. 1994a. The high and the mighty among man and beast: How universal is the relationship between height (or body size) and social status? In Lee Ellis (Ed.) *Social stratification and socioeconomic inequality, Volume 2: Reproductive and interpersonal aspects of dominance and status.* Westport, CT: Praeger, pp. 93–112
Ellis, Lee. 1994b. Relationships between height and social status (Plus birth weight, mental health, intelligence, brain size, and fertility); A broad theoretical integration. In Lee Ellis (ED.) *Social stratification and socioeconomic inequality, Volume 2: Reproductive and interpersonal aspects of dominance and status.* Westport, CT: Praeger, pp. 145–164.
Ellis, Lee. 1994c. Social status and health in humans: The nature of the relationship and its possible causes. In Lee Ellis (Ed.) *Social stratification and socioeconomic inequality, Volume 2: Reproductive and interpersonal aspects of dominance and status.* Westport, CT: Praeger, pp. 123–144.
Ellis, Lee. 1996a. Arousal theory and the religiosity-criminality relationship. L. Siegel & P. Cordella (Eds.) *Contemporary criminological theory.* Boston: Northeastern University Press.
Ellis, Lee. 1996b. The Role of perinatal factors in determining sexual orientation. In R. C. Savin-Williams & K. M. Cohen (Ed.) *The lives of lesbians, gays, and bisexuals.* Fort Worth, Tx: Harcourt Brace College Publishers, pp. 35–70.
Ellis, Lee, Donald Burke and M. Ashley Ames. 1987. "Sexual orientation as a continuous variable: A comparison between the sexes." *Archives of Sexual Behavior* 16: 523–529.
Ellis, Lee and Ashley Ames. 1987. "Neurohormonal functioning and sexual orientation: A theory of homosexuality-heterosexuality." *Psychological Bulletin* 101: 233–258.
Ellis, Lee and Phillis D. Coontz. 1990. Androgens, brain functioning, and criminality: The neurohormonal foundations of antisociality. Lee Ellis & Harry Hoffman (Eds.) *Crime in biological, social, and moral contexts.* New York: Praeger, pp. 162–193.
Ellis, Lee and William Peckham. 1991. "Prenatal stress and handedness among offspring." *Pre and Peri-Natal Psychology Journal* 6: 135–144.
Ellis, Lee and Robert Thompson 1989. "Relating religion, crime, arousal and boredom." *Sociology and Social Research* 73: 132–139.
Evans, T. David, Francis T. Cullen, R. Gregory Dunaway, Velmer S. J. Burton. 1995. "Religion and crime reexamined: The impact of religion, secular controls, and social ecology on adult criminality." *Criminology* 33: 195–225.
Fabianic, David. 1991. "Declining enrollments of sociology majors: Department responses." *American Sociologist* 22: 25–36.
Felson, Markus. 1992. "Farewell after 77 years." *Sociology and Social Research* 77: 169.
Felson, Richard B. 1993. Motives for sexual coercion. In Richard B. Felson & James T. Tedeschi (Eds.) *Aggression and Violence: Social interactionist perspectives.* Washington, D.C.: American Psychological Association, pp. 233–253.
Free, Martin D. J. 1992. "Religious affiliation, religiosity, and impulsive and intentional deviance." *Sociological Focus* 25: 77–91.
Freese, Lee. 1994. "The song of sociobiology." *Sociological Perspectives* 37: 337–373.
Gartner, J., D. B. Larson, G. D. Allen. 1991. "Religious commitment and mental health: A review of the empirical literature." *Journal of Psychology and Theology* 19: 6–25.
Goldberg, Steven. 1973. *The inevitability of patriarchy.* New York: Morrow.
Gordon, H. W. and P. A. Lee 1986. "A relationship between gonadotropins and visuospatial function." *Neuropsychologia* 24: 563–576.
Gordon, Robert A. 1980. "Implications of valid (and stubborn) IQ differences: An unstatesmanlike view." *Behavioral and Brain Sciences* 3: 343–344.
Gordon, Robert A. 1986. Scientific justification and the race-IQ-delinquency model. In Timothy F. Hartnagel & Robert A. Silverman (Eds.) *Critique and Explanation in Honor of Gwynne Nettler.* New Brunswick, New Jersey: Transaction Books, pp. 91–131.
Gordon, Robert A. 1987. "SES versus IQ in the race-IQ-delinquency model." *International Journal of Sociology and Social Policy* 7 (3): 30–36.
Gottfredson, Linda S. 1986. "Societal consequences of the g factor in employment." *Journal of Vocational Behavior* 29: 379–410.
Gottfredson, Linda S. 1994. "Egalitarian fiction and collective fraud." *Society* 31: 53–59.
Gottfredson, Linda S. and J. Crouse 1986. "Validity versus utility of mental tests: Example of the SAT." *Journal of Vocational Behavior* 29: 363–378.
Gove, Walter R. 1987. "Sociobiology misses the mark: An essay on why biology but not sociobiology is very relevant to sociology." *American Sociologist* 18: 258–277.
Gove, Walter R. 1994. "Why we do what we do: A biopsychological theory of motivation." *Social Forces* 73: 363–394.
Gove, Walter R. 1995. "Is sociology the integrative discipline in the study of human behavior." *Social Forces* 73: 1197–1206.

Gove, Walter R. and Charles Wilmoth 1990. Risk, crime, and neurophysiologic highs: A consideration of brain processes that may reinforce delinquent and criminal behavior. In Lee Ellis & Harry Hoffman (Ed.) *Crime in biological, social, and moral contexts.* New York: Praeger, pp. 261–293.

Green, Penny A. 1994. "Toward a biocultural theory of class circulation: An application of Joseph Lopreato's sociology." *Revue Europeenne des Sciences Sociales* 98: 195–214.

Hagan, Frank E. 1994. *Introduction to criminology, third edition.* Chicago: Nelson-Hall.

Hall, R. H. 1994. The sociology GRE: Problems and prospects. *ASA Footnotes*, 22, 8.

Halpern, Carolyn T., J. Richard Udry, B. Campbell & C. Suchindran (1993). Relationships between aggression and pubertal increases in testosterone: A panel analysis of adolescent males. *Social Biology* 40: 8–24.

Halpern, Carolyn T., J. Richard Udry, Benjamin Campbell Chirayath Suchindran, George A. Mason. 1994. "Testosterone and religiosity and predictors of sexual attitudes and activity among adolescent males: A biosocial model." *Journal of Biosocial Science* 26: 217–234.

Harry, J. 1984. "Sexual orientation as destiny." *Journal of Homosexuality* 10:111–124.

Heller, Scott. 1990. Despite protests, Washington U. stands by decision to close its once-vaulted sociology department. *Chronicle of Higher Education*: A1, A24–A25.

Henry, B., Terry Moffitt, F. Earls, Lee Robins, P. Silva. 1993. "Early family predictors of child and adolescent antisocial behavior: Who are the mothers of delinquents?" *Criminal Behavior and Mental Health* 3: 97–118.

Hernnstein, Richard J. and Charles Murray 1994. *The bell curve: Intelligence and class structure in American life.* New York: Free Press.

Heyl, Barbara S. 1989. "Washington University's pig roast: Ending sociology and jeopardizing liberal arts." *American Sociologist* 20: 341–345.

Hirschi, T 1969. *Causes of delinquency.* Berkeley: University of California Press.

Hooks, Bonnie Lori L. and Penny A. Green 1993. "Cultivating male allies: A focus on primate females, including homo sapiens." *Human Nature* 4: 81–107.

Horowitz, Irving L. 1993. *The decomposition of sociology.* New York: Oxford University Press.

Horowitz, Irving L. 1995. "The Rushton File: Racial comparisons and media passions." *Society* 32: 7–17.

Howery, Carla B. 1994. "Important changes with the GRE exams: Chairs and departments need to act now!" *ASA Footnotes* 22 (December)(9): 5.

Hsieh, K. and R. L. Burgess 1994. "Marital role attitudes and expected role behaviors of college youth in Mainland China and Taiwan." *Journal of Family Issues* 15: 405–423.

Jeffery, C. Ray. 1977. *Crime Prevention.* Beverly Hills: Sage Publications.

Jeffery, C. R. (1979). Biology and Crime: The new neo-lombrosians. In C. R. Jeffery (Ed.) *Biology and Crime.* Beverly Hills: Sage Publications, pp. 7–18.

Jeffery, C. Ray. 1980. Sociobiology and criminology: The long lean years of the unthinkable and the unmentionable. In Edward Sagrin (Ed.) *Taboos in Criminology.* Beverly Hills, CA: Sage, pp. 115–124.

Joubert, Charles E. 1994. "Religious nonaffiliation in relation to suicide, murder, rape, and illegitimacy." *Psychological Reports* 75: 10.

Kantrowitz, B. 1992. "Sociology's lonely crowd." *Newsweek* (Feb. 3): 55.

Kelly, Dennis, 1991. Sociologists track surge in their field. *USA Today*: ID.

Kemper, Theodore D. 1987. "How many emotions are there? Wedding the social and the autonomic components." *American Journal of Sociology* 93: 263–289.

Kemper, Theodore D. 1990. *Social structure and testosterone.* New Brunswick, NJ: Rutgers University Press.

Kemper, Theodore D. 1990. *Social structure and testosterone: Essays on the socio-bio-social chain.* New Brunswick, NJ: Rutgers University Press.

Kemper, Theodore D. 1994. Social stratification, testosterone, and male sexuality. In Ellis (Ed.) *Social stratification and socioeconomic inequality, Volume 2: Reproductive and interpersonal aspects of dominance and status.* Westport, CT: Praeger, pp. 47–62.

Kerbo, Harold R. 1991. *Social stratification and inequality, second edition.* New York: McGraw-Hill.

Kirsten, Larry. 1981. *The love exchange.* New York: Fredrick Fell.

Kirsten, Larry. 1988. *Marriage and the family: Studying close relationships.* New York: Harper & Row.

Kitcher, Philip, 1985. *Vaulting ambition, sociobiology and the quest for human nature.* Cambridge: MIT Press.

Kitchner, Phillip. 1985. *Vaulting ambition.* Cambridge: MIT Press.

Knottnerus, J. David and Brendan Maguire. 1995. "The status of sociology departments: An assessment of their current and future prospects." *Sociological Spectrum* 15: 17–38.

Kostowski, W., M. Plewako, A. Bidzinski. 1984. "Brain serotonergic neurons: Their role in a form of dominance-subordination behavior in rats." *Psychological Behavior* 33: 365–371.

Lauritsen, Janet L. 1995. "Book review." *Contemporary Sociology* 24: 89–90.

Lenski, Gerald. 1993. "Are our troubles unavoidable or have we brought them on ourselves? *Footnotes* 21 (April): 5.

Lester, David. 1988. "Religion and personal violence (homocide and suicide) in the USA." *Psychological Reports* 62: 618.

Levin, B. J. and G. B. Schalmo 1974. "Self-related liberalism is correlated with sensation-seeking." *Psychological Reports* 23: 298.

Lightcap, J. L., J. A. Kurland, Robert L. Burgess. 1982. "Child abuse: A test of some predictions from evolutionary theory." *Ethology and Sociobiology* 3: 61–67.

Lipset, Seymour M. 1994. "The state of American sociology." *Sociological Forum* 9(2): 199–220.

Lopreato, Joseph. 1981. "Toward a theory of genuine altruism in Homo sapiens." *Ethology and Sociobiology* 2: 113–126.

Lopreato, Joseph. 1984. *Human nature and biocultural evolution.* Boston: Houghton Mifflin.

Lopreato, Joseph. 1986. "Notes on human nature and biocultural evolution." *Revue Europeenne des Sciences Sociales* 24: 97–123.

Lopreato, Joseph. 1988. "Human nature and morality: A sociobiological perspective." *Politics and the Life Sciences* 6: 208–213.

Lopreato, Joseph. 1990. "From social evolution to biocultural evolutionism." *Sociological Forum* 5: 187–212.

Lopreato, Joseph. 1994a. "Book review." *Social Forces* 73: 316–318.

Lopreato, Joseph .1994b. "The ecological demography of the fertility-mortality quasi-equilibrium." *Population and Development Review* 21: (in press).

Lopreato, Joseph. 1994c. "Why women live longer." *II Campanile* 2: 5–12.

Lopreato, Joseph and Penny A. Green. 1990. The evolutionary foundations of revolution. In J. van der Dennen & S. E. Falger (Eds.) *Sociobiology and Conflict.* London: Chapman and Hall, pp. 107–121.

Lopreato, Joseph and J. Houghton. 1981. "Protestantism and capitalism: A biosocial emendation of Weber's thesis." *Revue Europeenne des Sciences Sociales* 19: 55–78.
Lynch, D. M., J. Richard. McFerrron, Lee H. Bowker, A. C. Beckford. 1993. "A discipline in trouble: Why more sociology departments may be closing shortly." *Footnotes* (published by the American Sociological Association) 21 (February)(2): 3–7.
Machalek, Richard 1995. "Basic dimensions and forms of social exploitation: A comparative analysis." *Advances in Human Ecology* II: (in press).
Machalek, Richard and Lawrence E. Cohen. 1991. "The nature of crime: Is cheating necessary for cooperation?" *Human Nature* 2: 215–233.
Maryanski, A. 1987. "African ape social structure: Is there strength in weak ties?" *Social Networks* 9: 191–215.
Maryanski, A. 1993. The elementary forms of the first protohuman society: An ecological/social network approach. In Lee Freese (Ed.) *Advances in Human Ecology.* Greenwich, CT: JAI Press, pp. 215–241.
Maryanski, A. 1994. "The pursuit of human nature in sociobiology and evolutionary sociology." *Sociological Perspectives* 37: 375–389.
Maryanski, A. and Jonathan H. Turner. 1991. Biological functionalism. In J. Turner (Ed.) *The Structure of Sociological Theory.* Belmont, CA: Wadsworth Publishing, pp. 152–177.
Maryanski, A. and Johnathan H. Turner. 1992. *The social cage: Human nature and the evolution of society.* Stanford, California: Stanford University Press.
Mazur, Allan. 1978. "Biological explanation in sociology." *Sociological Quarterly* 19: 604–613.
Mazur, Allan. 1985. "A biosocial model of status in face-to-face primate groups." *Social Forces* 64: 377–402.
Mazur, Allan. 1994. A neurohormonal model of social stratification among humans: A microsocial perspective. In Lee Ellis (Ed.) *Social stratification and socioeconomic inequality, Volume 2: Reproductive and interpersonal aspects of dominance and status.* Westport, CT.: Praeger, pp. 37–46.
Mazur, Allan and T. A. Lamb. 1980. "Testosterone, status and mood in human males." *Hormones and Behavior* 14: 236–246.
Mazur, Allan and Ultrich Mueller. 1996. Channel modeling: From West Point cadets to general. *Public Administration Review* (in press).
Mazur, Allan and Leon S. Robertson. 1972. *Biology and Social Behavior.* New York: Free Press.
Mazur, Allan, Eugene Rosa, Mark Faupel, Joshya Heller, Russel Leen, Blake Thurman. 1980. "Physiological aspects of communication via mutual gaze." *American Journal of Sociology.* 86: 50–74.
McMillian, M. and K. McKinney. 1985. "Reorganizing sociology undergraduate curricula." *Teaching Sociology* 12: 425–448.
Mitchell, Jim, Richard A. Dodder, Terry D. Norris. 1990. "Neutralization and delinquency: A comparison by sex and ethnicity." *Adolescence* 25: 487–492.
Molotch, Harvey. 1994. "Going out." *Sociological Forum* 9(2): 221–239.
Mueller, U. 1991. *Social and reproductive success: Theoretical considerations and a case study of the West Point class of 1950.* Mannheim: ZUMA.
Mueller, U. 1992. Birth control as a social dilemma. In G. Haag, U. Mueller, & Troitzsch, K. G. (Eds.) *Economic evolution and demographic change.* New York: Springer.
Mueller, U. & Mazur, Allan. 1995. "Facial dominance in West Point cadets predicts military rank 20+ years later." *Social Forces* (in press).
Nagin, D. and R. Paternoster. 1991. "The preventative effects of the perceived risk of arrest: Testing an expanded conception of deterrence." *Criminology* 29: 561–587.
Newcomer, S. and Richard Udry. 1984. "Mothers' influence on the sexual behavior of their teenage children." *Journal of Marriage and Family* 45: 477–485.
Nielsen, Francois. 1994. "Sociobiology and sociology." *Annual Review of Sociology* 20: 267–303.
Pearson, Paul R., Leslie J. Francis, Trevor J. 1986. "Impulsivity and religiosity." *Personal and Individual Differences* 7: 89–94.
Pearson, Paul R. and B. Scheffield. 1975. "Social attitude correlates of sensation-seeking in psychiatric patients." *Perceptual and Motor Skills* 40: 482.
Piliavin, Jane Allyn and Hong-Wen Charng. 1990. "Altruism: A review of recent theory and research." *Annual Review in Sociology* 16: 27–65.
Pittman, David J. and D. Boden. 1989. "Sociology a Washington University in St. Louis: History and reflections, 1906–1989." *American Sociologist* 20: 305–321.
Porter, Jack Nusan. 1993. "Sociology at Harvard: Toward a paradigm shift." *Footnotes* 21:7.
Rahav, Giora. 1990. "Cross-national variations in violence." *Aggressive Behavior* 16: 69–76.
Rahav, Giora and Lee Ellis. 1990. International crime rates and evolutionary theory: An application of the r/K selection concept to human populations. In Lee Ellis & Harry Hoffman (Eds.) *Crime in biological, social, and moral context.* New York: Praeger Publishers, pp. 115–120.
Raine, Adrian. 1993. *The psychopathology of crime: Criminal behavior as a clinical disorder.* San Diego: Academic Press.
Retherford, Robert D. and William H. Sewell. 1988. "Intelligence and family size reconsidered." *Social Biology* 35: 1–40.
Retherford, Robert D. and William H. Sewell. 1989. "How intelligence affects fertility." *Intelligence* 13: 169–185.
Rhoades, Lawrence J. 1981. "Duke overcomes creative retrenchment: Keep your dukes up." *Footnotes* 9: 10–11.
Robins, Lee N. 1978. "Sturdy childhood predictors of adult antisocial behaviour: Replications from longitudinal studies." *Psychological Medicine* 8. 611–622.
Robins, Lee N. and James L. Mills. 1993. "Effects of in utero exposure to street drugs." *American Journal of Public Health* 83: 1–32.
Robins, Lee N., P. A. West, B. Herjanic. 1975. "Arrests and delinquency in two generations: A study of black urban families and their children." *Journal of Child Psychology and Psychiatry* 16: 125–140.
Rosa, E. and Allan Mazur. 1979. "Incipient status in small groups." *Social Forces.* 58: 18–37.
Rosa, E. A. 1979. "Sociobiology, biosociology, or vulgar biologizing." *Sociological Symposium* 27: 29–49.
Rossi, Alice S. 1977. "The biosocial perspective on parenting." *Daedalus* 106: 1–31.
Rossi, Alice S. 1978. "The biosocial side of parenting." *Human Nature* 1: 72–79.
Rossi, Alice S. 1981. "On the reproduction of mothering: A methodological debate." *Signs: A Journal of Women in Culture and Society* 6: 492–500.
Rossi, Alice S. 1984. "Gender and parenthood." *American Sociological Review* 49: 1–19.
Rossi, Alice S. 1986. "Sex and gender in an aging society." *Daedalus* 115(1): 141–169.

Rossi, Alice S. 1994. Eros and Caritas: A biopsychosocial approach to human sexuality and reproduction. In Alice S. Rossi (Ed.) *Sexuality Across the Life Course.* Chicago: IL: University of Chicago Press, pp. 3–36.

Rossides, Daniel W. 1990. *Social Stratification: The American class system in comparative perspective.* Englewood Cliffs, NJ: Prentice Hall.

Rothenberg, Paula S. 1995. *Race, Class, and Gender in the United States.* New York: St. Martin's Press.

Rothman, Robert A. 1993. *Inequality and stratification: Class, color, and gender.* Englewood Cliffs, NJ: Prentice Hall.

Rowe, David C. and Donald W. Osgood. 1984. "Heredity and sociological theories of delinquency: A reconsideration." *American Sociological Review* 49: 526–540.

Rushton, J. Philippe. 1994. *Race, evolution and behavior: A life history perspective.* New Brunswick, NJ: Transaction Publishers.

Sampson, R. J., & Laub, J. H. 1992. "Crime and deviance in the life course." *Annual Review of Sociology* 18: 63–84.

Sanderson, Stephen K. 1991. *Macrosociology: An introduction to human societies, 2nd edition.* New York: HarperCollins Publishers.

Sanderson, Stephen K. and Lee Ellis 1992. "Theoretical and political perspectives of American sociologists in the 1990s." *American Sociologists* 23: 26–42.

Shepher, J. 1983. *Incest: A biosocial view.* Orlando, FL: Academic Press.

Shepher, J. and J. Reisman. 1985. "Pornography: A sociobiological attempt at understanding." *Ethology and Sociobiology* 6: 103–114.

Shepherd, G. 1985. *Neurobiology.* New York: Wiley.

Siegel, Larry J. (1989). *Criminology, Third edition.* St. Paul, MN: West.

Sloane, Douglas M. and Raymond H. Potvin. 1986. "Religion and delinquency: Cutting through the maze." *Social Forces* 65: 87–105.

Stone, Richard. 1992. "Yale plan draws faculty fire." *Science* 255: 398.

Thiessen, Delbert. 1990. Hormonal correlates of sexual aggression. In Lee Ellis & Harry Hoffman (Eds.) *Crime in biological, social, and moral contexts.* New York: Praeger, pp. 153–161.

Tiger, Lionel. 1979. *Optimism: The biology of hope.* New York: Touchtone (Simon & Schuster).

Tiger, Lionel. 1985. "Survival of the faithful." *The Sciences* (March/April): 61–63.

Turner, Stephen Park and Johnathan H. Turner. 1990. *The impossible science: An institutional analysis of American Sociology.* Newbury Park, CA: Sage.

Udry, J.R. 1988. "Biological predispositions and social control in adolescent sexual behavior." *American Sociological Review* 53: 709.

Udry, J.R. 1990. "Biosocial models of adolescent problem behaviors." *Social Biology* 37: 1–10.

Udry, J.R. 1994. "The nature of gender." *Demography* 31: 561–573.

Udry, J.R. 1995. "Sociology and biology: What biology do sociologists need to know?" *Social Forces* 73: 1267–1278.

Udry, J.R. and J.O.G. Billy. 1987. "Initiation of coitus in early adolescence." *American Sociological Review* 53: 709–22.

Udry, J.R., J.O.G. Billy, N. M. Morris, T. R. Groff, M. H. Raj. 1985. "Serum androgenic hormones motivate sexual behavior in adolescent human males." *Fertility and Sterility* 43: 90.

Udry, J.R., L. M. Talbert, N. M. Morris. 1986. "Biosocial foundations for adolescent female sexuality." *Demography* 23: 217.

Udry, J. R. and L. M. Talbert. 1988. "Sex hormones effects on personality at puberty." *Journal of Personality and Social Psychology* 54: 291–295.

U.S. Department of Education (1992). *Digest of Education Statistics.* Washington, D.C.: U.S. Government Printing Office.

Van den Berghe, P. and J. Whitmeyer. 1990. "Social class and reproductive success." *International Journal of Contemporary Sociology* 27: 29–48.

Van den Berghe, Pierre L. 1974. "Bringing beasts back in: Toward a biosocial theory of aggression." *American Sociological Review* 39: 777–788.

Van den Berghe, Pierre L. 1978. *Man in Society: A Biosocial View.* New York: Elsevier.

Van den Berghe, Pierre L. 1978. *Man in Society: A Biosocial View (Second Edition).* New York: Elsevier.

Van den Berghe, Pierre L. 1978. "Race and ethnicity: A sociobiological perspective." *Ethnic and Racial Studies* 1: 401–411.

Van den Berghe, Pierre L. 1979. *Human Family Systems: An Evolutionary View.* New York: Elsevier.

Van den Berghe, Pierre L. 1980. "Incest and exogamy, a sociobiological reconsideration." *Ethology and Sociobiology* 1: 151–162.

Van den Berghe, Pierre L. 1983. "Human inbreeding avoidance: Culture in nature." *Behavioral Brain Sciences* 6: 91–123.

Van den Berghe, Pierre L. 1984. A sociobiological view. *Family and Work: Comparative Convergences.* Westport, Conn.: Greenwood Press, pp. 31–41.

Van den Berghe, Pierre L. 1986. "Book review." *Contemporary Sociology* 15: 675–676.

Van den Berghe, Pierre L. 1987. *The ethnic phenomenon.* New York: Praeger.

Van den Berghe, Pierre L. 1987. Incest taboos and avoidance: Some African applications. In C. Crawford, M. Smith, D. Krebs (Eds.) *Sociobiology and Psychology.* Hillsdale, NJ: Lawrence Erlbaum, pp. 353–372.

Van den Berghe, Pierre L. 1988. The family and the biological base of human sociality. In Erik E. Filsinger (Ed.) *Biosocial Perspectives on the Family.* Beverly Hills, CA: Sage Publications, pp. 39–60.

Van den Berghe, Pierre L. 1990. "Why most sociologists don't (and won't) think evolutionarily." *Sociological Forum* 5: 1873–1875.

Van den Berghe, Pierre L. and David Barash. 1977. "Inclusive fitness and human family structure." *American Anthropologist* 79: 809–823.

Van den Berghe, Pierre L. and Peter Frost. 1986. "Skin color preference, sexual dimorphism, and sexual selection: A case of gene-culture co-evolution?" *Ethnic and Racial Studies* 9: 87–113.
Van den Berghe, P. and J. Whitmeyer. 1990. "Social class and reproductive success." *International Journal of Contemporary Sociology* 27: 29–48.
Vergnes, M., A. Depaulis, A. Boehrer, E. Kempf. 1988. "Selective increase of offensive behavior in the rat following intrahypothalamic 5, 7-DHT-induced serotonin depletion." *Behavioral Brain Research* 29: 85–91.

Vila, Bryan J. and Lawrence E. Cohen 1993. "Crime as strategy: Testing an evolutionary ecological theory of expropriative crime." *American Journal of Sociology* 98: 873–912.

Wallace, Walter L. 1983. *Principles of Scientific Sociology.* New York: Aldine.

Walsh, Anthony. 1980. "The prophylactic effect of religion on blood pressure levels among samples of immigrants." *Social Science and Medicine* 14B: 59–63.

Walsh, Anthony. 1983. "Neurophysiology, motherhood, and the growth of love." *Human Mosaic* 17: 51–62.

Walsh, Anthony. 1987. "Cognitive functioning and delinquency: Property versus violent offences." *International Journal of Offender Therapy and Comparative Criminology* 31: 285–289.

Walsh, Anthony. 1991a. "Genetic and environmental explanations of juvenile violence in advantaged and disadvantaged environments." *Aggressive Behavior* 18: 187–199.

Walsh, Anthony. 1991b. *Intellectual imbalance, love deprivation and violent delinquency: A biosocial perspective.* Springfield, Illinois: Charles C. Thomas.

Walsh, Anthony. 1993. "Love styles, masculinity/femininity, physical attractiveness, and sexual behavior: A test of evolutionary theory." *Ethology and Sociobiology* 14: 25–38.

Walsh, Anthony. 1995. *Biosociology: An emerging paradigm.* Westport, CT: Praeger.

Walsh, Anthony and Patricia Ann Walsh. 1989. "Love, self-esteem, and multiple sclerosis." *Social Science & Medicine* 29: 793–798.

Whitam, Frederick. 1983. "Culturally invariable properties of male homosexuality: Tentative conclusions from cross-cultural research." *Archives of Sexual Behavior* 12: 207–226.

Wilterdink, N. 1976. "Biology and sociology." *Netherlands' Journal of Sociology* 12: 19–37.

Wood, Peter B., John K. Cochran, Betty Pfefferbaum. 1995. "A sensation-seeking approach to delinquent substance use." *Journal of Drug Use* (in press).

Wood, Peter B., John K. Cochran, Betty Pfefferbaum, Bruce J. Arnekley. 1995. "Sensation-seeking and delinquent substance use: An extension of learning theory." *Journal of Drug Issues* 25: 173–193.

Wood, Peter B., Walter R. Gove, John K. Cochran. 1994. "Motivations for violent crime among incarcerated adults: A consideration of reinforcement processes." *Journal of the Oklahoma Criminal Justice Research Consortium* 1: 75–93.

Zuckerman, Marvin. 1979. *Sensation seeking: Beyond the optimal level of arousal.* Hillsdale, New Jersey: Lawrence Erlbaum.

Zuckerman, Marvin. 1983. *Biological bases of sensation seeking, impulsivity and anxiety.* Hillsdale, N.J.: Erlbaum.

Zuckerman, Marvin., M. S. Buchsbaum, S. Monte, D. L. Murphy. 1980. "Sensation seeking and its biological correlates." *Psychological Bulletin* 88: 187–214.

Zuckerman, Marvin and M. Neeb. 1980. "Demographic influences in sensation-seeking and expression of sensation-seeking in religion, smoking, and driving habits." *Personality and Individual Differences* 1: 197–206.

Zuckerman, Marvom and P. L. Myer. (1983). "Sensation seeking in homosexual and heterosexual males." *Archives of Sexual Behavior* 12: 347–356.

FRAME the DEBATE

Form at end of book

WiseGuide Wrap-Up

A mountain of evidence suggests that genetics does play a role in criminality. The extent to which genetics is a factor, however, is unclear. Further, the implications of this type of research are profound.

For example, if we say that social factors cause people to commit crimes, then we discount the role of a person's genetic makeup in contributing to deviance. However, this position suggests that society is somehow responsible for crime because we create the social conditions and environment in which criminals live.

On the other hand, shifting blame to offenders and their genetic makeup reduces the blame that society must bear. This happens when we consider crime not as a function of the environment, but as an inevitable action of a pathological offender.

A criminal justice system premised on the notion that the problem is inherent in the offender might be more inclined to offer rehabilitation and leniency. On the other hand, a system of justice that assumes that individual offenders are not predisposed to committing crime treats offenders as rational individuals who must be punished to deter them from subsequent offending.

Scientific inquiry is fostering major advancements in our understanding of the relationship between genetics and criminality. The Human Genome Project and other research endeavors will provide criminologists with more evidence regarding the relationship between genetics and deviance, which, in turn, may lead to better crime prevention strategies.

R.E.A.L. Sites

This list provides a print preview of typical **Coursewise** R.E.A.L. sites. (There are over 100 such sites at the **Courselinks**™ site.) The danger in printing URLs is that web sites can change overnight. As we went to press, these sites were functional using the URLs provided. If you come across one that isn't, please let us know via email to: webmaster@coursewise.com. Use your Passport to access the most current list of R.E.A.L. sites at the **Courselinks** site.

Site name: *Crime Times*

URL: http://www.crime-times.org/

Why is it R.E.A.L.? *Crime Times* is an online journal that focuses on the study of biological causes of criminal, violent, and psychopathic behavior. Numerous articles are available at this site.

Key topics: biological causes of crime, crime

Try this: Read several of the recent articles on the biological causes of violent behavior.

Site name: Human Genome Project

URL: http://www.ornl.gov/TechResources/Human_Genome/

Why is it R.E.A.L.? The goal of the U.S. Human Genome Project is to identify and better understand the roles that genes play in our DNA. Additionally, the U.S. Human Genome Project will address the ethical, legal, and social issues that may arise from the project. The possible implications for understanding biologically based criminality as a result of this endeavor are endless!

Key topics: biological causes of crime, research

Try this: Listen to some of the audio presentations and read about the Human Genome Project that is in progress.

Site name: Scientific Testimony

URL: http://www.scientific.org/

Why is it R.E.A.L.? At this site are articles, news reports, and commentary about the use of scientific evidence in legal proceedings. The site also offers an archive of information useful to lawyers, forensic scientists, and expert witnesses.

Key topics: scientific evidence, law

Try this: Read some of the articles from the online journal.

What Is the Best Way to Deter Criminals from Offending?

ISSUE 2

Take a Closer Look

1. What are some of the implications of conservative crime policies?
2. What are some of the implications of liberal crime policies?
3. What attempts, if any, have been made to advance crime policies in a bipartisan or apolitical nature?
4. Can Bennett's key to prevention (moral education) help reduce crime?
5. Can you think of a way in which boot camps could be more successful in reducing recidivism?
6. What role do you think criminologists should play in the formation of criminal justice legislation?

WiseGuide Intro

One of the most pressing issues that criminal justice professionals face is determining appropriate sanctions for dealing with criminals. Everyday, in every city across the United States, criminal justice professionals and policy-makers struggle with the issues of punishment and deterrence. Unfortunately, what people feel ought to be done about crime and criminals is often determined by personal political viewpoints, and not the criminological literature.

No other criminal justice issue alienates liberals from conservatives more than does the topic of deterrence. Typically, conservatives support harsher penalties and tougher sanctions for criminal offenders, while liberals promote rehabilitation as an alternative to incarceration and punishment.

What to do about criminals is a tough question. We know a lot about crime and criminal offending, yet we often don't apply that knowledge. The good news is that there are better ways to deal with criminals, and criminal justice research has shown us many of these alternatives. The bad news is that, due to a lack of bipartisan support, legislatures often fail to approve these alternatives.

The readings for Issue 2 clearly articulate how approaches to dealing with the criminal population are as different as the criminals and the crimes they commit. William Bennett's article, "Shut the Criminals' Revolving Door," takes a hard stance against criminals. Bennett advocates for preventing at-risk children from becoming criminals, preventing innocent people from becoming victims, and restraining convicted criminals from recidivating.

In "Thinking Your Way Out of Prison," James Byrne and Mary Brewster suggest that programs focusing on offender rehabilitation are working, as opposed to those that merely "monitor" an offender. Examples of such rehabilitation programs are boot camps with extensive after-care, intensive supervision, house arrest, and community service sentences.

R E A D I N G 3

Issue 2: What is the best way to deter criminals from offending?

Shut the Criminals' Revolving Door

Influenced by those opposed to punishment, government has failed to keep citizens safe from known repeat violent offenders.

William J. Bennett

William J. Bennett, a former secretary of Education, is a fellow at the Heritage Foundation and the co-chairman of the National Council on Crime in America.

During the past 25 years, much of the crime debate has been dominated by criminologists who are philosophically opposed to punishment. In an attempt to advance their agenda, they have perpetrated a wide array of myths. The recently released report of the bipartisan Council on Crime in America is an attempt to provide an alternative: a rigorous, empirical, real-world analysis of the current state of crime and punishment. The report tells us that the nation faces at least three distinct but related crime challenges: preventing at-risk children from becoming criminals, protecting innocent people from becoming crime victims and restraining convicted criminals who are under the "supervision" of the criminal justice system (on probation, parole or pretrial release) from committing additional crimes.

Prevention

We know that children born into poor families—matter their race, region, religion, demographic stripe or socioeconomic status—they have decent families and grow up with responsible, caring adults in their lives, are far less likely to become either victims or victimizers. We also know that not all children are born so lucky.

America is now home to nearly 70 million children 18 or under. As many as 15 million of them are growing up in relative poverty, often in places where the institutions of civil society—families, churches, schools, voluntary associations—are in near-complete collapse. The report argues that neither more spending by government nor the mere withdrawal of government can prevent today's at-risk 4- to 7-year-old boys from becoming next decade's 14- to 17-year-old predatory street felons or the next century's first big class of adult career criminals. The key to prevention is moral education. That, in turn, depends on reviving the character-forming institutions of civil society. But we know that there is no easy way to accomplish that.

Protection

The recent widely reported drops in serious crime in New York, Houston and other cities were due largely to innovative community policing strategies, citizen anti-crime initiatives and continued "target-hardening" or increased security and personal safety measures by individuals and businesses. But these drops in crime may be merely a lull. The storm is gathering in the form of a demographic bulge of highly crime-prone boys. During the next 10 years, enormous upward pressure will be exerted on crime rates. Redoubling crime protection efforts will not keep the storm offshore. But it can help to minimize the damage and reduce the human and financial cost.

Restraint

The criminal justice system imprisons only one criminal per 100 violent crimes. Most violent prisoners serve less than half their time in prison before being released. In 1993, there were 43.6 million criminal victimizations in America, more than 10 million of them violent. Between 1985 and 1993, the rate at which boys 14 through 17 committed murder increased by about 50% for whites and 300% for blacks. A third of all violent crimes, including murders, are committed by felons out on probation, parole or pretrial release. What is involved here is more than a failure of public safety; it is a massive failure of governmental obligation. Citizens should not have to accept their government's prolonged, persistent failure to restrain violent and repeat criminals. A government incapable of restraining known, violent, repeat criminals within its custody cannot be trusted to take on more complicated and costly public functions.

There is also the matter of eroding public trust in our political insti-

"Shut the Criminals' Revolving Door" by William J. Bennett as appeared in *The Los Angeles Times,* January 16, 1996. Reprinted by permission of the author.

tutions. A government that, amid much fanfare, passes wave after wave of get-tough anti-crime laws but proves toothless in the execution of those laws eviscerates public confidence in the integrity of lawmakers and the criminal justice system. Indeed, in 1993 and again in 1994, there was only one public institution in which the American people had less confidence than in Congress: the criminal justice system. No representative democracy can long survive this deep and disheartening lack of public trust. And the only way to restore public trust is to shut the revolving door.

A final point: A society tells as much about itself by what it punishes as what it praises, by what it condemns as well as what it encourages, by what receives reprobation as what receives approbation. The message of our justice system is all too clear to criminals and victims: Too often, for too many, it says "nobody cares" and "nothing matters." That has to change soon or the carnage and violence that have become almost permanent features of America's landscape will worsen.

FRAME the DEBATE

Form at end of book

Issue 2: What is the best way to deter criminals from offending?

Thinking Your Way Out of Prison

Demographics predict crime will increase over the next decade in the United States, further straining an already burdened correctional system. To prepare for the future, policy-makers should take a fresh direction in punishment. This approach must try new ways to rehabilitate criminals that are less reliant on prison and more reliant on the community and treatment.

James Byrne and Mary Brewster

Across the country, legislators and correctional administrators are faced with a difficult dilemma: how best to deal with the immediate problem of correctional crowding while offering a vision for the future of state and local correctional programs. Inevitably, both short- and long-term corrections strategies will be based on predictions of the future: Will crime and victimization rates increase in this decade? Will arrest trends change for various types of crime? Will government prosecute, convict and sentence offenders in the same manner? And, most importantly to corrections policy-makers and practitioners, will the corrections populations continue to grow, requiring even more resources than today?

After considering these basic questions, John DiIulio, a professor of Politics and Public Affairs at Princeton University, has offered a number of predictions about the future of criminal justice and corrections in this country.

A Pessimistic View

In 1991, John DiIulio wrote a book entitled *No Escape—The Future of American Corrections,* in which he offered a bleak assessment of the future based on the notion that the recent past is probably the best predictor of the immediate future. DiIulio's analysis is based on his review of research on demographic trends (in particular the size of the young adult population) and changes in the way the criminal justice system processes the various groups of offenders (in particular, drug offenders, property offenders, mentally ill offenders and drunken drivers).

DiIulio offers four predictions. First, he argues the nation will have a much larger correctional system. "By the year 2000 . . . the total number of citizens in the charge of corrections officials will easily surpass 4 million" (DiIulio, 1991: 3–4). Because the country has already passed this point, it appears that—barring a sudden shift in sentencing practices—DiIulio's prediction is conservative. An expected increase in overall correctional population at the end of the century is not surprising; it is an inevitable consequence of the size of the "at risk" adult population. According to a recent report, *Americans Behind Bars,* released by the Edna McConnell Clark Foundation (1992: 7), "(O)ver 60 percent of the people who were arrested and charged for crimes in 1991 . . . were between the ages of 13 and 29." As the children of the "baby boom" generation (the echo boomers) reach that age of life when they are most likely to commit offenses, crime rates are likely to rise. The effects of this increase will be noticed throughout the criminal justice system. So unless there is a dramatic shift in policy and practice, we should expect a larger correctional population.

The second prediction DiIulio makes is that more prison and jail space is needed because "we are already working near the limits of our capacity to manage offenders in the community" (DiIulio, 1991: 5). The United States spent about $25 billion on corrections in 1992; and in 1993, a total of 120,207 additional beds will be added to the federal and state prison systems. (Edna McConnell Clark Foundation, 1992) Despite these expenditures, the institutional system—prisons and jails—remains crowded beyond capacity. And the community-based system, which includes those sentenced to house arrest and community service, is in even worse shape. DiIulio has correctly observed that the community corrections system is more crowded than

"Thinking Your Way Out of Prison" by James Byrne and Mary Brewster from *Spectrum: Journal of State Government,* Fall 1993, Vol. 66, No. 4, pp. 50–58. Reprinted with permission from Spectrum. Copyright Council of State Governments, 1993.

our institutional system, and that it does not have the resources to adequately supervise its offenders. Rather than suggest that policy-makers might want to re-evaluate how they slice the correctional resource pie, DiIulio has resigned himself to the need for a larger institutional system.

DiIulio's third prediction is that prisons and jails will be crowded because the demand for space always seems to outstrip the building of correctional facilities. Along with crowding will come "(a) rise in . . . violence behind bars, as well as . . . deterioration in the quantity and quality of . . . educational and work opportunities available to inmates" (DiIulio 1991: 5). In other words, the nation will not build its way out of the crowding crisis; and as a result, many offenders will leave the prison system in worse shape than when they arrived. DiIulio argues that it may be possible to lessen the negative consequences of crowding through better management, but overall the scenario he presents is bleak.

Many offenders will leave the prison system in worse shape than when they arrived.

The last prediction offered by DiIulio is that policy-makers will have to look closely at community-based corrections programs and identify programs that deter repeat offenders. DiIulio appears to be predicting a comeback for the panacea of community-based offender rehabilitation programs. If DiIulio's assessment is correct, it portends a major change in correctional policy in this country: a rediscovery of correctional rehabilitation. Despite (or perhaps because of) DiIulio's gloomy predictions about the need to expand the capacity to incarcerate, he argues that the only hope for the future is to solve this problem by looking at promising alternatives to incarceration and determining what types of programs rehabilitate offenders. DiIulio argues that social science research has yet to provide answers to precisely the kinds of questions that federal, state and local officials need to ask: What works? With whom? And why?

However, some recent reviews of the research on the newest wave of community corrections programs, such as boot camps, intensive supervision, house arrest and community service sentences, have focused on precisely these questions (Byrne, Lurigio and Petersilia, 1992; Palmer, 1992). And as a result, a consensus seems to be forming that programs focusing on offender rehabilitation are working, while those that only monitor an offender in the community are not.

Is DiIulio correct in each of his four predictions about the future of American corrections? While each seems plausible, he may or may not be correct, based on what governments do during the next few years. As legislators and correctional administrators at the federal, state and local levels develop new programs, they will shape the future of corrections in this country. The question is: How will they answer basic questions about the purpose of corrections as they rethink the punishment for various types of offenders, such as drug and alcohol offenders, mentally ill offenders and property offenders. To answer this question, legislators and correctional administrators need to consider the four basic purposes of any sanction: (1) Punishment/Retribution, (2) Deterrence, (3) Rehabilitation and (4) Control. The key to understanding where our correctional system is headed is to determine the priority given to these various aims by policymakers at the federal, state and local levels.

Punishment of Offenders

In an assessment of correctional policy, the first area to consider is the notion of punishment. If the nation continues in the direction it's headed, with the echo boom generation coming of age and the increase of the size of the minority poor population, DiIulio will be correct. There will be more prisons and jails than ever before because many policy-makers equate punishment with incarceration. However, it is a good time to reassess the effectiveness of the "punishment by incapacitation" strategy, particularly in the use of incarceration for property offenders, drunken drivers, drug users, small-time drug dealers and mentally ill offenders. As some corrections experts have observed, there are other ways to punish offenders besides locking them up. (Austin and Irwin, 1993)

During the next couple of years, particularly in the 20 or more states that have sentencing guidelines, policy-makers will take a much closer look at "exchange rates." An exchange rate is the number of days under various forms of community supervision that would be equal to a single day of incarceration. For example, a sentencing guideline commission might decide that the exchange rate for house arrest might be 3:1 (three days under house arrest equals one day of incarceration). Policy-makers are now thinking about how to redefine punishment and exchange a period of incarceration for a period of supervision in the community. How punishment is defined in terms of both incarceration and non-incarceration will come down to this notion of exchange. How will it be built into sentencing guidelines? And how will the value of incarceration in exchange for a time in the community be determined? We suspect that similar changes will be proposed regarding the mandatory sentencing laws found in 46 states. For example, a mandatory one-year prison sentence might be "exchanged" for three years under intensive supervision in the community.

Any discussion about appropriate punishments depends on how punishment is defined in terms of sanctions. Should punishment be defined exclusively in terms of a stigma associated with a conviction status? Or are community service, loss of income because of fines, or some sort of community work forms of punishment? And given the definition of punishment in a community setting, how do you define what the exchange rate with incarceration will be? Answers to these questions will determine the movement towards non-incarceration sanctions in the states.

Deterrence by Incarceration

Offenders are sentenced to prison, jail and various community-based sanctions (including fines, community service, probation and intermediate sanctions) to punish them. But punishment is only one of the aims of sentencing. Another purpose is to deter both the offender (which we call "specific deterrence") and everyone else (known as "general deterrence") from committing crime. To many, the best way to deter crime is to punish offenders by locking them up. Between 1980 and 1992, the size of the state and federal prison population in the United States increased 267.9 percent, to 883,593 offenders from 329,821 offenders. The nation's reliance on incarceration does not appear to be abating. For example, only five states reported that their prison populations decreased in 1992. These states were Maine, New Jersey, North Dakota, Oregon and Wyoming. Prison population rose in the remaining states, with Texas (18.4 percent increase), West Virginia (16.2 percent), New Hampshire (15.9 percent), Idaho (15.5 percent) and Wisconsin (15.4 percent) reporting the largest increases between 1991 and 1992 (see Bureau of Justice Statistics *Bulletin* 1993).

How effective is a strategy of deterrence by incapacitation? The overall crime and victimization rates remained stable during the past decade, which suggests that increased reliance on incarceration did not deter crime as many conservative policy-makers had suggested (Steffensmeier and Harer, 1993; Byrne, Lurigio and Petersilia, 1992). In terms of stopping repeat offenders, research suggests that time in prison or jail actually increases the risk of subsequent crimes once these individuals are released to the community (Byrne and Kelly, 1989). In short, while a strong case can be made for prisons and jails to punish offenders, legislators and correctional administrators will find little or no support for claims that incarceration deters crime. Given that institutional corrections is the second fastest-growing area in state budgets after Medicaid (Edna McConnell Clark Foundation, 1992)—pressure has been mounting to justify the benefits of prison and jail construction and to consider community-based alternatives.

Of course, deterrence-based assumptions also have been used to develop community corrections programs. In community corrections, the idea that surveillance programs will deter offenders from criminal behavior has been tried for several years. However, the evidence is in from the 1990s' get-tough surveillance-oriented community supervision programs, such as boot camps, intensive supervision, home detention and day reporting centers. Overall, surveillance-oriented programs have not reduced cost, overcrowding or recidivism (Byrne, Lurigio, and Petersilia, 1992). These results are likely to depress people in favor of getting people out of prison who feel that "get tough" community sanctions offer one way to do it. But if specific deterrence is an important goal of sentencing, surveillance-oriented community sanctions are not the route to take.

Policy-makers and program managers are going to move away from these surveillance-oriented programs because there is little evidence they work. Thus, any predictions about the future of American corrections must take this movement into account. If DiIulio's assessment is correct, the pendulum may swing back in the direction of an earlier panacea—offender rehabilitation. If this occurs, the corrections system may or may not be larger, depending on the effectiveness of this strategy. Research on new prison and jail admissions shows the continuous movement of offenders between institutional and community control. For example, a recent Bureau of Justice Statistics *Bulletin* (May, 1993), reported that the percentage of people who entered state prisons because they violated probation or parole conditions increased from about 17 percent of all admissions in 1980 to 30 percent of all admissions in 1991 (p. 1). One thing is certain: Deterrence-oriented intermediate sanction programs have not interrupted this cycle; in fact, they appear to have made matters worse. In the next few years, we may discover whether a new wave of rehabilitation-oriented sanctions will produce different results.

Rehabilitation

A third dimension of sentencing is offender treatment. Recent discussions have stated that the individual goal of treatment is offender change, and the social goal of treatment is community protection through the reduction of crime (Palmer, 1992). The difference between the two lies in the means used to attain the goal. We need to determine what institutional and community-based treatment programs are available and then evaluate the extent these treatment programs reduce an offender's risk of recidivism. Focusing on community-based programs, there is evidence that offenders who receive treatment for substance abuse, employment and individual or family problems have lower recidivism rates than offenders who do not get treatment. An example is the study of 14 sites around the country conducted by RAND Corporation researchers Joan Petersilia and Susan Turner. Although the researchers

Based on the results of this research, it appears that the treatment aspects of a community supervision program need to be beefed up to provide both fair punishment and a higher level of community protection and control.

found no overall differences in recidivism across those 14 intensive supervision programs, within each of them the offenders who received treatment had significantly lower recidivism rates (Petersilia and Turner, 1993).

Similar findings have been reported by other researchers. For example, an evaluation of intensive probation supervision in Massachusetts found that offenders who receive help with substance abuse, employment and individual or family problems had significantly lower recidivism rates than offenders who did not receive treatment (Byrne and Kelly, 1989). Based on the results of this research, it appears that the treatment aspects of a community supervision program need to be beefed up to provide both fair punishment and a higher level of community protection and control. The same statement can be offered regarding the need for improved treatment in institutions, including boot camps.

Control's Double Edge

It is one thing to discuss the philosophy of sentencing offenders to either institutional or community-based programs; it is another to discuss the practical aspects of managing offenders in both settings. In community corrections, policy-makers need to decide what to do with offenders who do not comply with the conditions of their sentence. This can perhaps be described best as the control dimension of these programs. The most interesting trend of the next 10 years or so will be the increased use of technology to monitor offenders who have, for example, been sentenced to house arrest. Technology can monitor offenders' lifestyles, where they go, what they do, whether they are using drugs and whether they are violating their curfews. There also is more knowledge about the types of offenders and how to link offenders to various forms of treatment.

So the question is what to do with the information. As Donald Cochran, commissioner of probation in Massachusetts has observed, new information systems are great in theory, but policy-makers have to decide what programs are going to do in response to the information they give—particularly the negative information about offenders (Cochran, 1992). This is especially true in a surveillance-oriented program, where attempts are made to monitor offenders' movements in the community. As we noted earlier, one in three state prison admissions in 1992 was a probation or parole violator. In this respect, the issue of revoking parole is critical to predictions about the future size of the institutional system. Prisons and jails already are filled by probation and parole failures. But if policy-makers develop policies and programs that result in fewer failures, then there would be less demand for prison and jail space.

The Georgia Legislature recently tried to deal with the many offenders coming back into the system who had violated a technical condition of parole. Lawmakers limited the ability of community corrections programs to place an offender directly in prison or jail for violating a technical condition of probation. Instead, the offender must be placed in another type of community program first. Georgia's response to the problem forces program developers to rethink their approach to technical violators, using a structured hierarchy of intermediate sanctions in lieu of incarceration. Although it is difficult to predict whether other states will follow Georgia's lead, we suspect that the issue of control is going to be critical to the future viability of the next wave of community-based programs.

Can We Envision a Different Correctional Future?

How policy-makers answer these questions will determine whether, in the next 10 years, the nation goes in the direction DiIulio predicts, which is more of the same (with a nod toward alternatives to incarceration and rehabilitation), or whether the system will move in another direction altogether. The question is: If the system is going to move in a direction other than more crowding and more offenders, what will policy-makers, practitioners, researchers and the public have to do? The answer should be obvious. There needs to be a fundamental change in thinking about punishment, corrections and the dynamics of community control.

There is going to be increasing pressure on state legislatures to consider alternatives to incarceration and alternatives to traditional probation.

There are three changes in community corrections practice that we envision by 2000. First, there is going to be increasing pressure on state legislatures to consider alternatives to incarceration and alternatives to traditional probation. For this reason, we anticipate an increased use of non-supervision sanctions—such as day fines and community service. At least 10 percent to 20 percent of the correctional population can be sanctioned in this manner with no increased threat to the community. This change would result in significant reductions in the size of the traditional probation population. Successful day fine programs are operated in New York, Connecticut and Arizona; while community service programs also are making a comeback.

Second, we expect state and local corrections systems to embrace unique, stand-alone intermediate punishments. These intermediate sanctions will combine elements of punishment and treatment, reinforced by a hierarchy of punishments for offenders who do not comply with their sentence. Although less than 5 percent of the correctional population is in these programs, we predict that, by the end of the decade, one of every three convicted offenders will be in an intermediate punishment program. These programs will likely draw their population from two sources: the "high risk" offender types under supervision and certain offenders (like drug and alcohol) who are currently incarcerated. Along with the shift of offenders there will have to be a reallocation of correctional resources.

In addition to creating more intermediate sanctions, the nation needs to redefine traditional probation strategies. This could be done by borrowing from the concept of community-oriented policing, which itself borrows from the probation and parole practices of the late 1960s and early 1970s. This would address the problems and needs of offenders and their victims within the same local area. In this community-based model, traditional probation programs would move out of the office and into the streets. Many practitioners recognize that, while formal deterrence might be a good public focus for any corrections system, it is informal deterrence mechanisms that work the best (Cochran, 1992). The relationships between probation officers and offenders, the relationships between offenders and family members, and the relationships between offenders and their friends, have the most impact on behavior. Traditional probation practices should focus on improving these informal mechanisms. The best way to accomplish this is by reintroducing probation officers to the community. Probation officers need to spend less time in the courthouse and more time at the offender's house.

To the extent that increased informal community control results in less demand for formal criminal justice involvement, the turn of the century may be marked by lower, not higher, crime rates, despite demographic trends. If this occurs, the trickle-down effect on the correctional system should be obvious. Ultimately, the question becomes: Can the nation continue to muddle through, relying on assumptions about the effectiveness of incarceration and formal deterrence that are not true? The answer is no, and new approaches must be developed to deal with various types of offenders (such as property offenders, drug users, drunken drivers and mentally ill offenders). To quote DiIulio (1991: 270): "The future of American corrections permits no escape from [the] delicate moral balancing act" . . . between "punishment and hate one moment, reform and love the next" (p. 210). It is time for federal, state and local corrections policy-makers to assess how the scale is balanced in their own system and to act accordingly.

Sources

Austin, James and John Irwin. 1993. *Does Imprisonment Reduce Crime? A Critique of "Voodoo" Criminology.* San Francisco, CA: National Council on Crime and Delinquency.

Bureau of Justice Statistics. 1993. *Bulletin: Prisoners in 1992.* Washington, D.C., U.S. Department of Justice.

Byrne, James M. and Linda Kelly. 1989. *Restructuring Probation as an Intermediate Sanction. An Evaluation of Massachusetts Intensive Probation Supervision Program.* Washington, D.C., National Institute of Justice—Final Report.

Byrne, James, Arthur Lurigio and Joan Petersilia, editors. 1992. *Smart Sentencing. The Emergence of Intermediate Sanctions.* Newbury Park, CA: Sage Publications.

Cochran, Donald. 1992. "The Long Road From Policy Development to Real Change In Sanctioning Practice," pp. 307–318 in Byrne, Lurigio and Petersilia, editors. 1992. *Smart Sentencing. The Emergence of Intermediate Sanctions.* Newbury Park, CA: Sage Publications.

DiIulio, John I., Jr. 1991. *No Escape: The Future of American Corrections.* New York, NY: Basic Books.

Kramer, John H. 1992. "The Evolution of Pennsylvania's Sentencing Guidelines." *Overcrowded Times,* 3(4): 6:9.

McConnell, Edna Clark Foundation. 1992. *Americans Behind Bars.* New York, NY: Edna McConnell Clark Foundation.

Palmer, Ted. 1992. *The Re-Emergence of Correctional Intervention.* Newbury Park, CA: Sage Publications.

Petersilia, Joan and Susan Turner. 1993. "Evaluating Intensive Supervision Probation/Parole: Results of a Nationwide Experiment." *Research In Brief,* Washington, D.C.: U.S. Department of Justice.

Steffensmeier, Darrel and Miles Harer. 1993. "Bulging Prisons, An Aging U.S. Population and The Nation's Violent Crime Rate." *Federal Probation,* Vol. LVIII (2): 3–11.

FRAME the DEBATE

Form at end of book

WiseGuide Wrap-Up

Readings 3 and 4 show how approaches to crime control policy vary according to political beliefs. For example, Bennett's approach is clearly more conservative in nature in that he argues for a revival of character-forming institutions and for harsher restrictions for those convicted of crimes. Much more liberal are the alternative sanctions that Byrne and Brewster support.

Also interesting is the approach that each side takes in framing the argument. Bennett appeals to a "moral high ground" supported by his beliefs on what a just and fair system of justice would resemble. Byrne and Brewster, on the other hand, submit evidence from criminological research as to the best alternatives available to deal with crime. While an argument based on empirical support from criminological research seems to be the most appropriate way to advance crime policy, it isn't clear if that is the way criminal justice policy is formed.

In addition to thinking about how you would respond to crime, think about how crime legislation is passed, and given the nature of our political system, how you would seek to change the way in which the criminal justice system seeks to deter criminals. Do you see politicians debating crime issues from a moral standpoint or from a perspective based on criminological research? Is the former an appropriate and responsible way to address the crime issue, which is one of the most pressing issues facing our country?

R.E.A.L. Sites

This list provides a print preview of typical **Coursewise** R.E.A.L. sites. (There are over 100 such sites at the **Courselinks**™ site.) The danger in printing URLs is that web sites can change overnight. As we went to press, these sites were functional using the URLs provided. If you come across one that isn't, please let us know via email to: webmaster@coursewise.com. Use your Passport to access the most current list of R.E.A.L. sites at the **Courselinks** site.

Site name: *The Atlantic Monthly*

URL: http://www.theatlantic.com/politics/crime/crime.htm

Why is it R.E.A.L.? This site has a section on crime that hosts several well-written pieces.

Key topics: news, crime

Try this: Read some of the articles at this web site.

Site name: Preventing Crime: What Works, What Doesn't, What's Promising

URL: http://ncjrs.aspensys.com/works/index.htm

Why is it R.E.A.L.? This is a very comprehensive report to the U.S. Congress by leading criminologists.

Key topics: research, crime

Try this: Identify the approaches to crime that are successful, as well as those that are not working.

Site name: National Criminal Justice Reference Service

URL: http://www.ncjrs.org

Why is it R.E.A.L.? This extensive site provides abstract databases, links, reports, and more.

Key topics: research, reports

Try this: Search for a recent article on a topic of interest to you.

Why Is the Crime Rate Elusive?

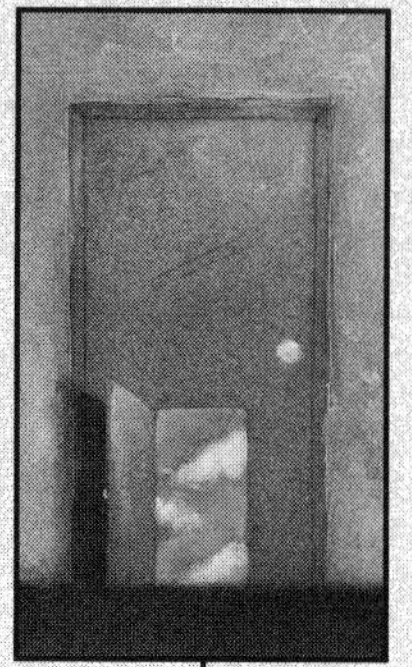

ISSUE 3

Take a Closer Look

1. What other factors can you think of that may help explain the decrease in the crime rate?
2. Has your local police department recently implemented any changes that may influence the reported crime rate?
3. Why would a police chief or sheriff report to the city council that crime is increasing in a jurisdiction, when, in fact, it has been decreasing?
4. Why would a police chief or sheriff report to the city council that crime is decreasing in a jurisdiction, when, in fact, it has been increasing?
5. How would you respond to a friend who says, "There is so much more crime lately, and each year it gets worse."

WiseGuide Intro

Mark Twain wrote, "There are lies, damn lies and statistics." While criminologists have not reached a clear consensus regarding why statistics indicate that crime rates have been declining as of late, the evidence presented makes the relationship unclear at best.

The Koch Crime Institute report entitled "The Falling Crime Rate" suggests that personal responsibility, sentencing policies, and community policing are associated with the declining crime rate. Also related to the drop in crime, according to the report, are the economy, demographic changes, and community involvement.

The problem is that crime data are extremely complicated and unreliable. In fact, crime data gathered from official reports such as the Uniform Crime Report (UCR) and the National Crime Victimization Survey (NCVS) are so inconclusive and contradictory that some criminologists rely on one main statistic to help them understand the crime picture: the homicide rate.

Criminologists have varying opinions as to why the crime rate is declining. In "As Crime Falls, Pressure Rises to Alter Data," newspaper reporter Fox Butterfield shows that some of the decline in the crime rate may not be due to criminals becoming good, but cops going bad! Butterfield explains that, for various reasons, cities may feel pressure to report a decrease in crime and that erroneous reporting of crime by various agencies may be contributing to the declining crime rate reported in the UCR.

Issue 3: Why is the crime rate elusive?

The Falling Crime Rate

Koch Crime Institute

Abstract

The consensus on the falling crime rate is that there is no singular event, policy implementation, or social action that can account for the decrease during the last six years. Individuals and organizations assessing the cause and implications of this decline are arriving at a unified theory attributing collective efforts and change as the reason or reasons.

Again there exists a consensus that the effective measures require further examination and definition, but that the current effect is temporary and will dissipate with the aging of the preteen and teen generation currently impacting the nation's juvenile justice systems.

Background

The media frequently make reference to America's declining crime rate. According to the Federal Bureau of Investigation's "Uniform Crime Reports," the crime index rate fell for the fifth straight year in 1996, and is down 10% from the rate of 1992.[1] The FBI's Uniform Crime Reporting Program is a city, county, and state law enforcement program that provides a nationwide view of crime based on the submission of information from local law enforcement agencies about crimes reported to police. The index includes several offenses: (a) Murder and Nonnegligent Manslaughter, (b) Forcible Rape, (c) Robbery, (d) Aggravated Assault, (e) Burglary, (f) Larceny-Theft, (g) Motor Vehicle Theft, and (h) Arson.

This reported decline is good news, but the reason for it is not understood. Surprisingly, no one seems to want to take credit for the decline. Crime is an issue similar to the weather: It is reportable, its effects are observable, everyone talks about it, a few try to predict it, and no one wants to claim responsibility for it. However, just as we now know a few things about what causes changes in the weather—some of which we can intentionally affect and some we cannot—we also know about crime.

The opinions expressed herein do not necessarily reflect the official position of the Koch Crime Commission concerning this issue.

"The Falling Crime Rate" from Koch Crime Institute White Paper Report, April 1998. Reprinted by permission of the Koch Crime Institute.

Discussion

Personal Responsibility

Do domestic violence initiatives such as hotlines, shelters, and education, as well as victims' assistance organizations and programs, have an impact in raising the awareness and ability to prevent these crimes?

The United States Department of Justice reports that 48% of all victims of violence in 1996 knew their offender. Seven out of 10 robberies were committed by strangers, compared to three out of 10 of all rapes/sexual assaults. Just over one-third of all rapes/sexual assaults were committed by nonrelatives well-known to the victim. Of murder victims, 45% were related to or acquainted with their assailants, 15% were murdered by strangers, and almost 40% had an unknown relationship to their murderer.[2]

Despite these statistics, the number of rape, sexual assault, robbery, aggravated assault, and simple assault victimizations at the hands of an intimate acquaintance declined from a 1992 high of 1.1 million to 840,000 in 1996. Bureau of Justice Statistics Director Jan Chaiken noted, "The victimization rates in 1996 are the lowest recorded by the National Crime Victimization Survey since its inception in 1973."[3]

The rise in assistance and awareness programs may have significantly contributed in helping potential victims remove themselves from dangerous situations.

Sentencing Policies and Incarceration

Robbery, theft, assault, burglary, and motor vehicle theft rates continue to decline. Is there a relationship between these types of crimes and those who are now incarcerated?

It is generally recognized that a minority of criminals commit a majority of the crimes; therefore, one offender may be responsible for multiple incidents within a type of crime. In defending the California legislation referred to as "Three Strikes You're Out," Governor Pete Wilson stated that two-thirds of violent crime is perpetrated by less than 10% of convicted felons. He further related that during the first three years of the law, 2,900 violent criminals in California were imprisoned, while overall crime dropped 20%, with violent crime down 9.3% and property crimes down 14%."[4]

Most states have initiated tougher sentencing for repeat offenders and for crimes that have a link to the commission of additional criminal acts. Since 1990, the number of people in custody has risen more than 577,100, or 1,708 inmates per week. Today, more than 1.7 million individuals are confined in state, federal, and local correctional facilities.[5] As the repeat offenders are taken off the streets, it is reasonable to expect that the repeatable crimes should decline.

Perhaps the state of Texas provides an example of this. In the 1980s, crime in Texas jumped 29%, creating a ratio of eight crimes for every 100 citizens. During the 1990s, after the creation of additional prison space and a concerted effort to fill it with repeat offenders, the rate dropped to 5.6 crimes per 100, the lowest since 1973.[6]

A recent article in the Washington Times reported that since 1991, when the rate of violent crime peaked at 758 offenses per 100,000 population, the rate has declined each of the following five years, reaching 634 offenses per 100,000 population in 1996, a cumulative decline of 16%.[7]

Concurrently, the incarceration rate increased from 479 per 100,000 in 1991 to 645 per 100,000 in 1997. How may crimes would have been committed by the 444,000 convicted felons who otherwise would not be incarcerated? Some estimates for the number of felonies committed by a career criminal range as high as 200 per year.[8]

Community Policing

Are the police having an impact on crime?

Years ago, police officers walked beats, where they were in close proximity to the people they served. The officers and community members in their beats were often on a first name basis and the beat officers were an integral part of the local community. As times have changed, patrol cars have taken over the foot beat, isolating officers from the public. In response to this, the nation's cities are now turning to community policing. Community policing is "a philosophy of full-service, personalized policing where the same officer patrols and works in the same area on a permanent basis, from a decentralized place, working in a proactive partnership with citizens to identify and solve problems."[9]

Crime and its impact on society are so complex that the problem cannot be solved by a single agency. In the analysis of this problem it can be recognized that an agency such as the police is not the only one responsible for finding solutions. The traditional approach to crime control directs all anticrime efforts to the police. Early on, the police embraced the role of crime fighter and have identified with the image but have retreated from responsibility for rising crime rates. As entities, departments have often taken credit for successes but have been hesitant in accepting responsibility for failures.

Policing techniques that were popular before the community policing trend caused the officers to be isolated from the communities they served and impaired crime-control efforts. Community policing allows law enforcement agencies to get back to their founding principles. Agencies and their officers are becoming reintegrated into the fabric of their communities so that the people come to the police for counsel and help before a serious problem arises, not after the fact.

The police are just one tool in crime-fighting. When an agency and its officers begin to tackle the problems of their communities (social and physical), those criminogenic conditions that foster and support criminal behavior begin to diminish. The total effect of improving quality of life and assisting the members of the community to resolve issues before they are problems reduces the levels of crime. The police, through these efforts, become better crime fighters.

The Economy

Is there a relationship between crime and employment?

Certainly for some, crime is a lifestyle. Others may find themselves involved, inexcusably, but by choice due to economic situations. Historically, crime trends have followed economic/employment trends.[10] Simply put, the more people who are working, the lower the crime rate, and vice versa.

Theorists and researchers have been hesitant to make a firm linkage between lower unemployment and lower crime. Everyone does agree that while paying for the services that attend to criminal behavior (courts, police, prisons, etc.) is not pleasant, it is undeniably necessary in some quantity. During the '90s, the law enforcement community has expanded in all facets, reaching record numbers of employees, facilities, and expenses. Having the capacity to shoulder these fiscal burdens is certainly easier in a vibrant economy.

Demographic Changes

How old is a criminal?

Through the analysis of crime data we can develop a profile of characteristics for past offenders. Two of these characteristics are age and sex of an offender who is most probable to commit crimes. Noted criminal justice author

R. J. Herrnstein believes that "the typical offender today, like the typical addict, is a young male probably between the ages of fifteen and twenty-four." Presently, there is a low point in the population of those in this group who would be sentenced as adults. The adult statistics have been declining. Juvenile rates have continued to increase in all categories. The present lull is limited in duration, as there is a large juvenile population on the horizon.[11]

The upcoming group of offenders have already demonstrated a disturbing capacity for violence. The coming crime wave reflects more a poverty of values than a poverty of material wealth.

Community Involvement

Who is responsible for solving the crime problem?

There has been a revitalization movement across the nation in terms of community, whether it is defined as block, neighborhood, city, or state. People have begun to stop relying on others to resolve their problems. It is the involvement of individuals in the conduct of their community that is the catalyst of change and leads to the improvement of their collective quality of life.

In his 1995 article, "Crime: The Real Root Causes," John J. DiIulio, Jr., summed up the position, saying, "Governmentally, locking the revolving door on criminals is vital. But so is opening the door to cooperation with law-abiding citizens. In the long run, nothing will buy America more public safety via government than reordering the justice system so that it does more to foster than to frustrate private (individual, community group, neighborhood, and business) anticrime efforts of all sorts."[12]

Conclusion

The "magic bullet" is not out there, but there are other reasons the crime rate is declining. The reasons mentioned here are not all inclusive but they merit discussion. While more police and prisons may help, the cure may lie in a renaissance of personal responsibility, and a reassertion of responsibility over rights and community over egoism. These are some of the issues being explored by the Koch Crime Commission. It is not sufficient when asked why crime is declining to reply, "I can't tell you why." The reasons it is declining are the same ones that will keep it from going up again. The continuing application and refinement of intentional and effective practices will be the tools required to face tomorrow's challenges.

Endnotes

1. Federal Bureau of Investigation. (1997, October 4). *Crime in the United States 1996.* (Press Release). (Online). Available: www.fbi.gov/pressrel.
2. U.S. Department of Justice. *Characteristics of Crime, Summary Findings 1995.* (Online). Available: www.ojp.usdoj.gov/bjs.
3. U.S. Department of Justice. (1997, November 15). *Criminal Victimization 1996.* (Press Release). (Online). Available: www.ojp.usdoj/bjs/pub/press.
4. Wilson, P. (1997, March 7). (Letter to the Editor). *USA Today.* (Online). Available: http://crime-free.org/newspapers.html.
5. U.S. Department of Justice. (1998, January 18). *Nation's Prisons and Jails Hold More Than 1.7 Million.* (Press Release). (Online). Available: www.ojp.usdoj.gov/bjs/pub/press.
6. Perspective. (1996, March 9). Crime's Cost. *Investor's Business Daily.* (Online). Available: www.ncpa.org/crime/pdcrm.
7. Crime and punishment. (1998, January 25). (Editorial). *Washington Times,* (Online). Available: http://crime-free.org/newspapers.html.
8. Crime and punishment. (1998, January 25). (Editorial). *Washington Times,* (Online). Available: http://crime-free.org/newspapers.html.
9. Trojanowicz, R., et al. (1994). Community Policing: A Survey of Police Departments in the United States. *Federal Bureau of Investigation, U.S. Department of Justice.*
10. Chiricos, T. G. (1997, April). Rates of Crime and Unemployment: An Analysis of Aggregate Research Evidence. *Social Problems, 34, No. 2,* 187–211; Freeman, R. B. (1983). Crime and Employment. In J. Q. Wilson (Ed.), *Crime and Public Policy.* San Francisco: ICS Press.
11. Herrnstein, R. J. (1995). Criminogenic Traits. In J. Q. Wilson (Ed.), *Crime and Public Policy.* San Francisco: ICS Press.
12. DiIulio, J. J., Jr. (1995, Winter). Crime: The Real Root Causes. *Milken Institute for Job & Capital Formation, Jobs & Capital, 4, Feature Article 7.* (Online). Available: www.mijcf.org/policy/jobs_capital.

FRAME the DEBATE

Form at end of book

READING 6

Issue 3: Why is the crime rate elusive?

As Crime Falls, Pressure Rises to Alter Data

Fox Butterfield

Senior police officials around the nation are concerned that the sharp drop in crime in recent years has produced new pressure on police departments to show ever-decreasing crime statistics and might be behind incidents in several cities in which commanders have manipulated crime data.

So far this year, there have been charges of falsely reporting crime statistics here, in New York, Atlanta and Boca Raton, Fla., resulting in the resignation or demotion of high-ranking police commanders.

In Boca Raton, for example, a police captain, with the knowledge of the police chief, systematically downgraded property crimes like burglaries to vandalism, trespassing or missing property, reducing the city's felony rate by almost 11 percent in 1997.

Experts say they believe these incidents do not mean that the nationwide drop in crime since 1992 is illusory.

But they are beginning to question whether politicians seeking office, the news media and the public should attach so much importance to the annual, and sometimes monthly, release of the latest crime figures.

In Philadelphia, the city has had to withdraw its crime figures from the national system maintained by the Federal Bureau of Investigation for 1996, 1997 and for at least the first half of 1998 because of underreporting and downgrading crimes into less serious incidents and sloppiness.

Because of Philadelphia's size—it accounts for 2 percent of all killings in the United States—the removal of its numbers could skew the crime rate for the whole nation. But Harlan McEwan, a Deputy Assistant Director of the F.B.I., said he was confident the agency had statistical methods to adjust the national rate even without Philadelphia's figures. The 1997 crime figures will be published this fall.

The impact on Philadelphia will be more telling. "I can guarantee you my crime is going to be way up this year," said John F. Timoney, who took over as Philadelphia's Police Commissioner in March. "But I don't care. If we are going to get this right and reduce crime, we have to start with accurate statistics."

Gil Kerlikowske, the former Police Commissioner of Buffalo, said the pressure on police departments to prove their performance through reduced crime figures, with promotions and pay raises increasingly dependent on good data, "creates a new area for police corruption and ethics," along with the traditional problems of brutality and payoffs.

Mr. Kerlikowske suggested that there had been too much focus on the eight major crimes counted by the bureau in its crime index: the violent crimes of murder, rape, robbery and aggravated assault along with the property crimes of burglary, theft, car theft and arson.

"There is too little focus on lesser crimes, which are not counted by the F.B.I.," Mr. Kerlikowske said, "like drug sales, prostitution and graffiti, which are more meaningful to the overall quality of life because there is so much more of them."

A common thread running through many of the incidences of police officials altering crime statistics has been that police commanders have downgraded felonies like aggravated assault and burglary, which are reported to the F.B.I., to misdemeanors like vandalism that are not reported to the bureau.

One of the first acts by Mr. Timoney, who was a career police officer in New York, where he helped pioneer the city's highly regarded computerized crime statistics system, was to set up a quality assurance division. It soon discovered that serious crimes throughout Philadelphia were being underreported by about 8 percent, he said in an interview. Much of this was the result of "stupidity or carelessness and was not intentional," Mr. Timoney said.

But Mr. Timoney discovered this month that the youngest district commander in the city, Capt. Daniel Castro, who had an excellent reputation for introducing community policing and aggressively eliminating drug dealers from the streets, had greatly exaggerated his reports of crime reduction.

Captain Castro reported an 80 percent drop in serious crime in his district over the past year. But a review found that Captain Castro had downgraded many robberies, burglaries and thefts to cases of "missing property." Captain Castro was removed from his command.

In New York, Kenneth Donohue, the head of the police department's Transportation Bureau, was forced to resign this year after Police Commissioner Howard Safir said he had presided over the bureau at a time when commanders carried out an elaborate scheme to reclassify incidents on the subway as street crimes. Mr. Safir said the manipulation had gone on for years and had underestimated crime in the subways by about 20 percent, but it had not affected New York City's overall crime rate because the crimes had been shifted to the streets and were reported by the regular precincts.

Problems have occurred at the precinct level as well. In 1996, the commander of the 41st Precinct, which covers Hunts Point in the Bronx, was forced to resign after he was charged with reclassifying a number of crimes as misdemeanors instead of felonies in an effort to make the decline in crime in the precinct more dramatic.

In the past, police officers here and in many other cities across the country had not attached much importance to collecting crime statistics beyond the need to report them to the F.B.I., Mr. Timoney said, and most commanders were more interested in issues like narcotics, training or forestalling corruption.

This casual attitude toward statistics, Mr. Timoney said, also stemmed from a "belief by the average police chief, in their heart of hearts, that they couldn't do anything about crime because they couldn't affect the root causes of crime." This was an idea that was popularized by academic criminologists in the 1970's and 1980's.

The success of New York in significantly reducing crime, with similar successes in cities from Boston to Houston, changed that old-fashioned mindset, Mr. Timoney said. Statistics have become as important a tool to the police as good accounting is to corporate executives.

But the change to placing a premium on keeping accurate statistics in a big police department is not easy. For years, the Philadelphia police counted crimes not when they occurred, but when officers logged them into their records, sometimes months later, meaning that some crimes that took place in one year were not reported to the F.B.I. until the next year, throwing off the national crime rate.

In Boca Raton, tips from low-level police officers led to an investigation by the Palm Beach County State Attorney's office last month that found that Capt. Jim Duke had systematically downgraded felonies, mostly property crimes, to misdemeanors "for the direct purpose of not having to report these crimes" to the F.B.I. In 1997, Captain Duke, who was later forced to resign, downgraded 385 felonies, 11 percent of the city's total of 3,635 serious crimes.

In most of the cases, Captain Duke personally reclassified the crimes by writing supplemental reports claiming new information showed that they were not as serious as originally recorded, according to the prosecutor's report. In one instance, Captain Duke downgraded a home burglary to vandalism, though it had occurred while the residents slept at 1 A.M. and someone broke in through a kitchen window and stole a purse.

In another incident originally labeled a burglary, a thief stole $5,000 in jewelry and did more than $25,000 in damage, the prosecutor said, but Captain Duke also reclassified the case as vandalism.

The prosecutor's office found that the "prevailing philosophy" at the Boca Raton Police Department regarding report classifications, from at least the level of Captain Duke down to the officer on the beat, was that the reports "should be classified at the lowest level possible."

The city's police chief, Peter Petracco, initially denied knowing about the changes, but was also forced to resign after it was discovered he had lied, said the city manager, Donna Dreska.

Debra Shannon, a spokeswoman for the Boca Raton Police Department, said the motives of the two in manipulating the crime report were still unknown. The prosecutor's investigation said the two had no criminal intent. An internal city police investigation is continuing.

In Atlanta, the City Council and the Georgia Bureau of Investigation are investigating accusations by a deputy police chief, Louis Arcangeli, that two other deputy chiefs pressured detectives and officers to write off unsolved crimes and misclassify violent crimes as nonviolent when preparing the city's crime statistics for 1996, the year the Olympics took place there. In a series of memorandums to Police Chief Beverly Harvard of Atlanta, Deputy Chief Arcangeli warned that the number of crimes reported as "unfounded," or without basis after an investigation, jumped 78 percent from 1995 to 1996.

Chief Harvard demoted Deputy Chief Arcangeli to captain after he wrote the memorandums, which were leaked to journalists, though she has insisted his demotion had nothing to do with the dispute.

Captain Arcangeli's lawyer, Bill McKenney, said the Atlanta Police Department's crime reporting procedure created ample room for the problem. Unless a crime is serious, like murder or rape, Mr. McKenney said, detectives do not investigate it in person but instead send postcards to the victims.

Alfred Blumstein, a criminologist at Carnegie Mellon University, said one reason to continue to have confidence in overall national crime figures reported by the police to the F.B.I. is that the downward trend reported had been mirrored by the country's other statistical program to measure crime, the National Crime Victimization Survey. Begun in 1973 as a check on the F.B.I. data, it measures crimes by a survey of 49,000 households.

The danger of sloppy reporting by the police, or outright fraud, is the reason most criminologists focus on murders as the most accurate crime statistic, Professor Blumstein said. It is hard to hide bodies.

FRAME the DEBATE

Form at end of book

WiseGuide Wrap-Up

Butterfield's work indicates that multiple factors, some of which are less than intuitive, influence the reported crime rate. While evidence suggests that the crime rate is declining, the reason for its reduction is not clear.

Police administrators assert that a main reason for the declining crime rate is the implementation of community policing efforts. While this explanation is plausible, current research that compares crime rates in cities with active community policing efforts to crime rates in similar cities without such programs should provide more useful information regarding the recent downward trends in official reports of crime.

So far, our examination of the crime rate has only looked at crimes reported/known to the police (that is, Uniform Crime Rate [UCR] statistics). Numerous crimes, however, never come to the attention of the police. The aggregate of all these unreported offenses is called the "dark figure of crime."

The total amount of crime (including the UCR crime rate and the "dark figure of crime") is probably at least ten times what the UCR reports. In addition, the true crime rate might even be greater than that for certain offenses, such as theft and assault. Because of the "dark figure of crime," some criminologists see the homicide rate as a reliable and valid measure of crime, as opposed to the statistics found in the UCR or National Crime Victimization Survey. The homicide rate can be determined with a fairly high level of certainty because criminologists can triangulate the homicide rate by arrests, bodies found, and missing person's reports.

R.E.A.L. Sites

This list provides a print preview of typical **Coursewise** R.E.A.L. sites. (There are over 100 such sites at the **Courselinks**™ site.) The danger in printing URLs is that web sites can change overnight. As we went to press, these sites were functional using the URLs provided. If you come across one that isn't, please let us know via email to: webmaster@coursewise.com. Use your Passport to access the most current list of R.E.A.L. sites at the **Courselinks** site.

Site name: The Koch Crime Institute
URL: http://www.kci.org/
Why is it R.E.A.L.? The Koch Crime Institute publishes the studies it conducts on crime and violence at this site.
Key topic: research
Try this: Read some of the articles and reports that are at this web site.

Site name: Uniform Crime Report
URL: http://www.fbi.gov/ucr.htm
Why is it R.E.A.L.? The Uniform Crime Report presents a nationwide view of crime based on statistics submitted by city, county, and state law enforcement agencies.
Key topics: research, crime rate, statistics
Try this: Look for trends in various offenses.

Site name: Sourcebook of Criminal Justice Statistics
URL: http://www.albany.edu/sourcebook/
Why is it R.E.A.L.? This is a huge reference tool that is now available online.
Key topics: crime rate, statistics
Try this: Look for trends in criminal offending.

Site name: Criminal Victimization, 1997

URL: http://www.ojp.usdoj.gov/bjs/abstract/cv97.htm

Why is it R.E.A.L.? The National Crime Victimization Survey is the nation's primary source of information on criminal victimization.

Key topics: victim, research, crime rate, statistics

Try this: Study the recent trends in crime victimization.

STAND! section 2

Critical Issues in Policing

Introduction

Given the controversies, differing viewpoints, and inconsistencies raised in Section 1, it is amazing that our criminal justice system is still in existence. One of the key elements of the criminal justice system is the police, and as we will see, the issues the police face are extremely complicated and often beyond their control.

Private citizens encounter the police frequently, whether to ask for directions or to receive a citation in violation of the vehicle code. Most of us have had some interaction with the police at one point in our lives. Therefore, most people have formed some opinion about the role of the police in our society and have an understanding of the services that the police provide.

Control of police abuse and corruption is of utmost concern for the management of law enforcement officers. Recent studies have shown that minorities have a greater level of distrust concerning the police. Readings 7 and 8, which were written exclusively for this volume of *Stand! Crime and Criminology,* attack this issue head-on.

Another critical issue in policing that impacts citizens daily is high-speed vehicle pursuits. Lately, the media have devoted more attention to police chases, probably because many police vehicles and helicopters are now equipped with video cameras, thus allowing such chases to be taped. Readings 9 and 10 examine the impact of these pursuits and look at some alternative measures and policy considerations aimed at reducing related accidents and injuries.

Given the strength of the economy in the private sector, coupled with budgetary constraints on government in general, and law enforcement in particular, privatization of the police may be inevitable. Reading 11 explores the challenges associated with privatization from a case study of a city that turned over its law-and-order duties to a private security firm. Reading 12 addresses many of the elements of police privatization and suggests that any notion of changing the fundamental way in which law enforcement services are delivered warrants critical analysis and discourse.

While not exhaustive, the issues discussed in Section 2 will give you a broad exposure to the exciting and controversial world of policing and to some of the challenges that the modern "protectors of the peace" face. Throughout the readings, contemplate the difficult situations that each police officer must deal with on a daily basis, and formulate a plan of action on how you would respond, given the circumstances. Then consider that police officers must often make these life-threatening decisions in a fraction of a second!

What Can Be Done to Reduce the Prevalence of Police Abuse?

ISSUE 4

Take a Closer Look

1. Do you feel that Kamau's approach to investigating police abuse raises any ethical issues?
2. What do you think about Kamau's assertion that half of the police are bad cops?
3. Do you agree with Holder that Kamau's techniques distract the police, thus placing police officers and others in greater danger?
4. How would you address police abuse if you were a police chief or sheriff?
5. Will hiring more minority police officers reduce the prevalence of police abuse?

WiseGuide Intro

The most pressing issue concerning the management of law enforcement personnel is police abuse. Not long ago, our country viewed discrimination, segregation, and racism as acceptable behaviors. Times may have changed, but have the people changed as well?

Both Readings 7 and 8 focus on how to reduce police abuse and were written exclusively for this volume of *Stand! Crime and Criminology* by two former police officers. Both Diop Kamau and Jack Holder agree that police abuse does occur and that something must be done to prevent future injustices. However, they disagree on the problem's prevalence and on how to remedy it.

How is it that two former cops can have such contrasting views on the police abuse issue? Jack Holder, a White police officer, served meritoriously for over 20 years and never had any problems with police abuse. However, Diop Kamau, a Black police officer, served for a shorter period of time and was victimized by the police on numerous occasions. In Readings 7 and 8, both ex-cops share their views on police abuse based on their real-life experiences.

Diop Kamau has a long history of observing police abuse. As a Black police officer, he observed firsthand the racism within the ranks of a Southern California police department. As a result, Kamau embarked on a long journey to expose police corruption and abuse of authority. In 1989, with a news crew following him, Kamau was assaulted by a police officer. Although the officer was never charged with a crime, Kamau's work led to the passage of legislation aimed at reducing the prevalence of police abuse.

Kamau covertly videotapes the police, and many people vehemently oppose his techniques. While agreeing with Kamau's belief that police abuse is a serious matter that needs to be addressed, Jack Holder, president of the National Police Defense Foundation, argues that Kamau's approach is unacceptable because it places police officers and others in danger.

What should be done about the problem of police abuse? The answer for Kamau is clear: Tenacious undercover surveillance of the police is a must, even if it poses a danger to officers and others. Holder believes that we must let the system handle the situation, even though the system has failed numerous times in the past.

Issue 4: What can be done to reduce the prevalence of police abuse?

Racial Conflict in Modern Policing: Resolution or Disaster?

Diop Kamau

Executive Director,
The Police Complaint Center

Allegations of excessive force and abuse by police officers have been a constant source of tension in minority communities across America for more than forty years. The complaints over excessive force and abuse fueled civil uprisings across America throughout the 1960s. In the past ten years, public disturbances related to complaints about police have taken place in Los Angeles, California, and St. Petersburg and Miami, Florida.

Over the past few months, new complaints have arisen about the behavior of police officers throughout the United States. The allegations that police officers are selectively targeting minority drivers have even prompted state investigations in Florida, Maryland, and New Jersey. In Maryland, after complaints of profiling were lodged with public officials, the state police were placed under court order. Maryland State police must now receive complaints from minority citizens about profiling on I-495. Recently, President Bill Clinton and United States Attorney General Janet Reno have commented on the issue and have discussed increased funding for police training and ethics education.

Among the worst cases of police misconduct, NYPD officers allegedly tortured and sodomized a Haitian immigrant while he was in their custody. In a second case, NYPD officers shot unarmed African immigrant Amado Diallo with forty-one rounds. In Riverside, California, a young woman, Taeysha Miller, was shot at nineteen times while sleeping in her vehicle. Officers killed Miller after she allegedly moved during her sleep. New Jersey State troopers on the New Jersey Turnpike shot four basketball players on their way to a try-out. The four young men were unarmed and were pulled over for allegedly meeting the profiling criteria. The troopers fired at the van when it supposedly lurched backward. All three shootings are reminiscent of past tragedies. Unarmed Leonard Deadwyler was shot in the head by a Los Angeles police officer in 1966 while rushing his pregnant wife to the hospital. Eula Love was shot multiple times two decades later by LAPD officers while holding a kitchen knife. Beatings and killings of Black motorists in Miami caused riots at about the same time.

Police and public officials sometimes discount the complaints by minorities about police abuse as the unfair political lynching of police officers. They claim that officers are simply doing a difficult job in the best manner that they can. Police supporters point out that nearly 700 police officers have given their lives in the line of duty over the past 10 years in the United States. While all this is true, it does not obviate the case that can be made about racism within law-enforcement or the misuses of police authority in regard to minorities.

Complaints about police misconduct in minority communities have substantial empirical and anecdotal evidence. Following the 1991 beating of motorist Rodney King, the Christopher Commission conducted exhaustive examinations of Los Angeles police department records. They found a substantial number of cases of excessive force against minority citizens. A review of complaints revealed several instances of careless investigations of abusive officers. Several officers had grievances expunged from their records prematurely. Moreover, some of the most abusive officers were routinely promoted, despite multiple complaints of abuse and misconduct. Similarly, the Kolts Commission, upon examining the records of Los Angeles County Sheriff Department, found that citizens were frequently prevented from filing complaints against officers. Investigating officers often refused to take witness statements if they supported allegations of abuse or misconduct. Witness statements would be taken only if they supported the officer's version of events.

In examining corruption and abuse in the New York City police department, the Mollen Commission

"Racial Conflict in Modern Policing: Resolution or Disaster?" by Diop Kamau, Executive Director of the Police Complaint Center, Tallahassee, FL. Reprinted by permission.

found similar patterns of excessive force, targeting of minorities, and routine policy violations. NYPD officers were also found to have stolen money from suspected minority drug dealers. These officers operated free from fear of detection as they consumed drugs themselves. It was not until another police agency arrested one of the principal officers, Michael Dowd, that an official probe interrupted the abuses. New York is not alone in this type of scandal.

In recent years, several cases of planted evidence, falsified confessions, and perjured testimony have shaken the court system in Philadelphia and Chicago. Philadelphia police officers routinely and systematically lied about evidence in order to obtain convictions against accused drug dealers and others who were completely innocent of any crime. In Chicago, a police captain is alleged to have forced confessions out of Black murder suspects by attaching wires from a live car battery to the suspects' testicles. These types of criminal violations and systematized injustices by police officers were uniformly directed at minorities. They lend credence to the view that police misconduct is frequently influenced by race and is not the result of isolated bad apples within particular law-enforcement agencies.

As in the case of the Philadelphia police, if officers felt confident that they could falsify evidence placing numerous innocent people in prison and get away with it, this goes beyond the random choices of a poorly trained police officer. The types of misconduct which ultimately lead to cases such as that of Luima in New York raise questions about the systemized injustice rather than corrupt individual officers within the system. After Luima was allegedly sodomized and tortured, not a single officer came forward to report the incident. In fact, Luima's family was not allowed to file a complaint when they went to the 70th precinct, where the incident had occurred the previous day. Similarly, following the 1991 beating of motorist Rodney King, not one of the twenty-seven officers on the scene reported that they had observed any misconduct, although King was savagely beaten with metal pr-24 batons by four officers. When King's family attempted to file a complaint, they were not allowed to report the incident.

Police officers have enormous power and authority. That authority is vested in the idea that officers will use discretion and will treat citizens equitably and fairly. However, in the case in which minorities are involved, police seem to follow a different set of rules. Common sense, reasonable discretion, and fairness may be set aside, and any outrageous behavior can be explained away in police jargon. In several cases, police claimed they saw movements from the deceased, which led them to fire multiple rounds into their bodies. Officers in the Rodney King beating claimed King was putting up a fight from the ground as they struck him more than fifty-one times with their batons. Malice Green in Detroit was beaten to death by two white officers, who claimed he was struggling as they beat him with their flashlights.

The excuse that the officers feared for their lives or that the suspect engaged in unusual behavior will often satisfy many folks in places where police misconduct and abuse by officers are the exception rather than the rule. These excuses ring hollow in minority communities. For many minorities, events such as these are viewed within the context of a history of indisputable antipathy by law enforcement's largely white officers and administrators. Police unions and strident police supporters support the apathy of law enforcement by failing to condemn obvious misconduct and by finding excuses for officers in even the most blatant cases of abuse. Moreover, no Wall Street executive has ever worried about being injured or killed by police and then having it explained to his or her family that the victim moved suddenly and forced the officers to fire. These excuses are reserved for the poor and minorities, who recognize that there is a history of racism behind many of today's police misconduct.

The History

The minority view of the police is that law enforcement does not care about the lives of Black citizens. Many police departments have no record of fairly administering the law. Historically, in disputes between Blacks and white officers, one can expect resolutions in favor of white officers. The behavior of police, especially in the South, hinged more often on race and status than on the equitable application of the law. This was especially apparent through the 1960s. Therefore, an encounter between a white police officer and a Black male on any street in America is not without contextual reference for both parties. These legacies between police and minority citizens fuel the level of suspicion and mistrust that can be seen in the eyes of police protesters today.

At the highest levels of law enforcement, American policing has proven its bias in antipathy. Civil rights investigations of killings, beatings, and lynchings of civil rights workers in the South were strongly resisted by J. Edgar Hoover. Hoover discounted the efforts of minorities for equality as the meddling of outside communist agitators. More than that, Hoover attempted to disrupt the movement by undermining the reputation of Martin Luther King and minority leaders. Hoover considered King and the efforts of other blacks for human rights a serious threat to democracy. His office initiated counterintelligence operations. One such operation, called cointelpro, worked under the auspices of the FBI in several major cities across the United States. The project was intended to destroy Black leadership and gather intelligence for the

FBI and other law-enforcement organizations. Organizations such as the Black Panthers were particularly irresistible targets. Their leaders were sometimes assassinated and in other cases framed by FBI informants, as in the case of recently released prisoner Geronimo Pratt. Pratt was released from prison in 1998 after serving nearly twenty-seven years for a murder conviction. Pratt was released after it was discovered that FBI informant Julius Butler gave false testimony during trial. Butler never disclosed that he was working as a paid FBI informant when he pinned a murder on Pratt. The FBI did not disclose this information, either. What is clear from this and other efforts by law enforcement is that the police were on the wrong side of the civil rights issue throughout the 1960s and for most of this century. They attempted to thwart the efforts of African Americans to achieve equality. No doubt many African Americans have neither forgiven nor forgotten the role of the police in this massive struggle for freedom.

Investigating the Issue

Police organizations must take serious steps to correct misconduct and patterns of excessive force by officers. Moreover, serious research in this area is needed. Detailed studies of police misconduct should provide data on the issue that can be used by police administrators to reduce the problem. Much of the research on police misconduct is based on observational studies. This type of research supplies limited results with respect to the actual behavior officers engage in relative to misconduct. Officers would be foolish to engage in illegal behavior in the presence of outside observers. The code of silence and exclusion of outsiders are traditions within the police subculture. Therefore, studies, which attempt to assess levels of misconduct using observational techniques, may be well off the mark. Studies that report that police abuse, racism, and excessive force rarely occur may underestimate the dark figure, which is hidden from observers, researchers, and police administrators.

Over the past ten years, I have attempted to uncover the truth behind these dark figures. Using hidden cameras, I tested both police patrol tactics and the complaint intake procedures of several police departments across the United States. Using hidden cameras, I twice videotaped my own arrest. In 1988, walking with six Black males through a white neighborhood in California resulted in our being stopped by several Los Angeles police officers. The officers ordered everyone to face the wall and place our hands behind the back of our heads. Everyone complied; however, I asked the officer why we were being detained. I was arrested and taken into custody on a charge of blocking the sidewalk. About one year later in a similar investigation, I was a passenger in a vehicle traveling through the city of Long Beach, California. Our car was traveling within the speed limit and there were no equipment violations. We found ourselves being followed by a Long Beach police car. The officers followed us for about three miles. We were stopped, allegedly for weaving. I stepped out of the car as the officers approached. The lead officer immediately began using profanity and ordered me to face a plate glass window. When I complied, my face was slammed through the window. I was subsequently beaten on the hood of the officer's car.

The beating stopped when the officers noticed an NBC camera crew recording the incident. We had not been weaving, and I offered no resistance to the officer. Nevertheless, I was charged with assault and battery on a police officer. The driver of the vehicle was cited for a traffic violation, which had not occurred. The officers in this case, as in many others, were using the law to cover their own illegal behavior. These types of events are invisible to most nonminorities. No one would have believed the story I told about either of these encounters had I not had video to support my claims. Unfortunately, the average African American trapped in these circumstances will not have video to record his or her mistreatment by police. Even those police supporters who agree that these events happen periodically claim they're so infrequent as to be dismissed as irrelevant. They would respond by saying 99 percent of the officers are honest and never lie on their reports. My investigations run contrary to that lofty figure. I suspect the figure is closer to 50-50. Without reliable state and national data collected on who is being stopped and for what reasons, we may never know just how frequently illegal traffic stops and subject stops occur across America.

I reference these incidents because they are not uncommon and they are precisely the types of complaints that African American leaders have most frequently sought to expose. Routinely, across America police officers make illegal stops, engage in abuse, and falsify reports to cover up their misconduct. My investigations documenting these incidents with video are intended to educate the public and to expose those officers who engage in this sort of conduct. They frequently complain that the officers are being set up. The video speaks for itself. In each case, no charge submitted against me by the police has ever withstood the scrutiny of a trial. In fact, in both the arrests, the charges were dropped before trial ever started.

Exposing police officers in this manner is almost too easy. It is less the case that I am a good undercover investigator than it is that the cases of misconduct among police officers across America are so pervasive that I could do this in almost any city with similar results. Police officers who routinely profile motorists frequently make up other reasons for the stop. But everyone knows it's really about race. European Americans are not being stopped in airports and accused of trafficking drugs. They are not being stopped on highways and having their property confiscated. They are not being subjected to traffic stops and ordered out of the vehicle for no reason other than that they looked suspicious. While these types of abuses seem small, they are rapidly corrupting the integrity of the criminal justice system.

Recently, my organization, The Police Complaint Center, has been conducting a hidden camera investigation of police complaint intake procedures. What we have found is as equally disturbing as my earlier investigations of police profiling and traffic stops have proven to be. In 1998, we conducted a hidden camera test of 40 percent of New York City's police department's precincts. We tested the precincts to see how citizens were treated when they attempted to file a complaint of police misconduct. In over 50 percent of the thirty-four stations we visited, we were given incorrect information, were subject to rudeness, or were thrown out of the station by officers at the front desk. If the nation's largest police department does not allow citizens to file complaints 50 percent of the time, how can anyone be surprised that the streets are filled with protesters? Can anyone be surprised that officers continue to engage in abuse and misconduct?

The results we uncovered at the NYPD mirrored our experiences with other police departments across the country. Police officers have modernized their techniques of obfuscation where complaints of misconduct are concerned. While citizens are not being beaten, as they might have been forty years ago for trying to file complaints, they are certainly being misled, harassed, and mistreated. The impact of this behavior, as one might expect, has fostered tremendous alienation in communities of color, where these events happen most frequently. Without a system for redress, pressure builds until one day it is unleashed, as in the case of the Rodney King verdict. The devastation which swept Los Angeles after the verdict had been bottled up for years. Officers who had escaped justice and had hidden within the cloak of police secrecy were responsible for the rage that was unleashed across Los Angeles, resulting in enormous property damage.

If we are to move forward from the current state of police minority relations, the police must take serious steps to investigate misconduct. Citizen review boards should be empowered to discipline officers and empowered to subpoena witnesses and records. Police unions must take a step back and resist the urge to protect abusive officers. These officers often receive greater support from unions than whistle-blowers within police ranks receive.

Some Solutions

Rules such as the forty-eight-hour rule in New York, which entitles officers to refuse to speak to investigators when they are accused of misconduct, must be done away with. Police unions should not promote such policies. They ultimately undermine the credibility of the investigations into the conduct of their own members. Police departments that have chronic patterns of abuse ought to conduct their own quality assurance testing using the same techniques that they would use to investigate similar serious offenses by ordinary citizens. If it is legitimate to investigate the drug dealers by using hidden cameras, police organizations should not be afraid to take serious investigative measures to address police misconduct. Police organizations should invest money on the front end in equipment such as video cameras in patrol cars and increased ethics training of officers. This is far cheaper than the millions of dollars paid out in lawsuits and lost careers. Until the public perceives the police as fair and believes that their behavior is held accountable, little progress will be made toward defining new relationships between police and the communities they serve.

FRAME the DEBATE

Form at end of book

Issue 4: What can be done to reduce the prevalence of police abuse?

Walk a Mile in My Shoes

Jack Holder

President, Police Defense Foundation

I was a New York City police officer for twenty years, and in all that time I appeared before the Civilian Complaint Review Board on only one occasion, and even then it was only as a witness. Does that mean I never used physical force? No! Does that mean I never used excessive force? Well, that depends on who is making the charge and what is considered by the accuser to be "unnecessary physical force." I'm quite sure that, of the literally hundreds of persons with whom I had negative dealings, some weren't too happy at the amount of force I was using. Some of them may even have considered my "necessary force" to have been police brutality. However, that's not how I, or my superiors, saw it. I did what was necessary to get the job done. And what exactly is the job of a police officer? To "protect and serve" is the motto and obligation of every law enforcement agency in the United States. Protect and serve!

The police officer is the first line of defense, and he or she is compensated by the public to protect and serve it, "John Q." The motto of the New York City Police Department, the department which I know best, is easily remembered by the code word Peter WEDS.

P = Protect
W = Warn
E = Enforce
D = Detect
S = Serve

The police cannot "protect and serve" if they are not able to control a situation. *Control* is an extremely important word in this equation. Once a police officer loses control of a situation, it is difficult, at best, to regain it. If control isn't regained, then all is lost. In keeping with this, every penal code in the United States provides law enforcement officers with special privileges and special powers—literally, the power of life and death. A police officer must be able to make a life and death decision in a split second. There is no time for delay and, unfortunately, little room for error. And, when an error occurs, whether an error in judgment or just an accident, the results are usually disastrous.

Police brutality is not an easy subject to discuss, especially today. Everyone has his or her own opinion, and the facts of a particular situation are usually relatively obscure and invariably come down to two opposing views—the view of the police officer involved and of his or her associates, who most likely have been in similar situations, and the view of the victim and his or her friends and family, the media, which are in the business of selling, and the politicians, who take advantage of a volatile situation.

Many factors must be taken into consideration, such as the actual guilt of the person involved and degree of crime being committed by the alleged victim of brutality. Narcotics traffickers, for example, frequently attempt to shift the blame. They believe that by focusing the attention on the police it will, perhaps, obscure their wrongdoings. These dealers have many cards in their deck. By its nature alone, drug trafficking operates in a violent setting. Fear of reprisal is on its side. Drug traffickers will get, and have gotten, people to come forth as supposed witnesses to back up their stories, which are on many occasions lies.

The media are interested in selling a story. "Man bites dog" sells. They are usually quick to pick up on a situation in which the police are involved in an incident in which the use of unnecessary force is alleged. The officer or officers involved fill the headlines for weeks and even months. In today's world of communication, how can you possibly have an allegedly impartial jury come to a fair decision when the officers involved have already been tried and convicted by the media? Their "knee jerk" reactions are also on many occasions wrong. Stories of alleged police brutality of a teenager will suddenly become justified force on an armed midtwenties felon. And where is the retraction printed, on page one? It is usually buried toward the back of the news session.

The views expressed here are those of the author's and do not necessarily reflect those of the Police Defense Foundation.

"Walk a Mile in My Shoes" by Jack Holder, president of the Police Defense Foundation. Reprinted by permission of the author.

Such names as Abner Louima, Anthony Baez, and Amadou Diallo suddenly become celebrities. And, when the race of the officers involved differs from that of the victim, there is more reason to exploit the situation. I'm not saying that race doesn't play a part in some instances. However, in my opinion, the problem between the races has been blown way out of proportion by opportunistic politicians who are looking to ride on the coattails of a horrific situation. Why? It gets their names in the paper. Just for a moment, let's forget about blame in the above tragedies. That's exactly what they are—tragedies. Whether or not they are actual crimes remains to be seen.

In today's climate, it is difficult to defend police accused of brutality. However, certain factors must be taken into consideration. There is another phenomenon to be considered—brutality against the police.

A number of police officers in the United States are killed in the line of duty each year. How are the sacrifices of these heroes repaid? Sure, the fallen officers are individually recognized, but in a short while their heroism is forgotten. The police in our nation soon become the scapegoats and targets of not only the media but also of overzealous prosecutors and politicians who attempt to atone for the failure of our crumbling criminal justice system by shifting the blame to the police. The police are easy targets. We must never fail to realize that these dedicated civil servants virtually lay their lives on the line daily in their never ending battle against those in our society who totally ignore the law for their own benefit. These miscreants are the real abusers. And, when they are caught, they use any and all derisive measures to aid their cause. The charge of police brutality is on the top of their list of defenses. The police are not the villains; they are the victims.

Now, it might appear that I condone the use of unnecessary force by the police. Nothing can be further from the truth. However, even in the rare situations in which there are charges of police brutality, they represent only a minute portion of the force. The media and some political opportunists ignore that fact and play on the sympathy of the public. On any given eight-hour shift, the New York City Police Department has several thousand officers patrolling the streets. If four of those officers are involved in one incident, that is less than 1 percent of the patrol force. The media make it look as if every police officer is a violent criminal with one thought in mind—terrorize the public. Does this excuse the four who allegedly have violated the public's trust? Absolutely not.

What is the answer? There must be a fair balance between "freedom of the press" and the "rights of the accused." Let's get all of the facts before going off half-cocked with a story that has been rushed out of the presses just to sell papers.

When we undermine the public's confidence in the police force, we create a situation in which the police have difficulty maintaining control. The cop on the beat will begin to hesitate when the use of force becomes an option. Then who will suffer? Police officers will not want to take chances when they might be viewed as being overly aggressive. They may face humiliation in the press or, even worse, criminal action, which, at the least, will drain their finances.

It's time that saner minds prevail and take a step back to view the entire situation before snap judgments and outrageous charges are made.

I would like to address the actions being undertaken by Diop Kamau. I've spoken with Mr. Kamau and I have debated him. I admire his zeal and I admire his efforts to root out acts of racial bigotry. Whether in the form of "profiling" or actual police brutality, racial bigotry cannot be allowed.

The situation in New York City involving the wrongful killing of a West African immigrant, Amadou Diallo, is probably the most horrific case in recent history in which the police have come under such scrutiny. I wasn't there and neither was Mr. Kamau. However, I watched him being interviewed on television and I detected hatred in his eyes. He is on a crusade and, although I commend him on his commitment, I disagree with his tactics. This brings me back to my original assertion regarding control. When a police officer stops and questions someone on the streets, it is probably the most dangerous encounter that police officer will face. It becomes more dangerous when the police officer has to look over his or her shoulder to keep an eye on someone who is videotaping the encounter or when an unknown third party approaches the police officer.

When a police officer stops someone, whether for a traffic violation or merely to question that person, cooperation is invaluable. An arrogant, uncooperative person only escalates an otherwise traumatic experience, traumatic for both the person being stopped and the police officer.

I must once again state that I agree with the rooting out of brutal police officers and racist police officers. However, I disagree with the methods being employed by Mr. Kamau. Do I have a better solution? I don't know. Perhaps with thorough investigations and the setting of examples of guilty parties, our common goals will be attained.

We have a criminal justice system. Let's allow this system to handle these cases unfettered by adverse reporting and political opportunism.

FRAME the DEBATE

Form at end of book

WiseGuide Wrap-Up

Issues faced by the criminal justice system are challenging, and police abuse is no exception. Diop Kamau has presented a great deal of anecdotal evidence about police abuse, and his work has provoked national debates and impacted criminal justice legislation. As the director of the Police Complaint Center in Tallahassee, Florida, Kamau has dedicated his life to exposing bad officers.

Kamau believes that nearly half of all the police officers he has encountered are not suited for law enforcement. He places the results of his investigations on the Internet (http://www.policeabuse.com).

Police work is dangerous, and bystanders videotaping a law enforcement situation may cause the average officer to become more nervous than normal. Jack Holder, citing police doctrine, articulates that police officers must be able to maintain control of a situation and that any threat to that control could create a dangerous situation for the police officers and citizens involved.

Holder's discussion of police abuse also addresses the rates of violence by cops. He contends that the rate is so low that it should be viewed within the context in which it belongs: atypical police behavior that warrants punishment by the proper authorities.

Finally, is race involved in police abuse? Evidence suggests that it is. In a recently released report, "Driving While Black: Racial Profiling on Our Nation's Highways," the American Civil Liberties Union presents a mountain of evidence that supports the notion that police abuse, especially against minorities, is a serious and persistent problem warranting immediate attention.

R.E.A.L. Sites

This list provides a print preview of typical **Coursewise** R.E.A.L. sites. (There are over 100 such sites at the **Courselinks**™ site.) The danger in printing URLs is that web sites can change overnight. As we went to press, these sites were functional using the URLs provided. If you come across one that isn't, please let us know via email to: webmaster@coursewise.com. Use your Passport to access the most current list of R.E.A.L. sites at the **Courselinks** site.

Site name: American Civil Liberties Union

URL: http://www.aclu.org/

Why is it R.E.A.L.? This site, sponsored by the American Civil Liberties Union (ACLU), has an enormous collection of materials related to the criminal justice system, as well as various other social issues. It is an outstanding site for gathering well-documented and scholarly materials. There is also a student's section.

Key topics: civil liberties, rights, freedom

Try this: Browse through the ACLU's special report, "Driving While Black: Racial Profiling on Our Nation's Highways."

Site name: Police Complaint Center

URL: http://www.policeabuse.com/

Why is it R.E.A.L.? The Police Complaint Center, a private, not-for-profit organization, collects complaints against the police online. In addition, the center conducts undercover operations in cities where the police have been known to unlawfully harass citizens. The investigations are published at this site. This is one of the most amazing web sites on the Internet.

Key topic: police

Try this: Watch the investigations that are on the web site. Also, look at the matrix of police complaints filed with the Police Complaint Center.

Site name: Police Officer's Internet Directory

URL: http://www.officer.com/

Why is it R.E.A.L.? This site provides a comprehensive list of police sites, worldwide police agencies, associations, training opportunities, listservs for law enforcement, and officers' personal homepages.

Key topic: police

Try this: View some of the web pages of agencies and officers in your community.

Site name: Human Rights Watch

URL: http://www.hrw.org/reports98/police/index.htm

Why is it R.E.A.L.? This site provides information regarding violations of human rights.

Key topics: rights, freedom, civil liberties

Try this: Read the entire report on police abuse by the Human Rights Watch.

Should the Police Engage in High-Speed Vehicle Pursuits?

ISSUE 5

Take a Closer Look

1. Are there other ways for the police to deal with people who attempt to flee?
2. How can technology help police to safely arrest people who attempt to flee?
3. What kind of pursuit policy would you implement if you were a sheriff or police chief?
4. Do you think that people would not stop if they knew that police departments only pursued serious felons?
5. What guidelines regarding high-speed vehicle pursuits does Hannigan suggest law enforcement agencies adopt?

WiseGuide Intro

Issue 5 examines the utility of policc pursuits. When you think of the phrases "cops and robbers," "the chase," and "catching the bad guy," you probably think about the fast-paced, action-packed career of a police officer. New recruits learn chasing and apprehension techniques at the police academy, where "making an arrest" is highly praised. After all, cops don't run from the criminals. In fact, it used to be legal to shoot fleeing felons, but the courts now require that fleeing felons pose an imminent threat to public safety before they can be shot. Basically, the attitude of policing is "get the bad guy at whatever cost."

However, not all police chases end in "Code 4—situation under control." In fact, high-speed vehicle chases not only place numerous lives in danger, but they often end in injury, even death.

Who are the police chasing, and for what offense? In "The Viability of Police Pursuits," Maurice Hannigan notes that most people who run from the police are wanted for either a felony or a serious misdemeanor. In "Hot Pursuit: The Cold Facts," however, Jan Lewis notes that simple traffic violations trigger most police pursuits.

Issue 5: Should the police engage in high-speed vehicle pursuits?

The Viability of Police Pursuits

Maurice J. Hannigan

Commissioner, California Highway Patrol, Sacramento, California

According to a U.S. Department of Transportation study, over 50,000 pursuits occur annually in the United States. Based on research conducted by the California Highway Patrol (CHP), the number of pursuits has increased significantly over the past several years. Although small in number compared to the large number of pursuits, some of them have resulted in death or serious injury to noninvolved citizens, pursuing officers, and pursued suspects. These collisions have drawn nationwide attention, with the public questioning the necessity of police pursuits.

Pursuits are necessary for the swift and efficient apprehension of violators. As experienced in California, pursuits can be successfully carried out with proper supervision, enhanced training and a comprehensive, consistently *enforced* written policy.

Pursuits are only one aspect of serving and protecting the public. CHP officers are trained to continuously assess the circumstances of any pursuit from a safety perspective and stop the pursuit when they believe the conditions may create an unacceptable degree of risk for themselves, noninvolved persons or even the fugitive.

Background

Vehicle pursuits are only one of many tasks performed by peace officers that may result in hazardous conditions. It is a critical function, but not without occasional consequences of public scrutiny, property damage or death.

Most recently, the number of pursuits has increased with the increase in crime nationwide. The media have focused primarily on those pursuits that have resulted in death, serious injuries and/or lawsuits. Less focus has been directed to the pursuits that have resulted in the apprehension of various felons, fugitives, murderers and serious misdemeanor offenders, such as a driver under the influence of alcohol and/or drugs.

CHP statistics show that over 70 percent of those involved in CHP pursuits were wanted for felony or serious misdemeanor offenses. Each year, CHP officers arrest numerous drug traffickers after observing them commit minor traffic violations. These individuals attempted to flee precisely because they had committed offenses more serious than a traffic violation. Based on this, and other law enforcement agencies' experience, I am convinced that *well-regulated* police pursuits are necessary. Otherwise, if law enforcement agencies were to adopt an absolute no-pursuit policy, more criminals would have an incentive to flee, and possibly go on to commit more crimes.

The Decision to Pursue

CHP, in conjunction with 10 municipal law enforcement agencies statewide, conducted a study in 1982 to identify the problems and characteristics associated with vehicle pursuits. Published in June 1983, the study found that CHP officers witnessing vehicle code violations and then attempting to stop the violators most commonly preceded pursuits. The study also indicated that the events preceding pursuits usually begin with a routine traffic stop and the officer not knowing anything about the violator.

In almost 37 percent of the 683 pursuits covered by the 1983 study, the pursued driver was driving under the influence. The fact that such a high proportion of traffic violators involved in the study were charged with driving under the influence of alcohol and/or drugs indicates the danger that exists in our society.

In 1989, almost 20 percent of drivers pursued by the CHP were wanted for felonies; 31 percent were wanted for other crimes; another 26 percent were driving stolen vehicles; and 29 percent of the pursued drivers were under the influence.

Pursuits in California

In 1989, CHP officers were involved in 935 pursuits, leading to the apprehension of 816 suspects (87 percent of the total). A review of these pursuits led to the following conclusions.

	% of Apprehensions	% of Pursuits
• 193 had outstanding felony warrants	24	21
• 189 were driving stolen vehicles	23	20
• 179 were driving under the influence	22	19
• 128 aborted for safety reasons		14
• 11 fatal collisions occurred		1
—7 suspects killed		
—7 passengers killed		
—1 innocent citizen killed (kidnap victim was in the suspect's vehicle.)		

Statistical information is available for only the first six months of 1990 because of a data base transition. The following analysis is based on the 644 pursuits that occurred during this period of time, resulting in the apprehension of 592 suspects (92 percent).

	% of Apprehensions	% of Pursuits
• 124 felony warrants	21	19
• 179 driving while under the influence	30	28
• 189 driving a stolen vehicle	32	29
• 76 aborted pursuits	13	12
• 3 fatal collisions		0.5
—No innocent persons killed		

The CHP has also evaluated pursuits involving its personnel from January 1, 1991, to August 31, 1991. The following conclusions were made on the basis of a projected 1,053 pursuits conducted during 1991 (approximately 10 percent higher than in 1989), based on previous years' statistics and the first eight months of 1991. Of the 1,053 pursuits, 834 (79 percent) ended with the apprehension of a suspect.

	% of Apprehensions	% of Pursuits
• 426 fugitives with felony warrants	51	40
• 239 driving stolen vehicles	29	23
• 157 driving under the influence	19	15
• 80 aborted pursuits	9	8
• 4 fatalities (3 suspects, 1 passenger)		0.3

In the 1983 study, a pursuit was defined as "an event involving one or more peace officers attempting to apprehend a suspect in a motor vehicle, while the suspect is trying to avoid capture using high-speed driving or other evasive tactics such as driving off a highway, making sudden or unexpected turning movements or maintaining a legal speed but willfully failing to yield to the officer's signal to stop."

Police pursuits generally follow certain patterns, progressing through similar stages before the pursuit is initiated. First, a driver commits a vehicle code violation or has been involved in some other activity that justifies police intervention. Second, an officer either observes the violation and decides to stop the vehicle, or is directed by dispatch to stop a certain vehicle. Third, the violator becomes aware of the officer's intention to stop him. Fourth, the violator decides to evade arrest—the first key event in a pursuit. Finally, the officer decides to pursue.

After the officer makes his decision, the violator may voluntarily stop or the officer may voluntarily terminate his participation in the pursuit. If neither occurs, three possibilities exist: the violator may escape or become involved in a traffic collision, or the officer himself may be involved in a collision.

Many factors are considered in an officer's decision to pursue a violator, including his vehicle's performance capabilities, the type of roadway(s) involved, weather conditions, other traffic, the seriousness of the offense and the risk involved in initiating a pursuit.

Problems in Pursuits

The media focus on police pursuits has been on the deaths and serious injuries of noninvolved citizens. Of course, all pursuits are potentially dangerous, and there is a risk to noninvolved citizens, the person being pursued and the

While it is true that all pursuits are potentially dangerous, and that there is a risk to noninvolved citizens, the person being pursued and the pursuing officer, in comparison to the number of high-speed pursuits conducted, only a small number have ended tragically.

pursuing officer. However, in comparison to the number of high-speed pursuits conducted, only a small number have ended tragically or resulted in the filing of lawsuits. The 1983 study provided evidence indicating that police pursuits do not typically end in death or injury to innocent persons, as the news media imply.

Law enforcement agencies should be as aggressive as possible in pursuing violators; nevertheless, their officers must use good judgment in the service and protection of the community.

Most problems associated with pursuits can be minimized with effective supervision and a comprehensive written pursuit policy, which is constantly refined and strictly enforced.

Pursuits should be controlled by a supervisor or senior officer who is responsible for the number of units involved and can make the decision to terminate the pursuit when conditions warrant. If the pursuit then results in a preventable traffic collision, the supervisor or officer in charge of the pursuit is held accountable to evaluate the incident and provide recommendations to management for deviation from the written pursuit policy.

A comprehensive written pursuit policy should include, as a minimum, provisions for how and when forcible stops are permitted; how and when to abort a pursuit; and disciplinary actions for officers and supervisors who fail to adhere to the policy.

An agency's pursuit policy should also contain guidelines for those supervisors or senior officers who are responsible for

1. determining the number of department units to participate in the pursuit;
2. coordinating operations with other jurisdictions;
3. using any available law enforcement aircraft when feasible;
4. determining when the interests of public safety and effective law enforcement justify a vehicle pursuit and when a pursuit should not be initiated or should be terminated; and
5. evaluating all pursuits and completing a written pursuit report following guidelines established by the agency.

The success of pursuits is also dependent upon the adequacy of an agency's pursuit and emergency driving training. The driving skills learned at the cadet level must be enhanced through ongoing evaluations and development of driving skills, both in the field environment and during pursuit and emergency driving. Training in pursuit and emergency driving should also be included in ongoing departmental training, since it is one of the most effective ways to increase rational decision making and reduce risk. More than simply driving skills, this training should encompass

1. the familiarization of officers and supervisors with department policy and its application.
2. the relationship and balance between an officer's mission in apprehending violators and the risk to noninvolved citizens.

Management's Role

When officers are regulated by a written pursuit policy and are properly supervised during pursuits, the potential for tragedies is greatly reduced. Proper supervision helps to ensure that the pursuing officer's decision-making process is sound and eliminates the possibility of the "pursuit at any cost" mindset.

If problems occur, the officer's behavior can be observed, reported and modified. Officers acting outside policy guidelines can be held accountable and given remedial training or disciplinary action. Since the officer cannot control the fleeing violator, it is important that he consistently and objectively evaluate the necessity of the pursuit and not hesitate to terminate it as established by the policy.

In December 1990, the CHP formed a task force to review its pursuit policy and report to executive management on the adequacy of the department pursuit policy, the adequacy of the department's pursuit and emergency driving training and the standard issuance of adverse actions for preventable traffic collisions during pursuits and emergency. The task force found the policy to be adequate and not overly restrictive. Indeed, it has been and continues to serve as a basis for court decisions and the drafting of legislation. It is also recognized as a model by federal, state and local agencies, as well as the FBI "Alert Committees" of 50 major agencies across the United States.

Conclusion

The CHP is not a proponent of damn-the-torpedoes, chase-'em-down-no-matter-what-the-circumstances school of pursuits. In our opinion, however, pursuits are necessary, as long as they are conducted in a responsible, controlled manner to enhance public safety through the apprehension of fleeing violators.

Most studies and published literature support the same basic conclusions: that a comprehensive written policy, enhanced training and effective supervision will reduce the potential for pursuits that end in tragedy.

Pursuits conducted by the CHP are regulated by an enforced written pursuit policy, which is reviewed every three months by all officers and supervisors. Executive management, commanders and supervisors emphasize accountability and responsibility in pursuit driving, as well as self-control, to achieve the swift, efficient apprehension of violators without compromising the public safety.

Officers acting *outside* the policy guidelines are held accountable and provided remedial training; when necessary, they are subject to disciplinary action. Officers acting *within* policy guidelines are not—and should never be—held responsible for actions of the pursued, regardless of the consequences.

FRAME the DEBATE

Form at end of book

READING 10

Issue 5: Should the police engage in high-speed vehicle pursuits?

Hot Pursuit:
The Cold Facts

Most police pursuits are triggered by simple traffic violations.

Jan Lewis

Jan Lewis is an attorney on the staff of The Exchange.

Citizens expect the police to keep their communities safe and to apprehend suspected lawbreakers without unnecessary risk to the public. When either a criminal suspect or a driver who has violated traffic laws uses a motor vehicle to flee, an officer's first instinct may be to pursue the driver at whatever speed is necessary. However, a police pursuit can quickly escalate into a deadly race that continues until one driver crashes.

Many localities have policies that regulate pursuits. Unfortunately, most give individual officers too much discretion in deciding when to begin and end pursuits. Officers may get caught up in the excitement of the moment or begin a potentially dangerous pursuit because of a contemptuous act by someone stopped for a minor traffic violation. Pursuit policies often give too much weight to the need to apprehend fleeing motorists, even those suspected of committing minor offenses, and not enough to protecting life and property.

Many experts believe that high-speed police pursuits should be allowed only when the fleeing motorist is considered violent or poses an immediate danger to the public, making nonpursuit a greater risk than pursuit.[1]

Escalated Risks

More than 300 people die each year as the result of high-speed police pursuits.[2] Thousands of others are injured. Studies over the past decade have found that between 18 and 44 percent of all pursuits end in collisions. The fleeing driver is the most likely to be killed or injured, but many innocent bystanders are also caught in the middle of pursuits and pay the price with their health or lives.[3]

Most police pursuits are triggered by simple traffic violations. Suspected felons are involved in only about 15 percent of all pursuits.[4] In many cases, the driver is a young man who panics or acts impulsively. When police pursue the driver, rather than simply identifying him for later apprehension, the driver's initial mistake in fleeing begins a rapidly escalating chain of foreseeable events that often ends with a crash.

The events described by the Florida Supreme Court in *City of Pinellas Park v. Brown*[5] illustrate the dangers of hot pursuit. Police began a high-speed chase of a driver who ran a red light. The pursuit continued through urban traffic for 25 miles at speeds up to 120 miles an hour. At times, as many as 20 police vehicles were involved. The pursuit ended when the fleeing motorist ran another red light and broadsided a car entering the intersection. The motorist and the two young women in the other car were killed.

The Florida court recognized that the high-speed pursuit increased the risk to other drivers and that the officers' conduct was a proximate cause of the crash, even though no police vehicles were directly involved in the crash. The court said that "experience and foresight support the conclusion that [the fleeing motorist) engaged in such reckless conduct primarily because he was being chased by police, and that this misconduct would have ceased had the police discontinued the pursuit."[6]

Too often, jurisdictions wait until a similar tragedy occurs to adopt policies that restrict the circumstances in which pursuits are permitted. For example, after seven people were killed in high-speed chases in one year in the District of Columbia, the police department limited pursuits to suspects believed to have committed felonies and who were considered dangerous.[7]

Three Policies

There are three types of pursuit policies currently in use.

- Judgmental or discretionary policies provide broad guidelines and list factors that officers should consider but leave all major

"Hot Pursuit: The Cold Facts" (The Exchange Report) by Jan Lewis from *Trial,* April 1993, Vol. 29, No. 4, pp. 78–80. Reprinted by permission of Association of Trial Lawyers of America.

decisions relating to pursuit initiation, tactics, and termination to individual officers.

- Restrictive policies remove some discretion from individual officers and place certain restrictions on their judgments and decisions. For example, these policies may forbid pursuits when the fleeing driver is a juvenile, a traffic offender, or a property offender. They may also limit pursuits to a specific speed, distance, or time.
- Policies of discouragement severely dissuade all pursuits except in clearly defined circumstances where the risks of nonpursuit outweigh the risks of pursuit. Examples include chasing a known murder suspect or a suspect an officer has observed committing a violent crime.[8]

The American Automobile Association Foundation for Traffic Safety recommends that police departments adopt policies of discouragement and provide officer training that covers attitudes toward pursuits, decision-making skills, and technical skills for pursuit driving.[9]

The International Association of Chiefs of Police (IACP) has adopted a model pursuit policy that is restrictive. Pursuits can be used only if the suspect has allegedly committed a felony or misdemeanor that normally would require a full custody arrest (thus excluding most traffic violations). The suspect, if allowed to flee, would present a danger to human life or cause serious injury.

In addition, the pursuing officer must determine that the immediate danger to the public created by the pursuit is less than the immediate or potential danger should the suspect remain at large. In reaching a decision, the officer must consider performance capabilities of the pursuit vehicle, condition of the road surface, amount of vehicular and pedestrian traffic in the area, and weather conditions.

Even if a pursuit is initially justified, changed circumstances may make the pursuit too risky to continue. The IACP policy specifies that pursuits should be immediately terminated when

- weather or traffic conditions substantially increase the danger of pursuit beyond the worth of apprehending the suspect,
- the distance between the pursuing and fleeing vehicles becomes so great that further pursuit is futile, or
- the danger posed to the public, the officers, or the suspect is greater than the value of apprehending the suspect would be.

The policy makes a field supervisor responsible for monitoring and controlling the pursuit. The policy also stresses the need for accountability. The supervisor must analyze the pursuit and determine whether it was handled properly and whether there was any deviation from policy.[10]

Some states have adopted statewide policies. In 1987, California passed a law that immunizes public agencies from liability for civil damages resulting from the collision of a fleeing vehicle with an innocent third party if the agency has adopted a written policy that meets minimum standards encouraging safe police pursuits.

The policy must have set procedures ensuring supervisory control of the pursuit, designating the primary pursuit vehicle and total number of vehicles permitted to participate, and coordinating operations with other jurisdictions. The policy is also required to outline guidelines for determining when the interests of public safety and effective law enforcement justify pursuit and when a pursuit should not be initiated or should be terminated.[11]

A recent California appellate court decision indicates that localities' policies will be scrutinized to ensure that they meet the minimum standards. In *Colvin v. City of Gardenia,*[12] the court had to determine the effect of the statute on a city's liability for the death of an innocent third party whose car was hit by a fleeing vehicle driven by a nine-year-old boy. The boy had been pursued by two police cars for about three miles through several red lights at speeds approaching 100 mph.

The city policy had a general provision that pursuits could be initiated whenever an officer had reasonable cause to stop a vehicle and the driver failed to stop. It did not provide any guidelines for determining when the gravity of a situation justified a pursuit.

The policy failed to mention obvious factors—such as traffic, weather and road conditions, and speed—that should be considered when deciding to start or continue a pursuit. A provision dealing with terminating pursuits weighed the risk of harm to the officer against the seriousness of the violations but failed to consider the safety of innocent third parties.

The court of appeal concluded that the city had purposely chosen not to set forth minimum standards but instead had tried to give its officers maximum discretion and flexibility. As a result, the city was not immune from liability.

Standard of Care

Police officers who are involved in pursuits or other emergencies are usually exempt from traffic regulations. However, they are generally required to exercise the care of a reasonable prudent person under the circumstances.[13] Some states base liability on simple negligence; others require that gross negligence be proved.[14]

Regardless of which standard is used, courts examine the same factors to determine whether police officers and their employers should be held responsible for injuries caused by a pursuit. These include reason for the pursuit, weather and driving conditions, evidence of excessive speed, presence of pedestrians and other traffic, use of warning signals such as a siren or flashing lights, and police adherence to traffic signals.[15]

However, the final decision to impose liability depends on legislative and judicial attitudes concerning two conflicting societal values: encouraging pursuits and arrests of lawbreakers versus discouraging the injuries and deaths that result from police pursuits.

Decisions not to impose liability often start from the premise that police officers have a duty to apprehend suspects and should not be responsible for the results of a fleeing driver's reckless behavior.[16] Courts have reasoned that officers had no duty to people injured during pursuits, that officers' actions were not the proximate cause of the crash, or that a fleeing driver's action was an intervening or superseding cause of the crash.[17]

Recent decisions imposing liability have stressed the importance of life and public safety over the immediate apprehension of a lawbreaker. In *Travis v. City of Mesquite,* for example, the Texas Supreme Court ruled that the decision to begin or continue a high-speed pursuit could be negligent when the heightened risk of injury to innocent third parties was unreasonable in relation to the state's interest in apprehending suspects.[18]

Duty to Passengers

A later decision by the Texas Court of Appeals made it clear that police officers owe a duty to passengers in the fleeing vehicle as well as to innocent third parties. In *Chambers v. City of Lancaster,* the court ruled that police had a duty to innocent bystanders who were unknown until the pursued vehicle crashed into them. Therefore, it was fair to place a similar duty on the police regarding apparently innocent passengers who were trapped in the fleeing vehicle.[19]

Courts that have imposed liability have recognized that police pursuits are the proximate cause of a crash if the police could have reasonably anticipated the crash as a probable consequence of their actions.[20] The fleeing driver's criminal behavior is not a superseding cause if the crash was a foreseeable result of the officers' negligence.[21]

In Nebraska, the legislature has determined that the need to protect innocent bystanders is of prime importance. It made political subdivisions strictly liable when an innocent third party suffers death, injury, or property damage proximately caused by the action of a law enforcement officer during a high-speed pursuit.[22]

Police pursuits escalate the danger presented by a fleeing motorist.

The Nebraska Supreme Court recently interpreted this statute in *Stewart v. City of Omaha.*[23] The city appealed from a judgment awarding damages to the parents of a motorcycle passenger killed during a police pursuit. An officer initially tried to stop the motorcycle because he mistakenly thought it was stolen. Before the pursuit began, however, he learned that it was not stolen and that the only violation was an expired license.

The motorcycle driver ran four stop signs during a two-minute chase that reached speeds of 50 to 70 mph in a residential neighborhood that had a 25 mph limit. The passenger was killed when the motorcycle crashed into another vehicle.

The trial court found that the passenger's parents were entitled to recover under the statute. The court also found the police officer negligent. The supreme court affirmed, ruling that the statute applied to the passenger because she was "an innocent third party" who neither assumed the risk of her injuries nor was negligent. The court also found that the officer's conduct in pursuing the motorcycle at high speeds through a densely populated neighborhood for a minor offense was the proximate cause of her death.

Recent decisions in Florida, Texas, California, and other states recognize that police pursuits escalate the danger presented by a fleeing motorist. To protect the safety of innocent bystanders, as well as police officers and suspects, pursuits should be allowed only when the risks of nonpursuit clearly outweigh the risks of pursuit.

Foregoing a pursuit does not mean letting a lawbreaker go free; it simply means delaying an arrest until it can be made safely.

Police department policies that discourage high-speed pursuits will help avoid the needless loss of life on streets and highways.

Notes

1. *See, e.g.,* Michael Charles et al., Police Pursuit in Pursuit of Policy: The Pursuit Issue, Legal and Literature Review, and an Empirical Study—Summary Report (Apr. 1992).
2. Bill Miller, *Officer Obeyed Rules in Chase, Wash. Post,* Jan. 20, 1993, at D1.
3. Charles et al., *supra* note 1, at 3, 6, 9.
4. *Id.* at 8.
5. 604 So. 2d 1222 (Fla. 1992).
6. *Id.* at 1228.

7. Veronica Jennings, *Montgomery to Reconsider Rules for Police Car Chases, Wash. Post,* Aug. 5, 1992, at D1.
8. Geoffrey Alpert & Roger Dunham, *Policing Hot Pursuits: The Discovery of Aleatory Elements,* 80 *J. Crim. L. & Criminology* 521 (1989).
9. Charles et al., *supra* note 1, at 18, 19.
10. International Ass'n of Chiefs of Police, Model Policy on Vehicular Pursuit (1989).
11. Cal. Veh. Code §17004.7 (West Supp. 1993).
12. 15 Cal. Rptr. 2d 234 (App. Ct. 1992).
13. 57 Am. Jur. 2d *Municipal, County, School, and State Tort Liability* §474 (1988).
14. *See* Jones v. Ahlberg, 489 N.W.2d 576 (N.D. 1992).
15. *Id.* at 581; 57 Am. Jur. 2d §474, *supra* note 13.
16. *See, e.g.,* DeWald v. State, 719 P.2d 643 (Wyo. 1986).
17. *See, e.g.,* Dickins v. Horner, 611 A.2d 693 (Pa. 1992); Kennedy v. Spring City, 780 S.W.2d 164 (Tenn. 1989).
18. 830 S.W.2d 94 (Tex. 1992).
19. 843 S.W.2d 143 (Tex. Ct. App., 1992), *application for writ of error filed* (Jan. 26, 1993).
20. *Jones,* 489 N.W.2d 576, 582.
21. *Chambers,* 843 S.W.2d 143, 148.
22. Neb. Rev. Stat. §§13-911 (1991).
23. 494 N.W.2d 130 (Neb. Jan. 15, 1993).

FRAME the DEBATE

Form at end of book

WiseGuide Wrap-Up

With regard to high-speed vehicle pursuits, are the police "damned if they do, damned if they don't"? There is room for compromise in the criminal justice system, and the trend seems to be that agencies, realizing the risks to their officers and others, are implementing pursuit policies that require more caution.

If a person shoots a police officer or kills someone, the police will do their best to apprehend the offender, even if they have to engage in a high-speed chase. However, in cases that pose less threat of injury to citizens, the police are likely to err on the side of caution.

New technologies, such as night vision devices in helicopters, and others that are currently being tested, such as engine kill devices, may allow police officers to arrest criminals in a safer manner. These advancements allow for greater enforcement of the law, while reducing risk of injury to all parties concerned.

R.E.A.L. Sites

This list provides a print preview of typical **Coursewise** R.E.A.L. sites. (There are over 100 such sites at the **Courselinks**™ site.) The danger in printing URLs is that web sites can change overnight. As we went to press, these sites were functional using the URLs provided. If you come across one that isn't, please let us know via email to: webmaster@coursewise.com. Use your Passport to access the most current list of R.E.A.L. sites at the **Courselinks** site.

Site name: Police Executive Research Forum
URL: http://www.policeforum.org/
Why is it R.E.A.L.? The goal of the Police Executive Research Forum is to disseminate criminal justice information throughout the policing community. The site has several articles and documents on policing.
Key topics: research, police
Try this: Look at some reports on topics in policing that interest you.

Site name: CJUST-L (Discussion List)
URL: listserv@cunyvm.cuny.edu
Why is it R.E.A.L.? This is the largest discussion list dedicated to justice issues. To subscribe, send email to <listserv@cunyvm.cuny.edu>, saying simply "subscribe CJUST-L FirstName LastName."
Key topics: justice, crime, criminal justice, discussion list
Try this: Join the discussion list, and participate in a lively discussion of criminal justice issues.

Site name: Community Policing Consortium
URL: http://www.communitypolicing.org/
Why is it R.E.A.L.? This is a mega-site of community policing materials! From newsletters to academic research projects to links, you'll find almost everything related to community policing here.
Key topic: community policing
Try this: Learn more about the COPS program by going to the "About COPS" section.

Site name: Law Enforcement Sites on the Web

URL: http://www.ih2000.net/ira/ira.htm

Why is it R.E.A.L.? This site has thousands of law enforcement links, which are updated daily.

Key topics: mega-site, links

Try this: Check out some of the stories that are at this web site.

The Pinkertons or the Police? What Is the Future of Law and Order in America?

ISSUE 6

Take a Closer Look

1. What do you feel would be the major challenge associated with the privatization of the police?
2. What benefits may emerge as a result of police privatization?
3. Describe the process of privatization as outlined by O'Leary.
4. According to Trojanowicz and Bucqueroux, how can the privatization of police facilitate community policing advancements?

WiseGuide Intro

Private security guards have been employed to protect property and people for a long time. Allan Pinkerton started the first security company in the mid-1850s. His security force, which became known as the Pinkertons, was hired to protect the railroads and shipments of materials as people began moving westward.

Abuse, corruption, and a variety of other problems emerged with the expansion of private security. States have recently begun to require that security guards undergo formal training, fingerprinting, and even background checks. As a result, the private security industry has become much more professional, and today, people can hire a security officer that is well trained and armed with weapons (including firearms) to protect their person, property, or employees. Some security officers are also K-9 qualified, and can provide the client with a police dog if necessary!

Currently, security guards outnumber police officers five to one. Although recent crime bills have provided funds for thousands of police officers across the country, businesses feel that they need additional security measures to ensure the protection of their property and employees.

In "Reflections on Police Privatization," Dennis O'Leary discusses some of the issues raised when his city privatized the police and hired a private security firm to serve as "keepers of the peace." While skeptical of the idea, O'Leary claims that if privatization of the police is to be successful, two critical issues must be addressed: accountability and qualifications.

While acknowledging that the privatization of police is already occurring, and will continue, Robert Trojanowicz and Bonnie Bucqueroux assert that the privatization of law enforcement is a grand opportunity to enhance the doctrine of community policing. Their treatment also addresses many of the constitutional safeguards that citizens lose when dealing with a private security officer as opposed to a police officer.

Issue 6: The Pinkertons or the police? What is the future of law and order in America?

Reflections on Police Privatization

Dennis O'Leary, J.D.

Across the Nation, budget-conscious communities explore the privatization of governmental operations as a way to contain costs while continuing to provide citizens with traditional municipal services. Some services, such as garbage collection, are routinely provided both as private functions and as functions of the government. Increasingly, however, communities are beginning to privatize services that were once *exclusively* within the realm of the public sector. Examples include food preparation in public schools, collection of delinquent parking violation penalties, and even vouchers for public education.

Recently, the Borough of Sussex, New Jersey, experimented with privatizing another service traditionally administered only by the public sector—the police department. In doing so, this small municipality of 2,500 residents became what may be the first modern American community to privatize its municipal law enforcement.

As the Sussex County Prosecutor, I witnessed firsthand the borough's experiment with private policing. Its experiences, both positive and negative, offer valuable lessons to community and law enforcement leaders around the Nation.

The Sussex Experiment

The Borough

Like many small communities in the Northeast, Sussex Borough has experienced a general economic decline during the past several decades. Founded before the advent of automobiles, its Main Street district offers very limited parking. As a result, people in the surrounding areas do the majority of their shopping at suburban malls rather than at local stores. Many merchants have found it difficult to survive this "Main Street syndrome," and the resulting vacant storefronts have proven to be something of a blight on the area. In addition, two once-fashionable hotels in the borough have degenerated into rooming houses that have, on occasion, attracted a criminal element.

Because Sussex Borough is a small, fully developed municipality, little opportunity exists to expand its tax base. In fact, during the past several years, the borough has experienced a decline in real-estate-based tax assessments that has brought the community to the brink of insolvency.

Disbanding the Police Department

For a number of years, the borough's governing body strongly considered closing the police department. Even though the four-member force patrolled only on a part-time basis and possessed almost no modern equipment, the borough found it increasingly difficult to afford.

The issue was, of course, a highly political one. Many residents feared that without a regular police presence, the criminal element in the Main Street area would overtake the business district. However, in early 1992, in the wake of a drug scandal that culminated in the indictment of the chief and another department officer, the borough's law enforcement operations were taken over by the Sussex County Prosecutor's Office for a period of several months.

With assistance from the county sheriff, we were able to provide borough residents with a law enforcement presence that they had heretofore not known. This was due, in large part, to the expanded personnel and resources available.

Still, because my statutory mission does not include providing local police coverage, I informed the borough's political leaders that the long-term issue of police coverage would be up to them. For primarily economic reasons, the borough elected to abolish the police department and to rely upon the State police for law enforcement services.

However, it soon became readily apparent that due to limited resources and slow response times, this option would not represent a satisfactory

"Reflections on Police Privatization" by Dennis O'Leary, J.D. from *FBI Law Enforcement Bulletin,* September 1994, pp. 21–25. Reprinted by permission.

permanent solution. The criminal element in the Main Street district and lawless flavor of the area posed enough of a problem that the residents demanded that the mayor and council enhance police protection within the borough.

Choosing Private Security

Having disbanded its police force for lack of funding, the borough now faced an impasse. Residents sought a more constant uniformed presence than the State police could provide. At the same time, political leaders considered a police department an expense the municipality could no longer afford.

The borough's leaders devised a unique response to this dilemma. They developed a plan to hire a private security company to provide a more constant uniformed presence within the borough. Specifications were drafted, a bid was submitted by a private security company, and a contract was signed between the firm and the borough.

While the security company's initial mission simply was to supplement the State police, it soon became clear that its true mission was to function as a fully independent municipal police department. From the outset, my office received reports of motor vehicles being stopped, summonses being issued, and persons being detained and arrested.

My concern was heightened when reports surfaced that the security guards had mishandled several incidents. In one case, they returned a knife to an individual suspected of assault. Information also came to light revealing that a number of the guards had minor criminal records, primarily for assault.

Partly for these reasons, the borough's experiment in private policing turned out to be a fairly short one. An injunction was obtained by the New Jersey attorney general's office on the basis that the Sussex Borough could not create a private police department without complying with existing State statutes relating to the creation of a police force. While this effectively resolved the issue as it related to Sussex Borough, the privatization of police services is an idea that undoubtedly will be studied closely by other communities in the future. As the residents of Sussex Borough learned, police privatization is a complex issue with a number of compelling arguments both for it and against it.

Privatization of Police Services

Not surprisingly, the Sussex experiment with privatization generated a great deal of interest from representatives of two distinct segments of government. Administrators of small municipal governments experiencing financial difficulties similar to those of Sussex Borough saw the experiment as an opportunity to save considerable sums of money without denying citizens a needed service. On the opposite end of the spectrum, the Police Benevolent Association and many law enforcement unions saw the Sussex experiment as a direct threat to their livelihood. While both sides professed their concerns in terms of good government and effective law enforcement, money clearly represented an underlying issue.

I personally opposed the action undertaken by Sussex Borough. However, my concern stemmed not so much from the concept itself as it did from the lack of safeguards provided in terms of accountability and qualifications.

Accountability

The statutes in New Jersey authorizing municipalities to provide police services are similar to those in other States. Once a police department is established, it operates more or less autonomously from the municipality's administration. The chain of command does not go through the mayor and political structure of the municipality, but rather directly to the county prosecutor and the attorney general, and ultimately to the courts. This arrangement was designed to "depoliticize" the administration of law enforcement, a laudable and desirable goal.

". . . political leaders considered a police department an expense the municipality could no longer afford."

The arrangement established in Sussex Borough completely circumvented this delicate balance. The private security company directly reported, and was technically responsible, only to the entity that awarded its contract. History is replete with instances in which police departments were used for dubious purposes by political bosses. This is not to say such a situation developed, or would have developed, in Sussex Borough. However, were such arrangements duplicated in other municipalities, the potential for corruption and abuse certainly would grow accordingly.

Qualifications

As county prosecutor, I was concerned also with the issue of qualifications. As in every State, an entire statutory framework exists in New Jersey relating to hiring qualifications for municipal police officers. Candidates undergo psychiatric testing prior to being offered employment, as well as intensive training on dealing with people in difficult situations, criminal law (including search and seizure), physical fitness, marksmanship, and various other matters relating to law enforcement work.

The training received by the private security guards was limited at best. In fact, the only real training the guards received focused on the use of guns. By contrast, firearms training generally represents a relatively minor component of the instruction provided to public sector law enforcement officers.

It is reasonable to assume that municipalities offering positions of authority, which include the carrying of a firearm, at relatively low salaries, will attract a wide spectrum of applicants. Some will be attracted to the job out of a sense of public commitment. Others will be motivated by other, less desirable factors.

Therefore, to ensure the integrity of any municipal law enforcement force, a psychological screening process is not only desirable but essential. However, this is only a first step. Training in areas such as search and seizure must keep personnel abreast of constant changes in the law. Even with intensive training, police officers, as well as attorneys and judges, make periodic mistakes in these areas.

The security guards in Sussex Borough received *no* training in these areas. The security firm explained this deficiency by claiming that, as private citizens, the guards were not bound to comply with the fourth, fifth, or sixth amendments (rights of defendants).

I vigorously disagree. While private citizens are not obliged to afford such rights to other private citizens, a convincing argument could be made that the security guards did not act merely as private citizens. They were, after all, duly hired agents of a municipality.

Nonetheless, the guards were seriously unprepared for their responsibilities. In short, the hiring of a private security firm in lieu of a municipal police department not only circumvented a longstanding statutory framework, it also constituted a giant step backward in terms of law enforcement professionalism.

Can Privatization Work?

Is it possible to have a professional qualified, responsible police department that operates fully within the private sector? As I have indicated, my objections to the Sussex Borough experiment centered on qualifications and accountability. Both areas could be addressed adequately by simply amending laws and regulations to provide accountability along a similar chain of command as those of public police agencies. In addition, legislatures could mandate that in order to win a bid for municipal policing, private security companies must meet the same screening and training criteria as public police departments.

". . . the only real training the guards received focused on the use of guns."

Could private security someday replace public policing? There seems to be a national trend among legislatures to grant greater police powers to private security. It is conceivable that the legal obstacles to private security firms assuming "public" policing powers could be overcome. In fact, from a legal perspective, this transition could be accomplished with little difficulty.

Whether municipalities embrace the concept depends on a number of factors. Communities should consider these factors carefully before embarking on the road to privatization.

Considerations

Like many private waste removal companies, large security firms could supply police coverage for several contiguous municipalities, and thereby affect economies of scale. Such an arrangement not only would keep costs down but also would provide greater promotional opportunities for law enforcement officers, because they would be working for a larger enterprise. In addition, the degree of professionalism theoretically would improve over small police departments that possess limited training resources and equipment.

The financial savings to municipalities could be dramatic. In the short-lived Sussex experiment, the borough realized a savings of over 50 percent. While I suspect that a portion of this amount resulted from a "loss leader" by the security firm in its effort to win the borough's initial bid, I believe that a practical savings of 25 to 30 percent could be realistic for many jurisdictions.

Clearly, however, such arrangements would not be without considerable drawbacks. The large amount of money private security companies would have to invest to hire and train qualified personnel would be reflected in any realistic bid. Further, while competition may serve to keep costs to municipalities down initially, once a security company becomes entrenched in a particular area, its proximity to nearby jurisdictions would allow it a distinct advantage to underbid other firms. The resulting monopoly could significantly erode any long-term savings that the municipalities anticipate.

Aside from costs, however, other important considerations remain. Under private security agreements, municipalities would possess considerably less control over their police force than afforded by the traditional public policing model. While public police departments enjoy some degree of autonomy, police chiefs often are appointed by municipal governing bodies. These bodies generally review and approve police budgets, as well.

But, more subtle "controls" also forge a link between a municipality and its police department. In many communities, for example, when the police department promotes a patrol officer to sergeant, a ceremony takes place before the town council meeting. Generally, despite periodic "rocky moments," a warm and friendly relationship exists between the governing body and the police department of a small town.

Municipalities that enter into private security arrangements suddenly would find themselves dealing with corporate America. The warm and friendly relationship as it once existed between local government and the police force would change forever. Because large private security firms could conceivably hire employees from anywhere and relocate them, municipal government officials and citizens may find themselves no longer dealing with police officers who are also friends, and in some cases, relatives. While this certainly could be seen on one level as a positive outcome, the fact remains that small town residents appreciate being afforded certain informal courtesies by their police department. They enjoy being known by name and feel secure being protected by members of their own community. To a large degree, the "personal touch" afforded by local public departments would become a casualty of police privatization.

Further, in the interest of efficiency and scheduling, private security guards in large firms might be assigned from municipality to municipality. This would allow little opportunity for guards to develop allegiance to any one community, let alone to individual residents or municipal officials. The unique advantages of local police coverage—intervening when an otherwise well-behaved youth becomes associated with the wrong crowd, checking on elderly residents, noticing a suspicious new person in town—would be missing.

In the final analysis, it may be these intangibles that form the basis for debate in municipalities considering the privatization issue. Communities must decide whether forsaking these intangibles is worth any monetary savings realized by privatizing the police function.

In the interest of accuracy, however, communities should keep the issue of police privatization in perspective. Private policing does not represent a radical new concept. Indeed, the idea of government-administered, or public, law enforcement is of relatively recent origin—occurring in most parts of the world within the past 100 years. Prior to the advent of public policing, groups of citizens wishing law enforcement protection organized it privately, without direct government intervention. During the formative years of the American frontier, citizen posses and private railroad guards provided essential law enforcement services. In many ways, the privatization of policing simply represents a new take on an American tradition.

Conclusion

Is it legally possible to create a private police department? Probably. But, more important questions remain. Would such an arrangement work? And would the savings be worth the effort? The Sussex Borough experiment may have been too brief to fully answer these questions. But, they will undoubtedly be asked by economically challenged communities around the Nation.

Although private policing may offer significant initial cost benefits to small municipalities, the savings would probably diminish as large security firms formed regional monopolies. Municipalities then may find that they lost far more than they gained.

Because many of the functions that local police departments perform relate to providing services to their communities in addition to mere code enforcement, ill-planned privatization could bring about unanticipated change. Communities should consider carefully the effects of all these changes when weighing the benefits of private, versus public, policing.

FRAME
the
DEBATE

Form at end of book

Issue 6: The Pinkertons or the police? What is the future of law and order in America?

The Privatization of Public Justice: What Will It Mean to Police?

Robert Trojanowicz

Director, School of Criminal Justice, Michigan State University, East Lansing

Bonnie Bucqueroux

Editor, Kennedy School of Government, Harvard University, Cambridge, Massachusetts

As the pace of change speeds up in our society, people can find themselves in the midst of a virtual revolution without fully realizing how profoundly different their world has become. A decade ago, research on pilot foot patrol projects showed that there appeared to be significant benefits in freeing creative police officers from the restraints of the patrol car and the incessant demands of the police radio, and putting them into direct, daily, face-to-face contact with the law-abiding people in the community. Yet no one thought that this decentralized and personalized delivery of police service would become the wave of the future—so much so that an article in the *New York Times* recently called what is now referred to as community policing as being on the "cutting edge" of police reform.

Not all change is positive, of course. It wasn't that many years ago that "crack" was a word that few of us had heard. Not that many years ago, even those who had heard about crack hoped that it would turn out to be an isolated problem, rather than the spark that has resulted in an epidemic of new drug abuse and drug-related crime and violence.

An equally dramatic and far-reaching change, for good or ill, taking place during this past decade has been the continued and increasing privatization of public justice—a profound change that has so far been both little researched and little understood. Almost invisibly, private for-profit and nonprofit corporations have been assuming roles that were once almost exclusively the province of the public criminal justice system. We have also seen a dramatic rise in the number of joint efforts involving some combination of public and private initiatives. A few examples follow:

- There are now almost twice as many people employed in private security as there are public police.
- In addition to for-profit prisons that house adults, we are also seeing a tremendous surge in the number of private initiatives that handle juvenile offenders.
- U.S. companies now spend an estimated $250 million each year on private undercover drug investigations of their employees.
- Litigants in civil suits can now choose to hire a private rent-a-judge-and-jury to settle claims, virtually bypassing the public courts.
- The federal Trademark and Counterfeiting Act of 1984 gave businesses expanded powers to protect their property and profits, including the right to conduct independent investigations, obtain search warrants, seize evidence, arrest suspects and pursue private criminal justice prosecutions.

A New Perspective

Viewed separately and independently of each other, any one of the examples might seem merely interesting. But viewed as part of the ongoing process of privatization, they raise the issue of whether we are on the brink of redefining what is meant by the concept of justice in this society. Is justice an ideal that we strive to achieve through public debate? Or is it yet another commodity that can be offered for sale in a free-market economy? Can it perhaps be some blend of both?

The moral, ethical, legal, political, economic and social implications of this apparent megatrend are obviously enormous. And, at present, we have far more questions than answers.

Will the motto for the future be "buyer beware" or "the customer is always right"?

Crucial Questions

As these examples demonstrate, the question is no longer whether the trend toward privatizing justice should continue; we are already too far down that road to turn back completely. Therefore, the crucial question is whether these changes will occur piecemeal and poorly or thoughtfully and well. What lines will be drawn, and who will draw them? The police, the frontline troops of the entire criminal justice system, face crucial questions that they must begin to address now—loudly and clearly and with one voice—if their input is to become part of the dialogue.

The police have valid concerns about what these changes portend. One important issue of immediate concern is the proper role of public police in private ventures. Some departments discourage their officers from moonlighting in private security, arguing that this can impair performance on the job by contributing to fatigue and burnout. Others encourage this practice, and some even allow the officers to use police equipment, including patrol cars, on their off-duty security jobs, in the belief that extending the visibility and presence of the police in the community is a plus.

Does the use of moonlighting police officers in private security substantially contribute to overall public safety?

Are police departments risking the possibility that this practice may unwittingly extend their liability to private ventures?

Should private firms be required to compensate departments for marketing the training and experience that the officers acquired at public expense?

Who should develop the models that communities can use to draft regulations for private security firms, to ensure that citizens have redress if they are harmed?

Should departments execute contracts detailing particulars concerning these issues whenever they allow their officers to moonlight for private firms?

To whom do moonlighting police officers owe their allegiance—the police department, the security firm or the company that hires these firms?

Should officers who moonlight receive guidance or written directives concerning proper conduct in their off-duty jobs?

How do officers handle situations when they may be asked to act improperly? There may be occasions, for example, when moonlighting officers will be asked to ignore drunk patrons staggering to their cars, or instructed to shoo away patrons on the basis of race or sexual preference.

Are departments putting their credibility on the line when officers work in part-time private security jobs?

Do they have a legal right to sanction employees who violate department rules in off-duty employment?

Does the general public understand the differences between public and private police?

Do citizens think that providing information about crime to a security guard ensures that it will be shared with the public police?

Balancing Conflicting Interests

A more general concern is whether police departments should form new links to private ventures and how these can be achieved. Consider the potential conflicts that can arise when a company hires a private firm to investigate possible drug trafficking or drug abuse among its employees. If the public police are not informed, such initiatives not only risk compromising ongoing police investigations, but may deny the police important information they need to do their job well. On the other hand, if the public police do become involved, are they lending their credibility and potential liability to enterprises over which they have little, if any, real control?

Private security guards need not adhere to the same procedural restraints as the public police. Where does a company's right to know about off-the-job behavior that could impair an employee's performance end, and the employee's right to privacy begin? Since private security operatives can testify in court, as private citizens, about what their investigations uncover, do they therefore actually have greater freedom to make cases against drug dealers than the public police? Or does this grant them undue license to trample on an individual's civil rights?

What legal and ethical responsibility does a private security firm have in sharing information about illegal activity? Many private firms are hired only to investigate drug problems among line workers, not management. But if a private investigation reveals that a valued and virtually irreplaceable employee is dealing drugs, whose rights will prevail if the company president orders the private security firm to hide this information? As states pass new laws to hold drug users more accountable, will companies have the right to divert employees into treatment without reporting them to the police?

Will it prove wiser for departments to forge links to private initiatives or do the dangers outweigh the benefits? Can the public police safeguard themselves from blame—or even from litigation? Who within the department should be responsible for such contacts? Is this a logical new role for community policing officers?

Underlying Issues

An overriding concern as well is whether the explosion in the number of private police initiative threatens the very future of public policing. A recent article in *New York* magazine on the city's crack problems inadvertently underscored the potential threat. The article took note of two success stories—one in which the police department's acclaimed Community Policing Outreach Program (CPOP) succeeded in helping a woman rid her Harlem apartment complex of drugs, and another that talked about how residents in a more affluent neighborhood had hired a private firm to patrol their streets to drive out the crack dealers.

An overriding concern is whether the explosion in the number of private police initiatives threatens the very future of public policing.

Are private initiatives serving a new niche in the market, or filling a vacuum that the public police should be providing? Does this portend a future where those who have the option choose to ignore the public police in favor of hiring private firms to provide them as much help as they want and can afford? Will taxpayers therefore become increasingly reluctant to support public services that they perceive as primarily serving the poor?

Will this intensify pressure to privatize the public police? In this budget-cutting era, many people argue that government agencies, such as the US. Postal Service, should become private, for-profit enterprises. Many believe that the private sector is more efficient, more effective and less costly. Will we soon see communities subcontracting for all or part of their police service from private sources?

The law provides private corporations protection from public scrutiny, whereas the hallmark of public initiatives is their openness and accountability to the public good. Private corporations are in the business to make a profit, which means their primary responsibility is to their stockholders. Public institutions are ultimately held accountable to the people they serve. If private enterprises continue to encroach on public functions, will corporations see their traditional freedoms eroded, to ensure they act in the public interest? Or will this instead mean that the increasing privatization of public justice poses a serious threat to our cherished liberties and civil rights?

Are we headed toward a future like the one portrayed in the movie "Robocop," where profitability was the sole measure of police performance, and cops-for-hire brutalized any unfortunates who happened to cross their path? Or are we on the brink of a new era in which police departments will strive to become more user friendly as a way of competing with private initiatives?

The Aurora, Colorado, Police Department is one of a growing number of police departments that is exploring how to extend the community policing philosophy department-wide. Not only have they deployed officers directly in the community, as the department's outreach specialists to all the people they serve, but they have challenged each element within the department to propose ways in which they can carry out the community policing mission.

No aspect of their service is exempt from this new mandate. Special divisions within the department are exploring ways to do a better job of meeting the needs of victims. And the overall effort even includes producing a new department directory, in the hope that anyone who calls will be directed to the proper person on the first try.

Many people still see their police department as a forbidding institution—or as a maddening bureaucracy. Private enterprises, in contrast, work hard at making people want to call them first for any job. Community policing may prove to be the vehicle that allows police departments to market themselves to the consumers on whose tax dollars they depend.

Choosing the Best Future

The police can choose to see the increasing privatization of public justice as either a threat or an opportunity. Competition from private sources may spell the end of public policing as we know it, but it may also be the goad that prods departments toward delivering the kind of police service that people want.

Perhaps the police should promote community policing as the affordable, do-it-yourself alternative to both traditional policing and private security. Just as one might save the expense of hiring outside contractors to paint one's home, citizens can be offered the option to become involved in a community policing approach as an affordable alternative to private security. In exchange for being allowed to have direct input into the police process, they will have to agree to donate their time in police-supervised initiatives designed to improve the safety and appearance of their communities.

The importance of the challenge facing the police cannot be overstated. The decisions about how best to contend with the increasing privatization of public justice will shape the world that our children will inhabit. As we enter the final decade of the 20th century, we must lay the proper groundwork for the kind of world we want to see tomorrow.

FRAME the DEBATE

Form at end of book

WiseGuide Wrap-Up

What is it that really bothers us about the privatization of the police? The paramedic profession is privatized, and we trust our lives to them. Is it because we see security guards who are untrained and unprepared, unprofessional, or lazy, and assume that those same people would become police officers charged with protecting our safety?

In reality, if agencies across the country start to privatize, most police officers probably won't quit the profession they love and become an accountant, nurse, or mechanic. Security firms that provide peace-keeping duties will most likely hire officers direct from the ranks of a police department.

People don't seek a career in policing because they want to be a cop. For the most part, people who seek a career in law enforcement want to make a difference in the lives of their neighbors, or they feel that they can help those who need assistance. Whether they wear the badge of the New York Police Department or the Pinkerton shield, their mission and duty in a police-privatized society would be the same: to protect and serve. The same outstanding (and yes, not so outstanding) police officers who currently protect us everyday would continue to do so; just the agency with which they are affiliated would change. And if we do undergo this transformation in American policing, we then must be able to adequately address the concerns that O'Leary, Trojanowicz, and Bucqueroux have raised—namely, increased standards and accountability, community policing principles, and constitutional protections.

R.E.A.L. Sites

This list provides a print preview of typical **Coursewise** R.E.A.L. sites. (There are over 100 such sites at the **Courselinks**™ site.) The danger in printing URLs is that web sites can change overnight. As we went to press, these sites were functional using the URLs provided. If you come across one that isn't, please let us know via email to: webmaster@coursewise.com. Use your Passport to access the most current list of R.E.A.L. sites at the **Courselinks** site.

Site name: The Legacy of Community Policing
URL: http://www.acsp.uic.edu/~ipsp/legacy/
Why is it R.E.A.L.? The Legacy of Community Policing explores the history, theories, operational challenges, and early evaluations of community policing in the United States.
Key topic: community policing
Try this: View lectures by some of the leading experts in community policing.

Site name: *Law and Order* Magazine
URL: http://www.lawandordermag.com
Why is it R.E.A.L.? *Law and Order* magazine is devoted to police issues. Many of its articles are available on the web site.
Key topic: police
Try this: Read some of the articles that interest you from *Law and Order* magazine.

Site name: Community Oriented Policing Services (COPS)
URL: http://www.usdoj.gov/cops/
Why is it R.E.A.L.? This site contains numerous links and documents related to community policing.
Key topic: community policing
Try this: Examine some of the new community policing initiatives.

Site name: Police Research at UNO

URL: http://cid.unomaha.edu/~police/

Why is it R.E.A.L.? This site provides an overview of the community policing movement and describes various community policing research projects.

Key topic: community policing

Try this: Learn how community policing research is being conducted.

STAND! **section 3**

Getting Tough on Criminals

Introduction

Sections 1 and 2 focused on why people commit crimes (causation) and the formal agents of social control (the police) that must respond when a crime is committed. We now look at some of the laws that have given the police the authority to arrest violators and at sanctions, such as the death penalty and the "three-strikes" law, that only come to bear upon an individual after arrest.

Although politicians create most crime legislation, the laws passed are not necessarily the most appropriate way to respond to criminal justice issues. In fact, some laws actually backfire, leading to terrible and unintended consequences.

Most politicians advocate tougher criminal justice legislation. Policymakers and criminal justice officials appear to be apathetic toward criminals, thus leading to harsher and more punitive crime policies. Policy proposals suggest that rehabilitation is a thing of the past and that the focus of the criminal justice system is revenge and deterrence.

Readings 13 and 14 examine the highly popular "three-strikes-and-you're-out" legislation. The crime rate has been declining, everyone is taking responsibility for it, and "three-strikes" advocates are no exception. The racial disparities that this policy manifests, coupled with its lack of empirical support concerning its deterrence value, mandate that the utility of "three-strikes" laws be investigated.

Almost every initiative that politicians and criminal justice practitioners endorse mandates that the criminal justice system respond more severely to criminals. A few politicians may break ranks and propose legislation seeking to reduce a penalty for a certain crime, but they are the exceptions to the rule. Legislation for decriminalizing an offense is rarely introduced. Readings 15 and 16 look at one issue, however, that has the potential to lead to the legalization of an offense: the debate over the decriminalization of drugs. However, even the legalization debate has strong opposition from some of our nation's leading moral scholars, such as James Q. Wilson.

As the war on drugs intensifies, another piece of criminal justice legislation relating to narcotic offenders has been passed. Readings 17 and 18 discuss this law, which relates to asset forfeiture of property that is connected to drug dealing.

Readings 19 and 20 analyze one of the most pressing and controversial pieces of criminal justice legislation of our time: the death penalty. Leading criminologists have spoken out against the death penalty, yet public support for capital punishment remains high. We'll explore why.

Finally, in Readings 21 and 22, we examine the Second Amendment and the right to bear arms. Recent research has suggested that carrying a firearm may protect an innocent person from being injured or killed.

As you read the articles in this section, think how you might respond to some of the issues raised if you were a police officer. How would you respond if you were a city manager? a concerned citizen? a politician? a criminologist? a victim? a police chief or sheriff?

Can "Three Strikes and You're Out" Legislation Create a Safer Community?

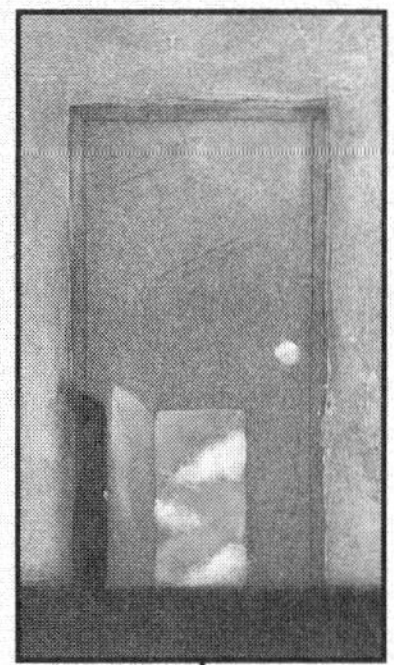

ISSUE 7

Take a Closer Look

1. Do you think that "three-strikes" legislation may be contributing to the decline of crime?
2. Do you see any legal problems with "three-strikes" legislation?
3. Should a juvenile conviction be counted as a "strike"?
4. Should nonviolent felonies be counted as a "strike"?
5. If you were a politician, what type of legislation would you introduce concerning repeat offenders?

WiseGuide Intro

Although many states had habitual offender statutes long before Polly Klaas was born, for numerous reasons, her kidnapping and murder led to what we now refer to as "three-strikes-and-you're-out" legislation. The goal of the measure is to selectively incapacitate the most serious and habitual of offenders.

Recently, the "three-strikes-and-you're-out" law has come under heavy attack. Moreover, the original supporters of "three strikes," such as Polly's father, Mark Klaas, have denounced the bill as an ineffective tool in the fight against crime. In "Three-Strikes-and-You're-Out—Pragmatic, Political, or Pacification," Morton Feldman claims that, if executed correctly, "three-strikes" legislation could have a significant impact on the ailing criminal justice system. He contends, however, that the legislation must be enacted in a manner that doesn't lead to a "net widening" effect, in which more prisoners are brought into the system than were intended.

In "Three-Strikes-and-You're-Out—Mandatory Life Imprisonment for Third Time Felons," Nkechi Taifa argues that this law is repetitive because many states already have habitual offender laws on the books. Also explored is the possibility that the economic, racial, and constitutional harms of this law outweigh its intention and may actually increase violent crime.

Issue 7: Can "three-strikes-and-you're out" legislation create a safer community?

"Three-Strikes-and-You're-Out"—Pragmatic, Political, or Pacification

Morton Feldman

Executive Vice-President, National Association of Chiefs of Police

I. Introduction

The "new" sound bite for politicians in 1994 was the "three-strikes-and-you're-out" proposal to reduce crime. Painted in broad, vague, and undefined terms, the plan calls for the incarceration for life of all "violent" three-time offenders. To a society plagued with random, violent crime (even though statistics show a decline in such crime), it is understandable that Americans believe that courts do nothing when criminals are caught and convicted, that there is no truth in sentencing (true), and that no criminal serves enough time in prison. The "three-strikes" proposal is music to the ears. A "cure" has been found, and I'm safe again.

Hold that thought. The United States incarcerates more people than any country in the western world—one of every 250. In 1992, there were 2.7 million adults on probation and 531,000 on parole. Adding those in jail and prison, there were 3.7 million adults under some type of "supervision" in our country. Those numbers should tell us that somebody, somewhere is doing something right. Unfortunately, the system has lost focus. As a result of badly flawed, hastily-crafted laws enacted to pacify the public in an attempt to show that we were waging a "war" on drugs, federal prisons are loaded to the seams with mid- to low-level nonviolent drug offenders. The laws as written took all discretion from judges. Laws that remove judges' discretion, such as the Federal Sentencing Guidelines, are under constant attack.

II. We Must Learn from the Past

The cost of incarceration (also known as the cost of protecting society from the criminal predator) is around $20,000 per inmate per year. When we expend this much money on the violent offender, the money is well spent—there is no dollar value to be placed on the lives of the victims of violent crime. The problem is that we have not learned from the past. Starting in the early 1920s and lasting until the early 1950s, we had a three-time loser act. That act failed as a result of indiscriminate targeting, and it was abandoned. The Department of Justice tells us that from 1979 to 1993, the rate of incarceration (per hundred thousand residents) rose from just under 150 to 350. These were the targets:

- Drug offenders: from 25% to 65%
- Violent offenders: from 15% to 35%
- Property offenders: from 10% to 20%
- Weapons offenders: from 5% to 10%
- Other offenders: from 10% to 20%

These figures should tell us two specific facts. First, we are not locking up the predators. Second, the "surgical strike," not the shotgun approach, is what we need.

III. Aim at the Right Target

It is axiomatic in the law enforcement community that between twelve and fifteen percent of the criminals commit between eighty and eighty-five percent of the crimes. Many public prosecutors' offices have created "career criminal units" that target habitual offenders. This is an excellent place to start. The next move is to identify, with total clarity and specificity, the nature of offenses that will be cited when invoking the new law. For example, when we cite the offense of rape, we must be careful to state forcible rape as opposed to statutory rape. We do not want to incarcerate for life an eighteen-year-old boy for having consensual relations with his sixteen-year-old partner simply because the law says that she cannot give consent until she is seventeen. Forcible rape is a matter of a subhuman entity using brute force or the threat of fear to victimize someone. It is not comparable to statutory rape, and the two should be distinguished. There is an absolute need for the ingredient of specificity. We do not want to expend the huge dollars, or even use the bed space, to incarcerate the nonviolent for life. The nonviolent can and must be dealt with at intermediate stages.

If our laws were properly aimed at the right targets, those immediately eligible for execution or life without parole would include those convicted of: (1) Murder; (2) Homicide of any law enforcement officer killed in the line of duty; (3) Homicide in any school, house of worship, airport, jail, prison, courtroom, or hospital; (4) Homicide during a forcible rape, armed robbery, armed burglary of an occupied dwelling, or home invasion kidnapping for ransom or with bodily harm; and (5) Homicide by any violent criminal competently diagnosed as sociopathic. We should not wait until the third such violent crime in most cases, as allowing the number of victims to multiply is not acceptable.

IV. To Serve What Purpose?

Incarceration serves a number of purposes. It incapacitates the offender, it protects society, it is acceptable retribution for the victim, and it punishes. Punishment, unlike brutality, is not a dirty word—it is the consequence of the criminals' choice of action; it is earned. Absent major mental disorder, there is no acceptable excuse for the actions of these predators. They have made a choice and now must pay the price. There are those that, by the repetition of their behavior, have demonstrated that they are not fit to live in a free society. This is an unfortunate but true fact.

V. The Devil Is in the Details

In the crafting of the "three-strikes" provision of the 1994 Crime Bill lies its potential success or failure. The cost of incarceration should not deter the plan's implementation. It should, however, create pause and thought that we must not repeat the failure of the past. The "shotgun" approach of the abandoned three-time loser law must be avoided, and the hastily-crafted mandatory drug sentences must not apply. With proper crafting, we have the intelligence and technology to strike the proper target.

For example, like all people, prisoners are subject to serious illness or injury, and medical costs are a serious burden added to the cost of incarceration. In the event an inmate suffers a medically confirmed incident that renders him incapable of inflicting additional harm, the court should commute his sentence to time served, release him, and let him take his place in line with the citizens who face this medical dilemma on a daily basis. To those who would say that this is a cold and unfeeling action, I would observe two things. First, Supreme Court Justice Louis Brandeis once said, "If we would guide by the light of reason, we must let our minds be bold."[1] In this case, the reasoned, bold approach is to release the inmate. Second, it is the criminals that have demonstrated by their violent acts that they are unworthy of compassion—the victims deserve our sympathy. Under current law, there is a gross obscenity in what we do for criminals in need as compared to how we help their innocent victims. This must change.

VI. An Idea Whose Time Has Been Long Overdue

"Three-strikes-and-you're-out" has the potential for being the first major positive step in criminal justice. Crafted properly, imposed effectively, and not diluted politically, the warning sign may soon be lighted: PREDATOR BEWARE.

Note

1. New State Ice Co. v. Liebmann, 285 U.S. 262, 311 (1932) (Brandeis, J., dissenting).

FRAME the DEBATE

Form at end of book

Issue 7: Can "three-strikes-and-you're out" legislation create a safer community?

"Three-Strikes-and-You're Out"— Mandatory Life Imprisonment for Third Time Felons

Nkechi Taifa

Legislative Counsel,
American Civil Liberties Union

I. Introduction

In 1994, politicians swept the nation with election-driven proposals that sounded snazzy but failed to have any real impact on crime. The catchy baseball metaphor "three strikes and you're out" is the latest expression of such nonreasoned, knee-jerk approaches to fighting crime.

Generally speaking, "three-strikes" provisions impose a mandatory life sentence without parole on offenders convicted of a third violent offense. In many instances such measures are constitutionally suspect, impose automatic life imprisonment for relatively minor crimes that may not warrant so harsh a penalty, and have the potential to disproportionately impact African Americans and other people of color. These proposals constitute bad public policy. They are unnecessary due to existing state habitual offender laws and federal sentencing guidelines for repeat or "career" criminals. They expensively retain low-risk geriatric prisoners without a corresponding benefit to society. They fail to effectively curb the crime rate, and, in some instances, may actually increase violent crime in America.

II. Early Congressional Proposals

Prior to final passage of "The Violent Crime Control and Law Enforcement Act of 1994" various "three-strikes" proposals were considered by the 103d Congress. Senator Trent Lott (R-Miss.) and Senator Phil Gramm (R-Tex.) introduced proposals which were adopted on November 19, 1993 as part of omnibus crime legislation passed by the Senate (H.R. 3355). On November 3, 1993 Representative Steny Hoyer (D-Md.) introduced the "Three-Time Loser Act of 1993" (H.R. 3424) in the House of Representatives.

These early proposals mandated the automatic life imprisonment of every defendant convicted of a third separate violent felony after two prior state or federal violent felony convictions. The definition of "violent felony" included offenses against property and crimes not actually involving violence. In describing the term "violent felony," these proposals referred to 18 U.S.C. § 16, which defines a violent felony as a crime involving the threatened or actual use of physical force against the person or the property of another; the term also includes any other offense that is both felonious and by its nature involves a substantial risk that force may be used against the person or property of another.

Thus, pursuant to this definition, malicious mischief to government property or contracts over $40,000 could be included as a "strike";[1] another "strike" could include impeding or intimidating an employee of the Federal Deposit Insurance Corporation, the National Credit Union Administration, or an FBI agent;[2] another could be sending a threatening letter to the President.[3] Any of these offenses, as well as other federal crimes such as stealing a radio from a federally-owned car, could be a strike that triggers automatic lifetime imprisonment for the third conviction.[4]

Senator Gramm's "three-strikes" proposal also counted felony drug offenses as a strike towards automatic life imprisonment. Thus, pursuant to this proposal, a person convicted of two separate offenses involving simple possession of 5.1 grams of crack cocaine[5] (the weight of two pennies), with an approximate value of $125, who thereafter takes a bicycle from someone in a national park, would spend the rest of his life in prison without parole.

Although "three-strikes" sponsors claim that their purpose is to protect society from only the most dangerous felons, these early congressional proposals were overly broad, encompassing a broad range of criminal conduct from murder to minor assaults and offenses against property.

State proposals were no better. In an open letter to the Washington state voters prior to passage of this country's first "three-strikes" law, more than twenty current and former prosecutors urged the public to vote against that state's "three-strikes" proposal. To illustrate why they opposed the law's passage, the following scenario was described:

> An 18-year-old high school senior pushes a classmate down to steal his Michael Jordan $150 sneakers—Strike One; he gets out of jail and shoplifts a jacket from the Bon Marche, pushing aside a clerk as he runs out of the store—Strike Two; he gets out of jail, straightens out, and nine years later gets in a fight in a bar and intentionally hits someone, breaking his nose—criminal behavior, to be sure, but hardly the crime of the century, yet it is Strike Three. He is sent to prison for the rest of his life.[6]

III. Current Federal Law

The "three-strikes" provision that prevailed in "The Violent Crime Control and Law Enforcement Act of 1994" was narrowed from the provision originally adopted by the Senate. It amends 18 U.S.C. § 3559 to require life imprisonment for a person convicted of a serious violent felony if that person has two or more final convictions for a serious violent felony or one prior conviction for a serious drug offense and one or more convictions for a serious violent felony. Each offense, including the offense subject to the enhancement, must have occurred on separate occasions and be separated by a conviction.

The definition of "serious violent felony" includes a federal or state offense

> punishable by a maximum term of imprisonment of ten years or more that has as an element the use, attempted use, or threatened use of physical force against the person of another or that, by its nature involves a substantial risk that physical force against the person of another may be used in the course of committing the offense.[7]

In addition, the definition enumerates certain offenses as "serious violent felonies," such as murder, manslaughter other than involuntary manslaughter, aggravated sexual abuse and sexual abuse, and arson.[8]

Although non-violent drug offenses remain as one of the "strikes" that can result in a mandatory life sentence, the legislation restricts its application to "serious drug offenses."[9] Although more limited than the extremely broad proposal encompassing any felony drug offense passed earlier by the Senate, the provision remains troubling. It categorizes "strikes" based upon the amount of drugs involved as opposed to culpability. As a result, a low level courier in a drug operation who is transporting a large amount of drugs faces the same threat of life imprisonment as the high level manager. Also, although automatic life imprisonment for simple possession of cocaine base (crack) will be excluded as a "strike," the law nevertheless maintains the hundred-to-one sentencing ratio between "crack" and powder cocaine distribution, which has an overwhelming disparate impact on African Americans.

Arson and robbery are exempted from consideration as "serious violent felonies" under certain circumstances. A robbery does not qualify as a serious violent felony if the defendant establishes by clear and convincing evidence that a firearm or other dangerous weapon was not used or threatened and no death or serious bodily injury occurred.[10] Arson is likewise exempted from consideration as a serious violent felony if the defendant establishes by clear and convincing evidence that there was not a threat to human life and the defendant reasonably believed the offense posed no threat to human life.[11] The robbery and arson exemptions are referred to as "non-qualifying felonies."

The government must comply with the procedures in 21 U.S.C. § 851 to provide notice of the predicate convictions and an opportunity for the defendant to challenge the validity of such convictions. In addition, the law allows for resentencing if a prior conviction upon which the life sentence was based is overturned.

In response to outcries that mandatory life imprisonment would keep people in prison well beyond the age of criminal activity and result in increased costs for care of elderly prisoners, the federal law includes a "geriatric exception" which allows for a seventy-year-old prisoner who has served at least thirty years under such a sentence to be released if the Bureau of Prisons determines that the prisoner is not a danger to the safety of any other person or the community.[12]

The law also includes a provision allowing the governing body of Indian tribes to elect whether this measure would apply to its members.[13]

Although narrowed from the original Congressional proposals, the "three-strikes" provision signed into law by President Clinton remains problematic. Not only is that law and state laws which have been enacted constitutionally dubious, they represent bad public policy as well. They fail to reduce crime, are costly with no corresponding return in public safety, and are unnecessary because of existing tough federal sentencing guidelines and mandatory minimum sentencing laws in most states.

IV. "Three Strikes" Violates the Eighth Amendment Proportionality Requirement

Under our system of criminal justice, the punishment must fit the crime. The requirement of mandatory life imprisonment thus raises serious constitutional problems of proportionality where neither the final crime nor the preceding two crimes would otherwise be serious enough to justify a life sentence. Individuals should not be executed for burglarizing a house nor incarcerated for life for committing relatively minor offenses, even when they commit several of them. This principle of proportionality, embodied in the Eighth Amendment, admonishes that "Excessive bail shall not be required, nor excessive fines imposed, nor cruel and unusual punishment inflicted." Punishment may be cruel and unusual if it is out of all proportion to the offense.[14] Many "three-strikes" proposals depart sharply from this rule of proportionality by failing to take into consideration the gravity of the offense.

Indeed, a California judge decided not to sentence a thirty-two-year old prisoner apprehended with two marijuana cigarettes under that state's new "three-strikes" sentencing guidelines.[15] Sonoma County Superior Court Judge Lawrence Antolini said that to sentence Jeffrey Dean Missamore to up to eight years in state prison would have been cruel and unusual punishment. Judge Antolini argued: "To send this man to a state prison . . . and take up space for a more violent felon is out of proportion for this crime."

Missamore was convicted in 1986 of burglary and auto theft charges. He was arrested in April 1994 on the marijuana possession charge when in county jail for petty theft. Although the law states that judges must double the sentence for two-time offenders, Antolini sentenced Missamore to a year in county jail and three years probation. The judge said that a loophole in the state Penal Code allows him to alter sentences "in the interest of justice."[16]

V. The Federal Sentencing Guidelines and State Recidivist Statutes Make "Three Strikes" Unnecessary

Although the life without parole aspect of "three strikes" is new, states have had habitual offender laws and recidivist statutes for years. These laws impose stiff penalties, up to and including life sentences, on repeat offenders. The 1987 Federal Sentencing Guidelines are also very tough on repeat offenders, providing enhanced penalties for repeat or "career" offenders[17] that are substantially similar to "three-strikes" proposals. The United States Sentencing Commission has characterized the sentences under the existing federal career offender guideline as "substantial," and has expressed that it is "not aware of any significant view, even among prosecutors, that [the career offender statute] is too lenient."[18]

The Sentencing Commission's analysis of the impact of "three-strikes" proposals is that such provisions would be "significant and disruptive" to the operation of the guidelines and to the Sentencing Reform Act's goals of uniformity and proportionality.[19] Under the Guidelines, for example, a defendant convicted of kidnapping who has two prior violent felonies or serious drug offenses, would receive, on the average, 364 months (over thirty years) of imprisonment. A defendant convicted of assault with the requisite two prior convictions, receives, on the average, sixty-eight months (more than six years) of imprisonment. Both the kidnapping and assault defendant receive substantial sentences, but the sentences are proportional to the seriousness of the offenses. Three-strikes proposals, on the other hand, impose life imprisonment for each defendant without regard to the relative seriousness of the instant offense.[20]

VI. "Three Strikes" Is Expensive without Any Corresponding Benefit to Public Safety

"Three-strikes" laws will keep people in prison well beyond the age of criminal activity at great fiscal expense to taxpayers, both for increased trial expenses as well as geriatric care in prison. Persons over the age of sixty, however, commit only one percent of all serious crimes.[21] Young defendants convicted of a third "truly violent" felony[22] are already required to serve lengthy sentences and emerge from prison well into their late middle age—a time when they pose little criminal risk to society. Although a "geriatric exception" has been adopted in the federal "three-strikes" law, its application is extremely limited, and will needlessly detain relatively harmless geriatric prisoners, at public expense, without substantially reducing crime.

The average cost of incarcerating a federal prisoner is $20,072 per year, or approximately $55 per day.[23] Incarcerating an aging prisoner is estimated to cost three times that amount—over $60,000 a year.[24] Three younger, more violent-prone offenders could be held in the place of one geriatric prisoner.[25]

Of course, more prisons could be built, at $100,000 per bed, or special geriatric prisons could be developed to house aging prisoners. There is no doubt, however, that the resources spent to keep elderly men and women incarcerated through their seventies, eighties, and nineties could be more effectively used to address the root causes of crime.

Finally, under a "three-strikes" law, trials will be more frequent and longer. Faced with a mandatory life sentence, repeat offenders will most likely go to trial, which is costly and time-consuming, rather than agree to plea bargaining. In the state of Washington, normal felonies resolved by a plea bargain cost about $600 to defend.[26] In contrast, defense in a full-blown criminal trial could cost as much as $50,000 per case.[27]

VII. "Three Strikes" Is Ineffective

Laws similar to "three-strikes" proposals have not been shown to lower the crime rate. Habitual offender laws have been found ineffective in those states that have them.[28] Independent studies of selected states which have habitual offender laws, such as Florida, Illinois, and Maryland, found no reduction in the crime rate.[29] Florida, for example, experimented with a similar law in 1987. As its prisons became overcrowded, Florida found it necessary to release first-time offenders—younger and more criminally-prone, in order to make room for recidivist offenders. A recently released report from the Rand Corporation predicts that California may have to release younger prisoners early to make room for permanent third-time offenders.

> If prison space is insufficient, courts may order the early release of prisoners. They may release those with a brief record in favor of retaining older criminals behind bars. This may not be the right choice from the point of view of crime reduction, as younger criminals have more of a criminal career ahead of them than older ones.[30]

Even prosecutors have admitted that there is no reliable way to identify violent criminal predators from their official records,[31] which is what "three-strikes" proposals would automatically do. Indeed, under the discretionary state repeat offender laws, only a small handful of people were actually charged. In Illinois, eighty-eight people in fifteen years were charged, while in Washington state, only sixty-three out of 16,000 felonies are expected to be affected.[32] Should discretion be completely eliminated, we could be incarcerating a lot of people who could benefit from rehabilitation programs and thereafter contribute to society.[33]

VIII. "Three Strikes" Could Disproportionately Strike Black Defendants

A federal "three-strikes" law will most likely have a disproportionate impact based on race. Dr. Lee P. Brown, director of the Office of Drug Control Policy, acknowledged in testimony before Congress that grim statistics reveal that "African-American males are disproportionately represented in all criminal justice statistics: arrests, victimization, incarceration, and executions."[34] Racial bias in the criminal justice system will thus have dramatic repercussions for a defendant facing a third, "violent" felony.

Studies have revealed that arrest and prosecution rates of Blacks are vastly disproportionate to their percentage in the population as a whole, raising the concern that race could be used as a significant factor in deciding whom to follow, detain, search, arrest or charge, as well as the length and type of sentence imposed.[35] Moreover, as a result of the "war on drugs," law enforcement resources are often concentrated in inner-city communities which have large numbers of people of color populations. Often, these factors combine to raise the likelihood that people of color will be arrested and prosecuted more often than their counterparts who reside in suburban areas, which, in turn, raises the potential for them to be subject to criminal convictions more often.

"Three-strikes" laws are also susceptible to prosecutorial manipulation. A Florida study which examined the backgrounds of 47,000 prisoners prosecuted under that state's habitual criminal law found that the decision to prosecute was "based on race and nothing but race. . . . [B]lacks had a rate of it being applied twice that of whites."[36] Similarly, the recently enacted Washington state "three-strikes" law is expected to be used against African American defendants twice as much as against Caucasians, although Blacks constitute only three percent of the population.[37]

IX. "Three Strikes" May Actually Lead to an Increase in Crimes

Many law enforcement professionals oppose "three-strikes" proposals out of fear such laws would spur a dramatic increase in violence against police, corrections officers and the public. A person facing the prospect of a mandatory life sentence will be far more likely to resist arrest, to kill witnesses or to attempt a prison escape. Dave Paul, a corrections officer from Milwaukee, Oregon, wrote: "Imagine a law enforcement officer trying to arrest a twice-convicted felon who has nothing to lose by using any means necessary to escape. Expect assaults on police and correctional officers to rise precipitously."[38] Police in Seattle are already reporting armed confrontations directly attributable to their new "three-strikes" law.[39] Ironically, these laws may cause more, not less, loss of life.

X. Conclusion

The federal "three-strikes" law incorporated in "The Violent Crime Control and Law Enforcement Act of 1994" as well as the various state laws and proposals are examples of ineffective, expensive bad law with constitutionally questionable sentencing consequences. Such legislation does nothing more than invite tougher-sounding proposals from politicians in their attempt to demonstrate to the public that they are "tougher than thou" on crime.

For more than twenty years, state and federal crime control policies have been based on the belief that harsh sentencing laws will deter people from committing crimes. But today, with the federal prison population having surpassed the one million mark and state budgets depleted by the huge costs of prison construction, we are no safer than before. It is clear, however, from already existing repeat offender laws and mandatory minimum sentences, that more stringent measures will not be instrumental in reducing crime. Legislation that could reduce crime must embody a more balanced approach which seriously addresses the need for prevention and imposes realistic sanctions as punishment.

Notes

1. 18 U.S.C. § 1361 (1988); U.S. Sentencing Guidelines § 2B1.3.
2. 18 U.S.C. § 111 (1988) (referencing a list of protected federal employees in 18 U.S.C. § 1114); U.S.S.G. §§ 2A2.2, 2A2.4.
3. 18 U.S.C. § 871 (1988); U.S.S.G. § 2A6.1.
4. Thus, pursuant to these proposals, a defendant convicted of sending a threatening letter to the President, where she already has previous separate convictions for damaging a nuclear weapon during a protest and resisting the arrest of an FBI agent during a demonstration, would automatically be sent to prison for the rest of her life.
5. Simple possession of crack cocaine is a felony, requiring a mandatory minimum sentence of five years and a maximum of twenty years for possession of: five grams for a first conviction, three grams for a second conviction, and one gram for a third conviction. *See* 21 U.S.C. § 844(a) (1988).
6. ACLU Department of Public Education, 10 Reasons to Oppose '3 Strikes, You're Out.' ACLU Briefer, produced by the ACLU Department of Public Education (on file with the *University of Dayton Law Review*).
7. 18 U.S.C.A. § 3559(c)(2)(F)(ii)(West 1994).
8. *Id.* § 3559(c)(2)(F)(i).
9. A "serious drug offense" is defined as a state or federal drug trafficking offense punishable by at least ten years as described in 21 U.S.C. §§ 84(b)(a)(A), 848, or 960(b)(1)(A)(1988).
10. 18 U.S.C.A. § 3559(c)(3)(A)(West 1994).
11. *Id.* § 3559(c)(3)(B).
12. *Id.* § 3582(c)(1)(A).
13. *Id.* § 3598.
14. *See* Solem v. Helm, 463 U.S. 277 (1983).
15. *See* Ron Sonenshine, Judge Defies '3 Strikes' Mandate, *S.F. Chron.*, Aug. 12, 1994, at A17; Tony Slaudes, County Judge Calls '3 Strikes' Law Insane, *Press Democrat*, July 20, 1994, at 1.
16. *See* discussion of this case in Halles, 5 National Drug Strategy Network Newsbriefs (Sept.–Oct. 1994).
17. U.S.S.G. § 4B1.1.
18. *See* U.S. Sentencing Commission Staff Analysis of Section 1008 of S.1356 (on file with the *University of Dayton Law Review*). As of the writing of the analysis, the Sentencing Commission consisted of five active and two ex-officio members. Serving on the Commission were a U.S. Circuit Court Judge; U.S. District Court Judge; U.S. District Court Judge and former assistant district attorney; former chief counsel for U.S. Senate's Subcommittee on Penitentiaries; Deputy U.S. Attorney General; Chairman of the U.S. Parole Commission; and law professor.
19. *See* United States Sentencing Commission Staff Analysis of Section 1008 of S.1356 and Issues of Concern Regarding H.R.3424 (on file with the *University of Dayton Law Review*).
20. *Id.*
21. U.S. Dep't of Justice, Bureau of Justice Statistics, Felony Sentences in State Courts (1988).
22. Truly violent felonies do not include property offenses. Indeed, even the U.S. Sentencing Commission does not include property offenses as violent crimes in its guidelines.
23. *See* Bureau of Prisons, State of the Bureau 1991, Summer 1992 (quoting FAMM Facts, Families Against Mandatory Minimums Foundation).
24. *See* Washington Association of Churches, Washington State Catholic Conference, American Civil Liberties Union of Washington, and Washington Association of Criminal Defense Lawyers, *Why We Oppose Initiative* 593 (Oct. 1993) (quoting *Wall St. J.*, Aug. 18, 1993). This figure does not include operations such as liver transplants or hip replacements which are not uncommon for elderly people to undergo. *Id.*
25. Bureau of Justice Statistics, U.S. Department of Justice, Felony Sentences in State Courts 1988.
26. Initiative 593 Might Bust Budgets, *Seattle Times*, Sept. 16, 1993, at B1.
27. *Id.*
28. See "Three Strike" Laws Strike Out Elsewhere. *Seattle Times*, Sept. 30, 1993, at 1 (describing Illinois and Florida laws) [hereinafter Three Strikes Out].
29. See H. Scott Wallace, *The Truth About "Three Strikes, You're Out,"* National Legal Aid and Defender Association (Jan. 25, 1994).
30. *See* The Rand Corporation, "Three Strikes and You're Out": Estimated Benefits and Costs of California's New Mandatory Sentencing Law 35 (Sept. 1994).
31. Prosecutors Say "No" to Three Strikes Initiative. Letter from 26 Washington State Prosecutors, Oct. 18, 1993.
32. Three Strikes Out, *supra* note 28.
33. *See* A "3 Strikes" Law Would Have Cost Him a 2nd Chance. *Seattle Times*, Oct. 6, 1993, at 1; Norman Edland, Trivial Inclusions in 593 Could Ruin Countless Lives, *Seattle Post-Intelligencer*, Oct. 21, 1993 (Letter to the Editor).
34. *See* Statement of the Honorable Dr. Lee P. Brown to the Congressional Black Caucus, Congressional Black Caucus Braintrust on Crime, Jan. 13, 1994, at 2.
35. *See* Gerald W. Heaney, The Reality of Guideline Sentencing: No End to Disparity, 8 *American Criminal Law Review* 203 (1991).
36. Three Strikes Out, *supra* note 28 (quoting Statement of James Austin of the National Council on Crime and Delinquency).
37. "Three Strikes" Would Impact Blacks Most, Records Show, *Morning News Tribune*, Oct. 16, 1993.
38. *See Portland Oregonian*, Mar. 1994.
39. *See* Testimony of the American Civil Liberties Union of Southern California before a Joint Hearing of the Assembly Committee on Public Safety and the Senate Committee on Criminal Procedure Regarding "Proposition 184: The Three Strikes Initiative," submitted by Samuel Mistrano, Legislative Director, Oct. 3, 1994, at 6.

FRAME the DEBATE

Form at end of book

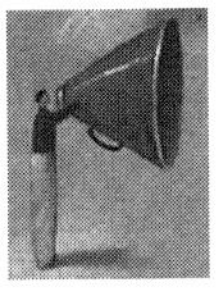

WiseGuide Wrap-Up

For the most part, crime in America has been declining. Some evidence suggests that harsher penalties and lengthier sentences inspired by "three-strikes" legislation have contributed to the slight decline in crime. In addition, it makes sense that, if we lock up our worst predators for longer time periods, we should expect to live in a safer society.

However, what cost are we willing as a society to pay to achieve a safer community? Are racial discrimination, increased taxes, and overcrowded prisons worth this luxury, especially if legislation is repressive to certain ethnic and social groups? Most politicians think that it is worth it, and even if most people agree, we must still ensure that "three-strikes" legislation is in the best interests of all society members.

While arguments on both sides of the issue are persuasive and compelling, justice can only be served with the passage of legislation that is based on what we know from the criminological literature. Further, policies must serve to advance the interests of the majority, as well as those of the minority.

R.E.A.L. Sites

This list provides a print preview of typical **Coursewise** R.E.A.L. sites. (There are over 100 such sites at the **Courselinks**™ site.) The danger in printing URLs is that web sites can change overnight. As we went to press, these sites were functional using the URLs provided. If you come across one that isn't, please let us know via email to: webmaster@coursewise.com. Use your Passport to access the most current list of R.E.A.L. sites at the **Courselinks** site.

Site name: American Bar Association's Criminal Justice Section
URL: http://www.abanet.org/crimjust/home.html
Why is it R.E.A.L.? A variety of information regarding criminal justice legislation is available at this site.
Key topics: law, criminal justice legislation
Try this: Read the report of the task force on the federalization of criminal law.

Site name: FindLaw
URL: http://www.findlaw.com/
Why is it R.E.A.L.? At this site, you can search for laws, legal cases, and other issues related to the legal field.
Key topic: law
Try this: Search for a legal topic of interest to you.

Site name: Preventing Crime: What Works, What Doesn't, What's Promising
URL: http://ncjrs.aspensys.com/works/index.htm
Why is it R.E.A.L.? This is a very comprehensive report to the U.S. Congress by leading criminologists.
Key topics: research, crime
Try this: Identify the approaches to crime that are successful, as well as those that are not working.

ISSUE 8

Should We Decriminalize Drugs?

ISSUE 8

Take a Closer Look

1. If you support decriminalization of drugs, do you favor legalizing all drugs, or only those considered the least harmful?
2. What kinds of laws would we need to regulate drugs if they were decriminalized?
3. If you do not support decriminalization of drugs, what are some of your main reasons?
4. How is the issue of decriminalization of drugs similar to and different from prohibition of alcohol?
5. Do you feel that it is becoming easier or harder to purchase illegal drugs?

WiseGuide Intro

All of the other issues in Section 3 are aimed at either reducing or taking away the rights, property, or life of an offender. Only in this issue do we consider decriminalizing an offense (drug use) and applying less punitive and alternative strategies to a social problem.

What is interesting about this debate is the widely held belief that decriminalization of drugs may be the best alternative to our failing war on drugs. Each year, the United States spends more money fighting drugs, but to no avail. Users continually report easy access to narcotics, and drugs are still a major problem in U.S. society. Even an occasional right-wing conservative will consider the idea of decriminalization of drugs, if only for a moment!

Perhaps decriminalization of drugs is a widely held belief because many people use drugs. Yet, many people assault others, and countless people steal, and we don't have public debates over legalizing assault and theft. This begs the question, "Is drug use not really a bad thing since many people are doing it and a lot of people support making it legal?"

In criminal law, the term *mala in se* refers to offenses that are crimes because they are inherently wrong (such as murder and rape), and the term *mala prohibitum* refers to offenses that are illegal only because society deems them inappropriate (for example, trespassing and drug use). Therefore, if drug use is illegal not because it is inherently wrong or evil, then it was codified as a crime because it was believed to be inappropriate behavior—ergo *mala prohibitum*. We have a dynamic criminal justice system that is designed to change with the times. If society is ready for change, as evidenced by the behavior and attitudes of its members, then the criminal justice system should consider new approaches.

In "Against the Legalization of Drugs," James Q. Wilson argues that widespread drug use will lead to a degradation of our society and that good character is less likely in a bad society. In "Should We Legalize Drugs? History Answers Yes," Ethan Nadelmann compares and contrasts the prohibition of alcohol with that of drugs. Nadelmann explains why alcohol has been decriminalized and drugs have not. Further, he denounces the criminalization of drugs, but points out that even decriminalization supporters disagree about how the laws should be changed to facilitate the legalization of narcotics.

R E A D I N G 1 5

Issue 8: Should we decriminalize drugs?

Against the Legalization of Drugs

James Q. Wilson

James Q. Wilson, Collins Professor of Management and Public Policy at UCLA, is the author of Thinking about Crime *and co-author (with Richard Herrnstein) of* Crime and Human Nature. *His latest book,* Bureaucracy, *has recently been published by Basic Books.*

In 1972, the President appointed me chairman of the National Advisory Council for Drug Abuse Prevention. Created by Congress, the Council was charged with providing guidance on how best to coordinate the national war on drugs. (Yes, we called it a war then, too.) In those days, the drug we were chiefly concerned with was heroin. When I took office, heroin use had been increasing dramatically. Everybody was worried that this increase would continue. Such phrases as "heroin epidemic" were commonplace.

That same year, the eminent economist Milton Friedman published an essay in *Newsweek* in which he called for legalizing heroin. His argument was on two grounds: as a matter of ethics, the government has no right to tell people not to use heroin (or to drink or to commit suicide); as a matter of economics, the prohibition of drug use imposes costs on society that far exceed the benefits. Others, such as the psychoanalyst Thomas Szasz, made the same argument.

We did not take Friedman's advice. (Government commissions rarely do.) I do not recall that we even discussed legalizing heroin, though we did discuss (but did not take action on) legalizing a drug, cocaine, that many people then argued was benign. Our marching orders were to figure out how to win the war on heroin, not to run up the white flag of surrender.

That was 1972. Today, we have the same number of heroin addicts that we had then—half a million, give or take a few thousand. Having that many heroin addicts is no trivial matter; these people deserve our attention. But not having had an increase in that number for over fifteen years is also something that deserves our attention. What happened to the "heroin epidemic" that many people once thought would overwhelm us?

The facts are clear: a more or less stable pool of heroin addicts has been getting older, with relatively few new recruits. In 1976 the average age of heroin users who appeared in hospital emergency rooms was about twenty-seven; ten years later it was thirty-two. More than two-thirds of all heroin users appearing in emergency rooms are now over the age of thirty. Back in the early 1970's, when heroin got onto the national political agenda, the typical heroin addict was much younger, often a teenager. Household surveys show the same thing—the rate of opiate use (which includes heroin) has been flat for the better part of two decades. More fine-grained studies of inner-city neighborhoods confirm this. John Boyle and Ann Brunswick found that the percentage of young blacks in Harlem who used heroin fell from 8 percent in 1970–71 to about 3 percent in 1975–76.

Why did heroin lose its appeal for young people? When the young blacks in Harlem were asked why they stopped, more than half mentioned "trouble with the law" or "high cost" (and high cost is, of course, directly the result of law enforcement). Two-thirds said that heroin hurt their health; nearly all said they had had a bad experience with it. We need not rely, however, simply on what they said. In New York City in 1973–75, the street price of heroin rose dramatically and its purity sharply declined, probably as a result of the heroin shortage caused by the success of the Turkish government in reducing the supply of opium base and of the French government in closing down heroin-processing laboratories located in and around Marseilles. These were short-lived gains for, just as Friedman predicted, alternative sources of supply—mostly in Mexico—quickly emerged. But the three-year heroin shortage interrupted the easy recruitment of new users.

Health and related problems were no doubt part of the reason for the reduced flow of recruits. Over the preceding years, Harlem youth had watched as more and more heroin users died of overdoses, were poisoned by adulterated doses, or acquired hepatitis from dirty needles. The word got around: heroin can kill you. By 1974 new hepatitis cases and drug-overdose deaths had dropped to a fraction of what they had been in 1970.

Alas, treatment did not seem to explain much of the cessation in drug use. Treatment programs can and do help heroin addicts, but treatment did not explain the drop in the number of *new* users (who by definition had never been in treatment) nor even much of the reduction in the number of experienced users.

No one knows how much of the decline to attribute to personal observation as opposed to high prices or reduced supply. But other evidence suggests strongly that price and supply played a large role. In 1972 the National Advisory Council was especially worried by the prospect that U.S. servicemen returning to this country from Vietnam would bring their heroin habits with them. Fortunately, a brilliant study by Lee Robins of Washington University in St. Louis put that fear to rest. She measured drug use of Vietnam veterans shortly after they had returned home. Though many had used heroin regularly while in Southeast Asia, most gave up the habit when back in the United States. The reason: here, heroin was less available and sanctions on its use were more pronounced. Of course, if a veteran had been willing to pay enough—which might have meant traveling to another city and would certainly have meant making an illegal contact with a disreputable dealer in a threatening neighborhood in order to acquire a (possibly) dangerous dose—he could have sustained his drug habit. Most veterans were unwilling to pay this price, and so their drug use declined or disappeared.

Reliving the Past

Suppose we had taken Friedman's advice in 1972. What would have happened? We cannot be entirely certain, but at a minimum we would have placed the young heroin addicts (and, above all, the prospective addicts) in a very different position from the one in which they actually found themselves. Heroin would have been legal. Its price would have been reduced by 95 percent (minus whatever we chose to recover in taxes.) Now that it could be sold by the same people who make aspirin, its quality would have been assured—no poisons, no adulterants. Sterile hypodermic needles would have been readily available at the neighborhood drugstore, probably at the same counter where the heroin was sold. No need to travel to big cities or unfamiliar neighborhoods—heroin could have been purchased anywhere, perhaps by mail order.

There would no longer have been any financial or medical reason to avoid heroin use. Anybody could have afforded it. We might have tried to prevent children from buying it, but as we have learned from our efforts to prevent minors from buying alcohol and tobacco, young people have a way of penetrating markets theoretically reserved for adults. Returning Vietnam veterans would have discovered that Omaha and Raleigh had been converted into the pharmaceutical equivalent of Saigon.

Under these circumstances, can we doubt for a moment that heroin use would have grown exponentially? Or that a vastly larger supply of new users would have been recruited? Professor Friedman is a Nobel Prize-winning economist whose understanding of market forces is profound. What did he think would happen to consumption under his legalized regime? Here are his words: "Legalizing drugs might increase the number of addicts, but it is not clear that it would. Forbidden fruit is attractive, particularly to the young."

Really? I suppose that we should expect no increase in Porsche sales if we cut the price by 95 percent, no increase in whiskey sales if we cut the price by a comparable amount—because young people only want fast cars and strong liquor when they are "forbidden." Perhaps Friedman's uncharacteristic lapse from the obvious implications of price theory can be explained by a misunderstanding of how drug users are recruited. In his 1972 essay he said that "drug addicts are deliberately made by pushers, who give likely prospects their first few doses free." If drugs were legal it would not pay anybody to produce addicts, because everybody would buy from the cheapest source. But as every drug expert knows, pushers do not produce addicts. Friends or acquaintances do. In fact, pushers are usually reluctant to deal with non-users because a non-user could be an undercover cop. Drug use spreads in the same way any fad or fashion spreads: somebody who is already a user urges his friends to try, or simply shows already-eager friends how to do it.

But we need not rely on speculation, however plausible, that lowered prices and more abundant supplies would have increased heroin usage. Great Britain once followed such a policy and with almost exactly those results. Until the mid-1960's, British physicians were allowed to prescribe heroin to certain classes of addicts. (Possessing these drugs without a doctor's prescription remained a criminal offense.) For many years this policy worked well enough because the addict patients were typically middle-class people who had become dependent on opiate painkillers while undergoing hospital treatment. There was no drug culture. The British system worked for many years, not because it prevented drug abuse, but because there was no problem of drug abuse that would test the system.

All that changed in the 1960's. A few unscrupulous doctors began passing out heroin in wholesale amounts.

One doctor prescribed almost 600,000 heroin tablets—that is, over thirteen pounds—in just one year. A youthful drug culture emerged with a demand for drugs far different from that of the older addicts. As a result, the British government required doctors to refer users to government-run clinics to receive their heroin.

But the shift to clinics did not curtail the growth in heroin use. Throughout the 1960's the number of addicts increased—the late John Kaplan of Stanford estimated by fivefold—in part as a result of the diversion of heroin from clinic patients to new users on the streets. An addict would bargain with the clinic doctor over how big a dose he would receive. The patient wanted as much as he could get, the doctor wanted to give as little as was needed. The patient had an advantage in this conflict because the doctor could not be certain how much was really needed. Many patients would use some of their "maintenance" dose and sell the remaining part to friends, thereby recruiting new addicts. As the clinics learned of this, they began to shift their treatment away from heroin and toward methadone, an addictive drug that, when taken orally, does not produce a "high" but will block the withdrawal pains associated with heroin abstinence.

Whether what happened in England in the 1960's was a mini-epidemic or an epidemic depends on whether one looks at numbers or at rates of change. Compared to the United States, the numbers were small. In 1960 there were 68 heroin addicts known to the British government; by 1968 there were 2,000 in treatment and many more who refused treatment. (They would refuse in part because they did not want to get methadone at a clinic if they could get heroin on the street.) Richard Hartnoll estimates that the actual number of addicts in England is five times the number officially registered. At a minimum, the number of British addicts increased by thirtyfold in ten years; the actual increase may have been much larger.

In the early 1980's the numbers began to rise again, and this time nobody doubted that a real epidemic was at hand. The increase was estimated to be 40 percent a year. By 1982 there were thought to be 20,000 heroin users in London alone. Geoffrey Pearson reports that many cities—Glasgow, Liverpool, Manchester, and Sheffield among them—were now experiencing a drug problem that once had been largely confined to London. The problem, again, was supply. The country was being flooded with cheap, high-quality heroin, first from Iran and then from Southeast Asia.

The United States began the 1960's with a much larger number of heroin addicts and probably a bigger at-risk population than was the case in Great Britain. Even though it would be foolhardy to suppose that the British system, if installed here, would have worked the same way or with the same results, it would be equally foolhardy to suppose that a combination of heroin available from leaky clinics and from street dealers who faced only minimal law-enforcement risks would not have produced a much greater increase in heroin use than we actually experienced. My guess is that if we had allowed either doctors or clinics to prescribe heroin, we would have had far worse results than were produced in Britain, if for no other reason than the vastly larger number of addicts with which we began. We would have had to find some way to police thousands (not scores) of physicians and hundreds (not dozens) of clinics. If the British civil service found it difficult to keep heroin in the hands of addicts and out of the hands of recruits when it was dealing with a few hundred people, how well would the American civil service have accomplished the same tasks when dealing with tens of thousands of people?

Back to the Future

Now cocaine, especially in its potent form, crack, is the focus of attention. Now as in 1972 the government is trying to reduce its use. Now as then some people are advocating legalization. Is there any more reason to yield to those arguments today than there was almost two decades ago?*

I think not. If we had yielded in 1972 we almost certainly would have had today a permanent population of several million, not several hundred thousand, heroin addicts. If we yield now we will have a far more serious problem with cocaine.

Crack is worse than heroin by almost any measure. Heroin produces a pleasant drowsiness and, if hygienically administered, has only the physical side effects of constipation and sexual impotence. Regular heroin use incapacitates many users, especially poor ones, for any productive work or social responsibility. They will sit nodding on a street corner, helpless but at least harmless. By contrast, regular cocaine use leaves the user neither helpless nor harmless. When smoked (as with crack) or injected, cocaine produces instant, intense, and short-lived euphoria. The experience generates a powerful desire to repeat it. If the drug is readily available, repeat use will occur. Those people who progress to "bingeing" on cocaine become devoted to the drug and its effects to the exclusion of almost all other considerations—job, family, children, sleep, food, even sex. Dr. Frank Gawin at Yale and Dr. Everett Ellinwood at Duke report that a substantial percentage of all high-dose, binge users become uninhibited, impulsive,

*I do not here take up the question of marijuana. For a variety of reasons—its widespread use and its lesser tendency to addict—it presents a different problem from cocaine or heroin. For a penetrating analysis, see Mark Kleiman, *Marijuana: Costs of Abuse, Costs of Control* (Greenwood Press, 217 pp., $37.95).

hypersexual, compulsive, irritable, and hyperactive. Their moods vacillate dramatically, leading at times to violence and homicide.

Women are much more likely to use crack than heroin, and if they are pregnant, the effects on their babies are tragic. Douglas Besharov, who has been following the effects of drugs on infants for twenty years, writes that nothing he learned about heroin prepared him for the devastation of cocaine. Cocaine harms the fetus and can lead to physical deformities or neurological damage. Some crack babies have for all practical purposes suffered a disabling stroke while still in the womb. The long-term consequences of this brain damage are lowered cognitive ability and the onset of mood disorders. Besharov estimates that about 30,000 to 50,000 such babies are born every year, about 7,000 in New York City alone. There may be ways to treat such infants, but from everything we now know the treatment will be long, difficult, and expensive. Worse, the mothers who are most likely to produce crack babies are precisely the ones who, because of poverty or temperament, are least able and willing to obtain such treatment. In fact, anecdotal evidence suggests that crack mothers are likely to abuse their infants.

The notion that abusing drugs such as cocaine is a "victimless crime" is not only absurd but dangerous. Even ignoring the fetal drug syndrome, crack-dependent people are, like heroin addicts, individuals who regularly victimize their children by neglect, their spouses by improvidence, their employers by lethargy, and their coworkers by carelessness. Society is not and could never be a collection of autonomous individuals. We all have a stake in ensuring that each of us displays a minimal level of dignity, responsibility, and empathy. We cannot, of course, coerce people into goodness, but we can and should insist that some standards must be met if society itself—on which the very existence of the human personality depends—is to persist. Drawing the line that defines those standards is difficult and contentious, but if crack and heroin use do not fall below it, what does?

The advocates of legalization will respond by suggesting that my picture is overdrawn. Ethan Nadelmann of Princeton argues that the risk of legalization is less than most people suppose. Over 20 million Americans between the ages of eighteen and twenty-five have tried cocaine (according to a government survey), but only a quarter million use it daily. From this Nadelmann concludes that at most 3 percent of all young people who try cocaine develop a problem with it. The implication is clear: make the drug legal and we only have to worry about 3 percent of our youth.

The implication rests on a logical fallacy and a factual error. The fallacy is this: the percentage of occasional cocaine users who become binge users *when the drug is illegal* (and thus expensive and hard to find) tells us nothing about the percentage who will become dependent when the drug is legal (and thus cheap and abundant). Drs. Gawin and Ellinwood report, in common with several other researchers, that controlled or occasional use of cocaine changes to compulsive and frequent use "when access to the drug increases" or when the user switches from snorting to smoking. More cocaine more potently administered alters, perhaps sharply, the proportion of "controlled" users who become heavy users.

The factual error is this: the federal survey Nadelmann quotes was done in 1985, *before* crack had become common. Thus the probability of becoming dependent on cocaine was derived from the responses of users who snorted the drug. The speed and potency of cocaine's action increases dramatically when it is smoked. We do not yet know how greatly the advent of crack increases the risk of dependency, but all the clinical evidence suggests that the increase is likely to be large.

It is possible that some people will not become heavy users even when the drug is readily available in its most potent form. So far there are no scientific grounds for predicting who will and who will not become dependent. Neither socioeconomic background nor personality traits differentiate between casual and intensive users. Thus, the only way to settle the question of who is correct about the effect of easy availability on drug use, Nadelmann or Gawin and Ellinwood, is to try it and see. But that social experiment is so risky as to be no experiment at all, for if cocaine is legalized and if the rate of its abusive use increases dramatically, there is no way to put the genie back in the bottle, and it is not a kindly genie.

Have We Lost?

Many people who agree that there are risks in legalizing cocaine or heroin still favor it because, they think, we have lost the war on drugs. "Nothing we have done has worked" and the current federal policy is just "more of the same." Whatever the costs of greater drug use, surely they would be less than the costs of our present, failed efforts.

That is exactly what I was told in 1972—and heroin is not quite as bad a drug as cocaine. We did not surrender and we did not lose. We did not win, either. What the nation accomplished then was what most efforts to save people from themselves accomplish: the problem was contained and the number of victims minimized, all at a considerable cost in law enforcement and increased crime. Was the cost worth it? I think so, but others may disagree. What are the lives of would-be addicts worth? I recall some people saying to me then, "Let them kill themselves." I was appalled. Happily, such views did not prevail.

Have we lost today? Not at all. High-rate cocaine use is not commonplace. The National Institute of Drug Abuse (NIDA) reports that less than 5 percent of high-school seniors used cocaine within the last thirty days. Of course this survey misses young people who have dropped out of school and miscounts those who lie on the questionnaire, but even if we inflate the NIDA estimate by some plausible percentage, it is still not much above 5 percent. Medical examiners reported in 1987 that about 1,500 died from cocaine use; hospital emergency rooms reported about 30,000 admissions related to cocaine abuse.

These are not small numbers, but neither are they evidence of a nationwide plague that threatens to engulf us all. Moreover, cities vary greatly in the proportion of people who are involved with cocaine. To get city-level data we need to turn to drug tests carried out on arrested persons, who obviously are more likely to be drug users than the average citizen. The National Institute of Justice, through its Drug Use Forecasting (DUF) project, collects urinalysis data on arrestees in 22 cities. As we have already seen, opiate (chiefly heroin) use has been flat or declining in most of these cities over the last decade. Cocaine use has gone up sharply, but with great variation among cities. New York, Philadelphia, and Washington, D.C., all report that two-thirds or more of their arrestees tested positive for cocaine, but in Portland, San Antonio, and Indianapolis the percentage was one-third or less.

In some neighborhoods, of course, matters have reached crisis proportions. Gangs control the streets, shootings terrorize residents, and drug-dealing occurs in plain view. The police seem barely able to contain matters. But in these neighborhoods—unlike at Palo Alto cocktail parties—the people are not calling for legalization, they are calling for help. And often not much help has come. Many cities are willing to do almost anything about the drug problem except spend more money on it. The federal government cannot change that; only local voters and politicians can. It is not clear that they will.

It took about ten years to contain heroin. We have had experience with crack for only about three or four years. Each year we spend perhaps $11 billion on law enforcement (and some of that goes to deal with marijuana) and perhaps $2 billion on treatment. Large sums, but not sums that should lead anyone to say, "We just can't afford this any more."

The illegality of drugs increases crime, partly because some users turn to crime to pay for their habits, partly because some users are stimulated by certain drugs (such as crack or PCP) to act more violently or ruthlessly than they otherwise would, and partly because criminal organizations seeking to control drug supplies use force to manage their markets. These also are serious costs, but no one knows how much they would be reduced if drugs were legalized. Addicts would no longer steal to pay black-market prices for drugs, a real gain. But some, perhaps a great deal, of that gain would be offset by the great increase in the number of addicts. These people, nodding on heroin or living in the delusion-ridden high of cocaine, would hardly be ideal employees. Many would steal simply to support themselves, since snatch-and-grab, opportunistic crime can be managed even by people unable to hold a regular job or plan an elaborate crime. Those British addicts who get their supplies from government clinics are not models of law-abiding decency. Most are in crime, and though their per-capita rate of criminality may be lower thanks to the cheapness of their drugs, the total volume of crime they produce may be quite large. Of course, society could decide to support all unemployable addicts on welfare, but that would mean that gains from lowered rates of crime would have to be offset by large increases in welfare budgets.

Proponents of legalization claim that the costs of having more addicts around would be largely if not entirely offset by having more money available with which to treat and care for them. The money would come from taxes levied on the sale of heroin and cocaine.

To obtain this fiscal dividend, however, legalization's supporters must first solve an economic dilemma. If they want to raise a lot of money to pay for welfare and treatment, the tax rate on the drugs will have to be quite high. Even if they themselves do not want a high rate, the politicians' love of "sin taxes" would probably guarantee that it would be high anyway. But the higher the tax, the higher the price of the drug, and the higher the price the greater the likelihood that addicts will turn to crime to find the money for it and that criminal organizations will be formed to sell tax-free drugs at below-market rates. If we managed to keep taxes (and thus prices) low, we would get that much less money to pay for welfare and treatment and more people could afford to become addicts. There may be an optimal tax rate for drugs that maximizes revenue while minimizing crime, bootlegging, and the recruitment of new addicts, but our experience with alcohol does not suggest that we know how to find it.

The Benefits of Illegality

The advocates of legalization find nothing to be said in favor of the current system except, possibly, that it keeps the number of addicts smaller than it would otherwise be. In fact, the benefits are more substantial than that.

First, treatment. All the talk about providing "treatment on demand" implies that there is a demand for treatment. That is not quite right. There are some drug-dependent people who genuinely want treatment and will remain in it if offered; they should receive it. But there are far more who want only short-term help after a bad crash; once stabilized and bathed, they are back on the street again, hustling. And even many of the addicts who enroll in a program honestly wanting help drop out after a short while when they discover that help takes time and commitment. Drug-dependent people have very short time horizons and a weak capacity for commitment. These two groups—those looking for a quick fix and those unable to stick with a long-term fix—are not easily helped. Even if we increase the number of treatment slots—as we should—we would have to do something to make treatment more effective.

One thing that can often make it more effective is compulsion. Douglas Anglin of UCLA, in common with many other researchers, has found that the longer one stays in a treatment program, the better the chances of a reduction in drug dependency. But he, again like most other researchers, has found that drop-out rates are high. He has also found, however, that patients who enter treatment under legal compulsion stay in the program longer than those not subject to such pressure. His research on the California civil-commitment program, for example, found that heroin users involved with its required drug-testing program had over the long term a lower rate of heroin use than similar addicts who were free of such constraints. If for many addicts compulsion is a useful component of treatment, it is not clear how compulsion could be achieved in a society in which purchasing, possessing, and using the drug were legal. It could be managed, I suppose, but I would not want to have to answer the challenge from the American Civil Liberties Union that it is wrong to compel a person to undergo treatment for consuming a legal commodity.

Next, education. We are now investing substantially in drug-education programs in the schools. Though we do not yet know for certain what will work, there are some promising leads. But I wonder how credible such programs would be if they were aimed at dissuading children from doing something perfectly legal. We could, of course, treat drug education like smoking education: inhaling crack and inhaling tobacco are both legal, but you should not do it because it is bad for you. That tobacco is bad for you is easily shown; the Surgeon General has seen to that. But what do we say about crack? It is pleasurable, but devoting yourself to so much pleasure is not a good idea (though perfectly legal)? Unlike tobacco, cocaine will not give you cancer or emphysema, but it will lead you to neglect your duties to family, job, and neighborhood? Everybody is doing cocaine, but you should not?

Again, it might be possible under a legalized regime to have effective drug-prevention programs, but their effectiveness would depend heavily, I think, on first having decided that cocaine use, like tobacco use, is purely a matter of practical consequences; no fundamental moral significance attaches to either. But if we believe—as I do—that dependency on certain mind-altering drugs *is* a moral issue and that their illegality rests in part on their immorality, then legalizing them undercuts, if it does not eliminate altogether, the moral message.

That message is at the root of the distinction we now make between nicotine and cocaine. Both are highly addictive; both have harmful physical effects. But we treat the two drugs differently, not simply because nicotine is so widely used as to be beyond the reach of effective prohibition, but because its use does not destroy the user's essential humanity. Tobacco shortens one's life, cocaine debases it. Nicotine alters one's habits, cocaine alters one's soul. The heavy use of crack, unlike the heavy use of tobacco, corrodes those natural sentiments of sympathy and duty that constitute our human nature and make possible our social life. To say, as does Nadelmann, that distinguishing morally between tobacco and cocaine is "little more than a transient prejudice" is close to saying that morality itself is but a prejudice.

The Alcohol Problem

Now we have arrived where many arguments about legalizing drugs begin: is there any reason to treat heroin and cocaine differently from the way we treat alcohol?

There is no easy answer to that question because, as with so many human problems, one cannot decide simply on the basis either of moral principles or of individual consequences; one has to temper any policy by a commonsense judgment of what is possible. Alcohol, like heroin, cocaine, PCP, and marijuana, is a drug—that is, a mood-altering substance—and consumed to excess it certainly has harmful consequences: auto accidents, barroom fights, bedroom shootings. It is also, for some people, addictive. We cannot confidently compare the addictive powers of these drugs, but the best evidence suggests that crack and heroin are much more addictive than alcohol.

Many people, Nadelmann included, argue that since the health and financial costs of alcohol abuse are so much higher than those of cocaine or heroin abuse, it is hypocritical folly to devote our efforts to preventing cocaine or drug use. But as Mark Kleiman of Harvard has pointed out, this comparison is quite misleading. What Nadelmann is doing is showing that a *legalized* drug (alcohol) produces greater social harm than *illegal* ones (cocaine and heroin). But of course. Suppose that in the 1920's we had made heroin and cocaine legal and alcohol illegal. Can anyone doubt that Nadelmann would now be writing that it is folly to continue our ban on alcohol because cocaine and heroin are so much more harmful?

And let there be no doubt about it—widespread heroin and cocaine use are associated with all manner of ills. Thomas Bewley found that the mortality rate of British heroin addicts in 1968 was 28 times as high as the death rate of the same age group of non-addicts, even though in England at the time an addict could obtain free or low-cost heroin and clean needles from British clinics. Perform the following mental experiment: suppose we legalized heroin and cocaine in this country. In what proportion of auto fatalities would the state police report that the driver was nodding off on heroin or recklessly driving on a coke high? In what proportion of spouse-assault and child-abuse cases would the local police report that crack was involved? In what proportion of industrial accidents would safety investigators report that the forklift or drill-press operator was in a drug-induced stupor or frenzy? We do not know exactly what the proportion would be, but anyone who asserts that it would not be much higher than it is now would have to believe that these drugs have little appeal except when they are illegal. And that is nonsense.

An advocate of legalization might concede that social harm—perhaps harm equivalent to that already produced by alcohol—would follow from making cocaine and heroin generally available. But at least, he might add, we would have the problem "out in the open" where it could be treated as a matter of "public health." That is well and good, *if* we knew how to treat—that is, cure—heroin and cocaine abuse. But we do not know how to do it for all the people who would need such help. We are having only limited success in coping with chronic alcoholics. Addictive behavior is immensely difficult to change, and the best methods for changing it—living in drug-free therapeutic communities, becoming faithful members of Alcoholics Anonymous or Narcotics Anonymous—require great personal commitment, a quality that is, alas, in short supply among the very persons—young people, disadvantaged people—who are often most at risk for addiction.

Suppose that today we had, not 15 million alcohol abusers, but half a million. Suppose that we already knew what we have learned from our long experience with the widespread use of alcohol. Would we make whiskey legal? I do not know, but I suspect there would be a lively debate. The Surgeon General would remind us of the risks alcohol poses to pregnant women. The National Highway Traffic Safety Administration would point to the likelihood of more highway fatalities caused by drunk drivers. The Food and Drug Administration might find that there is a non-trivial increase in cancer associated with alcohol consumption. At the same time the police would report great difficulty in keeping illegal whiskey out of our cities, officers being corrupted by bootleggers, and alcohol addicts often resorting to crime to feed their habit. Libertarians, for their part, would argue that every citizen has a right to drink anything he wishes and that drinking is, in any event, a "victimless crime."

However the debate might turn out, the central fact would be that the problem was still, at that point, a small one. The government cannot legislate away the addictive tendencies in all of us, nor can it remove completely even the most dangerous addictive substances. But it can cope with harms when the harms are still manageable.

Science and Addiction

One advantage of containing a problem while it is still containable is that it buys time for science to learn more about it and perhaps to discover a cure. Almost unnoticed in the current debate over legalizing drugs is that basic science has made rapid strides in identifying the underlying neurological processes involved in some forms of addiction. Stimulants such as cocaine and amphetamines alter the way certain brain cells communicate with one another. That alteration is complex and not entirely understood, but in simplified form it involves modifying the way in which a neurotransmitter called dopamine sends signals from one cell to another.

When dopamine crosses the synapse between two cells, it is in effect carrying a message from the first cell to activate the second one. In certain parts of the brain that message is experienced as pleasure. After the message is delivered, the dopamine returns to the first cell. Cocaine apparently blocks this return, or "reuptake," so that the excited cell and others nearby continue to send pleasure messages. When the exaggerated high produced by cocaine-influenced dopamine finally ends, the brain cells may (in ways that are still a matter of dispute) suffer from an extreme lack of dopamine, thereby making the individual unable to experience any pleasure at all. This would explain why cocaine users often feel so depressed after enjoying the drug. Stimulants may also affect the way in which other neurotransmitters, such as serotonin and noradrenaline, operate.

Whatever the exact mechanism may be, once it is identified it becomes possible to use drugs to block either the effect of cocaine or its tendency to produce dependency. There have already been experiments using desipramine, imipramine, bromocriptine, carbamazepine, and other chemicals. There are some promising results.

Tragically, we spend very little on such research, and the agencies funding it have not in the past occupied very influential or visible posts in the federal bureaucracy. If there is one aspect of the "war on drugs" metaphor that I dislike, it is its tendency to focus attention almost exclusively on the troops in the trenches, whether engaged in enforcement or treatment, and away from the research-and-development efforts back on the home front where the war may ultimately be decided.

I believe that the prospects of scientists in controlling addiction will be strongly influenced by the size and character of the problem they face. If the problem is a few hundred thousand chronic, high-dose users of an illegal product, the chances of making a difference at a reasonable cost will be much greater than if the problem is a few million chronic users of legal substances. Once a drug is legal, not only will its use increase but many of those who then use it will prefer the drug to the treatment: they will want the pleasure, whatever the cost to themselves or their families, and they will resist—probably successfully—any effort to wean them away from experiencing the high that comes from inhaling a legal substance.

If I Am Wrong . . .

No one can know what our society would be like if we changed the law to make access to cocaine, heroin, and PCP easier. I believe, for reasons given, that the result would be a sharp increase in use, a more widespread degradation of the human personality, and a greater rate of accidents and violence.

I may be wrong. If I am, then we will needlessly have incurred heavy costs in law enforcement and some forms of criminality. But if I am right, and the legalizers prevail anyway, then we will have consigned millions of people, hundreds of thousands of infants, and hundreds of neighborhoods to a life of oblivion and disease. To the lives and families destroyed by alcohol we will have added countless more destroyed by cocaine, heroin, PCP, and whatever else a basement scientist can invent.

Human character is formed by society; indeed, human character is inconceivable without society, and good character is less likely in a bad society. Will we, in the name of an abstract doctrine of radical individualism, and with the false comfort of suspect predictions, decide to take the chance that somehow individual decency can survive amid a more general level of degradation?

I think not. The American people are too wise for that, whatever the academic essayists and cocktail-party pundits may say. But if Americans today are less wise than I suppose, then Americans at some future time will look back on us now and wonder, what kind of people were they that they could have done such a thing?

FRAME the DEBATE

Form at end of book

Issue 8: Should we decriminalize drugs?

Should We Legalize Drugs? History Answers Yes.

Ethan A. Nadelmann

Ethan A. Nadelmann is assistant professor of politics and public affairs in the Woodrow Wilson School and the Department of Politics at Princeton University. He chairs the Princeton Working Group on the Future of Drug Use and Alternatives to Drug Prohibition.

The better title for this article, let me suggest at the outset, would be "Drug Prohibition: Con." Most opponents of "drug legalization" assume that it would involve making cocaine and heroin available the way alcohol and tobacco are today. But most legalization supporters favor nothing of the kind; in fact, we disagree widely as to which drugs should be legalized, how they should be controlled, and what the consequences are likely to be. Where drug-policy reformers do agree is in our critique of the drug-prohibition system that has evolved in the United States—a system, we contend, that has proved ineffective, costly, counterproductive, and immoral.

Efforts to reverse drug prohibition face formidable obstacles. Americans have grown accustomed to the status quo. Alcohol prohibition was overturned before most citizens had forgotten what a legal alcohol policy was like, but who today can recall a time before drug prohibition? Moreover, the United States has succeeded in promoting its drug-prohibition system throughout the world. Opponents of alcohol prohibition could look to successful foreign alcohol-control systems in Canada and much of Europe, but contemporary drug anti-prohibitionists must look further—to history.

The principal evidence, not surprisingly, is Prohibition. The dry years offer many useful analogies, but their most important lesson is the need to distinguish between the harms that stem from drugs and the harms that arise from outlawing them. The Americans who voted in 1933 to repeal Prohibition differed greatly in their reasons for overturning the system. They almost all agreed, however, that the evils of alcohol consumption had been surpassed by those of trying to suppress it.

Some pointed to Al Capone and rising crime, violence, and corruption: others to the overflowing courts, jails, and prisons, the labeling of tens of millions of Americans as criminals and the consequent broadening disrespect for the law, the dangerous expansions of federal police powers and encroachments on individual liberties, the hundreds of thousands of Americans blinded, paralyzed, and killed by poisonous moonshine and industrial alcohol, and the increasing government expenditure devoted to enforcing the Prohibition laws and the billions in foregone tax revenues. Supporters of Prohibition blamed the consumers, and some went so far as to argue that those who violated the laws deserved whatever ills befell them. But by 1933 most Americans blamed Prohibition.

If there is a single message that contemporary anti-prohibitionists seek to drive home, it is that drug prohibition is responsible for much of what Americans identify today as the "drug problem." It is not merely a matter of the direct costs—twenty billion dollars spent this year on arresting, prosecuting, and incarcerating drug-law violators. Choked courts and prisons, an incarceration rate higher than that of any other nation in the world, tax dollars diverted from education and health care, law-enforcement resources diverted from investigating everything from auto theft to savings-and-loan scams—all these are just a few of the costs our current prohibition imposes.

Consider also Capone's successors—the drug kingpins of Asia, Latin America, and the United States. Consider as well all the murders and assaults perpetrated by young drug dealers not just against one another but against police, witnesses, and bystanders. Consider the tremendous economic and social incentives generated by the illegality of the drug market—temptations so overwhelming that even "good kids" cannot resist them. Consider the violent drug dealers becoming the heroes of boys and young men, from Harlem to Medellin. And consider tens of millions of Americans being labeled criminals for doing nothing more than smoking a marijuana cigarette. In all these respects the consequences of drug prohibition imitate—and often exceed—those of alcohol prohibition.

Prohibition reminds us, too, of the health costs of drug prohibition.

"Should We Legalize Drugs? History Answers Yes" by Ethan A. Nadelmann from *American Heritage,* February/March 1993, pp. 42–48.

Sixty years ago some fifty thousand Americans were paralyzed after consuming an adulterated Jamaica ginger extract known as "jake." Today we have marijuana made more dangerous by government-sprayed paraquat and the chemicals added by drug dealers, heroin adulterated with poisonous powders, and assorted pills and capsules containing everything from antihistamines to strychnine. Indeed, virtually every illicit drug purchased at the retail level contains adulterants, at least some of which are far more dangerous than the drug itself. And restrictions on the sale of drug paraphernalia has, by encouraging intravenous drug addicts to share their equipment, severely handicapped efforts to stem the transmission of AIDS. As during Prohibition, many Americans view these ills as necessary and even desirable, but others, like their forebears sixty years ago, reject as perverse a system that degrades and destroys the very people it was designed to protect.

Prohibition's lessons extend in other directions as well. The current revisionist twist on that "Great Experiment" now claims that "Prohibition worked" by reducing alcohol consumption and alcohol-related ills ranging from cirrhosis to public drunkenness and employee absenteeism. There is some truth to this claim. But in fact, the most dramatic decline in American alcohol consumption occurred not between 1920 and 1933, while the Eighteenth Amendment was in effect, but rather between 1916 and 1922. During those years the temperance movement was highly active and successful in publicizing the dangers of alcohol. The First World War's spirit of self-sacrifice extended to temperance as a means of grain conservation, and there arose, as the historian David Kyvig puts it, "an atmosphere of hostility toward all things German, not the least of which was beer." In short, a great variety of factors coalesced in this brief time to substantially reduce alcohol consumption and its ills.

The very evidence on which pro-prohibition historians rely provides further proof of the importance of factors other than prohibition laws. One of these historians, John Burnham, has noted that the admission rate for alcohol psychoses to New York hospitals shrank from 10 percent between 1909 and 1912 to 1.9 percent in 1920—a decline that occurred largely before national prohibition and in a state that had not enacted its own prohibition law.

At best one can argue that Prohibition was most effective in its first years, when temperance norms remained strong and illicit sources of production had yet to be firmly established. By all accounts, alcohol consumption rose after those first years—despite increased resources devoted to enforcement. The pre-Prohibition decline in consumption, like the recent decline in cigarette consumption, had less to do with laws than with changing norms and the imposition of non-criminal-justice measures.

Perhaps the most telling indictment of Prohibition is provided by the British experience with alcohol control during a similar period. In the United States the death rate from cirrhosis of the liver dropped from as high as 10 per 100,000 population between 1910 and 1914 to 7 during the twenties only to climb back to pre-1910 levels by the 1960s, while in Britain the death rate from cirrhosis dropped from 10 in 1914 to 5 in 1920 and then gradually declined to a low of 2 in the 1940s before rising by a mere point by 1963. Other indicators of alcohol consumption and misuse dropped by similar magnitudes, even though the United Kingdom never enacted prohibition. Instead wartime Britain restricted the amount of alcohol available, taxed it, and drastically reduced the hours of sale. At war's end the government dropped restrictions on quantity but made taxes even higher and set hours of sale at only half the pre-war norm.

Britain thus not only reduced the negative consequences of alcohol consumption more effectively than did the United States but did so in a manner that raised substantial government revenues. The British experience—as well as Australia's and most of continental Europe's—strongly suggests not only that our Prohibition was unsuccessful but that more effective post-Repeal controls might have prevented the return to high consumption levels.

But no matter how powerful the analogies between alcohol prohibition and contemporary drug prohibition, most Americans still balk at drawing the parallels. Alcohol, they insist, is fundamentally different from everything else. They are right, of course, insofar as their claims rest not on health or scientific grounds but are limited to political and cultural arguments. By most measures, alcohol is more dangerous to human health than any of the drugs now prohibited by law. No drug is as associated with violence in American culture—and even in illicit-drug-using subcultures—as is alcohol. One would be hard pressed to argue that its role in many Native American and other aboriginal communities has been any less destructive than that of illicit drugs in America's ghettos.

The dangers of all drugs vary greatly, of course, depending not just on their pharmacological properties and how they are consumed but also on the attitudes and beliefs of their users and the settings in which they use them. Alcohol by and large plays a benign role in Jewish and Asian-American cultures but a devastating one in some Native American societies, and by the same token the impact of cocaine among "Yuppies" during the early 1980s was relatively benign compared with its impact a few years later in impoverished ghettos.

The culture helps determine the setting of drug use, but so do the laws. Prohibitions enhance the dangers not just of drugs but of the settings in which they are used. The relationship between prohibition and dangerous adulterations is clear. So too is its impact on the potency and forms of drugs. For instance, Prohibition caused a striking drop in the production and sale of beer, while that of hard liquor increased as bootleggers from Al Capone on down sought to maximize their profits and minimize the risks of detection. Similarly, following the Second World War, the enactment of anti-opium laws in many parts of Asia in which opium use was traditional—India, Hong Kong, Thailand, Laos, Iran—effectively suppressed the availability of opium at the cost of stimulating the creation of domestic heroin industries and substantial increases in heroin use. The same transition had occurred in the United States following Congress's ban on opium imports in 1909. And when during the 1980s the U.S. government's domestic drug enforcement efforts significantly reduced the availability and raised the price of marijuana, they provided decisive incentives to producers, distributors, and consumers to switch to cocaine. In each case, prohibition forced switches from drugs that were bulky and relatively benign to drugs that were more compact, more lucrative, more potent, and more dangerous.

In the 1980s the retail purity of heroin and cocaine increased and highly potent crack became cheaply available in American cities. At the same time, the average potency of most legal psychoactive substances declined: Americans began switching from hard liquor to beer and wine, from high-tar and nicotine to lower tar-and-nicotine cigarettes, and even from caffeinated to decaffeinated coffee and soda. The relationship between prohibition and drug potency was, if not indisputable, still readily apparent.

In turn-of-the century America, opium, morphine, heroin, cocaine, and marijuana were subject to few restrictions. Popular tonics such as Vin Mariani and Coca-Cola and its competitors were laced with cocaine, and hundreds of medicines—Mrs. Winslow's Soothing Syrup may have been the most famous—contained psychoactive drugs. Millions, perhaps tens of millions of Americans, took opiates and cocaine. David Courtwright estimates that during the 1890s as many as one-third of a million Americans were opiate addicts, but most of them were ordinary people who would today be described as occasional users.

Careful analysis of that era—when the very drugs that we most fear were widely and cheaply available throughout the country—provides a telling antidote to our nightmare legalization scenarios. For one thing, despite the virtual absence of any controls on availability, the proportion of Americans addicted to opiates was only two or three times greater than today. For another, the typical addict was not a young black ghetto resident but a middle-aged white Southern woman or a West Coast Chinese immigrant. The violence, death, disease, and crime that we today associate with drug use barely existed, and many medical authorities regarded opiate addiction as far less destructive than alcoholism (some doctors even prescribed the former as treatment for the latter). Many opiate addicts, perhaps most, managed to lead relatively normal lives and kept their addictions secret even from close friends and relatives. That they were able to do so was largely a function of the legal status of their drug use.

But even more reassuring is the fact that the major causes of opiate addiction then simply do not exist now. Late nineteenth-century Americans became addicts principally at the hands of physicians who lacked modern medicines and were unaware of the addictive potential of the drugs they prescribed. Doctors in the 1860s and 1870s saw morphine injections as a virtual panacea, and many Americans turned to opiates to alleviate their aches and pains without going through doctors at all. But as medicine advanced, the levels of both doctor- and self-induced addiction declined markedly.

In 1906 the first Federal Pure Food and Drug Act required over-the-counter drug producers to disclose whether their products contained any opiates, cocaine, cannabis, alcohol, or other psychoactive ingredients. Sales of patent medicines containing opiates and cocaine decreased significantly thereafter—in good part because fewer Americans were interested in purchasing products that they now knew to contain those drugs.

Consider the lesson here. Ethical debates aside, the principal objection to all drug legalization proposals is that they invite higher levels of drug use and misuse by making drugs not just legal but more available and less expensive. Yet the late-nineteenth-century experience suggests the opposite: that in a legal market most consumers will prefer lower-potency coca and opiate products to the far more powerful concoctions that have virtually monopolized the market under prohibition. This reminds us that opiate addiction per se was not necessarily a serious problem so long as addicts had ready access to modestly priced opiates of reliable quality—indeed, that the opiate addicts of late-nineteenth century America differed in no significant respects from the cigarette-addicted consumers of today. And it reassures us that the principal cause of addiction to opiates was not the desire to get high but rather ignorance—ignorance of their addictive qualities, ignorance of the alternative analgesics, and ignorance of what exactly patent medicines contained. The antidote to addiction in late-nineteenth century America, the historical record shows, consisted primarily of education and regulation—not prohibition, drug wars, and jail.

Why then was drug prohibition instituted? And why did it quickly evolve into a fierce and highly punitive set of policies rather than follow the more modest and humane path pursued by the British? In part, the passage of the federal Harrison Narcotic Act, in 1914, and of state and local bans before and after that, reflected a belated response to the recognition that people could easily become addicted to opiates and cocaine. But it also was closely intertwined with the increasingly vigorous efforts of doctors and pharmacists to professionalize their disciplines and to monopolize the public's access to medicinal drugs. Most of all, though, the institution of drug prohibition reflected the changing nature of the opiate- and cocaine-using population. By 1914 the number of middle-class Americans blithely consuming narcotics had fallen sharply. At the same time, however, opiate and cocaine use had become increasingly popular among the lower classes and racial minorities. The total number of consumers did not approach that of earlier decades, but where popular opinion had once shied from the notion of criminalizing the habits of elderly white women, few such inhibitions impeded it where urban gamblers, prostitutes, and delinquents were concerned.

The first anti-opium laws were passed in California in the 1870s and directed at the Chinese immigrants and their opium dens, in which, it was feared, young white women were being seduced. A generation later reports of rising cocaine use among young black men in the South—who were said to rape white women while under the influence—prompted similar legislation. During the 1930s marijuana prohibitions were directed in good part at Mexican and Chicano workers who had lost their jobs in the Depression. And fifty years later draconian penalties were imposed for the possession of tiny amounts of crack cocaine—a drug associated principally with young Latino and African-Americans.

But more than racist fears was at work during the early years of drug prohibition. In the aftermath of World War I, many Americans, stunned by the triumph of Bolshevism in Russia and fearful of domestic subversion, turned their backs on the liberalizing reforms of the preceding era. In such an atmosphere the very notion of tolerating drug use or maintaining addicts in the clinics that had arisen after 1914 struck most citizens as both immoral and unpatriotic. In 1919 the mayor of New York created the Committee on Public Safety to Investigate two ostensibly related problems: revolutionary bombings and heroin use among youth. And in Washington that same year, the Supreme Court effectively foreclosed any possibility of a more humane policy toward drug addicts when it held, in *Webb et al. vs. U.S.*, that doctors could not legally prescribe maintenance supplies of narcotics to addicts.

But perhaps most important, the imposition of drug prohibition cannot be understood without recalling that it occurred almost simultaneously with the advent of alcohol prohibition. Contemporary Americans tend to regard Prohibition as a strange quirk in American history—and drug prohibition as entirely natural and beneficial. Yet the prohibition against alcohol, like that against other drugs, was motivated in no small part by its association with feared and despised ethnic minorities, especially the masses of Eastern and Southern European immigrants.

Why was Prohibition repealed after just thirteen years while drug prohibition has lasted for more than seventy-five? Look at whom each disadvantaged. Alcohol prohibition struck directly at tens of millions of Americans of all ages, including many of society's most powerful members. Drug prohibition threatened far fewer Americans, and they had relatively little influence in the halls of power. Only the prohibition of marijuana, which some sixty million Americans have violated since 1965, has come close to approximating the Prohibition experience, but marijuana smokers consist mostly of young and relatively powerless Americans. In the final analysis alcohol prohibition was repealed, and opiate, cocaine, and marijuana prohibition retained, not because scientists had concluded that alcohol was the least dangerous of the various psychoactive drugs but because of the prejudices and preferences of most Americans.

There was, of course, one other important reason why Prohibition was repealed when it was. With the country four years into the Depression, Prohibition increasingly appeared not just foolish but costly. Fewer and fewer Americans were keen on paying the rising costs of enforcing its laws, and more and more recalled the substantial tax revenues that the legal alcohol business had generated. The potential analogy to the current recession is unfortunate but apt. During the late 1980s the cost of building and maintaining prisons emerged as the fastest-growing item in many state budgets, while other costs of the war on drugs also rose dramatically. One cannot help wondering how much longer Americans will be eager to foot the bills for all this.

Throughout history the legal and moral status of psychoactive drugs has kept changing. During the seventeenth century the sale and consumption of tobacco were punished by as much as death in much of Europe, Russia, China, and Japan. For centuries many of the same Muslim domains that forbade the sale and consumption of alcohol simultaneously tolerated and even regulated the sale of opium and cannabis.

Drug-related moralities have always been malleable, and their evolution can in no way be described as moral progress. Just as our moral perceptions of particular drugs have changed in the past, so will they in the future, and people will continue to circumvent the legal and moral barriers that remain. My confidence in this prediction stems from one other lesson of civilized human history. From the dawn of time humans have nearly universally shown a desire to alter their states of consciousness with psychoactive substances, and it is this fact that gives the lie to the declared objective of creating a "drug-free society" in the United States.

Another thing common to all societies, as the social theorist Thomas Szasz argued some years ago, is that they require scapegoats to embody their fears and take blame for whatever ails them. Today the role of bogeyman is applied to drug producers, dealers, and users. Just as anti-Communist propagandists once feared Moscow far beyond its actual influence and appeal, so today antidrug proselytizers indict marijuana, cocaine, heroin, and assorted hallucinogens far beyond their actual psychoactive effects and psychological appeal. Never mind that the vast majority of Americans have expressed—in one public-opinion poll after another—little interest in trying these substances, even if they were legal, and never mind that most of those who have tried them have suffered few, if any, ill effects. The evidence of history and of science is drowned out by today's bogeymen. No rhetoric is too harsh, no penalty too severe.

Lest I be accused of exaggerating, consider the following. On June 27, 1991, the Supreme Court upheld, by a vote of five to four, a Michigan statute that imposed a mandatory sentence of life without possibility of parole for anyone convicted of possession of more than 650 grams (about 1.5 pounds) of cocaine. In other words, an activity that was entirely legal at the turn of the century, and that poses a danger to society roughly comparable to that posed by the sale of alcohol and tobacco, is today treated the same as first-degree murder.

The cumulative result of our prohibitionist war is that roughly 20 to 25 percent of the more than one million Americans now incarcerated in federal and state prisons and local jails, and almost half of those in federal penitentiaries, are serving time for having engaged in an activity that their great-grandparents could have pursued entirely legally.

Examples of less striking, but sometimes more deadly, penalties also abound. In many states anyone convicted of possession of a single marijuana joint can have his or her driver's license revoked for six months and be required to participate in a drug-treatment program. In many states anyone caught cultivating a marijuana plant may find all his or her property forfeited to the local police department. And in all but a few cities needle-exchange programs to reduce the transmission of AIDS among drug addicts have been rejected because they would "send the wrong message"—as if the more moral message is that such addicts are better off contracting the deadly virus and spreading it.

Precedents for each of these penalties scarcely exist in American history. The restoration of criminal forfeiture of property—rejected by the Founding Fathers because of its association with the evils of English rule—could not have found its way back into American law but for the popular desire to give substance to the rhetorical war on drugs.

Of course, changes in current policy that make legally available to adult Americans many of the now prohibited psychoactive substances are bound to entail a litany of administrative problems and certain other risks.

During the last years of the Volstead Act, the Rockefeller Foundation commissioned a study by the leading police scholar in the United States, Raymond Fosdick, to evaluate the various alternatives to Prohibition. Its analyses and recommendations ultimately played an important role in constructing post-Prohibition regulatory policies. A comparable study is currently under way at Princeton University, where the Smart Family Foundation has funded a working group of scholars from diverse disciplines to evaluate and recommend alternative drug-control policies. Its report will be completed late in 1993.

History holds one final lesson for those who cannot imagine any future beyond drug prohibition. Until well into the 1920s most Americans regarded Prohibition as a permanent fact of life. As late as 1930 Sen. Morris Shepard of Texas, who had coauthored the Prohibition Amendment, confidently asserted: "There is as much chance of repealing the Eighteenth Amendment as there is for a hummingbird to fly to the planet Mars with the Washington Monument tied to its tail."

History reminds us that things can and do change, that what seems inconceivable today can seem entirely normal, and even inevitable, a few years hence. So it was with Prohibition, and so it is—and will be—both with drug prohibition and the ever-changing nature of drug use in America.

FRAME the DEBATE

Form at end of book

WiseGuide Wrap-Up

Many issues must be addressed and numerous challenges faced if drugs are to be decriminalized. The idea of decriminalizing narcotics is frightening to most people. However, we must consider that drug use is not a rare event.

If drugs were decriminalized, would many of the current laws regarding alcohol suffice to deal with those under the influence? Would we need new laws and tougher sanctions for those who couldn't responsibly use drugs? Even if drugs were decriminalized, stringent regulations would surely monitor their distribution and consumption.

The questions are tough, and the implications are profound. Perhaps as certain communities (such as California with medical marijuana) gradually reintegrate drugs into their environment, the long-term effects of drugs on individuals and communities can be studied. However, controlling for rampant drug use throughout the United States will be a challenging methodological task for criminologists as they study the impact of decriminalization of drugs on society.

R.E.A.L. Sites

This list provides a print preview of typical **Coursewise** R.E.A.L. sites. (There are over 100 such sites at the **Courselinks**™ site.) The danger in printing URLs is that web sites can change overnight. As we went to press, these sites were functional using the URLs provided. If you come across one that isn't, please let us know via email to: webmaster@coursewise.com. Use your Passport to access the most current list of R.E.A.L. sites at the **Courselinks** site.

Site name: Office of National Drug Control Policy (ONDCP)
URL: http://www.whitehousedrugpolicy.gov/
Why is it R.E.A.L.? This site has drug facts and figures, as well as the national drug control policy. Many resources are available at this site.
Key topic: drugs
Try this: Read the National Drug Control Strategy to see what the government is doing to combat drugs in America.

Site name: Drug Enforcement Agency
URL: http://www.usdoj.gov/dea/index.htm
Why is it R.E.A.L.? Gain a greater understanding of the Drug Enforcement Agency by visiting its web site. Data on drug usage and narcotics seizures are also available at this site.
Key topics: federal law enforcement agency, drugs
Try this: Review the schedules of controlled substances.

Site name: National Clearinghouse for Alcohol and Drug Information
URL: http://www.health.org/
Why is it R.E.A.L.? This site provides information about alcohol and substance abuse, with links to online research and resources.
Key topic: drugs
Try this: Read reports at this site on alcohol and drug use.

Site name: National Institute on Drug Abuse

URL: http://www.nida.nih.gov/

Why is it R.E.A.L.? The National Institute on Drug Abuse has numerous documents related to substance abuse and public policy at its web site.

Key topic: drugs

Try this: Read about alcohol and drug use by students in eighth, tenth, and twelfth grades in the "Monitoring the Future" study.

Should Drug Pushers Lose Their Property?

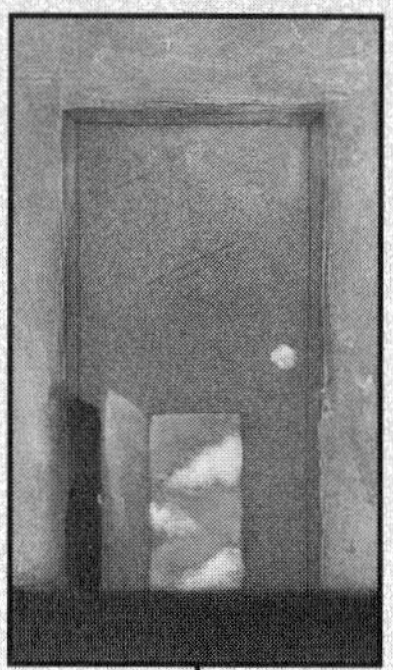

ISSUE 9

Take a Closer Look

1. Do you support forfeiture laws that allow the government to take away a person's property even if he or she is never convicted of a crime?
2. Should forfeiture laws be expanded to many other types of crimes?
3. What are the parameters of asset forfeiture laws, as explained by Schroeder?
4. According to Jensen and Gerber, what constitutional protections do asset forfeiture laws limit?

WiseGuide Intro

In a society with a healthy and responsible criminal justice system, most people would not object to drug dealers forfeiting property gained in connection with drug sales. However, we do not have such a system of justice, and to further complicate issues, many of the forfeiture laws are problematic at best.

William Schroeder's article, "Civil Forfeiture: Recent Supreme Court Cases," was written on behalf of the Federal Bureau of Investigation and law enforcement agencies across the United States. Schroeder's policy guideline provides moral support and the legal guidance necessary for law enforcement agencies to use asset forfeiture as a weapon in the war against drugs.

In "The Civil Forfeiture of Assets and the War on Drugs: Expanding Criminal Sanctions While Reducing Due Process Protections," Eric Jensen and Jurg Gerber argue that civil forfeiture actions proceed without the protection of an offender's due process privileges. They also find it troubling that a different set of standards is applied in asset forfeiture cases than in criminal proceedings.

READING 17

Issue 9: Should drug pushers lose their property?

Civil Forfeiture: Recent Supreme Court Cases

William R. Schroeder, J.D.

On February 12, 1996, the Attorney General of the United States issued a directive that urged all federal prosecutors and agents of the Federal Bureau of Investigation (FBI), Drug Enforcement Administration (DEA), and Immigration and Naturalization Service (INS) to reinvigorate their efforts in using asset forfeiture as a law enforcement tool. The Attorney General sought this additional commitment because asset forfeiture has proven to be one of the most effective methods available in the continuing battle against major drug traffickers, organized crime figures, and their criminal organizations. As the Attorney General pointed out in the directive, the failure to attack the economic infrastructure of criminals and their organizations seriously limits the effect that any prosecution of these criminals would have on improving the safety and welfare of the American public.[1]

A decline in the use of asset forfeiture by federal law enforcement over the past 2 years prompted this reinvigoration effort. Although a number of factors contributed to this decline, the loss of asset forfeiture's effectiveness in addressing serious crime and criminals is not one of them.

The forfeiture of property stifles the goals of those who, motivated by greed, engage in criminal activity. Forfeiture takes the profit out of crime, deprives the criminal of the money essential to finance future criminal conduct, and works to dismantle the financial underpinnings of the criminal organization.

This article discusses two recent Supreme Court cases affecting the use of civil forfeiture. The first case addresses one of the major reasons for the downward spiral in the use of asset forfeiture—the concern over double jeopardy. The second case addresses another issue that has contributed to the decline—the perception that civil forfeiture is unfair.

Double Jeopardy

One major reason for the decline in asset forfeiture has been the concern that its use may bar subsequent criminal prosecution. Civil forfeiture, unlike its criminal counterpart, involves procedures that allow pretrial seizure of assets, requires a relatively low burden of proof on the part of the government, and is not contingent on an owner's conviction. These factors lead to the basis for the concern—whether the combination of criminal prosecution and civil forfeiture may be successive punishment for the same crime, in violation of the Double Jeopardy Clause of the fifth amendment.

In the past 2 years, a significant number of opinions issued by the courts focused on this dilemma.[2] Two lower court rulings, in particular, led to the Supreme Court decision regarding double jeopardy discussed in this article. An adverse decision by the Court could have freed hundreds of drug dealers across the United States, required the return of millions of dollars of ill-gotten gain,[3] and prevented the future use of one of the most important law enforcement tools available to attack the organizational infrastructure of criminal cartels.

Lower Court Holdings

In September 1994, the U.S. Court of Appeals for the Ninth Circuit reversed a forfeiture order against various properties valued at approximately $1 million that had been seized from convicted methamphetamine dealers.[4] The court found that the civil forfeiture of drug proceeds and property used in money laundering,[5] which followed the dealers' convictions on drug trafficking and money laundering charges, constituted "punishment" under the Double Jeopardy Clause of the fifth amendment.[6]

The court based its finding in large measure on two recent Supreme Court decisions, one involving double jeopardy and the other involving the Excessive Fines Clause of the eighth amendment.[7] Both of these cases involved findings by the Court that certain government civil sanctions, despite the "civil" label, could constitute punishment under the Constitution and, therefore, require greater protections. The Ninth Circuit panel reasoned that because the civil forfeiture action was the second

"Civil Forfeiture: Recent Supreme Court Cases" by William R. Schroeder, J.D., from *FBI Law Enforcement Bulletin*, October 1996, pp. 28–32. Reprinted by permission.

punishment imposed for the same offense, the Double Jeopardy Clause required them to reverse the forfeiture order and return the property.[8]

In the other case, decided by the U.S. Court of Appeals for the Sixth Circuit, the government and Guy Ursery had agreed to settle a forfeiture action filed against his residence after the Michigan State Police discovered marijuana and marijuana-growing paraphernalia at the residence.[9] After the property, which had been used to facilitate the unlawful distribution of a controlled substance, was forfeited under federal drug laws,[10] Ursery was convicted of manufacturing marijuana and sentenced to 5 years' imprisonment. The appellate court reversed Ursery's conviction,[11] concluding that the Double Jeopardy Clause of the fifth amendment protects against multiple punishments and prohibits the government from punishing twice for the same offense.[12]

Supreme Court Finds Civil Forfeiture Is Remedial, Not Punitive

In *United States v. Ursery,*[13] a decision filed on June 24, 1996, the U.S. Supreme Court resolved the concern over double jeopardy in favor of law enforcement. The Court consolidated the two lower court cases for purposes of its opinion and, in an 8-to-1 ruling, demonstrated a strong consensus regarding the role of civil forfeiture in law enforcement.

In reversing both lower court decisions, the Supreme Court ruled that the government could use, in combination, the criminal law to prosecute someone and the civil forfeiture laws to confiscate that person's property, even where both actions were based upon the same underlying criminal offense. The Court held these "in rem civil forfeitures are neither 'punishment' nor criminal for purposes of the Double Jeopardy Clause."[14] In its analysis, the Court reviewed "a long line of cases [in which the] Court has considered the application of the Double Jeopardy Clause to civil forfeitures, consistently concluding that the Clause does not apply to such actions because they do not impose punishment."[15] The Court concluded that for over 50 years, in rem forfeiture has been found to be a remedial sanction, distinct and different from other potentially punitive in personam civil penalties, and does not constitute a punishment under the Double Jeopardy Clause.[16]

In 1984, the Supreme Court established a two-stage analysis to determine whether a forfeiture was punishment under the Double Jeopardy Clause or was remedial in nature and not subject to the multiple punishment prong of the clause. This analysis focused on whether Congress intended to establish a civil remedial sanction and whether, despite such intent, the civil forfeiture was so punitive in purpose or effect that its application constituted punishment.[17] Because nothing in its decisions had replaced this traditional understanding,[18] the Court used this same two-staged analysis and concluded that the civil forfeiture actions in question were remedial.

In the first stage of its analysis, the Court found "there was little doubt" that the laws involved in the forfeiture actions in question were intended by Congress to be civil actions, distinct from criminal sanctions in personam.[19] The Court supported this finding with the fact that Congress incorporated the in rem procedures of the customs laws, which target the property rather than the owner and include procedures for administrative forfeiture actions.[20]

The finding that Congress intended the civil forfeitures in these cases to be in rem actions established a presumption that they do not implicate double jeopardy. The Court noted that when Congress has intended a forfeiture action to be civil and, therefore, remedial, only the "clearest proof" that it is "so punitive either in purpose or effect" will overcome the presumption that double jeopardy does not apply.[21]

. . . the Supreme Court ruled that the government could use, in combination, the criminal law to prosecute someone and the civil forfeiture laws to confiscate that person's property. . . .

In the second stage, the Court found little evidence that the forfeitures under these statutes were so punitive, in form or effect, to render them punishment. The Court stated that the most significant factor in reaching this conclusion was that such civil forfeitures serve important nonpunitive goals. The important goals of civil forfeiture include encouraging property owners to take greater care in managing their property, ensuring that owners will not permit their property to be used for illegal purposes, and ensuring that "persons do not profit from their illegal acts."[22]

Forfeiture of Jointly Owned Property Upheld

Another reason for the decline in the use of asset forfeiture is the troubling perception that civil forfeiture can be unfair. This perception is based, in part, on the fact that a civil forfeiture of property can be obtained against an owner who was not involved in or aware of the criminal activity in which the property was involved.

In *Bennis v. Michigan,*[23] the Supreme Court examined such a forfeiture action under the light of constitutional scrutiny and upheld the confiscation. In *Bennis,* the Court found that a state forfeiture law that permitted forfeiture of property from an owner who was unaware of its illegal use by another in lawful possession of the property did not offend the constitutional rights of that owner.

Detroit police had arrested John Bennis after observing him engaged in a sexual act with a prostitute in his car, which was jointly owned by Bennis and his wife. After Bennis was convicted of gross indecency, the state had the car declared a public nuisance and abated (forfeited) under state law.[24]

The Circuit Court of Wayne County rejected the wife's challenge to the forfeiture on the grounds that she was innocent of any wrongdoing and that she had no knowledge her husband would use the vehicle to violate the law. Subsequently, on appeal, the Michigan Supreme Court upheld the forfeiture, finding that the state law did not provide for an innocent owner defense, and therefore, the state did not need to prove the owner knew or agreed that the car would be used illegally.[25]

The U.S. Supreme Court reviewed the case in order to determine whether Michigan's forfeiture of the vehicle deprived the wife of her interest in the car without due process in violation of the 14th amendment, or if it amounted to a taking of her interest for public use without compensation in violation of the fifth amendment, as incorporated by the 14th amendment. The Court affirmed the decision of the Michigan Supreme Court and upheld the forfeiture.

"Innocent Owner" Defense

Citing a long and unbroken line of cases holding that an owner's interest in property may be forfeited by reason of the property's use, even though the owner was unaware of that use, the Court concluded that the issue is "too firmly fixed in the punitive and remedial jurisprudence of the country to be now displaced."[26] The Court relied on the rationale of earlier decisions to find that even though Mrs. Bennis did not know her car would be used illegally, its forfeiture by the state did not offend the Due Process Clause of the 14th amendment.[27] The holdings of the earlier cases cited by the Court have generally been based on the concept that in a civil forfeiture it is the property itself that is being held accountable for its illegal use and thus the "innocence" of the owner is not relevant.

In its decision, the Supreme Court noted that the innocence of an owner has almost uniformly been rejected as a defense to forfeiture.[28] Additionally, the Court has consistently upheld the forfeiture of property from owners "without guilt" because such laws furthered "the punitive and deterrent purposes" of the legislature in enacting laws that "may have the desirable effect of inducing them (owners) to exercise greater care in transferring possession of their property."[29] The Court answered the fifth amendment "taking" question raised by *Bennis* by finding that the government may not be required to compensate an owner for property that has been acquired through a civil forfeiture action.

The Court, in reaching its conclusion, noted that civil forfeiture imposes an economic penalty on illegal use that is neither unconstitutional nor unfair. The Court balanced the increased responsibility for property owners against the need to deter criminal conduct and decided in favor of law enforcement. In this regard, civil forfeiture is no different than other laws based on important public interest precepts.

. . . the innocence of an owner has almost uniformly been rejected as a defense to forfeiture.

Civil forfeiture of property serves both remedial and deterrent purposes that are distinct from any punishment that may result from criminal prosecution of the owner. Such forfeitures help prevent future illegal use and impose an economic disincentive, rendering the behavior unprofitable.

Conclusion

The decision by the Court in *Ursery* permits federal and state law enforcement to resume the seizure and forfeiture of property under the civil procedures without fear that such action will bar subsequent prosecution of the owner. It also provides a clear signal that the Supreme Court recognizes and supports the strong "nonpunitive goals" of civil forfeiture that serve law enforcement in combating crime.

The significance of *Bennis,* however, lies more in the rationale employed by the Court than in the outcome.[30] It was a precursor to the Court's analysis in *Ursery* and returned the historical perspective of in rem forfeiture actions that seemed to have been changed in *Austin v. United States.*[31]

The *Bennis* decision should not be seen, however, as an unqualified justification for forfeiture where the owner is known to be innocent of any wrongdoing. In *Bennis,* an associate justice in a concurring opinion warned that "[i]mproperly used, forfeiture could become more like a roulette wheel employed to raise revenue from innocent but hapless owners whose property is unforeseeably misused, or a tool wielded to punish those who associate with criminals, than a component of a system of justice." He noted that the Constitution assigns to states and federal agencies that use the forfeiture tool the primary responsibility for avoiding that unwanted result.[32] Failure to use this authority consistent with its purpose could result in legislative disapproval.

The seizure of property from one who is truly innocent does not serve the goals of civil forfeiture, i.e., taking the profit out of crime and acting as a deterrent to future criminal activity. In fact, Congress has provided an innocent owner exception to most federal civil forfeiture laws that would, under similar facts, have allowed Bennis to recover her interest in the car by showing her lack of knowledge of the intended illegal use of the vehicle by her wayward husband, and her lack of consent to that usage.[33]

As a result of these Supreme Court decisions, law enforcement is constitutionally permitted to use civil forfeiture, undeterred by double jeopardy concerns, to seek out and confiscate the ill-gotten gains of criminals and to dismantle their criminal organizations. Both federal and state law enforcement agencies working together will be able to use civil forfeiture to effectively take the profit out of crime and deter future criminal conduct motivated by greed.

Endnotes

1. Memorandum from Janet Reno, Attorney General, Louis J. Freeh, Director, FBI, and Thomas Constantine, Administrator, DEA, to all U.S. Attorneys, and others, dated Feb. 12, 1996.
2. *See, e.g., United States* v. *Tilley,* 18 F.3d 295 (5th Cir.) *cert. denied,* 115 S. Ct. 573 (1974) (forfeiture of drug proceeds does not constitute punishment); *United States* v. *Baird,* 63 F.3d 1213 (3d Cir. 1995) (administrative forfeiture does not implicate the Double Jeopardy Clause).
3. *United States* v. *$405,089.23 in U.S. Currency,* 56 F.3d 41 (9th Cir. 1995) (dissent from order rejecting rehearing en banc).
4. *See United States* v. *$405,089.23 in U.S. Currency,* 33 F.3d 1210 (9th Cir. 1994).
5. *See* 21 U.S.C. §881(a)(6) (forfeiture of property constituting or traceable to drug proceeds) and 18 U.S.C. §981(a)(1)(A) (property involved in money laundering).
6. "Nor shall any person be subject for the same offense to be twice put in jeopardy of life or limb. U.S. Constitution. Amend. V.
7. *See United States* v. *Halper,* 490 U.S. 435 (1989) (civil fine imposed for filing false medical claims following criminal prosecution on charges stemming from the same false claims could violate the Double Jeopardy Clause as a second punishment); *Austin* v. *United States,* 509 U.S. 602 (1993) (civil forfeiture of real and personal property under federal drug laws constitutes punishment for purposes of the eighth amendment and may violate the Excessive Fines Clause).
8. The Ninth Circuit denied a request by the Department of Justice (DOJ) for a rehearing *en banc.* In an unusual step, seven of the circuit judges filed a written dissent to the denial of the rehearing, disagreeing with the analysis and judgment of the other judges, stating that any departure from Supreme Court precedent upholding the remedial purpose served by civil forfeiture should be undertaken by the Supreme Court and not by the circuit court. *See United States* v. *$405,089.23 In U.S. Currency,* 56 F.3d 41 (9th Cir. 1995).
9. *United States* v. *Ursery,* 59 F.3d 568 (6th Cir. 1995).
10. 21 U.S.C. §881(a)(7) (forfeiture of real property used to commit a drug felony).
11. The district court denied Ursery's claim that the criminal conviction and sentence was a second punishment for the same drug offense in violation of double jeopardy.
12. *See Witte* v. *United States,* 115 S.Ct. 2199 (1995); *United States* v. *Dixon,* 509 U.S. 688 (1993).
13. *United States* v. *Ursery,* 116 S.Ct. 2134 (1996).
14. Id. at 2149.
15. Id. at 2140.
16. Id. at 2142. *See, e.g., Various Items of Personal Property* v. *United States,* 282 U.S. 577 (1931) (civil forfeiture is an action in rem against the property and no part of the punishment for the criminal offense that involves a prosecution in personam against the person).
17. *See United States* v. *One Assortment of 89 Firearms,* 465 U.S. 354 (1984).
18. "In sum, nothing in *Halper, Kurth Ranch,* or *Austin,* purported to replace our traditional understanding that civil forfeiture does not constitute punishment of the purpose of the Double Jeopardy Clause." Id at 2146–2147.
19. Id. at 2147. The laws under examination were 21 U.S.C. §881(a)(6) and (a)(7) and 18 U.S.C. §981(a)(1)(A).
20. "Congress specifically structured these forfeitures to be impersonal by targeting the property itself," Id. at 2147. The Court noted other mechanisms indicating Congress' intent that such actions be civil, including the shifting burden of proof in a civil forfeiture action once the government has shown probable cause that the property is forfeitable. Id. at 2147.
21. Id. n. 3, at 2148.
22. Id. at 2148. Secondarily relevant to its conclusion were the following: Civil in rem forfeiture has not historically been regarded as punishment; there is no requirement that the government show scienter in order to prove the property is forfeitable; these forfeitures act as a deterrent to future criminal conduct, which serves civil as well as criminal goals; the fact that a forfeiture statute has some connection to a criminal violation does not show that a proceeding is criminal. Id. at 2149.
23. 116 S.Ct. 994 (1996).
24. Michigan Comp. Laws Ann., §§600.3801, 600.3805, 600.3810(2).
25. Michigan law provides that "proof of knowledge of the existence of the nuisance on the part of the defendants or any of them, is not required." Mich. Comp. Laws Ann. §600.3815(2).
26. *Bennis* v. *Michigan,* at 1000 (citing *J. W. Goldsmith Jr. Grant Co. v. United States,* 254 U.S. 505 at 511).
27. *See* The Palmyra, 12 Wheat 1 (1827) (forfeiture of a ship used as privateer without the conviction of the owner); *Van Oster* v. *Kansas,* 272 U.S. 465.47 S. Ct. 133 (1926) (upholding the forfeiture of a car from an owner who had entrusted the vehicle to another who then used it to transport liquor in contravention of Kansas law); *Calero-Toledo* v. *Pearson Yacht Leasing Co.,* 416 U.S. 663.94 S.Ct. 2080 (1974) (upholding the forfeiture of a lessor's interest in a yacht used by the lessee to transport one marijuana cigarette in contravention of the laws of Puerto Rico).
28. *Bennis* v. *Michigan,* at 998 (citing *Calero-Toledo* v. *Pearson Yacht Leasing Co.,* at 683); 686 and 687–688.
29. *Calero-Toledo* v. *Pearson Yacht Leasing Co.,* at 686, 688.
30. The rationale used by the Court in *Bennis,* however, undermines the foundational basis for the constitutional "innocent owner" defense that began appearing in federal appellate court decisions shortly after *Calero-Toledo* v. *Pearson Yacht Leasing Co.* was decided. *See, e.g., United States* v. *One 1973 Buick Riviera Automobile,* 560 F.2d 897, 900-01 (8th Cir. 1977) (". . . the Court *may* have left open the possibility of an innocent owner raising a due process claim based on his innocence in certain narrow factual situations").

31. *See Austin* v. *United States,* at 616 ("In none of these cases did the Court apply the guilty-property fiction to justify forfeiture where the owner had done all that reasonably could be expected to prevent the unlawful use of his property.").
32. Justice Thomas, in his concurring opinion in *Bennis,* observed that it was not always clear what property could be forfeited under various forfeiture statutes. As a result, the limits of the law should be applied strictly, adhering to historical standards for determining whether specific property is "used" illegally.
33. *See, e.g.,* 21 U.S.C. §881(a)(4)(C) ("No conveyance shall be forfeited under this paragraph to the extent of an interest of an owner, by reason of any act or omission established by that owner to have been committed or omitted without the knowledge, consent, or willful blindness of the owner."). One notable exception is the authority to forfeit property that has been used in an interstate gambling business. *See* 18 U.S.C. §1955(d), but it is the official policy of the FBI not to seize property for forfeiture from innocent owners.

FRAME the DEBATE

Form at end of book

Issue 9: Should drug pushers lose their property?

The Civil Forfeiture of Assets and the War on Drugs:

Expanding Criminal Sanctions While Reducing Due Process Protections

The War on Drugs has resulted in some of the most extensive changes in criminal justice policy since the due process revolution of the 1960s. Asset forfeiture has been used as a criminal sanction but has been camouflaged as a civil procedure, thus in effect limiting the due process rights of those accused. The state has extended its control over citizens and has simultaneously weakened the rights of individuals to protect themselves against state intrusion. The potential for excess with a civil asset forfeiture policy absent adequate due process protections render this policy unacceptable in a society based on the rule of law.

Eric L. Jensen

Professor of Sociology, Department of Sociology/Anthropology, University of Idaho, Moscow, ID.

Jurg Gerber

Assistant Professor and Associate Dean for Undergraduate Studies, College of Criminal Justice, Sam Houston State University, Huntsville, TX.

The 1986 War on Drugs has resulted in some of the most extensive changes in criminal justice policy and the operations of the justice system in the United States since the due process revolution of the 1960s. Whereas the U.S. Supreme Court due process decisions of this earlier era sought to ensure protections of individuals against the authority of the state, the legacy of the War on Drugs has been the opposite; the powers of the state to intrude into the lives of individuals for the purpose of fighting the illegal drug trade have been expanded while due process protections against these punitive state actions have simultaneously been reduced.

The changes in criminal justice policy and the resulting effects on the justice system have been numerous: jurisdictions that decriminalized possession of cannabis products have "recriminalized" this behavior, more mandatory minimum sentences have been enacted for drug offenses, sentences for crack-related offenses have been enhanced, drug courts have been created, women's behaviors during pregnancy have been criminalized (Farr 1995), major increases in prison populations have been related to the punitive trend in drug law enforcement and sentencing practices (Gordon 1994), selected civilian law enforcement functions have been turned over to the military (Nadelmann 1993), and American anti-drug enforcement tactics have been internationalized (Levi and Osofsky 1995). Furthermore, the research has shown that these severe sanctions for drug offenses have fallen disproportionately on people of color (Gordon 1994).

In addition to these direct ramifications of the War on Drugs on criminal justice policy, the civil powers of the state have been expanded to fight the drug war. One of these actions is the use of child protection statutes to remove children from the custody of mothers accused of drug use during pregnancy (Farr 1995), and another is the civil seizure and

A revised version of this article was presented at the annual meeting of the American Society of Criminology, Phoenix, AZ, October 1993. The authors would like to thank Don C. Gibbons for his comments and suggestions.

"The Civil Forfeiture of Assets and the War on Drugs: Expanding Criminal Sanctions While Reducing Due Process Protections" by Eric L. Jensen and Jurg Gerber from *Crime & Delinquency*, Vol. 42, No. 3, July 1996. Reprinted by permission of Sage Publications.

forfeiture of assets allegedly related to illegal drug trafficking, which is the topic of this article.

The History of the Asset Forfeiture Policy

Asset forfeiture dates back at least to British common law. The legal basis of forfeiture in the United States is found in the British Navigation Acts of 1660. This legislation required that most commodities be shipped in English vessels. "Violations of the Acts resulted in the forfeiture of the illegally carried goods as well as the ship that transported them" (*Austin* v. *United States,* 43 S.Ct. 2801, 2807 [1993]). The 1990 Supplemental Rules for Certain Admiralty and Maritime Claims are based on these early maritime laws and provide the legal grounds for civil seizure and forfeiture proceedings today (Wilson 1991–1992).

The civil forfeiture of assets related to the illegal drug trade began with the Comprehensive Drug Abuse and Control Act of 1970. This legislation was enacted at a time when Congress was responding to the "crime wave" mentality of the late 1960s and early 1970s and in concert with the Nixon-era war on drugs. The original RICO statute (Organized Crime Control Act of 1970) that included civil forfeiture was also enacted at this time.

Both of these laws were based on a premise that organized crime and illegal drug trafficking were motivated by the economic rewards reaped from these illegal activities. Thus both were designed to deter the targeted crimes by reducing, if not eliminating, their economic rewards (Nelson 1992).

Compared to current policies, the drug-related asset forfeiture legislation was limited in scope as originally enacted in 1970. Section 881 of the Comprehensive Drug Abuse and Control Act stated that the following were forfeitable: all controlled substances, all raw materials and equipment used or intended for use in manufacturing illegal drugs, and all vehicles that are used or intended for use to distribute illicit drugs. This statute was not widely used in its first 10 years of existence. From its passage to 1979, less than $30 million in assets had been forfeited, while nearly the same amount was forfeited in 1985 alone (Nelson 1992, p. 1315).

In 1978, Congress greatly expanded the scope of drug-related asset forfeiture statutes with the addition of subsection (a)(6) to section 881. Forfeiture was extended to the following:

> All monies, negotiable instruments, securities, or other things of value furnished or intended to be furnished by any person in exchange for a controlled substance in violation of this [subchapter], all proceeds traceable to such an exchange, and all monies, negotiable instruments, and securities used or intended to be used to facilitate any violation of this subchapter. (21 U.S.C. §881[a][6] [1988])

Thus all profits from drug trafficking and all assets purchased with these profits became subject to forfeiture. The scope of the statute was further broadened substantially with the addition of all monies or financial instruments *intended* to be used in exchange for illegal drugs, a provision that allows "the forfeiture of property never actually involved with illegal activities" (Stahl 1992, p. 277). Following this change in the statute, forfeiture by the DEA increased 20 times over the previous year (Nelson 1992, pp. 1315–16).

In line with the developing Reagan-Bush War on Drugs, the statute was amended to add other assets in 1984. Subsection (a)(7) of section 881 added the following:

> All real property, including any right, title, and interest [including any leasehold interest] in the whole or any lot of land and any . . . improvements, which is used, or intended to be used, in any manner or part, to commit, or to facilitate the commission of, a violation of this title. (Comprehensive Crime Control Act of 1984, Public Law No. 98-473, § 306, 98 Stat. 1837, 2050)

All real property that was used in or intended to be used in a drug trafficking offense was now included in the forfeiture statute. Furthermore, as pointed out by Nelson (1992), "since there is no longer any state drug offense not covered by federal law, every drug offense under federal *or* state law, from simple possession to mass distribution, triggers the forfeiture statute" (p. 1318).

In addition to federal forfeiture policies, the individual states have also enacted asset forfeiture laws. The Bush administration advocated the passage of state civil forfeiture laws in its 1989 National Drug Strategy Report. The intended objectives of state statutes included the following: "Asset forfeiture laws should sanction both casual users and drug traffickers" (cited in Yoskowitz 1992, p. 570). By 1990, 49 states and the District of Columbia had statutes that allowed civil forfeiture of assets believed to be connected with illegal drug activity (Flanagan and Maguire 1992).

The Economic Returns from Forfeitures

With the expanded scope of drug-related asset forfeiture statutes in the 1984 legislation, the use of forfeitures increased dramatically. Asset forfeiture receipts grew from $27.2 million in fiscal year 1985 to $874 million in fiscal year 1992, nearly a fortyfold increase, before declining in 1993 and 1994 to approximately the 1991 level (see table 1). Drug-related forfeiture is obviously big business.

The Distribution of Forfeiture Receipts

With the expansion of asset forfeiture legislated in section 881(a)(7), the Department of Justice created the Asset Forfeiture Fund in 1985 (Stahl 1992). This fund is a depository and distribution mechanism for a substantial share of the assets seized. Noncash property may be held by the Department of Justice for investigative purposes or turned over to any law enforcement agency that directly participated in the seizure or forfeiture actions. The remaining property is sold, and proceeds are deposited in the Asset Forfeiture Fund (Nelson 1992, p. 1322).

The revenue in this fund can be distributed in a number of ways. Under the Department of Justice "equitable sharing" program, any law enforcement agency that participated in the seizure of assets may request part of the monies related to the action. In 1990, about 41% of the nearly 12,000 local law enforcement agencies in the nation participated in the equitable sharing program. Over 90% of the agencies serving jurisdictions with populations exceeding 250,000 received funding from the program in the same year. Furthermore, the proportion of funds transferred to state and local law enforcement agencies increased from 18% of forfeiture proceeds in 1986 to 43% in 1991 (Nelson 1992, pp. 1322–25). Monies in the Asset Forfeiture Fund are also used by the Federal Bureau of Prisons, by law enforcement for incidental expenses related to forfeitures and investigations, and for special federal drug enforcement activities as part of the National Drug Control Strategy (Nelson 1992, p. 1323).

State governments were apparently interested in the potential for generating revenue through asset forfeiture rather than fighting the drug war per se: "many states . . . do not funnel all or even most forfeiture proceeds back into law enforcement" (Nelson 1992, p. 1329). While California directed about 65% of the proceeds from drug-related asset forfeiture to law enforcement, other states such as Indiana and Missouri allocated all of the revenue obtained from this source to their state general funds (Nelson 1992, p. 1329).

Thus drug-related asset forfeiture represents a new, relatively unregulated source of revenue for federal, state, and local law enforcement agencies. It is our contention that this policy has created several serious procedural problems and has diminished the accountability of law enforcement.

Table 1 **Asset Forfeitures, 1985–1994**

Fiscal Year	Forfeiture Receipts (in millions of dollars)
1985	27.2
1986	93.7
1987	177.6
1988	207.3
1989	580.8
1990	459.6
1991	644.0
1992	874.9
1993	688.7
1994	649.7

Source: Nelson (1992, p. 1324), Maguire and Pastore (1994, p. 465), Maguire and Pastore (1995, p. 423).

Procedural Problems with Asset Forfeiture

A number of procedural problems have been identified by critics of this new policy. These problems include violations of constitutional protections and issues of procedural fairness.

In Rem Proceedings

The legal doctrine that allows the civil seizure and forfeiture of assets is *in rem*. Although criminal seizure of property is also possible, it can only take place after a criminal conviction. *In rem* proceedings are based on "an antiquated legal fiction" that can force property owners to forfeit their property despite the fact that criminal charges are never brought or that defendants are eventually acquitted of such charges (Yoskowitz 1992, p. 572). The state in effect sanctions a suspected offender by seizing the property itself, rather than by prosecuting the alleged perpetrator of the crime and then appropriating that person's assets (*in personam* proceedings). The latter would mandate full constitutional protections, while the former does not:

> Civil forfeitures are *in rem* proceedings. The government proceeds against property, and, by resort to a legal fiction, the property is held guilty and condemned. *Because the property itself is the defendant, the guilt or innocence of the property owner is irrelevant.* (Edwards 1994, p. 259, emphasis in original)

Courts have justified this "guilty" fiction on the notion that the owner has been negligent in allowing his or her property to be misused and he or she therefore should be punished for that negligence (*Austin v. United States,* 43 S.Ct. 2801, 2808 [1993]).

The Standard and Burden of Proof

Two of the major legal debates surrounding the forfeiture of drug-related assets concern the standard and the burden of proof issues. Because asset forfeiture is defined as a civil action in section 881 (21 U.S.C. § 881[b][4]), the standard of proof required of the government to initiate a seizure and the subsequent forfeiture proceedings is *probable cause,* instead of *beyond a reasonable doubt* as in criminal cases. Furthermore, as noted by Yoskowitz (1992), "As a practical matter, the government usually meets the initial burden of proof of probable cause simply by filing a verified complaint" (p. 575). With this lesser evidentiary standard, the government may use hearsay, circumstantial evidence, or facts obtained after the seizure of assets to justify the forfeiture (Yoskowitz 1992).

Once the government has established probable cause and has seized the assets,

> *the burden of proof shifts to the claimant to prove by a preponderance of evidence that the property is not used in such a manner.* Every federal circuit has interpreted section 881 as shifting the burden of proof to the claimant once the government establishes probable cause. . . . The standard effectively leaves claimants *with the burden of providing their innocence* or losing their homes and other property. (Stahl 1992, pp. 284, 286, emphasis added)

In a similar vein, Yoskowitz (1992) stated, "Indeed, the civil forfeiture proceeding denies the owner one of the most fundamental foundations of the criminal law by placing the most difficult burden of proof on the accused" (p. 584).

The standard of proof has traditionally been lower in civil proceedings than in criminal cases because the interests at stake are thought to be less important (i.e., the stakes do not involve liberty and life). Because the statute has defined drug-related asset forfeiture as a civil matter, the courts have upheld the probable cause standard (Stahl 1992, pp. 284–85). It can be argued, however, that because asset forfeiture in illegal drug cases is based on alleged criminal actions, the standard of proof should be beyond a reasonable doubt. The potential loss of all of one's property on the basis of an alleged connection with illegal drug activities is a serious matter. In fact, the seizure of one's home, other real property, monies, and vehicles can be said to be more harmful and intrusive than almost any fine imposed by criminal courts. Nevertheless, property can be taken from individuals without the full constitutional protections applicable in criminal proceedings: "the civil courts were not designed to allow the government to circumvent the U.S. Constitution in criminal matters, but such an occurrence is possible under asset forfeiture legislation" (Holden 1993, p. 3). Commenting on the government's ability to avoid constitutional protections in such proceedings, Yoskowitz (1992) stated, "This ability to bypass criminal constitutional rights is not simply fortuitous circumstances for the government; rather, it is precisely the reason these civil forfeiture actions are chosen" (p. 585).

Stigma and Criminal Punishment

Another issue associated with the severity of actions taken against an individual by the state is the stigma involved. Stigma is one of the outcomes of the criminal sanctioning process. Some believe that being labeled with the stigma of criminal serves as both a specific and general deterrent. Certainly, stigma results from the loss of one's property due to seizure by law enforcement. The public and agents of the justice system perceive the person whose assets have been seized to be guilty of a drug-related offense, even though the individual may not have been convicted of a crime in court. As Stahl (1992) has noted, "Merely labeling a procedure as civil in nature does not eliminate the possibility that the interests involved necessitate a higher burden of proof" (pp. 292–93).

Although section 881 defines asset forfeiture as a nonpunitive civil procedure, and federal courts have accepted this definition of the situation until relatively recently, there is evidence that Congress intended forfeiture to be a punitive action. According to one explanatory statement,

> *Due to the penal nature of forfeiture statutes,* it is the intent of these provisions that the property would be forfeited only if there is a substantial connection between the property and the underlying criminal activity which the statutes seek to prevent. (Act of October 13, 1978, Public Law No. 95-633, 8551, 1978 U.S.C.C.A.N. [92 Stat.] 9518, 9522, emphasis added)

Furthermore, a congressional panel reviewing the purpose of the 1984 amendments noted,

> Today few in the Congress or the law enforcement community fail to recognize that the traditional sanctions of fine and imprisonment are inadequate to deter or *punish* the enormously profitable trade in dangerous drugs, with its inevitable attendant violence, which is plaguing the country. . . . Forfeiture is the mechanism through which such an attack may be made. (Act of October 11, 1984, Public Law No. 98-473 U.S.C.C.A.N. [98 Stat.] 3128, 3374, as cited in Stahl 1992, p. 309, emphasis added)

Stahl (1992, pp. 309–10) cited several court decisions that have also recognized the punitive intentions of Congress in drug-related forfeiture. One statement of the Supreme Court is particularly relevant. In the influential *Calero-Toledo v. Pearson Yacht Leasing Co.* decision, the Court stated,

> Plainly, the Puerto Rican forfeiture statutes further the *punitive deterrent purposes* that have been found sufficient to uphold, against constitutional challenge, the applications of other forfeiture statutes to the property of innocents. Forfeitures of the conveyances that have been used—and may be used again—in violation of the narcotics laws *foster the purpose served by the underlying criminal statutes,* both by preventing further illicit use of the conveyance and by imposing an economic penalty, thereby rendering illegal behavior unprofitable (416 U.S. 663, 686-87 [1974], as cited in Stahl 1992, p. 310, emphasis added)

Certainly, federal law enforcement organizations formally define the civil seizure of assets as serving a punishment function. The U.S. Attorney General's primary stated objectives for the asset forfeiture program are "to *punish* and deter criminal activity by depriving criminals of property used or acquired through illegal activities" (Department of Justice 1990, p. 2, as cited in Warchol and Payne 1995, p. 1, emphasis added).

Nearly a decade after the explosive escalation in asset forfeitures, the U.S. Supreme Court recognized the element of criminal punishment underlying this policy. In its 1993 *Austin v. United States* decision, the Court stated,

> "[A] civil sanction that cannot fairly be said *solely* to serve a remedial purpose, but rather can only be explained as also serving either retributive or deterrent purposes, is punishment, as we have come to understand the term," *Halper,* 490 U.S., at 448, 109 S.Ct., at 1982 (emphasis added). In light of the historical understanding of forfeiture as punishment, the clear focus of sections 881(a)(4) and (a)(7) on the culpability of the owner, and the evidence that Congress understood those provisions as serving to deter and punish, we cannot conclude that forfeiture under sections 881(a)(4) and (a)(7) serves a solely remedial purpose. We therefore conclude that forfeiture under these provisions constitutes "payment to a sovereign as punishment for some offense." (113 S.Ct. 2801, 2812 [1993])

Asset forfeiture is, then, intended to serve as a criminal sanction but has been camouflaged as a civil one, thus requiring a lower standard of proof, and shifting the burden of proof away from the state onto the accused. In addition, asset forfeiture stigmatizes defendants in a manner similar to a criminal trial. Thus the state has extended its control over citizens and *simultaneously weakened the rights of individuals to protect themselves against state intrusion.* Because the illegal drug trade has been the focus of a moral panic in the United States, legislators, the judiciary, and the public alike have largely failed to realize the far-reaching harm that can result from this forfeiture policy and the potential for expansion of it into other areas of state control over citizens.

The Exclusionary Rule

Another procedural problem in drug-related asset forfeiture cases is the loss of protection afforded by the exclusionary rule. This rule is a court-mandated check against law enforcement agents introducing into a criminal trial evidence seized in violation of the Fourth Amendment. The argument underlying the exclusionary rule is that law enforcement is deterred from using illegally obtained evidence in a trial under the threat of losing the conviction. Thus the exclusionary rule is intended to serve as a deterrent to illegal search and seizure.

If conviction is the primary goal of law enforcement officers, the exclusionary rule may be an effective protection against illegal search and seizure. However, if law enforcement officers pursue objectives other than conviction, "the fear that evidence may not be admissible at trial is too remote a concern to compel law enforcement agents to respect the boundaries of the Fourth Amendment" (Nelson 1992, p. 1336). In fact, an argument can be made that the exclusionary rule is not being adhered to in drug-related asset seizures for two reasons. First, with the advent of widespread asset forfeitures, law enforcement goals have shifted "from pursuing criminals to pursuing assets" (Nelson 1992, p. 1333). That is, the gains from forfeitures are sufficient to outweigh or substitute for convictions:

> Designed for criminal proceedings, the exclusionary rule can only generate a deterrent effect on police conduct in pursuit of forfeiture to the extent that it functions in forfeiture proceedings in a manner similar to its original design. It does not. (Nelson 1992, p. 1337)

Furthermore, although courts have consistently "held that the exclusionary rule is applicable in asset forfeiture proceedings" (Nelson 1992, p. 1339), illegal seizures do not threaten the eventual forfeiture of assets, since untainted evidence obtained after the seizure can be used to establish probable cause in the forfeiture proceedings.

Other Governmental Advantages over the Accused

Governmental agents not only have a lower standard of proof to meet, enjoy the reversal of the burden of proof, and can safely ignore the exclusionary rule, they enjoy numerous other procedural advantages in asset forfeitures as well. First, claimants have a very short deadline to observe in order to maintain a claim on the seized property. In most instances, this deadline is 10 days (Wilson 1991–1992). Thus an owner may lose any claim to the property due to a simple procedural oversight (Edwards 1994).

Second, fighting the government can be very expensive. Indigent defendants in criminal trials are entitled to legal counsel, but the civil nature of asset seizure removes this protection. Claimants are thus often not represented, or even if they can afford representation, the value of the claimed property may be less than the cost of legal counsel. Defendants may then be forced to give up their claim (Edwards 1994).

Third, innocent third parties are sometimes victimized by asset seizures (Yoskowitz 1992). Children who use their parents' house for selling drugs may jeopardize their parents' ownership of the house, even though the parents may not be aware of, or have consented to, the selling of drugs (Edwards 1994). Furthermore, the innocent families of alleged drug offenders lose their ownership of any property that is seized and forfeited (e.g., houses, land, vehicles) (Wilson 1991–1992).[1]

Fourth, law enforcement agencies need not establish that the property seized was in any sense instrumental in the drug-related activity (e.g., a house can be seized even if no drugs are ever stored there, but the house is used for negotiating a transaction). Similarly, until mid-1993 there was no need to establish proportionality between the drug transaction and the value of the seized property.

In sum, in an attempt to deter and punish drug trafficking, congressional mandates have circumvented the protections afforded individuals charged with criminal activity. The state has expanded its powers by levying what is essentially a fine without providing most of the constitutional protections to those who would be assumed to be innocent until proven guilty in criminal court.

Diminished Control over Law Enforcement Agencies

The existence of this civil asset forfeiture policy and the sharing of proceeds by police agencies may also affect the internal workings of such agencies, as well as societal and governmental control over them. Holden (1993) pointed out that police priorities may have been affected:

> It may be that for many police agencies, asset forfeiture causes drug enforcement activities to increase because of a shift in police priorities. For these agencies, drug enforcement becomes a profit-making enterprise where traffic enforcement and theft investigations do not. (p. 3)

Such a shift is problematic in and of itself, but another unanticipated consequence of "policing for profit" is that the police become more autonomous. Depending on the magnitude of revenue they obtain through asset forfeitures, the public loses some degree of control over police agencies through the regular budget allocation process:

> The problem is basically one of accountability. The police department has income for which there is little external control. . . . Generally speaking, as the ability of the police to generate external resources increases, the capacity of the elected officials to maintain control of the agency decreases. (Holden 1993, pp. 3, 24)

In fact, as Miller and Selva (1994) pointed out, not only do the police become more autonomous, they may no longer see the pursuit of justice as their main objective, but due to their dependence on raising revenue, they become beneficiaries of the existence of the illegal drug trade. In a manner, drug traffickers and enforcers become reliant upon each other.

> Asset forfeiture has given drug enforcers a powerful incentive to maintain and manage economic mechanisms that allow the illegal market to continue. In this market, the drug enforcers and the drug traffickers become symbiotic beneficiaries of the "War on Drugs." (Miller and Selva 1994, p. 333)

Recent U.S. Supreme Court Decisions: Limited Remedial Actions

It is in this context of lack of control over the police that the most recent U.S. Supreme Court decisions on asset forfeiture, *Austin v. United States* (1993) and *United States v. Good* (1993), can be understood. In the *Austin* case, the defendant met an undercover agent at his body shop and agreed to sell the officer cocaine. Austin then went to his mobile home to retrieve the substance and returned to the body shop where two grams of cocaine were sold to the agent. Later the federal government filed a civil forfeiture action seeking the body shop and the mobile home. The Court held in the *Austin* decision that the Eighth Amendment to the Constitution prohibiting excessive fines applies not only to fines that are the result of criminal proceedings, but also to civil asset forfeiture. In effect, it ruled that the constitutional protection against excessive fines must be obeyed by law enforcement officials when confiscating property in drug cases. The Court stated that asset forfeiture and the fine imposed are meant to be partly punitive and thus must be proportional to the severity of the offense. The lack of proportionality between offense and punishment that critics such as Yoskowitz (1992) have discussed has, in theory, been corrected.

Although the Court expressly declined in *Austin* to formulate a test for determining whether a forfeiture action constitutes an excessive fine, it instructed the lower courts to do so. The primary consequence of this ruling was that law enforcement officials were now required to provide a justification for the seizure of property and to show some degree of proportionality between the alleged offense and the value of the forfeiture.[2] Unfortunately, due to the absence of Court guidelines for a test, much confusion has arisen among the lower courts. A variety of standards have been set forth, but no national standard has been established (Giffuni 1995).

In a related decision, which addressed procedural needs for the civil seizure of assets, the Court ruled in *Good* that the constitutional protections afforded defendants in the Fourth Amendment (unreasonable seizures) and Fifth Amendment (due process clause) are applicable to civil asset seizures. In this case, without notifying him prior to the action, the government seized the defendant's residence and surrounding property 4 years after he pled guilty to drug charges. A majority of the justices held that defendants are entitled to notice and an adversarial hearing before assets can be seized, unless exigent circumstances are present (e.g., vehicles can be seized without a hearing or notice as they are mobile and may be moved or hidden).

Conclusions and Policy Implications

Given the substantial due process problems with civil asset forfeiture policies and the related reduction in the accountability of law enforcement agencies, on balance this policy is severely flawed. The integrity of the state and the liberties of citizens are threatened by the imposition of criminal sanctions through civil proceedings without full due process protections for the accused. Thus we recommend that the civil forfeiture of assets in drug cases be abolished. If asset forfeiture is to remain a component of the justice system's War on Drugs, we recommend that it be invoked only after relevant criminal charges have been proven in court, as is the case in the United Kingdom (Levi and Osofsky 1995). This revision in the policy would add assurance that the accused is indeed guilty of a drug trafficking offense before assets are forfeited (Yoskowitz 1992). In addition, all rights of due process guaranteed in a criminal trial should be available to the defendant in asset forfeiture proceedings.

Furthermore, we recommend that the provision in the Comprehensive Crime Control Act of 1984 that allows the forfeiture of all real property "which is used, or intended to be used, in any manner" to violate the statute be eliminated. This provision has allowed the state to expand its authority to seize property that was not purchased with the proceeds of illegal drug transactions and, as a result, has created the potential for severe disproportionality between fines and punishments in relation to the seriousness of the offense. Although the *Austin* decision should result in controls over the disproportionality of these seizures of real property, the spirit of the law would remain overly broad and punitive. In addition, the statute is open to interpretation by the thousands of law enforcement agencies throughout the nation absent a national test for excessive fines. If the state wishes to continue seizing real property purchased with the proceeds of illegal drug transactions, these actions can be achieved under 18 U.S.C. § 1963 (1992) (RICO) and 21 U.S.C. § 853 (1992)—the criminal forfeiture provision of the Comprehensive Crime Control Act of 1984 (Yoskowitz 1992, p. 571).

In summary, the state has expanded its power of criminal sanctions into the civil arena with the objectives of deterring and punishing drug traffickers. The potential for excess with this asset forfeiture policy absent adequate due process protections renders it unacceptable in a society based on the rule of law. Once again, a moral panic has influenced public policy in a manner that is antithetical to the maintenance of civil liberties and the fundamental principle of fairness in criminal justice policy. Although recent U.S. Supreme Court rulings have begun to rein in some of the problems with this public policy, comprehensive change is needed now.

Notes

1. One indication of this problem is the formation of groups such as F.E.A.R. (Forfeiture Endangers American Rights) protesting the negative effects of asset forfeiture on families.
2. These rulings may account for the reductions in civil forfeitures of assets, particularly those of real property, since 1993.

References

Austin v. United States, 113 St. Ct. 2801 (1973).

Calero-Toledo v. Pearson Yacht Leasing Co., 94 S. Ct. 2080 (1974).

Department of Justice, 1990. *Annual Report of the Department of Justice Asset Forfeiture Program.* Washington, DC: Office of the U.S. Attorney General.

Edwards, E. E. 1994. "Review of Federal Asset Forfeiture Program" (Testimony before the Legislation and National Security Subcommittee of the Committee on Government Operations, House of Representatives, 103rd Cong., 1st Sess., June 22, 1993). Washington, DC: U.S. Government Printing Office.

Farr, Kathryn Ann. 1995. "Fetal Abuse and the Criminalization of Behavior during Pregnancy." *Crime & Delinquency* 41:235–45.

Flanagan, Timothy J. and Kathleen Maguire, eds. 1992. *Sourcebook of Criminal Justice Statistics—1991.* Washington, DC: U.S. Department of Justice, Bureau of Justice Statistics.

Giffuni, Matthew Q. 1995. "Civil Forfeiture and the Excessive Fines Clause Following *Austin v. United States.*" *Criminal Law Bulletin* 31:502–33.

Gordon, Diana R. 1994. *The Return of the Dangerous Classes: Drug Prohibition and Policy Politics.* New York: Norton.

Holden Richard N. 1993. "Police and the Profit-Motive: A New Look at Asset Forfeiture." *ACJS Today* 12:1, 3, 24–25.

Levi, Michael and Lisa Osofsky. 1995. *Investigating, Seizing and Confiscating the Proceeds of Crime.* London: Home Office Police Department, Police Research Group.

Maguire, Kathleen and Ann C. Pastore, eds. 1994. *Sourcebook of Criminal Justice Statistics—1993.* Washington, DC: U.S. Department of Justice, Bureau of Justice Statistics.

Maguire, Kathleen and Ann C. Pastore, eds. 1995. *Sourcebook of Criminal Justice Statistics—1994.* Washington, DC: U.S. Department of Justice, Bureau of Justice Statistics.

Miller, J. Mitchell and Lance H. Selva, 1994. "Drug Enforcement's Double-Edged Sword: An Assessment of Asset Forfeiture Programs." *Justice Quarterly* 11:313–35.

Nadelmann, Ethan A. 1993. *Cops Across Borders: The Internationalization of U.S. Criminal Law Enforcement.* University Park, PA: Pennsylvania State University Press.

Nelson, William P. 1992. "Should the Ranch Go Free Because the Constable Blundered? Gaining Compliance with Search and Seizure Standards in the Age of Asset Forfeiture." *California Law Review* 80: 1309–59.

Stahl, Marc B. 1992. "Asset Forfeiture, Burdens of Proof and the War on Drugs." *Journal of Criminal Law and Criminology* 83:274–337.

United States v. Halper, 109 S.Ct. 1982 (1989).

United States v. James Daniel Good Real Property et al., 114 S.Ct. 492 (1993).

Warchol, Gregory and Dennis M. Payne. 1995. "Exploring the Impact of Federal Asset Forfeiture: A Cross-Sectional Analysis." Paper presented at the annual meeting of the American Society of Criminology. Boston, November.

Wilson, Derrick. 1991–1992. "Drug Asset Forfeiture: In the War on Drugs, Is the Innocent Spouse the Loser?" *Journal of Family Law* 30:135–53.

Yoskowitz, Jack. 1992. "The War on the Poor: Civil Forfeiture of Public Housing." *Columbia Journal of Law and Social Problems* 25:567–600.

FRAME the DEBATE

Form at end of book

WiseGuide Wrap-Up

It seems logical that the proceeds from a criminal transaction should be forfeited only after an individual is convicted of a crime. However, many forfeiture laws provide for property to be confiscated from an offender without litigation and even before the criminal trial. Most amazing is that the government can permanently confiscate property it believes to be connected to drug sales, even if the suspect is never charged with a crime!

One final consideration: If the police and courts vigorously go after minority drug dealers and tenaciously seek to confiscate their personal belongings, even though Whites are dealing and using drugs at comparable rates, is the criminal justice system exacerbating the oppression of minorities?

R.E.A.L. Sites

This list provides a print preview of typical **Coursewise** R.E.A.L. sites. (There are over 100 such sites at the **Courselinks**™ site.) The danger in printing URLs is that web sites can change overnight. As we went to press, these sites were functional using the URLs provided. If you come across one that isn't, please let us know via email to: webmaster@coursewise.com. Use your Passport to access the most current list of R.E.A.L. sites at the **Courselinks** site.

Site name: Forfeiture Endangers American Rights
URL: http://www.fear.org/
Why is it R.E.A.L.? This site is dedicated to reform of federal and state asset forfeiture laws to restore due process and protect property rights in the forfeiture process.
Key topics: asset forfeiture, due process
Try this: Read some of the stories that victims of asset forfeiture laws wrote.

Site name: National Clearinghouse for Alcohol and Drug Information
URL: http://www.health.org/
Why is it R.E.A.L.? This site provides information about alcohol and substance abuse, with links to online research and resources.
Key topic: drugs
Try this: Read reports at this site on alcohol and drug use.

Site name: National Institute on Drug Abuse
URL: http://www.nida.nih.gov/
Why is it R.E.A.L.? The National Institute on Drug Abuse has numerous documents related to substance abuse and public policy at its web site.
Key topic: drugs
Try this: Read about alcohol and drug use by students in eighth, tenth, and twelfth grades in the "Monitoring the Future" study.

Site name: Office of National Drug Control Policy (ONDCP)

URL: http://www.whitehousedrugpolicy.gov/

Why is it R.E.A.L.? This site has drug facts and figures, as well as the national drug control policy. Many resources are available at this site.

Key topic: drugs

Try this: Read the National Drug Control Strategy to see what the government is doing to combat drugs.

Site name: Drug Enforcement Agency

URL: http://www.usdoj.gov/dea/index.htm

Why is it R.E.A.L.? Gain a greater understanding of the Drug Enforcement Agency by visiting its web site. Data on drug usage and narcotics seizures are also available at this site.

Key topics: federal law enforcement agency, drugs

Try this: Review the schedules of controlled substances.

ISSUE 10

Does the Death Penalty Deter Crime?

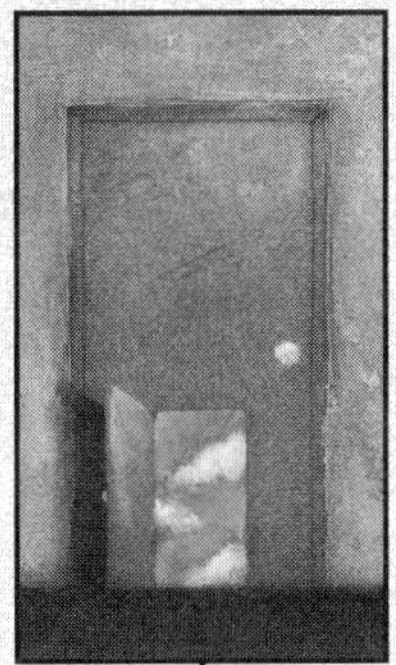

Take a Closer Look

1. Why is there strong public support for the death penalty, despite clear opposition by leading criminologists?
2. Do you think that the death penalty would be a greater general deterrent to crime if it were implemented quickly?
3. What are the main reasons that Radelet and Akers cite as to why most criminologists do not favor the death penalty?
4. Why do Berns and Bessette feel that the death penalty is fair?

WiseGuide Intro

The most controversial issue in the criminal justice system is the death penalty and its application. Unfortunately, criminological research has shown that the death penalty is applied discriminatorily against Blacks and the poor. Moreover, capital punishment is most likely to occur when a Black person kills a White person. Finally, the deterrence value of the death penalty has not been established, and there is no empirical support for its application. The death penalty appears to serve only one purpose: revenge.

Given these facts, and others, Michael Radelet and Ronald Akers report in "Deterrence and the Death Penalty: The Views of the Experts" that most criminologists do not support the death penalty. Leading criminologists agree that, even if the death penalty were applied more often, and in shorter intervals, general deterrence effects would still not be achieved.

In "Why the Death Penalty Is Fair," Walter Berns and Joseph Bessette contend that procedural safeguards are working. They assert that the death penalty is only initiated in rare circumstances when the offenders are the worst of a very bad group of offenders.

READING 19

Issue 10: Does the death penalty deter crime?

Deterrence and the Death Penalty:
The Views of the Experts

Michael L. Radelet and Ronald L. Akers

Abstract

The goal of this research is to determine if there is consensus among expert criminologists on whether the death penalty has been, is, or could be a general deterrent to criminal homicide. To assess expert opinion, we surveyed 67 of the 70 current and former presidents of three professional criminology organizations: The American Society of Criminology, Academy of Criminal Justice Sciences, and Law and Society Association. Over 80 percent of these experts believe the existing research fails to support a deterrence justification for capital punishment. Over three-quarters believe that increasing the frequency of executions, or decreasing the time spent on death row before execution, would not produce a general deterrent effects.

The American public has long been favorably disposed toward capital punishment for convicted murderers, and that support continues to grow. In a 1981 Gallup Poll, two-thirds of Americans voiced general approval of the death penalty. That support rose to 72 percent in 1985, to 76 percent in 1991, and to 80 percent in 1994 (Moore, 1994:5). Although these poll results need to be interpreted with extreme caution, it is clear that there are few issues on which more Americans agree: in at least some circumstances, death is seen as a justifiable punishment for the worst sorts of criminal homicides.

Part of the support for capital punishment comes from the belief that the death penalty is legitimate under a theory of "just desserts" (Bedau, 1978; Finckenauer, 1988). This justification suggests that murderers should be executed for retributive reasons; "Murderers should suffer, and life imprisonment is insufficient suffering as retribution for taking a life." While such views are important and worthy of debate, no empirical research can tell us if the argument is "correct" or "incorrect." Empirical studies cannot answer the question of what specific criminals (or non-criminals) "deserve," or settle debates over the moral issues surrounding capital punishment.

On the other hand, much of the public and political support for capital punishment rests on its presumed value as a general deterrent: we need the death penalty to encourage potential murderers to avoid engaging in criminal homicide. Unlike the issue of retribution, empirical studies can answer questions about the death penalty's general deterrent effects.

Politicians and prosecutors are often quick to use some version of the deterrence rationale in their cries for more and quicker executions when they see such appeals as a promising way to attract votes (Bright, 1995; Pierce and Radelet, 1990–91). Examples are not difficult to find. Rep. Newt Gingrich, Speaker of the House of Representatives, believes that mass executions of "27 or 30 or 35 people at a time" will reduce the importation of illegal drugs into America (Taylor, 1995). When signing legislation that returned the death penalty to New York in 1995, Governor George Pataki said, "This bill is going to save lives" (Dao, 1995). Governor William Weld, who is trying to get his state of Massachusetts to return the death penalty to its law books, bolsters his belief in the deterrent value of the death penalty with data he gets from his "gut." "Beyond a certain point, I think you have got to make a choice and go with your gut. My gut is that . . . capital punishment is a deterrent" (Lehigh, 1991). Ken Nunneley, an Alabama assistant attorney general in charge of the state's capital litigation division, obtains his data from the same source. "My gut tells me it has a deterrent effect, let me put it that way" (Lehr, 1993).

While opinion polls regularly find broad public and political support for the death penalty, there are significant pockets of abolitionist sen-

"Deterrence and the Death Penalty: The Views of the Experts" by Michael L. Radelet and Ronald L. Akers. Reprinted by special permission of Northwestern University School of Law, *Journal of Criminal Law and Criminology*, Vol. 87, Issue 1, 1996.

timents. Many of the nation's largest newspapers, such as the *New York Times, Washington Post, Los Angeles Times,* and the *Boston Globe* have editorial positions against the death penalty (Bedau, 1979). Among professional organizations that have gone on record as opposing the death penalty are the American Public Health Association (1987), the National Council on Crime and Delinquency (1964), the American Correctional Association, the American Orthopsychiatric Association (Bedau, 1979), and the American Society of Criminology (ASC, 1988). The fight against the death penalty in the 1960's and 1970's was led by the NAACP Legal Defense and Educational Fund (Meltsner, 1973), and today virtually all civil rights organizations in the United States stand opposed to the death penalty. Organizations such as the American Civil Liberties Union and Amnesty International, the 1977 Nobel Peace Prize recipient (see, e.g., Bedau, 1992; Amnesty International, 1989; 1995), feel the same way. The Catholic Church, as well as mainline Protestant and Jewish organizations, are also on record as opposing the death penalty (National Coalition to Abolish the Death Penalty, n.d.). This opposition is often based on moral principles. But just like belief in the death penalty's deterrent effects tends to correlate with pro-death penalty attitudes, most groups and individuals who oppose the death penalty are not convinced that the punishment is an effective deterrent to homicide (Gallup, 1991).

Whether or not the threat or use of the death penalty is, has been, or could be a deterrent to homicide is an empirical question that cannot be answered on the basis of gut feelings or on moral or political grounds. It is an empirical question that scores of researchers, dating back to a young Edwin Sutherland (Sutherland, 1925), have examined.

Has this long history and sizeable body of research served to support sound general conclusions? Can any factual statement be made about the death penalty's general deterrent effects, or are the published studies such that no conclusions can be reached? At least two valid methods can be used to answer this question. One is to examine individual scholarly opinions, as is done in most published research reports. Here researchers review the empirical research on deterrent effects of capital punishment and reach a conclusion based on the evidence from previous research by others and from their own research. A second approach is to gauge the considered and reasoned opinions of a group of scholars or experts. Indeed, much research-based public policy rests on known or presumed consensus of "expert" opinions. It is the aim of this paper to address the question of the death penalty's ability to deter homicides using this second approach: by gauging the judgments and opinions among one set of top criminological experts.

Literature Review

Gauging sentiment on the death penalty is not as easy a task as at first it might appear. When opinion polls ask respondents whether they support the death penalty, often no alternative punishments are given, and respondents are left to themselves to wonder what might happen if a particular inmate was not executed. Often respondents erroneously believe that absent execution, offenders will be released to the community after serving a short prison sentence. Even the most ardent death penalty abolitionists might support capital punishment if the alternative was to have dangerous murderers, such as Charles Manson or Ted Bundy, released to live in their neighborhoods. In one study, a sample of registered voters in Florida estimated that if a person convicted of first degree murder were not executed, s/he would be free and on the streets within ten years (Fox et al., 1990–91:513–14; see also Bowers, 1993:167–71). In reality, between 1972 and 1994, anyone convicted of first degree murder in Florida and not sentenced to death was not eligible for parole for at least 25 years. When respondents are asked if they would support the death penalty over an alternative of life without parole, support for the death penalty decreases significantly (Fox et al., 1990–91:515; Bowers, 1993). In 1991, Gallup found that 76 percent of Americans supported the death penalty, but that support would drop to 53 percent if life imprisonment without parole were available as an alternative (Gallup, 1991).

While most deterrence research has found that the death penalty has virtually the same effect as long imprisonment on homicide rates (for review, see Paternoster, 1991: 217–45), in the mid-1970's economist Isaac Ehrlich reported that his research had uncovered a significant deterrent effect. He estimated that each execution between 1933 and 1969 had prevented eight homicides (Ehrlich, 1975). This research gained widespread attention, in part because Solicitor General Robert Bork used it to defend the death penalty in the 1970's when the Supreme Court was considering whether to make permanent its 1972 ban of the death penalty (Bedau, 1981:95). Although Ehrlich's work was strongly criticized for methodological and conceptual shortcomings by scholars (e.g., Forst, 1983; Waldo, 1981) and even a panel appointed by the National Academy of Sciences (Klein et al., 1978), it continues to be cited by some as more or less conclusive proof that the death penalty has a deterrent effect on homicide (e.g., Sowell, 1994). A student of Ehrlich's, Stephen Layson, later reported his estimation that each execution deterred approximately 18 homicides (Layson, 1985). This research, too, was criticized as fatally flawed (Fox and Radelet, 1989), but nonetheless it continues to be embraced by proponents of the death penalty (e.g., Cassell, 1993).

It could very well be that the mere existence of a critique is more important than the quality of that critique. One researcher finds one thing, and another claims to refute it. What is left is a net gain of zero: politicians who never read or understand the original studies can select either position and cite only those studies that support their position.

Some research has asked the general public whether the death penalty acts as a deterrent to murder. Such a question is regularly asked to national samples in Gallup Polls (Gallup, 1985; 1986; 1991). In the mid-1980's, just over 60 percent of the respondents in Gallup polls said they believed the death penalty was a deterrent. Furthermore, these polls show that the deterrence rationale is an important death penalty justification. In 1986, 70 percent of the respondents supported the death penalty, but only a bare majority—53 percent—supported it when the alternative was life without parole. Gallup further asked if the respondents would still support the death penalty "if new evidence proved that the death penalty does not act as a deterrent to murder." Support for capital punishment then dropped to 43 percent (Gallup Report, 1986).

In his 1991 poll, where 76 percent of the respondents indicated support for the death penalty, Gallup asked a followup question on deterrence to those who favored the death penalty.

The pro-death penalty respondents were asked:

> Suppose new evidence showed that the death penalty does not act as a deterrent to murder, that it does not lower the murder rate. Would you favor or oppose the death penalty?

Here it was found that only 69 percent of the death penalty supporters would still maintain their support; 26 percent would change and oppose the punishment. Clearly, if the public were convinced that the death penalty failed to produce deterrent benefits, support for the death penalty would decline precipitously.

Ellsworth and Ross (1983) mailed questionnaires measuring attitudes toward the death penalty to 500 northern California respondents. Among their findings was that 82 percent of the death penalty proponents, but only 3.1 percent of the opponents, either strongly or slightly agreed with the statement, "We need capital punishment to show criminals that we really mean business about wiping out crime in this country" (Ellsworth and Ross, 1983:151). The Gallup and Ellsworth/Ross surveys show that the deterrence argument is one of the most important foundations for death penalty support in America. Questions from both the Gallup and the Ellsworth/Ross surveys were used in our own research, so precise comparisons will be made when our results are discussed below.

Two surveys have been conducted that examine how experts, as opposed to the general public, view the deterrence rationale for capital punishment. The first is limited but instructive. In September 1984, all criminologists (N=11) at the University of Florida released a statement saying that the empirical research on the death penalty did not support the deterrence hypothesis. The statement read:

> On numerous occasions Florida's Governor Graham has stated that his fundamental rationale for capital punishment is to reduce the state's homicide rate. As criminologists at the state's leading university, we feel a professional and ethical responsibility to report that there is no credible scientific research that supports the contention that the threat or use of the death penalty is or has been a deterrent to homicide. Other justifications of capital punishment are possible. However, whether or not the death penalty reduces the homicide rate is an empirical question which cannot be answered on moral or political grounds. The question has been clearly answered by numerous research projects conducted over the last 50 years. This deterrence research does not provide a legitimate basis for our state's death penalty policy.

After widespread newspaper publicity throughout the state, Florida's governor responded with the claim that crime statistics are an unreliable gauge for determining whether the death penalty prevents murder. In effect, he took the position that research could never evaluate the deterrent effects of the death penalty. "This is an issue that is inherently beyond what empirical research can validate. The deterrent effect of capital punishment is found in the homicides that are prevented and never get into the statistics" (*Gainesville Sun,* Sept. 7, 1984:10A).

A second survey of experts was conducted in 1995 by the Washington, D.C. based polling firm, Peter D. Hart Research Associates (Dieter, 1995). Telephone surveys were conducted with 386 randomly selected police chiefs and county sheriffs from throughout the continental United States. Among the "primary" ways to reduce violent crime, only one percent of the respondents chose the death penalty, which ranked this item last among six options. The most effective crime-reduction techniques included "reducing drug abuse" (favored by 31 percent); 17 percent selected "better economy and more jobs." Simplifying court rules, longer sentences, more police officers, and reducing the number of guns were also deemed as more important than expanding the use of the death penalty as ways of reducing violent crime. When asked to consider the statement "The death penalty significantly reduces the number of homicides," 67 percent of the chiefs felt the statement was inaccurate and 26 percent said it was accurate. Reacting to the poll, former New York Police Chief Patrick V. Murphy wrote, "Like the emperor's new clothes, the flimsy notion that the death penalty is an effective law enforcement tool is being exposed as mere political puffery" (Murphy, 1995). For comparative purposes, some of the questions we posed to our sample (reported below) were taken from this survey.

Methodology

To assess what the "experts" think about the deterrent effect of the death penalty, we must first answer the question of how to define "expert." One plausible definition is anyone who has published peer-reviewed research on the death penalty and deterrence. Surely those who have been active researchers in an area over many years are experts. However, such an approach has limited utility because (1) it is possible that only death penalty abolitionists, for whatever reasons, are motivated to conduct such research, (2) there would be a problem in differentially weighing the opinions of scholars who have published several acclaimed deterrence studies in major criminology journals from those whose research is less abundant or respected, and (3) surveying researchers in the field of deterrence would ask them to, in effect, evaluate their own work.

For this project we define "expert" as one who has achieved visibility and recognition as a leader among criminologists in the United States. Our operational definition is one who has been recognized by peers to the extent of being elected to the highest office in scholarly organizations. We contacted all present and former presidents of the country's top academic criminological societies. This small and elite group includes many of the country's most respected criminologists. As such, although few of these scholars have done research on capital punishment in general or deterrence in particular, they are generally well versed in central criminological issues, such as crime causation, crime prevention, and criminal justice policy. The presidents of three associations were surveyed: the American Society of Criminology, Academy of Criminal Justice Sciences, and the Law and Society Association.

The American Society of Criminology (ASC), founded in 1941, is the country's largest association of professional and academic criminologists, with a 1994 membership of 2,500 (Schwartz and Turner, 1994:10685), dominated by academics from graduate and research institutions. The Academy of Criminal Justice Sciences (ACJS), founded in 1963 under the name it held until 1971, The International Association of Police Professors, includes 2,400 members. Its primary goal is the advancement of the criminal justice system through research and education (Schwartz and Turner, 1994:10627). Its membership overlaps to a considerable extent with the ASC, but its leadership (taken primarily from undergraduate teaching programs) does not. Only one person in the history of the two societies has served as president of both. The Law and Society Association (L&SA), founded in 1964, includes more law professors and legal scholars among its 1,400 members than either the ASC or ACJS. Again there is overlapping membership with ASC and some with ACJS, but no one has served as president of L&SA and either of the other two. Its goal is to explore "the relationships between law and society in order to contribute to the understanding of law as a social and political phenomenon and to expedite the use of law as an instrument of public policy" (Schwartz and Turner, 1994:5318). These three associations are all interdisciplinary and publish what are among the most respected scholarly journals in criminology and criminal justice: *Criminology* (ASC), *Justice Quarterly* (ACJS), and *Law and Society Review* (L&SA).

Each organization elects officers, including a president, by a ballot sent to all members. While in the past some presidents served two-year terms, today all elections are for a one-year tenure. To be elected president, one must generally have high visibility in the field, be well-respected, and have been active in programmatic and organizational activities.

We began by writing to the offices of each of these three organizations and obtaining lists of their current and former presidents. Through letters and phone calls to some of those on the list, and to other criminologists, we were able to identify which of the former presidents were still living, and to obtain addresses for each. A total of 71 individuals was identified: 29 from the Academy of Criminal Justice Sciences, 27 from the American Society of Criminology, and 15 from the Law and Society Association. As noted, one person had served as president of two of the associations, reducing our sample to 70. Drafts of the questionnaire were examined and critiqued by three scholars who have conducted deterrence research. After revisions, numbered questionnaires were mailed to our respondents in August 1995, and followups (eventually preceded by phone calls), were sent throughout the fall. A total of 67 responded (95.7 percent): 27 from ACJS, 26 from the ASC, and 15 from L&SA.

The presidents were asked to answer the questions "on the basis of your knowledge of the literature and research in criminology." We did not ask for their personal opinions on the death penalty. Eleven questions relating to deterrence issues were included on the questionnaire, and the responses to all eleven are reported below.

Results

A. General Questions on Deterrence

The first question to be explored concerns the general question of how the presidents of the criminological associations generally view the deterrence question. Table 1

Table 1 Comparison of Responses of Criminologists and General Public to Identical Questions on Deterrence

A. Do you feel that the death penalty acts as a deterrent to the commitment to murder—that it lowers the murder rate, or what?

	Criminology Presidents (%)	Gallup 1985 (%)	Gallup 1991 (%)
Yes:	11.9	62	51
No:	83.6	31	41
No opinion:	4.5	7	8
N	67	1,523	990

B. Abolishing the death penalty (in a particular state) would not have any significant effects on the murder rate (in that state).

	Criminology Presidents (%)	Ellsworth and Ross, 1983
I'm sure it is true	32.8	10.2
I think it's true	53.7	35.8
I have no idea whether it is true or false	10.4	32.6
I think it's false	3.0	18.0
I'm sure it's false	0	3.4
N	67	500

C. Over the years, states which have had the death penalty have had lower murder rates than neighboring states which did not have a death penalty.

	Criminology Presidents (%)	Ellsworth and Ross, 1983:141 (%)
I'm sure it is true	0	4.6
I think it's true	6.0	22.4
I have no idea	14.9	6.0
I think it's false	40.3	32.0
I'm sure it's false	38.8	5.0
N	67	500

begins by replicating the question asked in the Gallup polls, "Do you feel that the death penalty acts as a deterrent to the commitment to murder—that it lowers the murder rate, or what?" It can be seen that the experts are more than twice as likely as the general population to believe that the death penalty does not lower the murder rate—41 percent of the population held this belief in 1991, the last year that Gallup published responses to this question, compared to 83.6 percent of our experts. Among the 64 experts who voiced opinions on this question, 56 (87.5 percent) believe the death penalty does not have deterrent effects.

Table 1 also compares responses to deterrence questions between the expert criminologists and the members of the general public in northern California surveyed by Ellsworth and Ross. Here 86.5 percent of the criminologists and 46 percent of the general public say they are "sure" or "think" that "Abolishing the death penalty (in a particular state) would not have any significant effects on the murder rate (in that state)." As would be expected, substantially more members of the general public than the criminologists (32.6 percent vs. 10.4 percent) say they have no idea whether this statement is true or false.

Similarly, as shown in the third part of Table 1, the criminologists are much less likely than members of the general public to agree that "Over the years, states which have had the death penalty have had lower murder rates than neighboring states which did not have a death penalty." Nearly 80 percent of the criminologists said that they were sure or they thought this was not true, compared to 37 percent of the general public. Interestingly, more criminologists stated that they had no idea whether this statement was true or false than did members of the general public (14.9 vs. 6.0 percent).

The results of Table 1 clearly show that approximately eighty percent of the experts in criminology believe, on the basis of the literature and research in criminology, that the death penalty does not have significant deterrent effects. In addition, no matter how measured, it is clear that the criminologists are much more likely than the general public to dismiss the deterrence argument.

Table 2 compares the beliefs of our experts to those of top criminal justice administrators, specifically to the beliefs of the police chiefs surveyed by Peter D. Hart Research Associates in 1995 (discussed above). Overall there is widespread agreement between the criminologists and the police chiefs on the deterrent value of the death penalty (or lack thereof), with the criminologists even less likely than the chiefs to see any deterrent value. As seen in Table 2, all of the criminologists, and 85 percent of the police chiefs, believe it is totally or largely accurate that "Politicians support the death penalty as a symbolic way to show they are tough on crime." Almost 87 percent of the criminologists and 57 percent of the chiefs find it totally or largely accurate to say "Debates about the death penalty distract Congress and state legislatures from focusing on real solutions to crime problems." None of the criminologists, and only about a quarter of the chiefs, believe there is any accuracy in the statement, "The death penalty significantly reduces the number of homicides." These statements indicate that both academic criminologists and police chiefs view the death penalty as more effective in political rhetoric than as a criminal justice tool.

Table 3 asks general questions about deterrence in two different ways. We developed the wording for these questions ourselves, so no comparisons with other opinion polls are possible. However, we believe these questions word the issue more precisely than the questions taken from other surveys. Given the widespread availability of "life without parole" as an alternative to the death penalty (Wright, 1990), the first question displayed in Table 3 is perhaps the clearest statement of the deterrence issue as actually faced by researchers and policy makers today. Only three of our respondents (4.5 percent) agreed, and none strongly agreed, with the statement, "Overall, over the last twenty years, the threat or use of the death penalty in the United States has been a stronger deterrent to homicide than the threat or use of long (or life) prison sentences." Ninety two point six percent of the respondents, and 96 percent of those with an opinion, disagreed or strongly disagreed. Responses to the next question indicate that only three respondents felt the empirical support for the deterrent effects of the death penalty had moderate support; none believed it had strong support. Instead, 94 percent of the criminologists felt the argument had weak or no support.

Table 2 **Comparison of Responses of Criminologists (N=67) and Police Chiefs to Same Questions (N=386) (in percents)**

A. Politicians support the death penalty as a symbolic way to show they are tough on crime.

	Presidents	Police Chiefs
Totally accurate	38.8	33
Largely accurate	61.2	52
Largely Inaccurate	0	10
Totally inaccurate	0	6
Not sure	0	2

B. Debates about the death penalty distract Congress and state legislatures from focusing on real solutions to crime problems.

	Presidents	Police Chiefs
Totally accurate	49.3	11
Largely accurate	37.3	46
Largely inaccurate	11.9	30
Totally inaccurate	0	11
Not sure	1.5	2

C. The death penalty significantly reduces the number of homicides.

	Presidents	Police Chiefs
Totally accurate	0	4
Largely accurate	0	22
Largely inaccurate	41.8	45
Totally inaccurate	52.2	22
Not sure	6.0	7

B. The Question of Reform

Proponents of the death penalty might concur with the critics of the deterrence argument, but say that the lack of a clear deterrent effect is a result of the fact that only a small proportion of those on death row are executed each year, or that the wait on death row between condemnation and execution is too long. Increasing the frequency and decreasing the celerity of the death penalty could produce a deterrent effect. The experts responding to our survey, however, disagree with such a position. Almost eighty percent disagree or strongly disagree with the statement, "If the frequency of executions were to increase significantly, more homicides would be deterred than if the current frequency of executions remained relatively stable." As seen in the second portion of Table 4, nearly three quarters (73.2 percent) of the experts disagreed or strongly

Table 3 Responses of Criminologists to General Questions on Deterrence (N=67) (in percents)

A. Overall, over the last twenty years, the threat or use of the death penalty in the United States has been a stronger deterrent to homicide than the threat or use of long (or life) prison sentences.

Strongly agree	0
Agree	4.5
Disagree	43.3
Strongly disagree	49.3
Missing	3.0

B. Overall, how would you evaluate the empirical support for the deterrent effects of the death penalty?

Strong support	0
Moderate support	4.5
Weak support	44.8
No support	49.3
Missing	1.5

Table 4 Responses of Criminologists to Belief That Reforms Could Produce a Deterrent Effect (N=67) (in percents)

A. If the frequency of executions were to increase significantly, more homicides would be deterred than if the current frequency of executions remained relatively stable.

Strongly agree	3.0
Agree	14.9
Disagree	44.8
Strongly disagree	34.3
Missing	3.0

B. The average time on death row between sentence and execution is now between eight and ten years. If that period was reduced significantly, there is reason to expect that the death penalty would deter more homicides than it does today.

Strongly agree	4.5
Agree	22.4
Disagree	44.8
Strongly disagree	28.4

disagreed with the position that decreasing the time on death row would deter more homicides. Much of the research that informs these experts' opinions was done with data from the 1930s, 1940s, and 1950s, when the frequency of executions was higher and the average time spent on death row was shorter than it is today. Hence, criminologists do have some research at their disposal that would enable accurate predictions of what would happen if these proposed death penalty reforms were actually enacted.

C. Support for the Brutalization Hypothesis

In a final question, the experts were asked how they felt about the so-called "brutalization hypothesis." This argument, supported by some research (Bailey, 1979; Bailey, 1983; Bowers and Pierce, 1980; Cochran et al., 1994), suggests that the death penalty tends to devalue human life and send a message that tells citizens that killing people under some circumstances is appropriate. However, as shown in Table 5, this hypothesis does not have widespread support among experts. Two-thirds (67.1 percent) of the respondents either disagree or strongly disagree with the statement, "Overall, the presence of the death penalty tends to increase a state's murder rate rather than to decrease it."

The responses to this item help us address some possible reservations about our overall findings: Is there anti-capital punishment bias among our respondents? Were the responses made based on an understanding of the research or are our respondents merely liberal academics who object to the death penalty on moral grounds and would report opinions that might undermine it, even if the empirical evidence showed otherwise? The responses to the question on brutalization suggest that the answers to these questions are negative. If our respondents simply respond to any question in a way that buttresses the abolitionist position, there should be strong agreement with the notion that the death penalty actually increases the homicide rate, since this is an anti-capital punishment argument. It appears, instead, that the respondents were responding on the grounds we asked—their appraisal of existing research. The brutalization hypothesis, in fact has not been tested very well and the research supporting it remains more suggestive than definitive. As on the other questions, our respondents appear to be reacting to the state of knowledge on this question, not to their personal preferences.

Conclusions

The results of this project clearly show that there is a wide consensus among America's top criminologists that the death penalty does, or can do, little to reduce rates of criminal violence in our society. These results chisel away at one of the most important justifications for the death penalty in modern society. To the degree that well-intentioned voters support the death penalty as a last-

Table 5 **Criminologists' Responses to the Brutalization Hypothesis (N=67) (in percents)**

Overall, the presence of the death penalty tends to increase a state's murder rate rather than to decrease it.	
Strongly agree	4.5
Agree	23.9
Disagree	52.2
Strongly disagree	14.9
Missing	4.5

resort effort to reduce crime rates, this study should have an impact on the public's support for the executioner.

The study also suggests that political debates about how to reduce criminal violence in America should shift away from debates about the death penalty. Politicians or prosecutors who continue to support the death penalty on deterrence grounds may be able to point to their "gut" feelings or to individual studies that support their position. However, given that so few expert criminologists give credence to the deterrence hypothesis, the results of this project challenge political discourse that points to the death penalty as a crime-fighting tool. Our findings support a shift in political discussions about crime away from the death penalty and in the direction of more promising crime-reducing policies.

This assumes that public policy makers in the United States actually look to, and care about, what criminologists think about public policies that might in one way or another relate to crime. To be sure, some policy makers do care what criminologists think about some issues. For example, in 1994 Attorney General Janet Reno asked the American Society of Criminology for input on crime control policy options, and twelve task forces were developed (American Society of Criminology, 1995). However, none of these task forces had anything to do with the death penalty, even though General Reno is herself a death penalty opponent who nonetheless has authorized several federal capital prosecutions.

Capital punishment will continue to generate much public debate in the early decades of the next century and various bodies of opinion will be consulted. The results of our research show that the question of whether or not the death penalty can reduce criminal violence, at least in the eyes of the presidents of the major scholarly societies in criminology, is a settled issue. Future research should investigate whether it is a settled issue in expert opinion defined in other ways, such as among the membership of ASC, ACJS, and L&SA, or among criminology faculties. Furthermore, just as results of direct research on deterrence and surveys of public opinion should be and are communicated to policy makers, research findings on expert opinion on the death penalty should be communicated to policy makers. Perhaps the ASC or other scholarly organization could form a task force on capital punishment to make formal recommendations in a manner similar to that of the ASC's 1995 recommendations to Attorney General Reno (American Society of Criminology, 1995). In the end, hopefully this study will encourage politicians to stop using the death penalty as a simplistic means to create the false impression that they are actually doing something about our high rates of criminal violence.

References

American Public Health Association. 1987. Policy statement 8611: Abolition of the death penalty. *American Journal of Public Health* 77:105–6.

American Society of Criminology. 1988. Resolutions considered during annual meeting. *The Criminologist,* Jan.–Feb., p. 15.

———. 1995. Special Issue. *The Criminologist,* Nov./Dec., pp. 1–16.

Amnesty International. 1989. *When the State Kills. . . .* London: Amnesty International Publications.

———. 1995. *The Machinery of Death: A Shocking Indictment of Capital Punishment in the United States.* New York: Amnesty International U.S.A.

Bailey, William C. 1979. Deterrence and the death penalty for murder in Oregon. *Willamette Law Review* 16:67–85.

———. 1983. Disaggregation in deterrence and death penalty research: The case of murder in Chicago. *Journal of Criminal Law and Criminology* 74:827–59.

Bedau, Hugo Adam. 1978. Retribution and the theory of punishment. *The Journal of Philosophy* 75:601–20.

———. 1979. The death penalty in the United States: Imposed law and the role of moral elites. In Sandra B. Burman and Barbara E. Harrell-Bond (eds.), *The Imposition of the Law.* New York: Academic Press.

———. 1981. *The Death Penalty in America.* Third Edition. New York: Oxford University Press.

———. 1992. *The Case Against the Death Penalty.* New York: American Civil Liberties Union.

Bowers, William J. 1993. Research note: Capital punishment and contemporary values: People's misgivings and the Court's misperceptions. *Law and Society Review* 27:157–75.

Bowers, William J., and Glenn L. Pierce. 1980. Deterrence or brutalization: What is the effect of executions? *Crime and Delinquency* 26:453–84.

Bright, Stephen B. 1995. The politics of crime and the death penalty: Not 'soft on crime,' but hard on the bill of rights. *Saint Louis University Law Journal* 39:479–503.

Cassell, Paul G. 1993. Testimony before the House Committee on the Judiciary, subcommittee on Crime and Criminal Justice, on H.R. 3131, October 22.

Cochran, John K., Mitchell B. Chamlin, and Mark Seth. 1994. Deterrence or brutalization? An impact assessment of Oklahoma's return to capital punishment. *Criminology* 32:107–134.

Dao, James. 1995. Death penalty in New York reinstated after 18 years: Pataki sees justice served. *New York Times,* March 8, p. 1A.

Dieter, Richard C. 1995. *On the Front Line: Law Enforcement Views on the Death Penalty.* Washington, D.C.: Death Penalty Information Center.

Ehrlich, Isaac. 1975. The deterrent effect of capital punishment: A question of life and death. *American Economic Review* 65:397–417.

Ellsworth, Phoebe C., and Lee Ross. 1983. Public opinion and capital punishment: A close examination of the views of abolitionists and retentionists. *Crime and Delinquency* 29:116–69.

Finckenauer, James O. 1988. Public support for the death penalty: Retribution as just desserts or retribution as revenge? *Justice Quarterly* 5:81–100.

Forst, Brian E. 1983. Capital punishment and deterrence: Conflicting evidence? *Journal of Criminal Law and Criminology* 74:927–42.

Fox, James Alan, and Michael L. Radelet. 1989. Persistent flaws in econometric studies of the deterrent effect of the death penalty. *Loyola of Los Angeles Law Review* 23:29–44.

Fox, James Alan, Michael L. Radelet, and Julie L. Bonsteel. 1990–1991. Death penalty opinion in the post-Furman years. *New York University Review of Law & Social Change* 18:499–528.

Gallup Report. 1985. Support for the death penalty highest in half-century. *Gallup Report* 232–233 (Jan./Feb.):3–10.

———. 1986. The death penalty. *Gallup Report* 244–245 (Jan.–Feb.):10–16.

———. 1991. Death penalty support remains strong. *Gallup Report* 309 (June):40–45.

Klein, Lawrence R., Brian Forst, and Victor Filatov. 1978. The deterrent effect of capital punishment: An assessment of the estimates. In Alfred Blumstein, Jacqueline Cohen, and Daniel Nagin (eds.), *Deterrence and Incapacitation: Estimating the Effects of Criminal Sanctions on Crime Rates.* Washington, D.C.: National Academy of Sciences.

Layson, Stephen K. 1985. Homicide and deterrence: A reexamination of the United States time-series evidence. *Southern Economic Journal* 52:68–89.

Lehigh, Scot. 1991. Governor says he'll oppose hike in state cigarette tax. *Boston Globe,* Nov. 23, p. 28.

Lehr, Dick. 1993. Death penalty foes seek a new debate, see stronger case. *Boston Globe,* Jan. 10, p. 1.

Meltsner, Michael. 1973. *Cruel and Unusual: The Supreme Court and Capital Punishment.* New York: Random House.

Moore, David W. 1994. Majority advocates death penalty for teenage killers. *The Gallup Poll Monthly* 348 (Sept.):2–6.

Murphy, Patrick V. 1995. Death penalty useless. *USA Today,* Feb. 23, p. 11A.

National Coalition to Abolish the Death Penalty. n.d. *The Death Penalty: The Religious Community Calls for Abolition.* Washington, D.C.: National Coalition to Abolish the Death Penalty.

National Council on Crime and Delinquency. 1964. Policy statement on capital punishment. *Crime and Delinquency* 10:105–9.

Paternoster, Raymond. 1991. *Capital Punishment in America.* New York: Lexington Books.

Pierce, Glenn L., and Michael L. Radelet. 1990–1991. The role and consequences of the death penalty in American politics. *New York University Review of Law and Social Change* 18:711–28.

Schwartz, Carol A., and Rebecca L. Turner. 1994. *Encyclopedia of Associations,* 1995. Detroit: Gale Research Inc.

Sowell, Thomas. 1994. Death penalty is valid option. *St. Louis Post Dispatch,* Dec. 12, p. 11C.

Sutherland, Edwin H. 1925. Murder and the death penalty. *Journal of Criminal Law and Criminology* 15:522–36.

Taylor, Stuart Jr. 1995. The politics of death: Governing by tantrum. *Texas Lawyer,* Sept. 11, p. 1.

Waldo, Gordon P. 1981. The death penalty and deterrence: A review of recent research. In Israel L. Barak-Glantz and Ronald Huff (eds.), *The Mad, the Bad, and the Different.* Lexington, Mass.: Lexington Books.

Wright, Julian H., Jr. 1990. Life-without-parole: An alternative to death or not much of a life at all? *Vanderbilt Law Review* 43 (1990):529–68.

FRAME the DEBATE

Form at end of book

READING 20

Issue 10: Does the death penalty deter crime?

Why the Death Penalty Is Fair

Walter Berns and Joseph Bessette

Mr. Berns is a resident scholar at the American Enterprise Institute in Washington. Mr. Bessette is an associate professor of government and ethics at Claremont McKenna College in California.

The death penalty is much in the news. With jurors failing to agree on a sentence for Oklahoma City bombing conspirator Terry Nichols, he will escape the maximum legal punishment for his part in the deaths of eight federal agents (though an Oklahoma jury may eventually sentence him to die if he is convicted of murdering the 160 other victims). Meanwhile, Theodore Kaczynski's Unabomber prosecution continues its halting pace toward what all must now assume will be his execution—after, of course, excruciating delays while the case is appealed to various courts. The U.S. Supreme Court has already refused the last challenge to the execution of spree killer Karla Faye Tucker, who on Feb. 3 will become the first woman to receive Texas's lethal injection—unless, that is, Gov. George W. Bush decides not to sign her death warrant.

Gov. Bush faces an enormously weighty decision, and so may take some comfort in the knowledge that signing a death warrant was a problem, too, for Abraham Lincoln. "You do not know how hard it is to let a human being die," he said, "when you feel that a stroke of your pen will save him."

Lincoln's misgivings had nothing whatever to do with the legality of capital punishment; as he read it, the Constitution gave him the power to authorize a death sentence when it gave him the power to "grant reprieves." The opponents of capital punishment would applaud his all-too-human misgivings, but deplore his constitutional judgment—which, as it turned out, is today shared by the Supreme Court.

True, the court's 1972 decision in *Furman v. Georgia* held that, when imposed in an arbitrary or capricious manner, the death penalty violated the Eighth Amendment's prohibition of "cruel and unusual punishments." Because, under the state laws then in force, only an unfortunate few of those convicted of a capital crime were being sentenced to death, Justice Potter Stewart likened it to "being struck by lightning." The Constitution, he said, could not permit "this unique penalty to be so wantonly and so freakishly imposed."

But this did not put an end to capital punishment. Within a few years, 35 states rewrote their death-penalty statutes, and in 1976, in cases from Georgia, Texas and Florida, the Supreme Court upheld their constitutionality.

By narrowing the categories of murder for which the death penalty might be imposed, and by requiring separate sentencing hearings during which juries or judges would weigh evidence of aggravating or mitigating circumstances, the new laws ensured, again in Justice Stewart's words, that "sentences of death will not be 'wantonly' or 'freakishly' imposed."

But the issue of arbitrariness has not died. In 1986, Jack Greenberg, writing in the *Harvard Law Review*, complained that capital punishment continued to be imposed in an "infrequent, random, and erratic fashion." More recently, Hugo Adam Bedau, perhaps the nation's leading academic opponent of capital punishment, denied that the new laws succeeded in "winnowing the worst from the (merely) bad" offenders. The few actually sentenced to death—5,553 since 1976, of whom 403 have in fact been executed—are, he said, simply "the losers in an arbitrary lottery."

The opponents have now gained support from an unlikely quarter. Writing in these pages last month, Princeton Prof. John J. DiIulio repeated the lottery analogy, asserting that the administration of the death penalty in the U.S. is, and is likely to remain, "arbitrary and capricious," and thus ought to be abolished. Because he is known otherwise to be a proponent of harsh punishment, Mr. DiIulio's judgment ought to carry weight. On this subject, however, he is surely mistaken.

Rather than being arbitrary and capricious, the system now in place serves as a filter, reserving the death penalty for the worst offenders. This is demonstrably the case in Illinois. In August 1996, state prosecutors compiled a list of the 174 persons then on death row in Illinois, with a description of the murder (or murders) committed by each offender. A comparison of this information with the data on homicides collected by the FBI and the Justice Department's Bureau of Justice Statistics reveals the dramatic difference between the crimes committed by the offenders on death row in Illinois and other murderers:

- 20% of those on the Illinois death row committed murders during the commission of a rape or sexual assault, compared with well under 1% of all murderers;
- 10% of the condemned committed murders during a burglary or home invasion, compared with less than 1% of all murders;
- 13% of the condemned had murdered a child, compared with 4% of all murders;
- 37% of the condemned committed murders involving more than one victim, compared with 4% of all murders.

These statistics do not succeed in conveying the truly despicable nature of the crimes committed by those on death row in Illinois. The first offender in this (alphabetically ordered) list murdered two Chicago police officers; the second murdered a Chicago police officer by running him down with an automobile; the third beat to death an 86-year-old woman with her walking cane; the fourth shot and killed four persons during a drug-related robbery; the fifth murdered his girlfriend's 16-month-old daughter by denying her food and exposing her to subfreezing temperatures; the sixth shot to death an 86-year-old man during a robbery; the seventh, while dressed as a priest, committed a murder-for-hire of an 81-year-old widow by shooting her twice in the back of the head; the eighth, during an armed robbery, shot and killed one man and wounded another; the ninth raped and murdered a 34-year-old woman as she walked to catch a bus; and the 10th shot and killed three men in a dispute over money.

There are no barroom brawls here, no domestic disputes that got out of hand, no "heat of passion" crimes that are so common among homicides in the U.S. These are brutal, cold-blooded murders, often involving other felonies, and often committed against the most vulnerable of victims. An examination of the lists of those on death row in the other 37 capital-punishment states would probably show that they, too, reserve the death penalty for the worst offenders.

Indeed, it could hardly be otherwise. In the post-Furman era, and at the insistence of the Supreme Court, the death-penalty states have carved out from first-degree murder (already a subset of all homicides) a still narrower category of the most heinous killings and have rendered them alone subject to capital punishment. This system, which imposes the death penalty on a few hundred of the 12,000 persons convicted each year of homicide, cannot be described as arbitrary or capricious.

Nor can it be described as cruel. During his four years as president, and despite his misgivings, Lincoln authorized the executions of 267 soldiers and sailors, men sentenced to death for desertion or for sleeping on watch, but none of them so deserving of death as the men on the Illinois list—to say nothing of mass murderer John Gacey; Richard Allen Davis, the killer of 12-year-old Polly Klaas; or, to bring this up to date, the notorious Timothy McVeigh.

FRAME the DEBATE

Form at end of book

WiseGuide Wrap-Up

Even if the death penalty could be applied fairly with respect to race and socioeconomic status, capital punishment appears to have only one purpose: revenge. However, if society can accept that fact and administer the death penalty in good faith, knowing that its only value is revenge and that other equally appropriate sanctions are available, then that would at least satisfy some concerned criminologists.

Even if all things were equal, criminologists would still argue that the death penalty does not serve as a general deterrent to crime, given the current body of literature. The final question that we need to ask is, "Should we as a leading industrialized nation execute even the most egregious of offenders simply for the sake of revenge?"

R.E.A.L. Sites

This list provides a print preview of typical **Coursewise** R.E.A.L. sites. (There are over 100 such sites at the **Courselinks**™ site.) The danger in printing URLs is that web sites can change overnight. As we went to press, these sites were functional using the URLs provided. If you come across one that isn't, please let us know via email to: webmaster@coursewise.com. Use your Passport to access the most current list of R.E.A.L. sites at the **Courselinks** site.

Site name: Death Penalty Information Center
URL: http://www.essential.org/dpic/
Why is it R.E.A.L.? This site provides information on the death penalty.
Key topics: death penalty, punishment
Try this: Examine some of the information regarding the disparities that exist with the death penalty.

Site name: American Society of Criminology
URL: http://www.asc41.com/
Why is it R.E.A.L.? The American Society of Criminology seeks to foster criminological scholarship, research, education, and training within academic institutions and within the divisions of the criminal justice system. Their membership application is online, and students are encouraged to apply!
Key topics: research, professional organization, criminology
Try this: Read about the organization and consider joining!

Site name: Amnesty International
URL: http://www.rightsforall-usa.org/index.html
Why is it R.E.A.L.? Amnesty International is a worldwide voluntary activist movement primarily concerned with human rights violations. Their full report, Rights for All, is available at this site.
Key topics: civil liberties, rights, freedom
Try this: Find ways to participate in various social movements facilitated by Amnesty International.

Site name: Human Rights Watch

URL: http://www.hrw.org/reports98/police/index.htm

Why is it R.E.A.L.? This site provides information regarding violations of human rights.

Key topics: rights, freedom, civil liberties

Try this: Read the entire report on police abuse by the Human Rights Watch.

Site name: American Civil Liberties Union

URL: http://www.aclu.org/

Why is it R.E.A.L.? This site, sponsored by the American Civil Liberties Union (ACLU), has an enormous collection of materials related to the criminal justice system, as well as various other social issues. It is an outstanding site for gathering well-documented and scholarly materials. There is also a student's section.

Key topics: civil liberties, rights, freedom

Try this: Browse through the ACLU's special report, "Driving While Black: Racial Profiling on Our Nation's Highways."

ISSUE 11

Can Right-to-Carry Laws Reduce Crime?

Take a Closer Look

1. Do you feel that the Second Amendment of the U.S. Constitution was written to allow people the right to carry concealed firearms?
2. Do you think that concealed weapons laws could deter crime?
3. According to the National Rifle Association, what does the literature report concerning the link between crime and "right-to-carry" laws?
4. According to Sugarmann, what type of social issue is firearm-related deaths?

WiseGuide Intro

The Second Amendment of the U.S. Constitution is straightforward in its proscription that the right of the people to keep and bear arms shall not be infringed. However, the ensuing debate over the right to bear arms and the consequences of such behavior has been anything but simplistic.

The best-known proponent for the right to bear arms—the National Rifle Association (NRA)—has found an unlikely ally in traditionally liberal criminologists. In "The Right to Carry," the NRA adds to its constitutional stance key findings from a growing body of literature examining the crime-deterrence value of firearms. Primarily, the NRA notes that the crime rate is lower in "right-to-carry" states than in states without such provisions.

In "Reverse Fire," Josh Sugarmann claims that gun violence is a public health issue resulting in numerous deaths each year. Sugarmann also discusses how gun control laws don't provide any real solutions.

Issue 11: Can right-to-carry laws reduce crime?

The Right to Carry

From just a few states only a short time ago, nearly two-thirds of the states now have laws respecting the right of individual citizens to exercise their fundamental right of self-defense by carrying concealed firearms for protection against criminals. Among legislative issues related to the right to keep and bear arms, nothing so clearly represents the will of the American people as the Right to Carry movement sweeping the nation during the last decade. And nothing so disillusions "gun control" advocates, whose *control*-oriented philosophy the American people are implicitly rejecting.[1]

- ***31 states have Right to Carry laws.*** 127 million Americans—nearly half the U.S. population, including 60% of handgun owners—live in Right to Carry states. Twenty-two states have adopted Right to Carry laws since the mid-1980s; 19 states since 1995.[2]
- ***Right to Carry laws reduce crime.*** In their landmark study, Prof. John R. Lott, Jr., and David B. Mustard, of the Univ. of Chicago, found that "allowing citizens to carry concealed weapons deters violent crimes and it appears to produce no increase in accidental deaths. If those states which did not have Right to Carry concealed gun provisions had adopted them in 1992, approximately 1,570 murders; 4,177 rapes; and over 60,000 aggravated assaults would have been avoided yearly. . . . [T]he estimated annual gain from allowing concealed handguns is at least $6.214 billion. . . . [W]hen state concealed handgun laws went into effect in a county, murders fell by 8.5 percent, and rapes and aggravated assaults fell by 5 and 7 percent." ("Crime, Deterrence, and Right to Carry Concealed Handguns," 1996. See also, Lott, *More Guns, Less Crime,* Univ. of Chicago Press, 1998.)
- ***States with Right to Carry laws have lower violent crime rates.*** On average, they have a 24% lower total violent crime rate, a 19% lower homicide rate, a 39% lower robbery rate, and a 19% lower aggravated assault rate, compared to other states and the District of Columbia. The nine states with the lowest violent crime rates are all Right to Carry states. (Data: FBI)
- ***Restrictive carry laws have been on the books for decades, but have never reduced crime.*** Washington, D.C. and Chicago (which have banned handguns), Detroit and Baltimore are four of the five major U.S. cities with the highest homicide rates. Baltimore had more murders in 1998 than in 1997. Chicago reports that it had more murders in the first half of 1998, compared to 1997. Los Angeles remains among the 10 major U.S. cities with the highest homicide rates.
- ***Crime has decreased in America recently, but not because of restrictive carry laws.*** Restrictive carry laws have been on the books for decades, but crime didn't begin declining nationally until 1992. The N.Y.P.D. reduced crime by cracking down on criminals on the streets. Texas built prisons. Many states significantly increased their incarceration rates. In Richmond, Va., U.S. Attorneys launched "Project Exile," to increase prosecution of illegal gun possession.
- ***Carry permit holders are much more law-abiding than the rest of the public.*** Only a minuscule percentage of permit holders commit firearm crimes.

Before 1987, only Georgia, Indiana, Maine, New Hampshire, North Dakota, South Dakota and Washington had "shall issue" RTC laws, requiring law enforcement officials or courts to issue firearm carrying permits to applicants who meet fair statewide standards established by the Legislature. Alabama and Connecticut law allowed authorities to issue carry permits at their discretion, and for the most part they did so fairly. Vermont law respected the right to carry a firearm without a permit. In other states, however, law enforcement discretion over permits regularly resulted in permits being denied to eligible applicants, or carrying a firearm was prohibited and no permits were available.

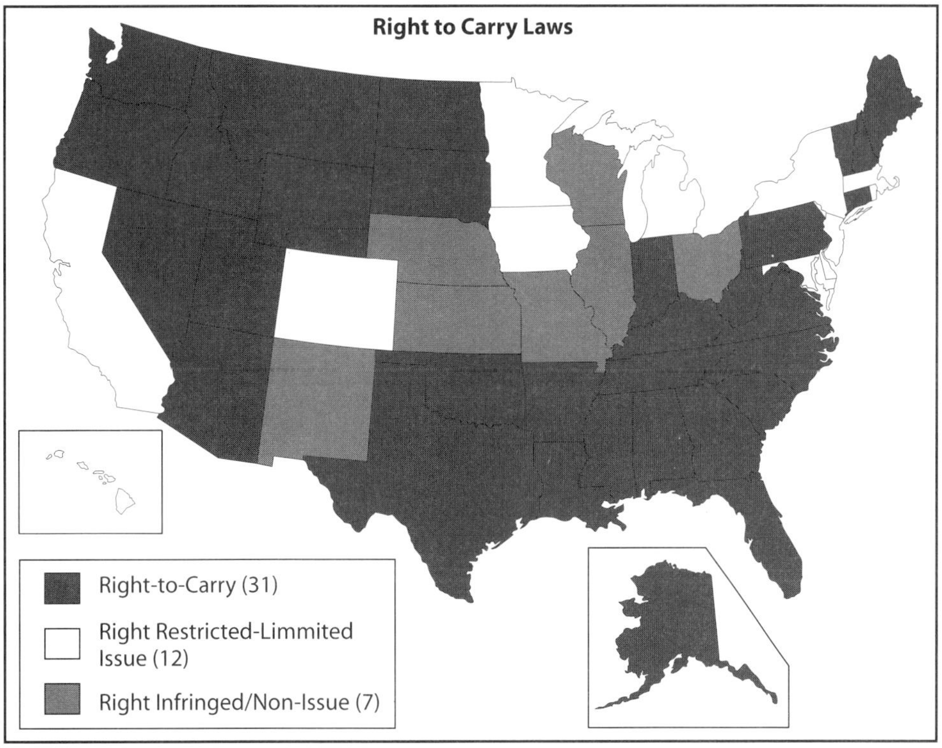

Right to Carry states: January 1999.

RTC in Florida

In 1987, Florida enacted a "shall issue" RTC law, now the framework for similar laws and legislative proposals in other states. The law was supported by the Florida Dept. of Law Enforcement, Florida Sheriffs Assn., Florida Police Chiefs Assn., and other law enforcement groups. Opponents waged a fear-based campaign, claiming crime would increase if law-abiding citizens carried guns. Anti-gun politicians predicted Florida would become the "GUNshine State." The news media forecast vigilante justice and "Wild West" shootouts on every corner. One newspaper said "[A] pistol-packing citizenry will mean itchier trigger fingers. . . . South Florida's climate of smoldering fear would flash like napalm when every stranger totes a piece, and every mental snap in traffic could lead to the crack of gunfire."

Those predictions were ultimately proven false. Florida's homicide rate has decreased 41% since the state adopted its RTC law. In the same period, the national rate has decreased 20%. Only 0.02% of Florida carry permits have been revoked because of firearm crimes committed by license holders. Florida's Licensing Division Director, John Russi, has said of the ratio, "When you compare that to the number of licenses that were issued, that's very small." The firearm crime rate among permit holders, is a fraction of the rate for the state as a whole. (FBI)

Though anti-gun activists claim that citizens are not capable of handling firearms safely and that allowing people to carry firearms will lead to an increase in accidents, Director Russi has stated that his Department has "no record of any accidents or incidents from a lack of training" and that "Florida's concealed weapon law has been very successful. All major law enforcement groups supported the original legislation and in the eight years the program has been in place, none of these groups has requested any changes. . . . [S]ome of the opponents of concealed weapon legislation in 1987 now admit the program has not created the problems many predicted." (Testimony before the Michigan House of Representatives Judiciary Committee, Dec. 5, 1995.)

Florida's Homicide and Total Violent Crime Trends Since RTC

As noted, Florida's homicide rate has decreased 41% since the state adopted its RTC law. Anti-gun activists claim that Florida's three-day waiting period is responsible for the state's homicide rate decrease. Historically, though, waiting periods have not caused reductions in homicide. California increased its five-day waiting period to 15 days in 1975. But from 1974, the last year before the 15-day wait took effect, to 1980, the state's homicide rate rose 53%. Even with the national decrease in crime during the

1990s, California's homicide rate remains 21% higher than the rate for the rest of the country; its total violent crime rate is 37% higher. States subject to the Brady Act's now-expired five-day "waiting period" experienced worse violent crime trends than states exempt from that provision. (Data: FBI) Anti-gun researcher David McDowell has observed that "waiting periods have no influence on either gun homicides or gun suicides." ("Preventative Effects of Firearm Regulations on Injury Mortality," prepared for presentation to the annual meeting of the American Society of Criminology, 1993.)

Anti-gun activists also claim that Florida's high total violent crime rate "proves" that RTC doesn't work. There are several reasons to reject that notion, however. First, firearms are involved in only 26% of "violent crimes" (homicides, rapes, robberies and aggravated assaults). Ninety-three percent of violent crimes are aggravated assaults and robberies, and firearms are used in only 20% of aggravated assaults and in 40% of robberies. (FBI) Second, Florida's violent crime rate was significantly higher than the national rate for decades before Florida's carry law went into effect. Third, while both the Florida and national violent crime rates have decreased 1% since Florida adopted its RTC law, Florida's decrease has been steady, while the U.S. rate rose during 1990–1992, before beginning to decrease in 1993.

More Law-Abiding Than the Rest of the Public

Attorney David Kopel has noted that "Whenever a state legislature first considers a concealed-carry bill, opponents typically warn of horrible consequences. Permit-holders will slaughter each other in traffic disputes, while would-be Rambos shoot bystanders in incompetent attempts to thwart crime. But within a year of passage, the issue usually drops off the news media's radar screen, while gun-control advocates in the legislature conclude that the law wasn't so bad after all." ("The Untold Triumph of Concealed-Carry Permits," *Policy Review,* July–August 1996, p. 9). The following reports show why RTC laws have not turned out as their critics predicted.

- ***Florida***—Only 0.02% of licenses issued (107 of 540,025) from 10/87–11/30/98 have been revoked due to firearm crimes by licensees. (Dept. of State, Div. of Licensing, www.dos.state.fl.us.—click on "The Department," "Licensing," "Statistical Reports.") In a 3/15/95 official correspondence to the governor and other state officials, Department of Law Enforcement Commissioner James T. Moore stated that "From a law enforcement perspective, the licensing process has not resulted in problems in the community from people arming themselves with concealed weapons."
- ***Louisiana***—0.2% of permits issued (21 of 10,309) through 12/98 have been revoked for *any* reason. (State Police)
- ***Oklahoma***—0.1% of permits issued (33 or 27,278) through Jan. 1999 have been revoked for *any* reason. (State Bureau of Investigation)
- ***North Carolina***—0.3% of permits issued (102 of 35,942) from 12/1/95–1/5/99 have been revoked for *any* reason. (State Bureau of Investigation)
- ***South Carolina***—0.3% of permits issued (56 of 18,496) from Aug. 1996–1/18/99 have been revoked for *any* reason. (State Law Enforcement Division)
- ***Texas***—0.4% of carry permits issued (718 out of 195,630) from 1/1/96–1/13/99, have been revoked for *any* reason. (Dept. of Public Safety) Then-DPS Director Col. James Wilson said, "It has impressed me how remarkably responsible the permit holders have been." (Bruce Tomaso, "Gun law's record impresses official," *Dallas Morning News,* 6/11/96.)
- ***Utah***—1% of permits issued (215 of 22,401) have been revoked for *any* reason.
- ***Virginia***—0.1% of permits issued (88 of 77,180) from 7/95–12/98 have been revoked for *any* reason. (State Police) Public Safety Secretary Jerry Kilgore said, "Virginia has not turned into Dodge City. We have not seen a problem."
- ***Wyoming***—only 0.2% of permits issued (10 of 5,288 from 10/1/94–1/11/99 have been revoked for *any* reason. (Attorney General's Office, Dept. of Criminal Investigation)

Handgun Control, Inc.'s Latest "Evaluation" of RTC Laws

In January, 1999, several months before Missouri's RTC referendum, HCI issued a "study" purporting to show that between 1992–1997, violent crime rates declined less in RTC states than in other states. On its face, the claim was noteworthy because it was a long overdue admission by the group that its previous notion, that RTC laws cause crime to rise, was erroneous.

There were serious flaws in the new HCI claim, however. In comparing the violent crime trends of RTC states to those of states with restrictive carry laws, the anti-gun group grossly miscategorized the states. HCI categorized the states according to whether they had RTC laws in

1997, but calculated the states' crime trends from 1992–1997. The error was obvious: Of the 31 states that had RTC laws in 1997, only 17 had their laws in 1992. Alaska, Arizona, Tennessee and Wyoming adopted their laws in 1994. Arkansas, Nevada, North Carolina, Oklahoma, Texas, Utah and Virginia adopted theirs in 1995. Kentucky, Louisiana and South Carolina adopted theirs in 1996. Since the benefits of RTC in a state are greater the longer the state has its law, a proper computation would take into account the very short period of time that some states have had RTC, especially Louisiana and South Carolina, which had very high crime rates before adopting RTC.

Also, HCI classified Alabama and Connecticut as "restrictive" states. Both states provide for law enforcement officials to have discretion over the issuance of permits, but permits are issued fairly, by and large. HCI counted the two states as restrictive, probably because they had very large decreases in their violent crime rates, and their inclusion in the restrictive states group exaggerated its decrease.

Also, HCI's 1992 starting point inevitably underrepresented the impact of RTC laws on violent crime. By 1992, many states had had RTC for many years and had already experienced significant decreases in crime. Only a small part of their decreases to date occurred after 1992. HCI erred by crediting restrictive carry laws with the decrease in crime in states that have such laws. Every state that has a restrictive carrying law has had it for many years, or in some cases many decades. However, crime did not begin to decline in those states until the 1990s, when a variety of things unrelated to carry laws occurred. Among them, New York City, which accounts for a significant portion of the nation's crime, began a massive city-wide crackdown on a broad range of crimes. Also, the violent aspect of the drug trade has subsided, with the aging of drug gang members. Further, many states have significantly increased their incarceration rates. Finally, many states with restrictive carry laws have historically had very high crime rates, thus allowing significant decreases in crime recently, due to the general factors noted.

HCI failed to mention that violent crime is lower in RTC states. In 1991, the last year before crime began to decline nationally, the then-17 RTC states had a 20% lower violent crime rate overall, compared to other states. The seven states with the lowest violent crime rates were RTC states.

Fifteen of the 17 RTC states had violent crime rates below the national rate. Ten of the 12 states with violent crime rates above the national rate were restrictive states, as was highest-crime D.C.

Similarly, in 1997, the most recent year of data available, the now-31 RTC states had a 24% lower violent crime rate, a 19% lower homicide rate, a 39% lower robbery rate, and a 19% lower aggravated assault rate, on average, compared to restrictive states. Nine of the 10 states with the lowest violent crime rates are states that have RTC laws.

Additional reason to question HCI's reliability as an evaluator of RTC laws, the group gives higher carry law "grades" to states with higher crime rates. As noted, nine of the 10 states with the lowest violent crime rates are states that have RTC laws. HCI gives these nine states an average grade of "F+."

The University of Maryland "Study"—Using Your Money to Fund Anti-Gun "Research"

In March 1995, David McDowell and some colleagues released a "study" paid for with *taxpayers' money* by the federal Centers for Disease Control and Prevention (CDC). ("Easing Concealed Firearm Laws: Effects on Homicide in Three States.") The CDC regularly uses tax dollars to fund anti-gun "research," though legislation to stop the CDC's misuse of funds has been passed by Congress. The "study" claimed gun homicide rates increased in Miami, Jacksonville and Tampa after Florida's carry law took effect. FDLE Commissioner James T. Moore has said that he doubts the researchers' figures. ("Gun Control: License to conceal," by David van Biema, *Time,* March 27, 1995, pp. 27–29.) For good reason: total homicide rates declined 10%, 18% and 20%, respectively, in those metropolitan areas, from 1987 until 1993, the latest available data when the "study" was released.

McDowell et al. came up with their figures by calculating Jacksonville and Tampa homicide trends from the early 1970s, when homicide rates were lower than in 1993, to create the false impression that Florida's 1987 carry law caused homicide to rise. Then they calculated Miami's trend from 1983 forward, since homicide rates before 1983 were higher, and their inclusion in the comparison would have shown that the city's homicide rate had decreased. Further rendering the study worthless, none of the homicides studied were committed by license holders, and no distinction was made between homicides that occurred in situations where a license would be required to carry a firearm and other homicides. McDowell's brand of math comes as no surprise. In a previous study, he claimed Washington, D.C.'s homicide rate decreased after its handgun ban, which took effect in 1977. In reality, D.C.'s homicide rate tripled after the ban. (FBI)

Through 1995, two-thirds of Florida cities of 10,000 or more population experienced decreases in homicide rates, one out of three experiencing a 100% reduction, having had no homicides in 1995 (improved from one-in-four during 1994). Eight of Florida's 10 largest cities experienced decreases. Through 1996, eight of Florida's 10 most populous cities showed decreases in homicide rates since 1987, with the aggregate homicide rate for the 10 cities decreasing 29.7% and the average reduction of the cities 21.9%. The seven largest Florida cities with the highest homicide rates in 1987 all had decreases through 1996. All of Florida's 10 largest cities showed decreases in robbery from 1987–1996. While the state's rate decreased 18.9%, the 10 cities as a group decreased 19.1% and averaged a 15.8% decrease. The biggest decrease was Jacksonville (34.3%), the state's most populous city. (FBI)

In 1997, one of every three Florida cities of 10,000 or more population experienced zero homicides. Of Florida's 10 largest cities, nine have experienced decreases in their homicide rates since the state adopted its Right To Carry law: Ft. Lauderdale (–71%), Orlando (–58%), Jacksonville (–54%), Tampa (–45%), Clearwater (–43%), Tallahassee (–34%), St. Petersburg (–26%), Miami (–21%) and Hialeah (–5%). The homicide rate for Florida's 10 largest cities as a group decreased 34%. (FBI)

Violence Policy Center "Study"

In 1995, a tiny, radical anti-gun group calling itself the Violence Policy Center (VPC), led by gun-ban advocate Josh Sugarmann, released a "study" claiming that Florida's carry law "puts guns into the hands of criminals." ("Concealed Carry: The Criminal's Companion.") The claim was preposterous, since the law relates only to the carrying of firearms already lawfully possessed; not the acquisition or ownership of firearms. VPC also claimed that "criminals do apply for concealed carry licenses" in Florida, without noting that Florida naturally rejects such applications, just as banks reject loan applications from people with bad credit ratings. VPC itself underscored the point by including in its "study" a list of alleged criminals who, after their applications were rejected, wanted the rejections reconsidered.

Florida's Secretary of State, Sandra B. Mortham rejected the VPC's allegations, blaming them on the group's "zeal to attack the National Rifle Association." To "set the record straight," Secretary Mortham stated that "As of November 30, 1995, the Department had denied 723 applications due to criminal history. The fact that these 723 individuals did not receive a license clearly indicates that the process is working." Secretary Mortham added, "The statistics show the majority of concealed weapon or firearm licensees are honest, law-abiding citizens exercising their right to be armed for the purpose of lawful self-defense." (Letter to the *St. Petersburg Times,* January 11, 1996.) FDLE Commissioner James T. Moore had previously noted that "The strict provisions of 790.06, Florida Statutes, preclude the licensing of convicted felons, etc., thus allowing the permitting of law-abiding citizens who do not routinely commit crimes or otherwise violate the law." (March 15, 1995.)

The VPC has since continued its practice of releasing headline-grabbing claims, but with similarly mixed results. In 1997, the group attacked NRA's Eddie Eagle Gun Safety Program only to be lambasted in newspapers normally supportive of severe restrictions on the right to arms. In 1998, the group attacked Texas' successful firearm carrying law, only to be similarly rebuked by state officials. The group's tactics come as no surprise, given the ethics of its leader, Josh Sugarmann. In 1988, Sugarmann authored "Assault Weapons in America," a primer on that issue for anti-gun activists, which suggested: "[T]he issue of handgun restriction remains a non-issue with the vast majority of legislators, the press, and public. . . . Assault weapons . . . are a new topic. The weapons' menacing looks, coupled with the public's confusion over fully automatic machine guns versus semi-automatic assault weapons—anything that looks like a machine gun is assumed to be a machine gun—can only increase the chance of public support for restrictions on these weapons."

Right to Carry Legislation Since the Mid-1980s

Since the mid-1980s, 22 state legislatures have enacted new "shall issue" carry laws (where no permit system previously existed), changed from discretionary permit issue to "shall issue," or re-affirmed a "shall issue" law through judicial ruling. Other states improved existing "shall issue" laws.

1987: Florida enacted new "shall issue" law.

1989: Oregon, Pennsylvania and West Virginia enacted new "shall issue" laws. Georgia confirmed "shall issue" by judicial ruling.

1990: Idaho and Mississippi enacted new "shall issue" laws.

1991: Montana enacted new "shall issue" law. Idaho improved its "shall issue" law.

1994: Alaska, Arizona, Tennessee, and Wyoming enacted new "shall issue" laws.

1995: Arkansas, North Carolina, Oklahoma and Texas enacted new "shall issue" laws. Nevada, Utah and Virginia changed from discretionary to "shall issue." Florida and Idaho improved their RTC laws. Pennsylvania brought Philadelphia under state law.

1996: Kentucky enacted "shall issue" law (effective Oct. 1). Louisiana (effective April 19) and South Carolina (effective August 22) changed from discretionary laws to "shall issue." West Virginia reaffirmed "shall issue" legislatively, after the state Supreme Court ruled that the state's system of issuing permits through circuit court judges was unconstitutional. Georgia, Idaho, Oklahoma and Tennessee improved their RTC laws.

1997: Arkansas, Georgia, Mississippi, North Dakota, Oklahoma, Tennessee, Texas, Utah and Virginia improved their RTC laws.

1998: Alaska improved its RTC law.

Citizens Can Defend Themselves Safely

The National Center for Health Statistics and National Safety Council report that fatal firearm accidents dropped to an all-time low in 1996, among the total population and children in particular. Since 1930, the annual number of fatal firearm accidents has decreased 65%, while the U.S. population has more than doubled and the number of firearms owned has more than quadrupled. (National Center for Health Statistics: "Deaths from 282 selected causes, 1996"; National Safety Council: *Accident Facts, 1997 Edition,* pp. 42–43; U.S. Population: Bureau of the Census; Firearm numbers: BATF. See also, NRA "Firearm Safety Fact Sheet.")

Criminologist Gary Kleck's analysis of National Crime Victimization Survey data shows that "robbery and assault victims who used a gun to resist were less likely to be attacked or to suffer an injury than those who used any other methods of self-protection or those who did not resist at all." (*Point Blank: Guns and Violence in America,* Aldine de Gruyter, 1991, p. 124.)

Kleck's research has also shown that firearms are used for self-protection about 2.5 million times annually. (Kleck and Marc Gertz, "Armed Resistance to Crime: The Prevalence and Nature of Self-Defense with a Gun," *Journal of Criminal Law and Criminology,* 86:150–187, Fall 1995.) Evaluating Kleck's work, the late criminologist Marvin E. Wolfgang, who described himself as "as strong a gun-control advocate as can be found among the criminologists in this country" who would "eliminate all guns from the civilian population and maybe even from the police," said, "It is hard to challenge the data collected. We do not have contrary evidence. . . . [T]he methodological soundness of the current Kleck and Gertz study is clear. I cannot further debate it. . . . I do not like their conclusions that having a gun can be useful, but I cannot fault their methodology. They have tried earnestly to meet all objections in advance and have done exceedingly well." ("A Tribute to a View That I Have Opposed," *Journal of Criminal Law and Criminology,* Fall 1995, pp. 188–192.)

A 1986 study for the U.S. Department of Justice found that 34% of felons had been "scared off, shot at, wounded or captured by an armed victim," and 40% of felons have not committed particular crimes for fear their potential victims were armed. (James D. Wright and Peter H. Rossi, *Armed and Considered Dangerous: A Survey of Felons and Their Firearms,* Aldine de Gruyter, 1991.)

The Right to Self-Protection Has Been Recognized for Centuries, and Remains So Today

The great Roman philosopher, senator, and lawyer, Cicero, argued 2000 years ago that "There exists a law, not written down anywhere but inborn in our hearts; a law which comes to us not by training or custom or reading but by deprivation and absorption and adoption from nature itself; a law which has come to us not from theory but from practice, not by instruction but by natural intuition. I refer to the law which lays it down that, if our lives are endangered by plots or violence or armed robbers or enemies, any and every method of protecting ourselves is morally right. When weapons reduce them to silence, the laws no longer expect one to await their pronouncements. For people who decide to wait for these will have to wait for justice, too—and meanwhile they must suffer injustice first." (Stephen P. Halbrook, *The Every Man Be Armed: The Evolution of a Constitutional Right,* Albuquerque: Univ. of New Mexico Press, 1984, p. 17.)

Many centuries later, the great English jurist, Sir William Blackstone, observed that the English Bill of Rights signified that Englishmen possessed "the right of having and using arms for self-preservation and defense." (Halbrook, p. 45.) Blackstone believed that "having arms suitable for their defence" was one of the five auxiliary rights people possessed "to protect and maintain inviolate the three great and primary rights," the first of which is "personal security." (Halbrook, p. 54.) Sir Michael Foster, judge of the Court of King's Bench, wrote in the late 18th century that the Common Law recognized that "The right of self-defense . . . is founded in the law of nature, and is not, nor can be, superseded by any law of society." (Robert Dowlut and Janet Knoop, "State Constitutions and The Right to Keep and Bear Arms," *Oklahoma City University Law Review,* 1982, p. 183.)

The Supreme Court of the United States, in *U.S. v. Cruikshank,* recognized that the right to arms preexisted the Constitution (92 U.S. 542, 1876. The Court stated that the right to arms "is not a right granted by the Constitution. Neither is it in any manner dependent upon that instrument for its existence.") In *Beard v. United States,* the Court approved the common-law rule that a person "may repel force by force" in self-defense, and concluded that when attacked a person "was entitled to stand his ground and meet any attack made upon him with a deadly weapon, in such a way and with such force" as needed to prevent "great bodily injury or death." (158 U.S. 550, 1895.) The laws of all 50 states, and the constitutions of most states, recognize the right to use armed force in self-defense. In the Gun Control Act (1968) and the Firearms Owners' Protection Act (1986), Congress affirmed the right of citizens to possess firearms for protection, stating that the law was not intended to "place any undue or unnecessary Federal restrictions or burdens on law-abiding citizens with respect to the acquisition, possession, or use of firearms appropriate to the purpose of hunting, trapshooting, target shooting, personal protection, or any other lawful activity. . . ." (Public Laws 90-618 and 99-308.)

The Police Are Not Obligated to Protect Citizens

Courts have held that the police are under no obligation to provide protection to individual citizens. In *Warren v. District of Columbia* (444 A.2d 1, 1981), the District of Columbia Court of Appeals ruled that "official police personnel and the government employing them are not generally liable to victims of criminal acts for failure to provide adequate police protection . . . this uniformly accepted rule rests upon the fundamental principle that a government and its agents are under no general duty to provide public services, such as police protection, to any particular citizen . . . a publicly maintained police force constitutes a basic governmental service provided to benefit the community at large by promoting public peace, safety and good order." In *Bowers v. DeVito* (686 F.2d 616, 1982), the Court of Appeals for the Seventh Circuit ruled that "[T]here is no constitutional right to be protected by the state against being murdered by criminals or madmen."

Handgun Control, Inc's., and Other Gun-Control Supporters' Views on Self-Defense

Gun control activists have claimed that women shouldn't resist attackers. Then-Handgun Control, Inc., Chair, the late Pete Shields, advised that, if attacked, people should "put up no defense—give them what they want." (*Guns Don't Die—People Do,* N.Y.: Arbor House, 1981.) According to Dennis Henigan, the director of Handgun Control, Inc.'s Center to Prevent Handgun Violence Legal Action Project, self-defense is "not a federally guaranteed constitutional right." (*USA Today,* November 20, 1991, p. 11A.)

According to anti-gun researchers George D. Newton and Franklin E. Zimring, "women generally are less capable of self-defense and less knowledgeable about firearms." (*Firearms and Violence in American Life,* National Commission on the Causes and Prevention of Violence, n.d., p. 64.) Gun control supporters cite a small study of King's County (Seattle), Washington, claiming a gun in the home is "43 times more likely" to be used to kill a family member than to kill in self-defense. (Arthur L. Kellermann, "Protection or Peril?: An Analysis of Firearm-Related Deaths in the Home," *New England Journal of Medicine,* 314: 1557–1560, 1986.) To reach that ratio, however, self-defense firearms uses were grossly undercounted by counting only cases in which criminals were killed. In most protective firearms uses, criminals are scared off, captured or non-fatally wounded. Additionally, suicides were counted as family member killings, increasing the suicide count more than 500%. The claim that women use handguns to kill few criminals, but are more often killed by criminals with handguns, is misleading, again, because criminals are rarely killed in self-defense and because it is based upon police reports only, excluding fatal shootings ruled self-defense or justifiable by the courts.

Rep. Stearns' National Right to Carry Reciprocity Bill

In February 1999, Rep. Cliff Stearns (R-Fla.) introduced H.R. 492, the Right to Safety and Personal Protection Act (introduced in the previous Congress as H.R. 339). H.R. 492 proposes to allow any person with a valid firearm carrying permit or license, issued by a state, to carry a firearm in any other state, as follows: In states that issue firearm carry permits, each state's laws governing where firearms may be carried would apply within its own borders. In states that do not issue carry permits, a federal "bright-line" standard would permit carrying in places other than police stations; courthouses; public polling places; meetings of state, county, or municipal governing bodies; schools; passenger areas of airports; and certain other locations. H.R. 492 applies to D.C., Puerto Rico and U.S. territories, though D.C. residents are prohibited from purchasing handguns. Rep. Stearns has noted that the Lott/Mustard study shows that RTC laws deter crime and that reciprocity is needed "to greatly expand the security individuals enjoy in their own states when they travel or simply cross state lines." Under H.R. 492, people who have carry permits issued by their home states would be able to carry lawfully in any other state, under either the laws of the state they are carrying in (if the state issues permits) or under the federal standard (if the state doesn't issue permits). People who live in states that do not issue permits would be allowed to carry in any state, provided they possess a carry permit issued by any state, under either the state or federal law, as noted.

Notes

1. *U.S. News & World Report* reported August 19, 1996 (p. 18), that "Handgun Control, Inc., . . . is said to be worried that it is losing the public relations war to the National Rifle Association, and plans to hire a public relations firm to 're-orient' its message. It is also considering a name change because, among other reasons, polls and focus groups show that many Americans are uncomfortable with the word *control.*" HCI now releases propaganda under the name of its "educational" wing, the Center to Prevent Handgun Violence, an organizational member of the HELP Network, which supports prohibiting the private ownership of handguns.
2. Additionally, 18 states adopted range protection measures (total, 29), five adopted preemption of local firearm ordinances (total, 42), four adopted "Instant Check" (total, 17), and two adopted hunter protection laws (total, 50). In 1998, Wisconsin voters approved a constitutional amendment protecting the right to arms, making theirs the 44th state to do so.

FRAME the DEBATE

Form at end of book

Issue 11: Can right-to-carry laws reduce crime?

Reverse Fire

The Brady Bill won't break the sick hold guns have on America. It's time for tougher measures.

Josh Sugarmann

Josh Sugarmann is executive director of the Violence Policy Center and author of NRA: Money, Firepower & Fear.

For seven years gun-control advocates have lobbied for the Brady Bill, which mandates a national waiting period for buying handguns. But ironically, the bill's passage may actually benefit the gun industry. Oversold by its supporters, the Brady Bill has become synonymous in American minds with gun control itself. If violence continues once a national waiting period goes into effect (as it likely will), the gun lobby will offer the Brady Bill as proof that gun control doesn't work.

With its passage, gun-control advocates find themselves at a crossroads. We can continue to push legislation of dubious effectiveness. Or we can acknowledge that gun violence is a public-health crisis fueled by an inherently dangerous consumer product. To end the crisis, we have to regulate—or, in the case of handguns and assault weapons, completely ban—the product.

The romantic myths attached to gun ownership stop many people from thinking of them as a consumer product. As a result, the standard risk analysis applied to other potentially dangerous products—pesticides, prescription drugs, or toasters—has never been applied to firearms.

Yet guns are manufactured by corporations—with boards of directors, marketing plans, employees, and a bottom-line—just like companies that manufacture toasters. What separates the gun industry from other manufacturers is lack of regulation.

For example, when a glut in the market caused handgun production to plummet from 2.6 million in 1982 to 1.4 million in 1986, the industry retooled its product line. To stimulate sales, manufacturers added firepower, technology, and capacity to their new models. The result: assault weapons, a switch from six-shot revolvers to high-capacity pistols, and increased use of plastics and high-tech additions like integral laser sights.

The industry was free to make these changes (most of which made the guns more dangerous) because guns that are 50 caliber or less and not fully automatic can be manufactured with virtually no restrictions. The Bureau of Alcohol, Tobacco, and Firearms lacks even the common regulatory powers—including safety-standard setting and recall—granted government agencies such as the Consumer Product Safety Commission, the Food and Drug Administration, and the Environmental Protection Agency.

Yet guns are the second most deadly consumer product (after cars) on the market. In Texas and Louisiana the firearms-related death rate already exceeds that for motor vehicles, and by the end of the decade firearms will likely supplant automobiles as the leading cause of product-related death throughout the United States.

But since Americans view firearm suicides, murders, and fatal accidents as separate problems, the enormity of America's gun crisis goes unrecognized. In 1990, American guns claimed an estimated 37,000 lives. Federal Bureau of Investigation data shows that gun murders that year reached an all-time high of 15,377; a record of 12,489 involved handguns.

In 1990 (the most recent year for which statistics are available), 18,885 Americans took their own lives with firearms, and an estimated 13,030 of those deaths involved handguns. Unlike pills, gas, or razor blades—which are of limited effectiveness—guns are rarely forgiving. For example, self-inflicted cutting wounds account for 15 percent of all suicide attempts but only 1 percent of all successful suicides. Poisons and drugs account for 70 percent of suicide attempts but less than 12 percent of all suicides. Conversely, nonfatal, self-inflicted gunshot wounds are rare—yet three-fifths of all U.S. suicides involved firearms.

In addition to the human toll, the economic costs of not regulating guns are staggering. The Centers for Disease Control (CDC) estimated that the lifetime economic cost—hospitalization, rehabilitation, and lost wages—of firearms violence was $14.4 billion in 1985, making it the third most expensive injury category. The average lifetime cost per person for each firearms fatality—$373,520—was the highest of any injury.

Such human and economic costs are not tolerated for any other product. Many consumer products from lawn darts to the Dalkon Shield have been banned in the United States, even though they claimed only a fraction of the lives guns do in a day. The firearms industry is long overdue for the simple, regulatory oversight applied to other consumer products. For public safety, the ATF must be given authority to control the design, manufacture, distribution, and sale of firearms and ammunition.

Under such a plan, the ATF would subject each category of firearm and ammunition to an unreasonable-risk analysis to weed out products whose potential for harm outweighs any possible benefit. This would result in an immediate ban on the future production and sale of handguns and assault weapons because of their high risk and low utility.

Because they are easily concealed and accessed, handguns hold the dubious honor of being our number-one murder and suicide tool. Assault weapons—high-capacity, semiautomatic firearms designed primarily for the military and police—pose a public-safety risk as the result of their firepower. A 1989 study of ATF data conducted by Cox Newspapers found that assault firearms were twenty times more likely to turn up in crime traces than conventional firearms.

In addition, a regulatory approach to firearms would exert far greater control over the industry and its distribution network. It would not, however, affect the availability of standard sporting rifles and shotguns, which would continue to be sold because of their usefulness and relatively low risk.

Such an approach is the industry's worst nightmare—conjuring images of an all-powerful "gun czar." And in a sense, gun manufacturers would be right: the ATF would become a gun czar in the same way that the EPA is a pesticide czar, the FDA is a prescription-drug-and-medical-device czar, and the Consumer Product Safety Commission is a toaster czar. Yet it is just such a regulatory approach that has dramatically reduced motor-vehicle deaths and injuries over the past twenty years.

Gun-control advocates cannot afford to spend another seven years battling over piecemeal measures that have little more to offer than good intentions. We are far past the point where registration, licensing, safety training, background checks, or waiting periods will have much effect on firearms violence. Tired of being shot and threatened, Americans are showing a deeper understanding of gun violence as a public-health issue, and are becoming aware of the need to restrict specific categories of weapons.

As America's health-care debate continues, discussion of the role of guns—from the human price paid in mortality to the dollars-and-cents cost of uninsured gunshot victims—can only help clarify that gun violence is not a crime issue but a public-health issue. This shift in attitude is apparent in the firearms component of Clinton's domestic violence prevention group, which is co-chaired not only by a representative from the Justice Department—as expected—but also by a CDC official.

Even if the only legacy of this current wave of revulsion is that gun violence will now be viewed as a public-health issue, America will still have taken a very first step toward gun sanity.

FRAME the DEBATE

Form at end of book

WiseGuide Wrap-Up

While it isn't clear if owning a gun can prevent a person from becoming a victim of a violent crime, it is fairly intuitive that the mere possession of a firearm in the home greatly increases the risk that someone will be killed in a shooting.

Therefore, is it better to prepare for a potentially fatal situation, or to wait for such an event to occur and respond accordingly? The chance of a person being involved in a violent crime is slim to begin with, and owning a firearm may increase the chance of being shot or killed. However, to many, the Constitution is clear—American citizens have the right to bear arms.

R.E.A.L. Sites

This list provides a print preview of typical **Coursewise** R.E.A.L. sites. (There are over 100 such sites at the **Courselinks**™ site.) The danger in printing URLs is that web sites can change overnight. As we went to press, these sites were functional using the URLs provided. If you come across one that isn't, please let us know via email to: webmaster@coursewise.com. Use your Passport to access the most current list of R.E.A.L. sites at the **Courselinks** site.

Site name: National Rifle Association

URL: http://www.nra.org/

Why is it R.E.A.L.? The National Rifle Association's site contains numerous articles on the Second Amendment and guns.

Key topic: Second Amendment

Try this: Examine some of the new legislative activity that the NRA is conducting.

Site name: Bureau of Alcohol, Tobacco and Firearms

URL: http://www.atf.treas.gov/

Why is it R.E.A.L.? In addition to providing reports and documents, the Bureau of Alcohol, Tobaco and Firearms also makes available data on various crimes that are under its jurisdiction.

Key topics: federal law enforcement agency, alcohol, tobacco, firearms

Try this: Look at some of the new techniques that the ATF is employing to combat crime.

Site name: American Civil Liberties Union

URL: http://www.aclu.org/

Why is it R.E.A.L.? This site, sponsored by the American Civil Liberties Union (ACLU), has an enormous collection of materials related to the criminal justice system, as well as various other social issues. It is an outstanding site for gathering well-documented and scholarly materials. There is also a student's section.

Key topics: civil liberties, rights, freedom

Try this: Browse through the ACLU's special report, "Driving While Black: Racial Profiling on Our Nation's Highways."

Site name: *Law and Order* Magazine

URL: http://www.lawandordermag.com

Why is it R.E.A.L.? *Law and Order* magazine is devoted to police issues. Many of its articles are available on the web site.

Key topic: police

Try this: Read some of the articles from *Law and Order* magazine that interest you.

STAND!

Section 4 Offender Rights

Introduction

We started our exploration of crime and criminology by first studying the causes of crime. Then we looked at the challenges the police face in responding to crime. Next, we focused on criminal justice legislation, hoping to find ways to keep people from ending up in prison. Unfortunately, there is no "cure" for crime, and as correctional personnel know all too well, our criminal justice revolving doors never close. In this section, we contend with the rights of offenders.

While not intuitively an offender rights issue, boot camps are examined in Readings 23 and 24, primarily because of the treatment offenders receive while incarcerated in boot camps and also because of the false promises on which boot camps are predicated. Returning offenders to society when they feel that they are ready for the real world—when, in fact, they are not prepared—can be devastating to youth. Boot camps have been a hot topic of debate lately. With major administrative changes, boot camps might plausibly function as a viable tool for the criminal justice system.

Readings 25 and 26 examine another right of the offender: whether or not chain gangs are legitimate correctional tools. Chain gangs are being brought back into the correctional system, and new technologies may further assist their utilization. However, the oppressive message that these work groups send to the community may not be in the best interest of society.

Readings 27 and 28 focus on a highly controversial issue of offender rights: community notification of sexual predators. The average child molester resides within the home of, or has close ties to, the victim. This being the case, we need to rethink how we deal with sexual predators as they are released back into the community. Another concern is that community notification laws have led to vigilante-type attacks on released offenders, thus placing them in harm's way.

Regardless of the crime committed, offenders still have certain constitutional, moral, and humanitarian rights that must be safeguarded. Granted, small doses of shamming may be good for criminals, based on what we know about deterrence, human behavior, and recidivism, but constant degradation, humiliation, oppression, and torture have no place in our correctional system.

While the punishment needs to be severe enough to ensure that the offender won't recidivate (specific deterrence), it also needs to have some broader deterrent value on other potential offenders (general deterrence). However, the punishment should not be so egregious and demoralizing as to permanently harm the individual.

As you read on, consider the actions of a sheriff in Arizona who makes his male inmates wear pink underwear. Think about the long-term psychological consequences that this type of punishment may lead to, especially without love and reintegration. Inmates are human beings who deserve to maintain their pride and self-respect, even though they have violated the law. The Constitution mandates proper treatment of offenders, while the principles of human rights require that they be treated with dignity.

Can Boot Camps Rehabilitate Youthful Offenders?

ISSUE 12

Take a Closer Look

1. How would you improve the typical boot camp to make it a more effective correctional program?
2. Are there certain types of criminals that you would not send to a boot camp? If so, what kind and why?
3. Do you think that the boot camp environment could be dangerous to youthful offenders?
4. Why might boot camp graduates experience high levels of recidivism?
5. Describe the characteristics of a boot camp as explained by Waldron.
6. What boot camp limitations does Sechrest note?

WiseGuide Intro

Boot camps, modeled after the military's primary induction phase for enlistees, are being used as intermediate sanctions for youthful offenders. The premise is that, if these offenders can be taught discipline, self-esteem, and job skills, such as the boot camp is designed to do for military soldiers, then the offenders can be returned to society, where they become productive, law-abiding citizens.

In "Boot Camp Prison Offers Second Chance to Young Felons," Thomas Waldron walks us through the daily regimen of a boot camp and explains how the program has positively changed the attitudes of some of the offenders. In "Prison 'Boot Camps' Do Not Measure Up," Dale Sechrest dismisses the assertion that these sanctions are effective rehabilitation programs and cautions that boot camps may cause various forms of harm to the participants. Sechrest suggests that, if these programs are to be effective, extensive after-care that follows into the community must be made available to offenders.

Issue 12: Can boot camps rehabilitate youthful offenders?

Boot Camp Prison Offers Second Chance to Young Felons

Thomas W. Waldron

Red Creek, N.Y.—In the old days, Freyn Anderson says, he sold crack in Queens, carried a gun and a bad attitude, and once shot a man during a robbery.

Now, after three weeks in a boot camp prison in upstate New York, 17-year-old Anderson talks about staying "focused," calls everybody sir and in his pocket packs a handful of soggy Cheerios.

"Sir, this inmate just has to carry the Cheerios, sir, because he didn't eat it all, sir," Anderson explains.

In the eight minutes you have to eat here at Butler Shock Incarceration Correctional Facility, you'd better clean your plate or you'll carry the leftovers in your pockets.

Butler is part of the newest fad in corrections—boot camp-style prisons. And Freyn Anderson is the kind of offender these prisons hope to turn around: first-time felons between the ages of 16 and 29 doing their first time in state prison. New York inmates are sent to the shock camp for a six-month term and if they make it through—about 88 percent do—they win parole, no matter how long a sentence they received from a judge.

Maryland plans to open a boot camp prison in Jessup July 1 and state officials have used New York as a model.

At Butler Shock, one of five such prisons in New York, about 90 percent of the inmates dealt or used drugs. The men, on average, read at a fifth-grade level. A majority come from New York City, seven hours away.

By all appearances, the thing inmate Steven Smith carried on his shoulder was a log, a big white-washed log.

But to everyone at Butler Shock, Smith carried a "learning experience."

Smith, baby-faced and 17 years old, claims he made $25,000 a week selling crack cocaine in Brooklyn before he arrived at Butler Shock, had his head shaved and learned there is a Butler way and a wrong way of doing everything.

Smith was given his learning experience after another inmate sat down to a meal the wrong way and six inmates, including Smith, had to stand up and try sitting down again. Irritated, Smith stood up. His chair made too much noise. An officer noticed and asked if Smith had a problem.

"I just told him, 'Yes sir,' because one of the rules is 'Tell the truth with compassion,' sir," Smith said. "Really, I wanted to tell him no."

"Inmate Smith," said the officer as he pointed to the log, "you will carry that learning experience with you for four days."

Smith doesn't complain. "They're going to give me tools to take care of stress, to deal with stress, to keep my attitude under control and don't let the attitude control me.

"I fight the program," he says, "but I meet the program in the middle."

A few minutes later, Butler Superintendent R. Harvey Penny approaches Smith.

"We do break them down and then build them back up. Everything we do is done for a purpose."

—Butler Superintendent R. Harvey Penny

"Is that learning experience heavy enough, Smith?" asks Penny, a huge affable man with 27 years in the New York prison system.

Smith pauses, trying to think of the right answer.

"No, sir," he says finally.

"Then go get that one," Penny says, pointing out a log one size larger.

"We do break them down and then build them back up," Penny says. "Everything we do is done for a purpose."

"Boot Camp Prison Offers Second Chance to Young Felons" by Thomas W. Waldron, *The Baltimore Sun*. Reprinted by permission.

The inmates' day at Butler begins at 5:30 every morning as fluorescent lights flash on, reveille blares over the intercom and drill instructors start screaming.

"Are you fired up?" shouts drill instructor Al Bielowicz in Squad Bay A.

"Fired up! Fired up! Fired up!" the men scream back, only seconds out of bed.

The inmates' entire day is accounted for, beginning with an hour of strenuous calisthenics in the early-morning dark, and moving through work, military drilling, drug counseling and study. They live the Butler way. Meals last eight minutes and there is no talking. They never look someone in the eye. They run. They stop and stand at attention when they approach an official. They ask permission to speak. They call themselves "This inmate."

On the other hand, Butler maintains a small dignity not common in prison: The restroom stalls have doors.

A three-foot-high fence, with no barbed wire, bounds the camp, which sits in a rural community a few miles south of Lake Ontario. The gate is always open.

Unlike other prisons, there are no televisions, radios or newspapers. The inmates have no idea how the local sports teams are doing or who is in the championship games.

"The DIs tell us all we need to know," says one inmate.

They never look someone in the eye. They run. They stop and stand at attention when they approach an official. They ask permission to speak. They call themselves "This inmate."

Twelve inmates from the rookie class at Butler work in a marshy field a couple of miles from the camp, sawing down dense shrubbery to make a duck-nesting area. A cold, steady drizzle falls. Two officers stand nearby. Many of the men kneel in the mud to saw the stubborn, three-inch-wide stumps. They work silently. Normally they would talk, but this afternoon they are in trouble.

"Some of the individuals started talking about New York and how it was," explains Carlos Rivera, a 22-year-old convicted drug dealer. "They started talking bad language. They started with the F word . . . talking about the good old days."

Inmates work outside the camp from about 8:30 A.M. to 3:30 P.M. four days a week. The fifth day they go to classes. There is no work on Saturday and Sunday, but inmates stay busy with the rest of the routine plus organized recreation.

One day, the work included cutting brush in the duck-nesting area, shoveling snow in Red Wing and spreading gravel in a park on Lake Ontario.

At the park site, the small crew works steadily. Men with wheelbarrows loaded with rocks jog from place to place. Many of the men work in shirt-sleeves despite the icy, lakeside weather.

Norman Brown, 23 years old and a month away from graduation from Butler Shock, shovels rocks.

"This isn't hard work. It's not hard enough," says Brown, a former drug dealer from Long Island. Brown was sentenced to three years in prison. By coming to shock camp, he will do six months, if he finishes.

"The impression I had when I first got to shock was I would do the six months and I'll get out of here, you know," Brown says. "It wasn't all about that. After they taught me little things about what shock was about, I knew what I wanted. I wanted to change."

Brown says he has changed. "I was the type of person who didn't like to take orders . . . I've never had an experience like this in my life. I never really held a job. I never in my life accomplished anything."

He started crying in a meeting when he started talking about leaving Butler Shock, he says. Such behavior would brand him a punk or a dupe on the streets in New York.

"I'm ready for it," he says. "I'm accepting. I'm learning how to accept things . . . I love it that I've changed."

The forum for change at the prison is the nightly Network meeting, an encounter group run military-style.

Inmates lead the meetings in small rooms with inspirational charts taped to cinderblock walls. Buzzwords such as "regressions" and "pullups" abound and the word "progress" has been turned into a verb.

"I'd like to progress myself for a highly motivated day at work," one inmate tells the group of about 30. The men join the inmate in loud applause.

Network groups discuss problems the men have. Their "fellow peers" offer suggestions. They rise and speak only when recognized. Each man is supposed to maintain military bearing at all times.

At a meeting, one young inmate complained that a drill instructor had harassed him. A couple of inmates recited the basic Network tenets the men had drilled on for months. Then another inmate rose with a new idea: "This inmate finds when he is in that situation that it helps to count to 10."

Butler's small cafeteria serves breakfast to 180 inmates in 45 minutes. These are hungry men: Each tray holds sprawling piles of pancakes, hash browns, bread and dry cereal.

No one talks except the drill instructors, who shout out occasional commands or insults. The phone on the wall by the door rings.

"Hey, Smith," one of the officers shouts to an inmate who has been dogging it a little. "It's for you. It's Attica."

The officers laugh. Attica, the site of a bloody riot in 1971, is one of New York's maximum security prisons and the officers regularly invoke its horrific image. Inmates who do not make it through shock camp return to a regular prison like Attica to finish their sentences. For some, that can mean several more years in prison.

Probably the only people who fear Attica more than the inmates are the officers. Nearly every officer at Butler has worked in a regular prison and nobody has anything nice to say about the experience.

"There was absolutely no job satisfaction. It was a war zone," says Stephen Van Son, a Butler drill instructor who worked at Attica for 4 ½ years. "A place like that all they do is make better criminals."

It is Graduation Day. After six months of Butler Shock, 28 men are going home. Their platoon started with 48. Twenty couldn't take it.

An inmate walks out grimly and embraces his mother without speaking for several minutes. Finally, she hands him a present, a religious medal, and mother and son weep.

The men get dressed in Squad Bay F, the last stop in the camp and the most prestigious. They wear their green fatigue jackets and green pants. But they put on white shirts and brown ties, gifts of the state of New York.

The mood is bright but a drill instructor can't resist.

"Give me 20," he barks. The inmates shout with joy as they flop down to do 20 quick push-ups.

The men assemble in formation on the asphalt walkway in front of their dorm. Carrying the platoon flag is Scott Patton, a blond, blue-eyed 21-year-old convicted cocaine dealer from Rochester. The inmates call him Opie. "This inmate was very greedy, sir," Patton says to explain his crime. "This inmate had a job making good money. It's just that this inmate was into instant gratification."

Patton's parents have driven the 60 miles from Rochester for the graduation. They join a group of about 60 other relatives and friends of the graduates.

At 10 A.M., the graduating class marches smartly onto the camp's outdoor basketball court.

Under Patton's command, the squad moves slowly and evenly across the court, doing intricate weaves and patterns. The men have learned a lot about marching in six months.

Gloria Hudgeon giggles. This is an incongruous sight—a bunch of young drug dealers from the city marching proudly, happily, on a cold morning on a basketball court in Wayne County.

Hudgeon has driven from Rochester to pick up her 18-year-old son, Chris Jackson, who was sentenced to three years for stealing cars.

Inside the gymnasium the graduation ceremony begins. Like a stern father, Henry Garvin, New York's assistant commissioner of corrections, tells the inmates to stay out of trouble and listen to their parents.

"We have a real, real problem taking direction from the ones we love the most," Garvin says in his most serious tone of voice, his eyes locked on the graduates.

"If you go back to the streets with the same mentality," he says, slowing, "you're . . . going . . . back . . . to . . . jail." From the relatives' side of the room, several women respond with "Amen" and "Uh-huh."

The men file forward to pick up the symbols of their success: certificates of graduation and parole papers. One last military touch: The platoon's flag, festooned with pennants symbolizing the group's top ranking in areas such as physical training and marching, is tied up and retired.

Back in their dorm, the men are almost free. They strip off the fatigues and put on tan pants, brown jackets, brown shoes and a tan knee-length raincoat.

A murmur starts in the room. "Push-ups!" The 28 graduates drop again and do their last 10 as the 2nd Platoon.

Finally, it becomes clear to them. There is no more schedule. They are free.

"Sir, yes sir, I'm missing it right now," an inmate says of Butler Shock. "But I know I got to go . . . I thank God for a second chance."

The men seem a little lost. Some dawdle in the dorm, keeping parents waiting.

Chris Jackson eventually comes out, smiling sheepishly and carrying a mesh bag with a few belongings. He hugs his mother and two brothers.

Scott Patton greets his parents and they quickly leave for Rochester.

Another inmate walks out grimly and embraces his mother without speaking for several minutes. Finally, she hands him a present, a religious medal, and mother and son weep.

Frank Barnes, 24, who did time for possession of cocaine, is one of the last to leave the dorm.

"Sir, yes, sir, I'm missing it right now," Barnes says of Butler Shock. "But, I know I got to go." Barnes' wife has come up from Brooklyn and waits outside. Barnes looks around at the remaining men and smiles. "I thank God for a second chance."

FRAME the DEBATE

Form at end of book

Issue 12: Can boot camps rehabilitate youthful offenders?

Prison "Boot Camps" Do Not Measure Up

Dale K. Sechrest[1]

Assistant Professor of Criminal Justice, Florida International University, North Miami

It pays to advertise, so they say, but is the product advertised the best product? Using available data, the principal objective of this paper is to lay to rest the idea that short-term "shock" incarceration, at least in its present form, is a valid response to the problems of young offenders. These types of programs are not the best response to the problem of improving offenders' lives or increasing the probability that they will not commit new crimes when they return to the community. They add to the fiction that short term, "quick-fix" panaceas can solve significant social problems.

Prison "boot camps," technically called "shock incarceration," known variously as Basic Training (Florida), Special Alternative Incarceration (Georgia), Regimented Inmate Discipline (Oklahoma), are flourishing in the United States. At last eight states now have such programs and at least eight more soon will have them. The National Institute of Justice (NIJ) completed a major report on them in 1989, and the U.S. General Accounting Office (GAO) published an earlier report on them in 1988. New York State has the largest program (500 beds), followed by Georgia (200 beds), which, along with Oklahoma, was one of the first to begin the programs in late 1983. The programs accept young offenders, aged 18 to 24 in most states, who have nonviolent criminal records. These convicted offenders are put through a program of strict discipline and military-style drills for a period of 90 to 120 days, although Louisiana and New York State operate 6-month programs. In New York State 180 days are seen as necessary to calm public fears about the early release of violent offenders and to do a better job of treatment. In exchange for completion of the program, the sentence, which could be up to 10 years, is reduced to the time served and the boot camp experience. In Florida this is an average of 245 days (8 months) and amounts to 20 percent of the sentence (an average of 3.5 years).[2] Four states have boot camp programs for women inmates—Oklahoma, Mississippi, South Carolina, and Orleans Parish and the State of Louisiana—with the largest having 60 beds (Mississippi).

The Florida profile of participants shows the typical offender to be under 20 at the time of prison admission, a user of illegal drugs, of average intelligence, convicted of a first- or second-degree felony (30- or 15-year maximum sentences, respectively). Participants may have no prior commitments to prison and their sentence must be 10 years or less. Selection for boot camp programs varies from state to state, although in most states the participants are convicted of felonies and sentenced to the department of corrections (DOC) and then selected for boot camp participation, often after several months in jail or prison. Judges are involved in the decision in about two-thirds of the program states. Most program descriptions do not point out the significance of the conviction, which precludes military service and carries with it all the problems of loss of rights subsequent to release.[3]

Shock Incarceration Techniques

Shock incarceration stresses discipline and purports to have the same results as military recruit training with respect to developing positive attitudes toward authority and providing physical conditioning. Official goals in Florida are "to divert offenders from long terms of imprisonment while at the same time deterring them from future criminal activity." Inmates "receive training in psychological methods that promote responsibility and improve decision-making."[4] Related goals that apply for most programs are providing inmates a chance for re-evaluation of their lives through working with others, learning to accept discipline, and improving their self-respect and ability to control their behavior; in the process they learn to seek realistic goals, and are taught how to live without committing crimes. While education and job training are not part of the Georgia and Florida programs, with voca-

"Prison 'Boot Camps' Do Not Measure Up" by Dale K. Sechrest from *Federal Probation,* September 1989, vol. 53, no. 3, pp. 15–20. Reprinted by permission.

tional training part of none, some programs emphasize education and job skills to a limited extent. As opposed to "rehabilitation," the New York State shock incarceration program purports to "habilitate," or properly socialize these offenders.[5] For most states system goals include reducing prison crowding and system costs, and ultimately recidivism and its related costs.[6]

The primary technique, or "treatment tool" is teaching discipline through the use of military "boot camp" techniques. A new "recruit" in Georgia (of "both races") is shouted at and referred to as a maggot, scumbag, boy, a fool, or a nobody, and repeatedly threatened with transfer to the main facility where he may be sexually abused, he is told, if he fails the program.[7] In Florida the "pukes" must pull together or they are all punished as a group, which is standard recruit fare. The NIJ report points out that the Army no longer uses these types of abusive and degrading techniques as part of their training, preferring to use "voice commands" and other forms of motivation.[8] Motivation in the Florida program is provided by moving through stages marked with different colored hats leading to graduation.

Shock incarceration programs appear to have less appeal to corrections officials than to the public or its representatives.[9] The programs have great media appeal, and are widely publicized as meeting the need to "do something" about the crime problem. The public appeal is similar to that for the "scared straight" and "shock" probation and parole concepts of the early 1980's, none of which have proven effective on close examination. Corrections officials' arguments are more practical, including better prison management, reduced crowding, and expanded sentencing options.

The Success of Shock Incarceration

What are the successes and failures of these programs? As with the other shock and scare programs, as well as other highly touted social panaceas, such as methadone maintenance, deinstitutionalization, determinate sentencing, and the like, early media and program reports are glowing. Early reports from Georgia claimed 80 percent success rates for graduates "staying out of trouble."[10] In 1986, Mississippi reported a return to prison rate "35 percent lower than the normal return rate," which would be about 5 percent, since the national return rate is about 40 percent over a 3-year followup period.[11] Florida always claimed a success rate of 75 to 80 percent which they can now document, as discussed below.[12]

In fact, about half the inmates selected for these programs complete them. Their return rates to prison are not better than the national average for most programs over a 3-year followup period. Georgia had a 23-percent return rate after 2 years (1986 figures) and the U.S. General Accounting Office reported a 39-percent return rate for Georgia inmates at 3 years compared with a 38-percent return rate for controls after 3 years (through July 1988).[13] The NIJ report cites the Georgia figure of 38.5 percent, indicating that those entering in their teens had a 46.8 percent return to prison rate. The NIJ report cites a study of Oklahoma's program in which return rates of shock incarceration (SI) graduates were compared with similar nonviolent offenders sentenced to their DCO; after 29 months almost half the SI graduates, but only 28 percent of the other group had returned to prison.[14] These data appear to indicate that the programs may have early successes, but in the long term they may not do any better than conventional methods. The real test, as always, is performance in the community. A recent NIJ 3-year followup study of released offenders nationally reported that 62.5 percent of former state inmates were rearrested for a felony or a serious misdemeanor within 3 years of their discharge from prison; 47 percent were convicted of new crimes, and 41 percent returned to prison.[15] Based on these findings, the GAO report conclusions concurred with those of the NIJ report in advising caution to states planning to move ahead with such programs, recommending further study.[16]

The Florida Study

Florida's recently completed study reports on a 1-year followup comparison of a "matched" group of (nonparticipant) offenders of the same age and general background as the boot camp graduates. Unfortunately, the "matched" sample had 257 more inmates than those graduating, a total of 400, which does not make it a truly matched group but more of a comparison pool of offenders with similar characteristics. And, since the possibility of any occurrence was greater in the larger group, comparisons of any kind will be flawed. Nonetheless, return-to-prison rates (probation revocations) after 1 year for the 143 graduates were 5.59 percent (8 graduates of 143) and 7.75 percent for the 400 "matched" offenders (31 of 400), a claimed "likelihood of returning to prison nearly 40 percent greater than that of Boot Camp graduates."[17] Since the size of these populations was reported, some statistical tests were possible. A chi-squared test revealed no significant difference between the two groups on return to prison ($X^2 = .73$, p M .39).[18] In addition to returns to prison, postrelease failures of all kinds were reported—absconding, or a new felony, misdemeanor, or technical revocation; these figures revealed a different picture. There were 13 failures of graduates and 69 in the comparison group, which proved significant ($X^2=5.5$, p M .012), indicating that overall failure rates show graduates doing better than the comparison group. However, there were no technical violations for the graduates and 22 for the matched group, which had 257 more inmates. When technical violations are treated as successes there is no significant difference between the two groups (X^2=.76, p M .38). The rate of absconders in the comparison group was also double that of the graduates (7.3 % v. 3.5%). These comparisons make it difficult to pronounce the program a success on prison return rates or failures at this time. Florida officials are reluctant to pronounce the program a complete success even with these findings in hand, citing too many unanswered questions at this time.[19]

The Florida report also compared program graduates (successes) with nongraduates (failures). Graduates (54% of all admissions) were older (19.5 v. 18.7 years), in better physical condition at program onset, more likely to have completed high school (31% v. 10.2%), lacking full-time employment at arrest (32.2% v. 44.8%), twice as likely to be convicted of a first-degree felony for armed robbery, violent crime(s) or drug sale/manufacture (44.1% v. 20%), and more likely to have had a prior term of probation or community control (42.7% v. 33.3%).[20] Statistically significant differences between the groups are not provided in the report, only tendencies based on percentages. Chi-squared comparisons reveal that significant differences existed for high school completion (favoring graduates; X^2 = 13.29, p M .001), employment at admission (less for graduates; X^2 = 4.1, p M .04), and convictions for armed robbery (greater for graduates; X^2 = 6.48, p M .02). The question of seriousness of the crimes is an important one. While armed robberies are reported as significantly greater for graduates, total crimes for economic gain (see table 1 footnote for types) are not significantly different for either group, and *include armed and unarmed robbery.*[21] In fact, when armed and unarmed robbery are combined and compared for the two groups there are no significant differences (X^2 = 2.2, p M .13). For economic crimes, also, there are no statistically significant differences between the two groups—80.4 percent graduates, 85.7 percent nongraduates (X^2 = 1.2, p M .28). The report itself, in discussing differences between participants and other inmates, as shown in table 1, states that "Boot Camp admissions are also less likely to have had a term of probation and more likely to have been involved in a crime for economic grain."[22]

Table 1 is extracted from the Florida Department of Corrections report and compares the characteristics of boot camp admissions with males under 25 admitted in 1987–88 and the general population of males admitted in 1987–88. No actual numbers are reported for the latter two groups, so statistical comparisons are not possible. However, armed robberies and "economic crimes" are shown for each group, and again, even though armed robberies are shown as greater for boot camp admissions, economic crimes are the predominate criterion for admission to the Florida program. These comparisons appear to indicate that boot camp participants in Florida are, in fact, a less serious group of offenders.

Interestingly, very few of the boot camp offenders in Florida have been tried on probation and, of those who have been, far fewer have violated community control. This concern is expressed in the NIJ report, which notes that many states have adopted the criteria used for shock probation sentences to target "persons believed most likely to be deterred—young, non-violent offenders who have not been confined before under sentence . . . most of whom would have gotten probation in the past."[23]

Space and Cost Factors

Costs are difficult when evaluating correctional programs. Institutions have fixed costs that do not vary a great deal when more inmates are added to the population. This is why the facilities can be crowded without major increases in costs; there are "economies of scale." Programs that claim great cost savings by reducing prison populations 200 to 400 inmates per year are not providing great savings. Georgia provides a cost of $3,523 per inmate/year for Special Alternative Incarceration (SAI), inclusive of probation supervision, compared to $13,450 per year for conventional incarceration.[24] An early report from New York State quoted a cost of $9,000 per inmate compared to $19,400 for regular prison inmates.[25] NIJ figures are for annual facility operations and simply do not support the notion that it costs less to operate these shock incarceration programs. Costs are at least the same.[26] In fact, New York State now reports higher costs for shock incarceration, which are no doubt indicative of the longer time spent in the program and the depth of the services provided. An early report from the Oklahoma program reported that the staff-inmate ratio was about four times greater than that for the general prison population.[27] The program acknowledges being more costly than a comparable living unit in the department, which could be due to its greater emphasis on educational and vocational programs.[28] A concern for Florida is that only 61.6 percent of the program beds are filled, on average, indicating that it is difficult to find inmates willing to undergo this type of program, especially when sentence reductions due to crowded prisons might make their sentence equally brief.[29] Still, shorter confinement times, even with more program expenditures, should produce some cost savings in the long term, but how much is unclear at this time. In fact, as the NIJ report points out, if these offenders had received probation, even greater savings could have been re-

Table 1 Boot Camp Admissions Compared to Youthful and Older Males Admitted during Fiscal Year 1987–88

	Boot Camp Admissions	Male Inmates 24 and Younger Admitted 1987–88	Male Inmates 25 and Older Admitted 1987–88
	N-Size	N-Size	N-Size
Race:			
White	51.1%	41.3	42.1%
Black	47.7%	57.2%	56.1%
Ethnic: Hispanic	5.3%	4.9%	6.7%
Marital: Single	88.5%	89.8%	54.1%
Completed high school*	17.9%	26.5%	47.8%
Employed at arrest*	38.9%	51.0%	64.2%
Uses illegal drugs	57.1%	57.8%	47.9%
Average I.Q.*	93.4%	88.3%	85.1%
Prior probation	25.9%	61.7%	86.3%
Prior violation of probation or community control	14.6%	43.1%	37.4%
Primary offense of:			
Burglary	31.8%	27.4%	18.5%
Armed robbery	16.8%	9.0%	4.6%
Narcotics (sale and manufacture)	9.0%	11.9%	17.4%
Total for:			
Physical injury crimes**	8.4%	12.0%	16.4%
Economic crimes***	82.2%	71.2%	61.1%
Sentence length	3.5	3.6	4.1
Class of felony:			
First degree	22.1%	16.1%	15.1%
Second degree	43.3%	44.0%	38.0%
Third degree	27.7%	37.4%	44.4%
Capital/life	0.0%	2.5%	2.5%
No prior prison commitments	100.0%	75.4%	61.1%

Source: "Characteristics of Boot Camp Admissions in Florida" from *Research Report, Boot Camp Evaluation,* p. 5. Reprinted courtesy Florida Department of Corrections.

*These figures are estimates based on samples.

**These include homicide, manslaughter, sexual crimes, assault, and battery. Note that no Boot Camp admission was for a sexual offense.

***These include robbery (armed and unarmed), burglary, larceny, fraud, narcotics (sale), receiving stolen property, possession of burglary tools, forgery and auto theft.

alized.[30] All factors must be carefully evaluated to really understand the savings possible—actual prison costs, not inflated daily figures based on original design capacities, the actual need for incarceration, and the effects of these programs on reduced crime and recidivism—the ultimate cost saving.

Problems with Boot Camps

Corrections officials do not appear to be as delighted with shock incarceration programs as are judges, law enforcement officers, legislators, and prosecutors.[31] Why is this? Perhaps the military emphasis makes them nervous. In one state the program was originally designed around programs of education, training, and the like. However, the director later became concerned that the military aspect had so much appeal that it became the rationale for the program, *not* providing emotional support, education, and job skills to these youngsters over the long term. It is further feared that the military style used by correctional officers may bring out their "dark side," or sadistic tendencies. There are possibilities for abuse of authority, especially since conventional disciplinary procedures are waived by the inmates coming into these programs.

The NIJ report suggests that this "discipline therapy" or confrontation style, which the military has abandoned, can and has gotten out of control in some instances. Experience with confrontational "T-groups" and "haircuts" used in drug treatment programs in the 1960's and 1970's tells us that some individuals find confrontation and abuse emotionally damaging and unlikely to build self-esteem. Further, most evaluations of "shock" programs, whether jail, prison or probation, have shown that gains are most often short term unless followup is available. Sometimes even more hostility toward the system is engendered. The NIJ report notes that program inmates did not object to profanity by officers as long as it was not directed at them—if so, it angered them.[32]

Abuses do occur, although there have been no legal challenges to the practices used because it would be difficult to see this as cruel and unusual punishment when it is used by the military. Nonetheless, NIJ investigators found the use of racial slurs in one program that led to transfer of some employees to other duties. It has been demonstrated in other types of programs that rules can be enforced, physical stress used, and firm discipline applied in contexts that will build self-esteem. The "wilderness programs," such as Outward Bound, use these techniques which, along with scared straight, appear to make up the roots of the boot camp concept. VisionQuest, a program that places chronic juvenile delinquents in rustic wilderness camps and other settings, appears to show success in reducing recidivism, reducing arrests to 55 percent for program participants compared to 71 percent for those in a conventional treatment facility after one year.[33] The NIJ report contains an appendix section that discusses "challenge" programs, which have the goals of increasing self-esteem, self-control, and respect for authority through vigorous physical and mental challenges. In fact, Outward Bound was founded by two former merchant seamen who saw the value of building personal confidence through the learning of survival skills and transposed this concept to the civilian world.[34]

Conclusions

Shock incarceration programs—"boot camps"—should not be created as a public relations gimmick. They may be good politics, but they could become programs that will not be good for corrections or society in the long run. Over the past 15 years corrections officials have been criticized repeatedly and resoundingly for failed programs. The "rehabilitation" programs they sold the public in the past were pronounced to be failures, i.e., "nothing works." Most corrections officials fell back into the incapacitation role, augmented by voluntary program participation, as a matter of simple self-defense. It is now almost unbelievable that these same corrections officials would allow the media to tout these untested programs as they did the old "failed" programs.

The boot camp programs are often underfunded, sometimes underused or poorly implemented, clearly untested, and mostly incomplete efforts to provide full correctional programs for young offenders. Followup programs that may exist are never mentioned by the media, probably because they appear to be little used by shock incarceration programs anyhow. Surely they are not newsworthy. Some probation departments have special programs for these individuals, but these do not appear to be well-organized or well-funded. New York State claims to have a treatment program that is "more extensive" than others, lasting 6 months, and involving drug treatment, which is a sound direction for the future. The program provides early contact with parole officers in an "aftershock," or intensive parole supervision, phase, but no extensive evaluation of that appears to be planned. Many probation officers report that offenders released from these programs are easier to manage, so continuity appears to be important. What about the program dropouts? No program appears to take positive steps with dropouts, although Oklahoma appears to move them into other programs that will assist them upon their release.[35] The NIJ study did not address this issue.

Unfortunately, the emphasis lies with the military aspects of the program, the notion that we can shock or scare young people out of crime by drilling it out of them! The programs are not unlike scared straight in their emphasis on fear and intimidation to transform offenders into upstanding citizens. Grueling exercise and labor are the bywords, and punishment surely occurs. After all, it works for the military—but those aren't criminal offenders, either. Further, the boot camps are not like the military, which has entirely different purposes. Military boot camps train people to kill other people; their dropout rates are considerably lower than the prison programs; and, they provide followup, i.e., young men and women stay in the service long enough to realize the benefits of their initial experience. Prison boot camp graduates cannot get into the military because the military won't accept either a G.E.D. certificate or a convicted felon. In fact, this is exactly what they don't want! Curiously, no shock incarceration program appears to be attempting to break down this barrier to military service, which may now be possible in view of upcoming personnel shortages in the military.

What Does the Future Hold?

Regardless of the media hype, there is no evidence that shock incarceration "works" for the offenders that need to be reached any more than scared straight or shock probation worked to any great degree. None. Yet these types of "quick-fix" solutions linger on. Shock programs like scared straight and boot camps appear to be "right" methods based on our middle class understanding of how punishment works. The American Correctional Association notes that "This deeply-rooted social problem [of juvenile delinquency] cannot be eradicated by exposing juveniles to threats of force, intimidation, verbal abuse, or other practices that are meant to shock youths out of delinquent-prone behavior." Generally, programs like these will not erase the social conditions under which these people must live upon release. Where are the community programs that are required both before and after incarceration? Corrections officials must demand these resources before committing themselves to a program that may produce only limited benefits in its present form and again show that "nothing works."

Most experts agree that without the help of the family, and without addressing social problems emanating from poor schools, unemployment, poverty, and racial discrimination, there is little likelihood that the "scare" or the "drill" will last for any length of time. Young men and women require well-rounded, community-based programs which will assist them in growth at home, in school, and in finding and financing training for jobs. Frightening or "discipline drilling" people who have resorted to crime will not have a long-term deterrent effect if these people cannot get satisfaction through legitimate alternatives in society. Nor will determinate sentencing, methadone programs, selective incapacitation, more prison space, better law enforcement, or increased punishments solve deeply rooted social problems.

This is not to say that properly used and evaluated, these programs may be successful for some types of inmates, although the possibilities of abuse are evident and the programs lack long-term commitments to the offenders involved. In the final analysis, properly run shock incarceration programs should be another of many tools for use in helping selected offenders. This may occur if they can be expanded to include education, job training, and skill development components starting in the facility and continuing into the community. Corrections staff may be learning how to evaluate offenders better for programs along some continuum of need. Now that corrections has the attention of its constituency, it would appear to be time to ask for sufficient resources to explore the full potential of this early intervention approach to young offenders. As Commissioner Coughlin of New York State says of shock incarceration, "It is a major step in recognizing that incarceration, on its own, is not necessarily the proper punishment for all offenders. Now we must look ahead to see if this alternative provides habilitation of inmates and protection of society."[36] But how will we know?

Notes

1. Research assistance for this article was provided by Mr. Carmelo J. Cabarcas.
2. Bureau of Planning, Research and Statistics, Florida Department of Corrections, *Research Report, Boot Camp Evaluation,* March 1989, p. ii.
3. Cf. Velmer S. Burton, Jr., Lawrence F. Travis III, and Francis T. Cullen, "Reducing the Legal Consequences of a Felony Conviction: A National Survey of State Statutes," *International J. of Comparative and Applied Criminal Justice* 12:1, Spring 1988, pp. 101–109; same authors, "The Collateral Consequences of a Felony Conviction: A National Study of State Statutes," *Federal Probation,* September 1987.
4. Florida Department of Corrections, p. 1.
5. American Correctional Association, 1988 Winter Conference, November 24, 1988:1.
6. Dale G. Parent, *Shock Incarceration: An Overview of Existing Programs,* National Institute of Justice *Issues and Practices,* U.S. Department of Justice (undated advance copy, May 1989): 21.
7. *People,* February 1, 1988, p. 25; *Life,* June 1988, p. 82.
8. National Institute of Justice, *Shock Incarceration,* p. 21.
9. Ibid., p. 3.
10. *People,* February 1, 1988, p. 25; Carmelo J. Cabarcas, telephone interview with Lt. James Combs, Georgia Shock Unit Supervisor, November 1988.
11. *Time,* August 11, 1986, p. 17.
12. Carmelo J. Cabarcas, telephone interview with Jim Mitchell, Florida Department of Corrections, November 1988.
13. *Prison Boot Camps. Too Early to Measure Effectiveness,* a Briefing Report to the Honorable Lloyd Bentsen, U.S. Senate, September 1987, p. 5.
14. National Institute of Justice, 1989, p. 4.
15. U.S. Bureau of Justice Statistics, April 1989. A useful benchmark for shock incarceration programs might be the 30 to 40 percent estimated lifetime recidivism rates for male offenders developed by the U.S. Bureau of Justice Statistics by Patrick A. Langan and Lawrence A. Greenfeld in "The Prevalence of Imprisonment," July 1985, p. 7.
16. U.S. General Accounting Office, p. 4.
17. Florida Department of Corrections, 1989, p. 26.
18. All chi-squared statistics are four-fold tables, df = 1; continuity corrections were used where cell sizes warranted.
19. *The Miami Herald,* April 12, 1989, p. 11A.
20. Ibid., p. 1.
21. Ibid., p. 9.
22. Ibid., p. 4.

23. National Institute of Justice, *Shock Incarceration,* 1989, pp. 3–4.
24. David C. Evans, Georgia Department of Corrections Probation Division, Report on Special Incarceration Units, undated (c. 1988).
25. *Corrections Today,* June 1988, p. 87.
26. National Institute of Justice, 1989, p. 16.
27. Al Pagel, "Doing a Tour of Duty in a 'Boot Camp' Prison," *Corrections Compendium,* November 1986, p. 10.
28. National Institute of Justice, *Shock Incarceration,* 1989, p. 7.
29. *The Miami Herald,* April 12, 1989: 11A; Florida Department of Corrections, 1989, p. 23.
30. National Institute of Justice, *Shock Incarceration,* p. 16.
31. Ibid., p. 3.
32. Ibid., p. 22.
33. *Criminal Justice Newsletter,* March 1, 1988, p. 5.
34. National Institute of Justice, 1989, p. 57.
35. Les Crabtree, "Military Discipline, Young Offenders Learn Accountability," *Corrections Today,* December 1985, pp. 38–39.
36. Commissioner's Commentary, *D.O.C.S. Today,* New York State Department of Correctional Services, April, 1988.

FRAME the DEBATE

Form at end of book

WiseGuide Wrap-Up

Politicians and corrections officials alike, desperate for a quick solution to the rampant crime problem, have turned to a program they know works: military-style boot camps. The U.S. military has often been seen as the premiere deterrence program in our country. It takes children and young adults between the ages of 17 and 23 (when young men are at their criminal offending peak) and instills confidence, discipline, and self-esteem while preoccupying so much of the individual's time that committing crimes is not feasible.

Once soldiers graduate from military boot camp, they are usually sent to a permanent duty station, where they begin a career, acquire job training and leadership skills, and become a contributing member of a productive society. When discharged, most soldiers are eligible for substantial financial assistance via the Montgomery G.I. Bill and various college funds as they pursue a college or vocational degree.

If prison boot camp programs are to succeed, they may need to emulate the military model and focus on extensive after-care—that portion of the supervision that takes places after incarceration—such as job training, education, and career advancement.

R.E.A.L. Sites

This list provides a print preview of typical **Coursewise** R.E.A.L. sites. (There are over 100 such sites at the **Courselinks**™ site.) The danger in printing URLs is that web sites can change overnight. As we went to press, these sites were functional using the URLs provided. If you come across one that isn't, please let us know via email to: webmaster@coursewise.com. Use your Passport to access the most current list of R.E.A.L. sites at the **Courselinks** site.

Site name: American Correctional Association
URL: http://www.corrections.com/aca/index.html
Why is it R.E.A.L.? This site has numerous sections, including an online version of the American Correctional Association magazine *Corrections Today.* The association also provides its application online. Students are encouraged to apply!
Key topics: corrections, professional organization
Try this: Browse through the magazine *Corrections Today.*

Site name: Corrections Connection
URL: http://www.corrections.com/
Why is it R.E.A.L.? This site has a huge depository of news and information for the corrections field.
Key topic: corrections
Try this: Go to the student section and post a question for a correction's expert.

Site name: NIC Corrections Exchange (Discussion List)
URL: http://www.nicic.org/cgi-bin/lyris.pl?enter=correx&text_mode=0
Why is it R.E.A.L.? This is an open listserv for discussion of corrections issues.
Key topics: corrections, discussion list
Try this: Join in a discussion of corrections issues.

Site name: Prison Law Page

URL: http://www.wco.com/~aerick/prison.html

Why is it R.E.A.L.? This web site is dedicated to advancing prisoners' rights and exchanging information throughout the prison community.

Key topic: corrections

Try this: Read some of the articles on prison life that inmates have written.

Site name: PRISON-L (Discussion List)

URL: listproc@lists.yale.edu

Why is it R.E.A.L.? This is a discussion list on prison issues and topics. To subscribe, send email to listproc@lists.yale.edu, saying simply, "SUBSCRIBE PRISON-L FirstName LastName."

Key topics: discussion list, corrections

Try this: Join the discussion list and engage in conversations on correction issues.

Are Chain Gangs Legitimate Correctional Tools or Institutional Slavery?

ISSUE 13

Take a Closer Look

1. Does the manner in which offenders are being restrained in a work group have ramifications?
2. How do you respond to the following assertions concerning chain gangs: If the criminals are not dangerous, then why are they in prison, and if they are dangerous, why are they released for work projects?
3. Would you want a chain gang working in your community?
4. What is different about the chain gang that Kilborn introduces?
5. According to the *Harvard Law Review,* how do chain gangs exacerbate racist stereotypes?

WiseGuide Intro

As criminal sanctions become more stringent and inmates start serving longer sentences, the prison population increases. Unfortunately, like all other government entities, prisons have a limited budget. Prison overcrowding and budgetary concerns push prison officials and legislators to search for practical solutions. Prison work crews and chain gangs have emerged as practical remedies to both problems. Allowing inmates to be rotated out of the prison temporarily reduces the burden and tension that overcrowded prisons cause, and work projects can bring in much-needed money for the institution.

In "Revival of Chain Gangs Takes a Twist," Peter Kilborn reports that correctional officers are monitoring chain gangs with a new tool: stun belts. According to Kilborn, stun belts could save money because fewer officers are required per work crew. They are also safer for inmates because a stun imposes no long-term harm, whereas shooting an inmate can cause serious injury or even death.

In "Florida Reintroduces Chain Gangs," the *Harvard Law Review* claims that the shift toward chain gangs and prison labor signals the end of our rehabilitative model of justice and leads the way to a retributive form of punishment. The article also suggests that this type of punishment can manifest racist stereotypes that are damaging to society.

Issue 13: Are chain gangs legitimate correctional tools or institutional slavery?

Revival of Chain Gangs Takes a Twist

Peter T. Kilborn

In many of the nation's prisons, time behind bars is no longer punishment enough. Prodded by a vengeful public and alert politicians, jailers in some states have cut down on hot meals and visiting hours and taken away furloughs, exercise gear, racy magazines and cable television. They dress inmates in black and white stripes again, and a county in Arizona dyes the men's underwear pink.

But Centreville, population 2,662, the wind-scrubbed seat of Queen Anne's County on the Maryland Eastern Shore, has bigger ideas. Starting next month, county authorities will become the latest to introduce chain gangs—and perhaps the first to make them chainless.

Rather than shackling the ankles of inmates on outdoor work crews, the county may buy devices called stun belts that would leave convicts writhing into the dirt if they tried to flee or fight.

The stun belts are the latest device in the booming corrections industry, and they are starting to generate as much debate as the chain gangs. Some jailers and local officials like the idea of the belts because they would save money: fewer guards would be needed to keep an eye on prisoners wearing them. And, these officials contend, there is no long-term physical damage to a prisoner who is stunned.

But human rights advocates and even some corrections officials around the country oppose the belts, portraying them as the most degrading new measure in a field that they regard as increasingly barbaric.

The belt comes with a battery and a receiver with electric prongs. From up to 300 feet away, an officer can press a button to detonate an eight-second burst of 50,000 volts of electricity and stun a fleeing inmate for up to 10 minutes. Once stunned, prisoners also lose control of their bladders and bowels.

"It overrides the body's neuromuscular system," said Dennis Kaufman, president of Stun Tech Inc. in Cleveland, which makes the belts. "Normally, you can open and close your hand twice in one second. This device makes it contract 20 times in a second. It wears the muscles down."

Mr. Kaufman said he has sold 1,100 to law-enforcement agencies, including 200 to the United States Marshals Service and 100 to the Federal Bureau of Prisons. Currently, he said, they are used in transporting dangerous prisoners or in court, replacing shackles.

Amnesty International has appealed to Washington to ban the belts, in part because it says they can be used to torture. It calls them "cruel, inhuman and degrading."

But Mr. Kaufman said they strike such terror in prisoners that a belt has been fired to subdue a prisoner only 14 times in the 30,000 occasions they have been worn. He said the belts cost $600 to $700 apiece and readily pay for themselves in reducing the number of officers needed to guard work crews.

Wisconsin plans to start using them soon. At Gov. Tommy G. Thompson's behest, the State Legislature ordered the adoption of chain gangs last year, joining Alabama, Arizona, Florida, Iowa and some county sheriff's departments. Bill Clausius, spokesman for the Department of Corrections, said that when the first Wisconsin gangs went out this spring, jailers would have the option of the belts or individual leg restraints.

It would be the first use of the belts for work-crew control, unless Queen Anne's County acts faster.

People in Centreville, a two-century-old town an hour's drive across the Chesapeake Bay Bridge from Washington and Baltimore, say their interest in the stun belts and in chains reflects their growing anger about rising crime in their town.

Rehabilitation does not work, say people in Centreville. And prisoners have it too easy, they add. A convict gets free room, board, medical care and television, while they have to earn their own keep and his. They want convicts, like welfare recipients, to work. But they also want to stigmatize and shame the people who shamelessly violate them.

"Give them public humiliation," said Deborah Steenken, a crew leader for a fast-food chain who was resting on a bench in the courthouse square. "They never think twice about committing a crime."

Last month, the three Queen Anne's County commissioners voted unanimously to institute chain gangs on April 1 for many of the 80-some inmates at the county detention center. The commissioners are considering the stun belts as well as the chains.

All but the most trustworthy inmates at the detention center, which holds minimum to maximum security prisoners for up to 18 months, would wear chains or the belt.

"If they try to take off," said Michael F. Zimmer, Jr., 45, the commissioner who proposed the gangs, "they could be zapped."

Mr. Zimmer said using chains or stun belts on prisoners also sent "a good message to children" when they spot convicts clearing brush and debris from roadsides.

" 'If you end up in trouble,' " Mr. Zimmer said he would tell children, " 'this could happen to you.' "

These attitudes trouble advocates of prisoner rights.

"We claim to be a civilized society and we return to these primitive methods of punishing people," said Mark Kappelhoff, legislative counsel for the American Civil Liberties Union in Washington. "We executed 54 people last year, and now we're dehumanizing them. It causes you to wonder what will satisfy this thirst for vengeance."

Most leading jailers have scruples about using restraints on work crews other than the customary shotgun-armed officer. In a position statement, the 20,000-member American Correctional Association, made up of wardens and corrections officers, has called upon Congress to oppose chain gangs.

The association says chaining and similar practices are "harsh and mean-spirited." Such practices, it says, "result in a hardening of criminal offenders," raise costs of incarceration and threaten inmate health.

Inmates are chained in one of two ways: They are bound together in groups, hitched at their waists six feet or so apart or at their legs with handcuff-like clasps, or they are bound individually by shackling both ankles with 14- to 18-inch chains—too short to let them run.

Prisons stopped using either form 30 years ago after 52 protesting convicts at a labor camp in Georgia took the sledgehammers they were using to break rocks and shattered their own legs. But over the last couple of years, individual chaining has revived.

Iowa began deploying individually shackled teams of 15 inmates last May for less violent prisoners as an alternative to segregation in a cell for misbehavior.

"We think it's successful in getting community support for corrections," said Sally Chandler Halford, Iowa's corrections commissioner.

Independent of state corrections departments, a small but undetermined number of counties has introduced the practice, and at least three—in Arizona, Indiana and Oklahoma—use group chaining. Maj. Joe Barger, commander of the Johnson County Jail in Indiana, binds his inmates in pairs at their legs.

"We use them every weekend," Mr. Barger said. "We ask for volunteers. They work out great. It gives them a chance to get outside, get some fresh air."

All are minimum-security prisoners, he said.

Alabama resumed group chaining two years ago, binding 300 men in groups of five to clear roads and break rocks. But problems arose. One convict on a chain attacked another. The victim could not escape, so a guard shot and killed the offender. The state discontinued group chaining last May to settle a lawsuit brought by the Southern Poverty Law Center that cited cruel and unusual punishment. It now uses individual shackling for work crews.

Many states forego both forms of chaining on humanitarian grounds or because of the cost of supervision, chaining's interference with efficient work and the risk of escape.

"Our view," said Roger Baungarten, spokesman for the Pennsylvania Department of Corrections, "is if they need to be enchained, they shouldn't be outside."

The proposed use of chains and stun belts is a response to a pique with prisoners, be they murderers, thieves or drunken drivers, that has seized Queen Anne's County.

Bruce Wakefield conducts a weekly poll for the Queen Anne's Record-Observer in Centreville by inviting residents to call in their answers to topical questions. He said last month's questions about prisoners generated the most calls he has received in his two years of polling. In response to the question of whether prisoners should be placed in chain gangs, Mr. Wakefield said, 232 callers said yes and 41 said no.

One reason for the get-tough attitude may be a crime rate that has risen along with the population of the county. Queen Anne's County has 37,500 people now, up from 35,000 in 1990. And reports of breaking and entering doubled in the last year, said George M. O'Donnell, president of the county commission and owner of a security-alarm business.

The county has also become more conservative. Mr. Wakefield said that in one decade, it has swung to 80 percent or 90 percent Republican, from 50 percent Republican and 50 percent Democrat.

But how far the county goes in getting tougher with convicts may depend on the views of their keepers. LaMonte Cooke, the detention center's warden and acting county administrator, and Rebecca Eason, the acting warden, will not say what they think of stun belts and chains.

But Ms. Eason, who was asked by the commissioners to estimate the cost of such changes, said the corrections department would need $110,000 this year, on top of its $1.7 million budget, to pay start-up costs including the purchase of two vans.

Mr. Zimmer, the commissioner who proposed the chain gangs, said the prison could make the changes for much less.

Some people raise questions on other grounds.

"If these guys are so dangerous," said Mary Chambers, a liquor store operator, "they shouldn't be out on those crews. And if they're not dangerous, why put them in chains?"

"I mean," Ms. Chambers said, "you have people in there for drunken driving. Maybe they have a problem. But do you put them in chains?"

FRAME the DEBATE

Form at end of book

READING 26

Issue 13: Are chain gangs legitimate correctional tools or institutional slavery?

Florida Reintroduces Chain Gangs

Conscious of the manifold costs of crime and faced with ever-tightening budgets, several states have recently adopted prison reform measures to reduce expenditures on corrections and to emphasize the punitive nature of incarceration.[1] With a one-sentence provision in an unnamed bill, Florida joined this harsh movement by reinstating use of the "chain gang" in its inmate labor system.[2] Premised on the notion that a high rate of recidivism is at least partially attributable to favorable prison conditions,[3] such reforms seek to inflict upon inmates deprivations and indignities—such as working long hours in leg-irons—that will make prison a degrading ordeal. Whatever the intuitive appeal of such a policy, the available evidence indicates that the reintroduction of chain gangs is unlikely to have an appreciable effect on recidivism and could exacerbate the current problem of intraprison violence. Moreover, the potential social consequences of resurrecting a practice synonymous with racial oppression and inhumane treatment of prisoners far outweigh the benefits from the speculative and, at most, limited deterrence of a few criminals.

The renewed interest in chain gangs is the latest manifestation of a steady shift away from rehabilitation and toward retribution as the primary justification for punishment.[4] Retributivists argue that society should punish each individual according to what she morally "deserves" for her behavior.[5] Today, retributive reasoning is often expressed in quasi-deterrence terms[6] because it is presumed that, if society would punish criminals according to their "just deserts," the resulting punishment would be severe enough to deter potential offenders and reduce recidivism. In a crime-ridden society that is as concerned with attaining safety as with meting out justice, this formulation of retributive theory is understandable. However, empirical evidence does not support the argument that severe prison conditions will result in lower rates of recidivism. For example, research on "boot camps"—penal programs analogous to chain gangs in their emphasis on providing participants with a grueling prison experience—indicates that neither the hard labor nor the martial atmosphere of these programs produces an appreciable reduction in recidivism.[7] Little evidence suggests that prison conditions are at the root of—or even figure significantly in—the complex processes that lead individuals to commit crimes after incarceration.[8] The lack of evidence linking recidivism to prison conditions, coupled with the failure of other penal programs targeted at prison conditions to reduce recidivism rates, strongly suggests that the logic behind the implementation of chain gangs as an antirecidivism measure is flawed.

Moreover, evidence exists that chain gangs may actually *increase* recidivism because of the negative impact of hostile prison environments on individual prisoners. Corrections officials, well aware of the deleterious physical and psychological effects of incarceration, are wary of reforms designed to make austere prisons harsher,[9] partly because intraprison violence—including violence among inmates and violence between inmates and corrections staff—is already endemic in most prisons.[10] The wearing of chains on a daily basis is likely to produce feelings of humiliation and degradation in inmates that will only exacerbate prison violence. Chain gangs could thus serve as an additional source of tension and a new arena for violent expression.[11] Equally troubling is the prospect that inmate hostility generated by chain-gang labor may extend beyond prison confines by inculcating in certain inmates a "revenge" motive that could make them even more likely to relapse into crime as a form of retaliation.[12]

Notwithstanding the lack of empirical evidence that the use of chain gangs reduces recidivism, proponents seem to argue that the symbolic value of chain gangs alone justifies their use.[13] Such an argument either ignores the racially divisive nature of this symbol or, more insidiously, attempts to take advantage of it by subtly scapegoating one segment of society.[14] Given the ignoble history of the chain gang, its reintroduction resurrects and reinforces racist stereotypes—a concrete harm that outweighs any symbolic benefit.

Public acceptance of any system of punishment depends upon its moral credibility, which in turn arises from the degree to which that system accurately embodies the values of those citizens. Indeed, in Florida, where public image translates directly into economic well-being as a result of tourism,[15] proponents advocate using chain gangs as a symbol of Floridians' attitude toward crime and criminals. As the sponsor of the Florida bill remarked: "I recall seeing chain gangs as a child while driving through the state with my parents. . . . The impression I had was one of hard labor and a law-abiding state. That's the image Florida needs today—instead of one of innocent citizens and tourists being robbed and raped every day."[16]

The potency of the image of men in chains undeniably draws power from the history of chain gangs, yet that history is one of racism and barbarism. Although its origins are difficult to pinpoint precisely, the practice of placing groups of inmates in chains while performing manual labor became widespread in the South after the Civil War.[17] A sentence of hard labor was not a function of the severity of the crime, but often depended upon the severity of the judge and the location of the crime.[18] The harsh conditions on chain gangs included starvation rations, regular whippings, and heavy iron chains that were soldered in place.[19] Not surprisingly, the death rate among members of chain gangs in various states was estimated at between 10% and 50% from the 1880s to the 1920s.[20] For African-Americans, chain gangs were a special hardship that reinforced the oppressive social order of the Jim Crow era. Due in large part to racially motivated laws that provided criminal sanctions for vagrancy, breach of contract, and unemployment, involuntary membership in a chain gang was a realistic possibility for African-Americans.[21] An extensive and intricate convict lease system enabled states to rent the largely African-American chain gangs to private businesses for labor-intensive projects such as picking cotton, building roads, or mining coal.[22] Convict labor was so widespread and essential to the Southern economy that local sheriffs commonly arrested able-bodied African-Americans, falsely charged them with vagrancy, and leased them to private entrepreneurs.[23] The eventual abolition of the convict lease system in Florida did little to redress the pervasive racism and inhumanity of its successor—the state-operated system of "road" prisons that housed the modern-day chain gang.[24]

The chain gangs of old operated in a racist and racialized context that both promoted and rested upon a widespread belief in the criminal nature of African-Americans.[25] Notwithstanding the considerable strides that have been made in bridging the racial divide since the initial introduction of chain gangs, revival of the practice may lend credence to these pernicious beliefs. The current composition of Florida's prison population suggests that the men in chains observed by thousands of passing citizens and tourists along Florida's highways will be mostly African-American.[26] Such a brief glimpse of the face of crime can convey neither the complex set of factors responsible for the disproportionate numbers of African-Americans nor the actual degree of danger that the members of chain gangs pose to the general public. At best, passersby will be able to gauge the age and the race of the men they see, characteristics that could bolster unfounded fears regarding the "dangerous" proclivities of African-Americans[27] and young men.[28]

The racializing potential of chain gangs extends beyond majority perceptions of criminals to minority perceptions of the criminal justice system itself. For many African-Americans, chains are the most potent symbol of racial oppression imaginable. The cultural insensitivity involved in resurrecting a practice that is inextricably linked to the oppression of an entire people will likely contribute to the steady erosion of confidence among African-Americans in the impartiality and racial neutrality of the criminal justice system.[29]

Ultimately, the minimal impact on recidivism that chain gangs will have as a penal policy renders the potential impact of chain gangs as a symbol especially salient. The moral legitimacy of the criminal justice system is its greatest and most enduring asset.[30] Enacting a practice steeped in an infamous and immoral history undermines the moral legitimacy of the system as a whole and impairs its efficacy. As long as those who perceive the system to be unrepresentative of their values resent and resist its administration, a policy designed to promote respect for the law may achieve precisely the opposite outcome.

Notes

1. *See*, e.g., Mark Curriden, Hard Time, *A.B.A. J.*, July 1995, at 72, 74; Peter Morrison, The New Chain Gangs, *NAT'L L.J.*, Aug. 21, 1995, at A1, A22–23.
2. The provision requires the department of corrections "to implement a plan by December 1, 1995, for inmate labor wearing leg irons in chain-gang workgroups." Act of June 15, 1995, ch. 283, 1995 Fla. Sess. Law Serv. 2080, 2081 (West). Alabama and Arizona adopted similar programs in the summer of 1995. *See* Chain Gangs Reinstituted, *NAT'L L.J.*, May 29, 1995, at A8.

   The failure of the Florida legislature to authorize funding has limited implementation of the chain-gang program to 7 prisons statewide, affecting a total of 140 inmates. Each chain gang consists of approximately 20 members connected by lightweight leg-irons and operates solely within state-owned facilities. *See* Telephone Interview with Lori Levings, Spokesperson, Florida Department of Corrections (Jan. 8, 1996).

3. "Until punishment is uncomfortable or painful enough to bring about a change in behavior, we will continue to see these same criminals as the main players in the game of the revolving door in . . . corrections." Curriden, *supra* note 1, at 73 (quoting a Hamilton, Tennessee, grand jury report) (internal quotation marks omitted).
4. *See,* e.g., Francis T. Cullen and Karen E. Gilbert, *Reaffirming Rehabilitation,* 80–125 (1982) (describing both conservative and liberal attacks on rehabilitation theory); James Q. Wilson, *Thinking about Crime* 162–77 (2d ed. 1983) (reviewing the decline of rehabilitative theory during the late 1960s and 1970s).
5. Although the moral paradigms used by retributivists to decide upon specific punishments may differ, all retributivists premise punishment upon moral rather than utilitarian considerations. *See generally* Ralph D. Ellis and Carol S. Ellis, *Theories of Criminal Justice* 55–60 (1989) (contrasting the various bases for different paradigms of punishment).
6. Pure deterrence theorists believe that the only justifiable punishment is that which is necessary to deter offenders and nonoffenders alike from future offenses: "Punishments that exceed what is necessary for protection of the deposit of public security are by their nature unjust." *Id.* at 4 (quoting Cesare Beccaria, *On Crimes and Punishments,* II (Henry Peolucci trans., 1963)) (internal quotation marks omitted). Thus, if the same punishment would be required to deter a thief as to deter a rapist, a deterrence theorist would find equivalent punishment justified for both, even though society might consider the act of rape morally "worse" than theft. This outcome is inconsistent with the retributive theorists' belief that punishment should be based upon moral and not utilitarian purposes. *See,* e.g., Ernest van den Haag, Punishing Criminals, 181–82 (1991) (discussing Kant's disapproval of using nonconsenting individuals to further social goals).
7. *See* Doris L. MacKenzie, Results of a Multisite Study of Boot Camp Prisons, *Fed. Probation,* June 1994, at 60, 64–65. Those programs that did produce a demonstrable drop in recidivism incorporated rehabilitative programs such as counseling and drug treatment. *See id; see also* Jerald C. Burns and Gennaro F. Vito, An Impact Analysis of the Alabama Boot Camp Program, *Fed. Probation,* Mar. 1995, at 63, 65–67 (examining the results of a longitudinal study of one boot camp program).
8. Penological literature typically assumes that individuals commit repeat offenses for reasons similar to those that lead them to commit their first offenses. Thus, discussions of the possible reasons for recidivism are often subsumed into broader theories of crime causation. *See,* e.g., Steven Box, *Recession, Crime and Punishment,* 47–48 (1987) (arguing that recessions lead to crime and recidivism because economic pressures make crime a rational choice for individuals).
9. *See,* e.g., Curriden, *supra* note 1, at 74–75; Morrison, *supra* note 1, at A22–23.
10. Currently, inmates face a higher risk of assault while in custody than they do before incarceration. *See* Jeff Potts, American Penal Institutions and Two Alternative Proposals for Punishment, 34 *S. Tex. L.J.* 443, 462 (1993). In addition, inmate assassinations are a leading cause of death, and sexual abuse among prisoners is widespread. *See Human Rights Watch, Prison Conditions in the United States,* 37–42 (1991).
11. Alabama's experience with chain gangs is illustrative. Within three weeks of the program's inception, numerous fights erupted among members of chain-gang workshops. One fight was so severe that guards were forced to fire shots overhead. *See* Second Amended Complaint at 5–6, Austin v. James, No. 95-T-637-N (M.D. Ala. filed Sept. 19, 1995) (on file with the Harvard Law School Library) (alleging that the use of chain gangs violates the Eighth Amendment).
12. Retributive punishment "puts inmates in an alienated posture and makes them more likely to take revenge against the whole system." Morrison, *supra* note 1, at A22 (quoting Prof. Marvin Wolfgang) (internal quotation marks omitted). The potential of chain gangs to contribute to recidivism should be understood in the context of a growing body of research indicating that incarceration itself, under certain conditions, promotes recidivism: "Take a group of people, strip them of possessions and privacy, expose them to constant threats of violence . . . deprive them of meaningful work—and the result is an embittered underclass more intent on getting even with society than on contributing to it." Potts, *supra* note 10, at 455–59 (quoting Charles Colson, Crime and Restitution: The Alternative to Lock-Them-Up Liberalism, 43 *POL'Y Rev.* 14, 15 (1988)) (internal quotation marks omitted).
13. The existence of less draconian policy alternatives strongly suggests that the symbolic value of chain gangs may have outweighed other policy considerations. For example, the recently proposed Prison Work Act would link receipt of federal monies for prison construction to a requirement that prisons extend the workweek to 48 hours. *See* S. 930, 104th Cong., 1st Sess. (1995). Given that the average inmate workweek is 34.5 hours, this proposal would significantly contribute to the unpleasantness of prison by reducing inmate recreation time by almost 14 hours, or two full seven-hour workdays. *See* Richard Lacayo, The Real Hard Cell, *Time,* Sept. 4, 1995, at 32, 32.
14. Charles Stuart and Susan Smith recognized the power of racial scapegoating. Both of these murderers generated national outrage when it was discovered that they had invented fictitious African-American assailants to cover up their own crimes. Despite the existence of contradictory evidence, law enforcement bodies and the nation alike initially believed them. *See,* e.g., Margaret Carlson, Presumed Innocent, *Time,* Jan. 22, 1990, at 10, 10–11; Nancy Gibbs, Death and Deceit, *Time,* Nov. 14, 1994, at 43, 45–47. Similarly, the 1988 Republican presidential campaign encouraged racial scapegoating with its successful use of television advertisements featuring Willie Horton, an African-American convicted murderer who raped a white woman during a one-day furlough. *See* Dan Goodgame, Why Bigotry Still Works at Election Time, *Time,* Nov. 25, 1991, at 44, 45.
15. *See* Julie Schmit and Rhonda Richards, Sunshine State in a Crime Storm, *USA Today,* Sept. 20, 1993, at 1B.
16. John Barry, Return of the Florida Chain Gang: New Justice or Old Cruelty? *Miami Herald,* May 30, 1995, at 1A, 8A (quoting Florida Senator Charles Crist) (internal quotation marks omitted).
17. The origins of the convict lease system—the predecessor of the state-operated chain gang—are difficult to trace. However, it is clear that the practice neither originated in, nor was exclusive to, the South. *See* Mildred Fierce, *Slavery Revisited: Blacks and the Southern Convict Lease System* 1865–1933, at 63–78 (1994).
18. For example, Robert Burns, the man immortalized in the film classic "I Am a Fugitive from a Chain Gang (Warner Bros. 1932), was sentenced to 10 years of hard labor for stealing $5.80. *See* Vincent G. Burns, *The Man Who Broke a Thousand Chains* 28 (1968).
19. *See* Fierce, *supra* note 17, at 90–109; Benno C. Schmidt, Jr., Principle and Prejudice: The Supreme Court and Race in the Progressive Era, Part Two: The Peonage Cases, 82 *Colum. L. Rev.* 646, 650–54 (1982).
20. *See* Fierce, *supra* note 17, at 90–109; Schmidt, *supra* note 19, at 650–54.

21. *See* Jennifer Roback, Southern Labor Law in the Jim Crow Era: Exploitative or Competitive?, 51 *U. Chi. L. Rev.* 1161, 1163–69 (1984).
22. *See* Fierce, *supra* note 17, at 85.
23. *See id.* Nor was it uncommon for the sentences of African-Americans to be extrajudicially extended for months or years as a result of the avarice or carelessness of their jailers. *See id.* at 85–87.
24. *See id.* at 207; Barry, *supra* note 16, 1A, 8A (reporting that the fire deaths of 38 shackled road chain-gang members in 1967 revealed the "squalid conditions" then prevalent in Florida's road prison system).
25. "Being indifferent as to the . . . punishments imposed, made, and inflicted under our laws, and also ignorant, indolent and naturally inclined to the ways of uncivilized people, the negro furnishes a criminal class in Alabama one thousand percent greater than the Whites." Fierce, *supra* note 17, at 114 (quoting John T. Milner in a letter to the *Montgomery Daily Advertiser* of January 28, 1883).
26. As of 1994, The Florida state prison system held 30,818 African-American males and 21,117 white males. If a Florida chain gang were drafted without regard to prior record or current offense, the chain gang would be 57.6% African-American. If Florida were to adopt the Alabama model and make only repeat offenders eligible for chain-gang duty, 9184 African-Americans and 5345 others would be eligible—a racial proportion of 63.2% and 36.8% respectively. *See* Florida Dep't of Corrections, 1983–94 *Annual Report: The Guidebook to Corrections in Florida* 70, 81 (1994).
27. *See* John C. Hill, Many Whites Can't Separate Issues of Race and Crime, *Atlanta Const.,* Dec. 26, 1993, at M6 (noting that many whites "leap from the fact that many criminals are black into a belief that many blacks are criminals—a conclusion unsupported by statistics or reason").
28. Widespread coverage of gang activities has heightened widely held fears of youths despite evidence that most victims of young offenders are their age peers. *See* Joe Sexton, Young Criminals' Prey: Usually Young, *N.Y. Times,* Dec. 1, 1994, at A1.
29. A 1994 poll revealed that 74% of African-Americans believe that the criminal justice system treats African-Americans "too harshly." Derrick Z. Jackson, So Who Really Gets the Juice? *Boston Globe,* July 29, 1994, at 19. The racially polarized reaction of the nation to the verdict in the O. J. Simpson trial underscored the deep racial division in perceptions of the criminal justice system. *See,* e.g., Sherry Stolberg, Will We Ever Get Along? *L.A. Times,* Oct. 10, 1995, at S3 (revealing large disparities between whites and African-Americans in their assessments of the outcome of the Simpson trial and the fairness of the criminal justice system as a whole).
30. *See* Paul H. Robinson and John M. Darley, *Justice, Liability and Blame: Community Views and the Criminal Law* 202 (1995).

FRAME the DEBATE

Form at end of book

WiseGuide Wrap-Up

The prison population is growing exponentially and shows no signs of decreasing in the near future. Prison overpopulation and budgetary restraints require practical solutions—one of which may be the prison work crew or chain gang. Prisoners, secured with either chains or stun belts, are taken outside the prison and required to perform arduous tasks. While this may fill a practical societal need, it also sends a message to the rest of the general population.

Questions to consider: If these offenders are so dangerous, then why are they allowed to work outside the prison? Conversely, if these inmates are not a danger to society or others, then why are they incarcerated?

R.E.A.L. Sites

This list provides a print preview of typical **Coursewise** R.E.A.L. sites. (There are over 100 such sites at the **Courselinks**™ site.) The danger in printing URLs is that web sites can change overnight. As we went to press, these sites were functional using the URLs provided. If you come across one that isn't, please let us know via email to: webmaster@coursewise.com. Use your Passport to access the most current list of R.E.A.L. sites at the **Courselinks** site.

Site name: Journal of Prisoners on Prisons

URL: http://www.jpp.org/

Why is it R.E.A.L.? This journal is a unique documentary of incarceration as told by prisoners.

Key topics: corrections, journal

Try this: Read some of the articles on prison life that inmates have written.

Site name: National Law Enforcement and Corrections Technology Center

URL: http://www.nlectc.org/

Why is it R.E.A.L.? This site contains several documents and updates on applying technology to enhance the criminal justice system.

Key topics: computers, technology

Try this: Find some of the new techniques that law enforcement and corrections are employing to combat crime and violence.

Site name: Prison Law Page

URL: http://www.wco.com/~aerick/prison.html

Why is it R.E.A.L.? This web site is dedicated to advancing prisoners' rights and exchanging information throughout the prison community.

Key topic: corrections

Try this: Read some of the articles on prison life that inmates have written.

Site name: PRISON-L (Discussion List)

URL: listproc@lists.yale.edu

Why is it R.E.A.L.? This is a discussion list on prison issues and topics. To subscribe, send email to listproc@lists.yale.edu, saying simply, "SUBSCRIBE PRISON-L FirstName LastName."

Key topics: discussion list, corrections

Try this: Join the discussion list and engage in conversations on correction issues.

Does the Harm Outweigh the Good with Public Notification of Sex Offenders?

ISSUE 14

Take a Closer Look

1. How would you implement a community notification program that protects the offender as well as his or her neighbors?
2. How might new technologies (for example, the Internet and email) help communities to protect themselves from convicts living in the area?
3. If the typical sexual predator is not a "stranger" but actually lives with the victim, or is a friend of the victim's family, then how would you implement an effective community notification program?
4. What did Turner do when he learned about a sexual predator living in his jurisdiction?
5. According to Steinbock, what are some of the problems with community notification policies?

WiseGuide Intro

The actions of sex offenders in general, and those who sexually violate the trust of children in particular, mandate a criminal justice system that responds with the utmost power, authority, and leadership. Community notification laws regarding sex offenders pose a classic criminal justice balancing act. On the one hand, the system must safeguard the rights of the offender, while on the other hand, it must also protect the interests of the community.

In "Community Notification of a Sex Offender: Creates Trust, Reduces Fear," police chief John Turner reveals the moral dilemma he faced after receiving knowledge that a "sexual predator" was living in his jurisdiction. As you read Turner's experience, you should gain an appreciation for the moral dilemma that offenders create for criminal justice professionals.

In "Megan's Law: A Policy Perspective," Bonnie Steinbock explains the challenges associated with community notification laws. According to Steinbock, community notification laws: (1) have proven ineffective, (2) have placed innocent people in harm's way, and (3) are misdirected.

As you read these articles, consider ways of ensuring the safety of the community while also protecting the rights and privacy of the offender.

READING 27

Issue 14: Does the harm outweigh the good with public notification of sex offenders?

Community Notification of a Sex Offender:

Creates Trust, Reduces Fear

John Turner

Chief, Mountlake Terrace Police Department

Mountlake Terrace, Wash. In 1989, I learned from a juvenile institution that an 18-year-old sex offender was about to be released into my jurisdiction. The institution informed me that authorities recently found a plan and a map on this individual's computer. The two items illustrated the sex offender's plan to *borrow* elementary school children for sexual purposes. The community he had targeted was Mountlake Terrace.

As Mountlake Terrace's police chief, I asked myself what to do with this kind of information, especially in light of potential civil litigation. My gut reaction was to go public. I kept thinking, "What happens if I sit on this information and the offender re-offends?" I saw this as a classic case of "damned if you do, damned if you don't!" Since my gut hunches have served me well in the past, I decided to publicize the information. I intended to do more than just identify the offender's name. Making this decision was easier because I had the support of my city manager and city council.

I informed the citizens of Mountlake Terrace, and as was expected, the outcry over the sex offender's release was enormous. But the community's strong reaction eventually helped to bring state passage of the Community Protection Act of 1990.

I knew that once the offender was released, he planned to move in with an older sister living in Mountlake Terrace. A few days after his release, I drove by the sister's house and observed the young man using binoculars to watch what appeared to be a 9- or 10-year-old boy riding a bicycle. I immediately contacted the sister who was concerned because she found baby clothes and photos of nude children hidden under her brother's bed. With our fears justified, the state agreed to help protect society from this offender.

The Washington state legislature passed the Community Protection Act of 1990, an act that provides for:

- sex offender registration;
- increased penalties;
- civil commitment of offenders, based on probability of future offenses; and
- police chief indemnity for community notification.

The act, while it doesn't require it, does allow law enforcement officers to notify communities, and protects them from liability for doing so. Since 1990, Mountlake Terrace, a city of 20,000, has had 22 registered sex offenders. We have gone public four times.

According to Mike Hawkins, juvenile parole officer for the Washington State Department of Juvenile Rehabilitation, "Community notification meetings are just one more tool in our tool box that can and do get utilized by public agencies, be they law enforcement or parole." These meetings, in some cases, have allowed community members to confront offenders face-to-face. And in each situation, citizens have been empowered to keep the offender on the "straight and narrow."

The decision to go public is based on a level-one, -two or-three notification as established in guidelines prepared by the Washington Association of Sheriffs and Police Chiefs (WASPC). A level-three notification (the highest level) is for offenders with a history of sex offenses whose victims were strangers. A level-three notification also indicates that the offender did not willingly participate in therapy while incarcerated.

In Mountlake Terrace, a level-three community notification takes shape the following way: After deciding to go public, the department prepares a news release for the media that contains the offender's name, address, criminal history and photograph.

"Community Notification of a Sex Offender: Creates Trust, Reduces Fear" by John Turner from *Community Policing Exchange,* Phase IV, No. 22, September/October 1998. Reprinted by permission of the Community Policing Consortium.

Volunteer senior citizens distribute flyers door-to-door, focusing on a six-block area surrounding the offender's residence. Next, we alert schools, parks and businesses in the targeted vicinity. Finally, we use flyers to notify citizens of a scheduled community meeting.

Attendance at the notification meetings has been good, with as many as 200 citizens participating. When community members first arrive, they are usually mad at me because they believe I am responsible for setting the sex offender free. Once I clarify my role, their anger usually shifts to the Department of Correction's representative, who reads the conditions of the offender's parole. At the core of their anger is frustration over why a person like this doesn't remain locked up forever, and how it is possible that he can't be barred from moving into their neighborhood. (History has shown that in many cases, a sex offender returns to the neighborhood where he lived before incarceration and where former victims often still reside.)

The message communicated to community members is (1) know who the offender is and (2) know the conditions of his release. This knowledge minimizes the offender's opportunity to reoffend. Before community notification, a lack of public awareness provided the offender a veil of secrecy that made it easier for him to recommit. "Frequently, offenders *appear* to act within established guidelines but in reality are living a secret life of deviant behaviors that may go undetected unless offense factors are understood by all involved," explains Mike Hawkins.

What about vigilantism? In the five years we have practiced community notification, Mountlake Terrace has never had a single case of vigilantism. The best news is that since implementing this program, there have been no reoffenses.

FRAME the DEBATE

Form at end of book

Issue 14: Does the harm outweigh the good with public notification of sex offenders?

Megan's Law:
A Policy Perspective

Bonnie Steinbock

Bonnie Steinbock, author of Life before Birth, *is Professor of Philosophy at the State University of New York, Albany.*

On July 29, 1994, Jesse Timmendequas invited seven-year-old Megan Kanka into his home to see his puppy. Once inside, Timmendequas forced Megan into his room, strangled her with a belt, and sexually assaulted her. She died from asphyxiation. Only after Megan's death did authorities reveal that Timmendequas had two previous convictions for child sexual abuse. Timmendequas had been sentenced to ten years at the Adult Diagnostic and Treatment Center, known as Avenel. With time off for good behavior, Timmendequas was released after serving only six years. At the time of Megan's murder, Timmendequas lived across the street from the Kankas with two other convicted sex offenders whom he had met at Avenel.

The outrage of community members that convicted sex offenders could live anonymously in their communities led to the passage of "Megan's Law" in New Jersey. In 1990, Washington State enacted its Community Protection Act[1] after a seven-year-old Tacoma boy was lured into a wooded area by a recently released sex offender who orally and anally raped the boy and then cut off his penis. The man had a twenty-four-year record of assaults on young people, including the kidnapping and assault of two teenage girls and involvement in the murder of a fifteen-year-old schoolmate.[2]

Registration of sex offenders with police is relatively unproblematic.[3] It is community notification that has sparked the greatest controversy. In arguments before New Jersey's Supreme Court, lawyers opposed to Megan's Law criticized the law as stigmatizing and humiliating for offenders. They also said it was punitive, increasing the punishment to which offenders had originally been sentenced, and was therefore unconstitutional.[4] In addition, they said that the law was an invasive measure that infringed the privacy and liberties of convicted sex offenders who had supposedly paid their debt to society. Other commentators point out that the stigma attached to sex offenders by society, and reinforced by notification laws, interferes with their ability to find jobs and places to live and to resume a normal life.

Whatever the merit of these objectives as a matter of law—an issue I leave to those with legal backgrounds—they do not have much moral force. As Megan's mother, Maureen Kanka, expressed it, "I have a dead little girl. How can they sit there and worry about if it's punishment? What about our kids? That's ultimately what it comes down to. Our kids have rights and it's time someone started addressing them."[5] It seems to me that Mrs. Kanka has framed the issue correctly. When a little boy has been raped and had his penis cut off, or when a little girl has been raped and murdered, worry about humiliating the people who committed these crimes seems a little overly sensitive.

I start then with the assumption that the paramount issue is the protection of children, that their rights to be safe from violent sexual assault certainly outweigh the rights of sexual predators not to be stigmatized. The trouble is that notification laws will not protect children. They are at best ineffective and at worst create a false sense of security that may actually expose children to risk. In addition, there is the danger of vigilantism that risks harming innocent bystanders and is contrary to the rule of law even when directed at the guilty.

First, Megan's Law focuses on a tiny percentage of those who commit sexual crimes against children, namely, dangerous strangers. Between seventy-five and eighty-nine percent of child sexual abuse is committed by relatives and friends.[6] Yet Megan's Law explicitly targets for community notification sexual predators whose "sexual preference is for minor children *outside his or her immediate family*."[7] Thus, it fails to protect children from the most common kind of sexual abuse, that inflicted by friends and relatives. Indeed, such laws may "promote a false sense of security, lulling parents and kids into the big-bad-man mindset when many molesters are in fact trusted authority figures or family members."[8]

"Megan's Law: A Policy Perspective" by Bonnie Steinbock from *Criminal Justice Ethics*, Vol. 14, No. 2, Summer/Fall 1995, pp. 4–9. Reprinted by permission of The Institute for Criminal Justice Ethics, 899 Tenth Avenue, New York, New York, 10019–1029 and the author.

It might be objected that it is not unreasonable to focus on the dangerous stranger even though this accounts for a very small percentage of child sexual abusers, simply because the dangerous stranger is likely to inflict greater harm on the child than a relative or family friend. Although all sexual abuse of children is undesirable, there is a much greater need to protect children from violent sexual predators than from pedophiles who fondle children or expose themselves.[9]

However, this raises the question whether it is possible to determine who are the truly dangerous sex offenders. At first glance, this might seem simple. Columnist Suzanne Fields notes that Jesse Timmendequas had served just six years after two convictions for sexually assaulting two young girls and asks rhetorically, "Was there any doubt that he would strike again?"[10] Yet while it may seem obvious, with 20–20 hindsight, that Timmendequas would commit more crimes if released, in fact it is not easy to predict either dangerousness or the propensity to reoffend. Studies indicate that predictions of an offender's dangerousness or propensity to reoffend average only a one-third accuracy rate.[11] Thus, it is relatively arbitrary which offenders are placed into tier three and subject to community notification. This is the second reason why Megan's Law is not a good bet for protecting children. Inevitably, some sex offenders who would not have committed future crimes will be placed erroneously in the third tier, and unfairly stigmatized, while others who will go on to harm other children will escape community notification.

Nevertheless, perhaps some offenders are so clearly sociopaths that professionals can tell with a high degree of certainty that they are dangerous, violent, and likely to repeat their crimes. Then the question has to be, why on earth do we release such people? Worse, why do we release them *without supervision?* Under current law, once sex offenders complete their sentences at Avenel, they do not have to attend outpatient therapy or report to any authorities. In a psychiatric evaluation in February 1988, shortly before he was released, Timmendequas himself said that he needed more therapy and expressed fears about adjusting to life outside of the center.[12] His therapist also urged that he remain institutionalized, or at least undergo "intensive psychotherapy in the community following release," but this was not done since Timmendequas had completed his sentence. "[W]e have no legal jurisdiction over anyone who has completed a jail sentence," says Grace Rogers, acting superintendent of the Avenel prison. "There's absolutely nothing we can do."[13] Why has there not been community outrage and a "Megan's Law" about this absurd flaw in the law?

Aside from the epistemological problem of correctly identifying recidivists, some dangerous sex offenders escape notification because they have not been convicted of a crime. Some just were never caught, but there are other ways to escape notification. For example, the suspect arrested in the Polly Klaas kidnapping case, Richard Allen Davis, had spent more than fifteen years in prison since 1973 for sex convictions, but because he had avoided sex offense charges through plea bargains, he was exempt from registration and notification.[14]

Megan's Law fails to protect children from the most common kind of sexual abuse, that inflicted by friends and relatives.

A third reason why Megan's Law will not protect children is that notifying community members of the presence of convicted sex offenders will not prevent offenders from reoffending. "Released sex offenders . . . who experience a compulsion to offend, will find a victim regardless of whether the victim resides in a notified or unnotified community."[15] In some jurisdictions, neighbors within a three-block radius must be notified of the presence of a paroled sex offender.[16] What's to stop an energetic pedophile from walking four or five blocks to find a victim? One demonstrated effect of community notification laws is that sex offenders tend to flee the notified community.[17] Thus, even if notification provides some measure of protection to one community, it may be at the expense of another. Offenders are likely to relocate in areas that either do not have notification laws or that do not enforce them. "In particular, sex offenders find large cities and inner city areas attractive because law enforcement agencies in these areas usually lack the time and resources to enforce community notification laws."[18] Community notification simply transfers the problem of dangerous sex offenders from middle- and upper-class communities to poor inner-city neighborhoods.

Fourth, the success of Megan's Law depends on the cooperation of convicted sex offenders. Although they are required by law to register with the police, not all do.[19] Some register under a phony address. Many move frequently. Police lack the resources to track down those who fail to comply, in part because New Jersey legislators passed Megan's Law without appropriating any funds for its enforcement.[20] The inevitable conclusion is that the legislators were not really serious about protecting children, but did what was likely to be politically popular.[21]

However, even if there is little reason to think that Megan's Law will protect children, is there any harm from such laws, which are, after all, wanted by many voters? Quite aside from the problem of promoting false security, the greatest harm posed by notification laws is vigilantism. In Washington, notification laws have prompted several incidents of vigilantism. The family home of Joseph Gallardo, a convicted child rapist, was burned down by angry neighbors who had heard he was about to be released from prison. Not only the convicted offenders, but their relatives have been subjected to death threats, eggs thrown at their homes, and eviction.[22] Worse, in Warren County, New Jersey, a father and son broke into a house, looking for a convicted child molester whose address was made public, and beat an innocent man who happened to be staying there.[23] Thus, Megan's Law is not harmless pandering to voter preference, but is itself a threat to innocent people and a law-abiding society.

Some commentators oppose notification because it does not address the root problems of child abuse. One writes:

> [N]otifying community members of released sex offenders neither confronts the causes of child sexual abuse nor looks to help offenders control their deviant behavior. Thus, Megan's Law represents a short-term solution that will not deter convicted sex offenders from reoffending.[24]

But can sex offenders be taught to control their behavior? This is extremely controversial. A 1989 article in the journal *Psychological Bulletin,* reviewing studies of treatment for sex offenders before 1985, concluded that there was no successful treatment. Andrew Vachss, a lawyer who represents children, characterizes sexual predators as crafty sociopaths who "laugh behind their masks at our attempts to understand and rehabilitate them." He calls rehabilitation for chronic sexual predators "a joke":

> A 1992 study of 767 rapists and child molesters in Minnesota found those who completed psychiatric treatment were arrested more often for new sex crimes than those who had not been treated at all. A Canadian survey that tracked released child molesters for 20 years revealed a 43 percent recidivism rate regardless of the therapy.[25]

However, a new generation of more sophisticated therapies is challenging the conventional wisdom that sex offenders cannot be rehabilitated. "The new view is that, as with alcoholism, there is no complete 'cure' for sex offenders, but that with help they can manage their sexual impulses without committing new crimes."[26] The new treatment, called "relapse prevention," focuses on helping sex offenders control the cycle of troubling emotions, distorted thinking, and deviant sex fantasies that lead to their sex crimes, whether rape, child molesting, exhibitionism, or voyeurism. A first step is helping the men develop empathy for their victims by reading accounts and watching videotapes from the victims' perspective. Proponents claim that the recidivism rate of those who complete programs in relapse prevention is about half that of offenders who receive no treatment.[27]

A new generation of more sophisticated therapies is challenging the conventional wisdom that sex offenders cannot be rehabilitated.

There is probably truth in the claims of both sides. Therapy is probably helpful for some sex offenders, but unlikely to rehabilitate sexual sociopaths who are incapable of empathy.[28] Psychologists agree that sex offenders must be highly motivated for the therapy to work, and some offenders have no interest in changing their behavior.[29] In any event, relatively few convicted sex offenders (about twenty-five percent) receive any treatment at all. Consider what has occurred at Avenel, once a model treatment center. When it opened in 1976, it provided inmates with individual and small group therapy, sometimes on a daily basis, and was headed by a superintendent with an expertise in mental health. However, its budget was reduced, staff was cut, and quality of therapy declined, and the inmate population, designed to be 594, grew to 681. By 1989, Avenel had changed from a treatment center into a maximum-security prison.[30] "What passes for treatment is one and one-half hours of group therapy per week. There are no bilingual counselors and no one-to-one therapy."[31]

It is beyond the scope of this essay to attempt to determine whether it is worthwhile to put resources into treatment programs for sex offenders. The evidence of success in Vermont and California suggests that further research and experimentation should be tried. Nevertheless, it seems likely that some sex offenders—the hard-core, violent sexual predators—cannot be rehabilitated. They should get longer sentences and be released, if at all, only under strict supervision.

The remaining avenues for protecting children are supervision and education. Indeed, notification is supported by some partly because they think it will motivate parents to educate their children about sex crimes.[32] However, this is a weak argument for notification, in light of all its problems. Parents will be motivated to educate their children simply by understanding that this is the best way to protect them. But what should be the content of the education? I dissent from the view that we should be educating young children about sex crimes. It seems to me that this is more likely to frighten them than to protect them. Nor will pointing out individuals the children should avoid provide adequate protection. Mrs. Kanka said, "If I had known that three sex perverts were living across the street from me, Megan would be alive today." Perhaps so, but notification would not prevent another Megan in another neighborhood from becoming a victim. Nor would notification protect Megan from a sex pervert who was not registered or who had escaped tier-three classification. A better way to protect children is by giving them sensible safety rules, for example, that they are not to go with strangers: not into their houses, in their cars, or into the woods. Parents should role-play various situations with children, such as, "What if a stranger says that I'm hurt, and I've asked him to come get you? Would you get into a car with him then?" or "What if he says he has candy or a toy or a puppy for you to play with? Would you go into his house then?" Parents can teach these safety rules to children in a non-frightening way, without scarring them with the details of rape and sexual mutilation. Such rules can protect children not only from tier-three offenders, but from those in tiers one and two as well as those who have not yet committed or been convicted of a sexual offense.

Children also need to be protected from the vastly more common form of sexual abuse, that committed by friends and relatives. Children must feel that they can tell their parents, or other trusted adults, about anything that is bothering them, that they will not be dismissed or ridiculed. It is often shame or the fear of being disbelieved that makes children reluctant to reveal sexual abuse. They need to know that they will not be blamed or punished if they tell, but will be protected.

Nevertheless, it seems likely that some sex offenders—the hard-core, violent sexual predators—cannot be rehabilitated.

Education is only part of the story. As parents, we are responsible for supervising our children. How closely a child needs to be supervised depends on several factors, such as the child's age and maturity, and the kind of community in which one lives. Parents in New York City cannot safely let six-year-olds out of their sight; parents in suburbs and small towns can let children play by themselves with only periodic checks so long as they do not leave the yard or block. There are no hard and fast rules, and it is often a matter of judgment as to what is safe.

The difficulty that parents face is to strike a balance between teaching our children to be prudent and cautious while not making them excessively dependent or timid. After all, neighborliness is also an important virtue we want our children to learn. My children are in and out of the houses of their playmates on our street; their friends frequently visit in our house. We permit this even though it is possible that, unbeknownst to us, their friends' parents are sexual predators. That risk is too minute to worry about, any more than I would keep my children indoors to protect them from lightning (though I would call them inside if there was a thunder storm in the area) or refuse to let them ride bicycles (though they must wear helmets). Instead, we tell them that we need to know where they are, and so they must tell us before they go to play with their friends.

It may be that Megan thought of Jesse Timmendequas as a friend. Apparently, he was considered a gentle man, and the neighborhood children often played with his puppy. We do not know if Megan asked permission from her parents before going inside Timmendequas's house, but probably it never occurred to her to do so. It may not have occurred to her parents to teach her to do so. Unfortunately, in today's world, parents must be a little more suspicious than was necessary in the past. We need to have our antennae up. A childless adult who makes friends with children may be perfectly harmless, but it does not hurt to tell children that they are not allowed to go inside a grown-up's house without first getting permission. Had Megan been taught this rule, she would probably be alive today.

Supporters of community notification ask, "But wouldn't you want to know if there was a dangerous sex offender in your neighborhood?" This is not the right basis for making law or policy. Some people would want to know the HIV-status of their doctor or dentist even though the risk to patients from HIV-infected doctors is miniscule and the dangers of such notification very great indeed. We should not ask, then, what people are likely to want to know, but rather, what are the effects of community notification? If, as I have argued, it does not increase safety but rather promotes a false sense of security and furthermore is likely to lead to vigilantism, then we need to find more effective, less dangerous ways of achieving the paramount goal of protecting children.

Notes

1. 1990 Wash. Laws ch. 3, §§ 101-1406 (codified as amended in scattered sections of Wash. Rev. Code).
2. Recent Legislation: Criminal Law—Sex Offender Notification Statute—Washington State Community Protection Act Serves as Model for Other Initiatives by Lawmakers and Communities, 108 *Harv. L. Rev.* 787 (1995) [hereinafter cited as Recent Legislation].
3. Registration is unlikely to lead to vigilantism, does not infringe offenders' privacy rights, and serves some useful purposes. It may help police to catch offenders when they strike again. The knowledge that their names are on a list of possible suspects at the police department may also serve as a deterrent for some offenders. Jerusalem, *Note:* A Framework for Post-Sentence Sex Offender Legislation: Perspectives on Prevention, Registration, and the Public's "Right" to Know, 48 *Vand. L. Rev.* 219, 238.
4. Hanley, New Jersey Supreme Court Hears Bitter Legal Argument Over "Megan's Law," *N.Y. Times,* May 3, 1995, B5.
5. Montana, *Note:* An Ineffective Weapon in the Fight Against Child Sexual Abuse: New Jersey's Megan's Law, 3 *J.L. & Pol'y* 569, 581 (1995).
6. *Id.,* at 591.
7. As explicated in the New Jersey Attorney General's Guidelines for Law Enforcement for Notification to Local Officials and/or

the Community of the Entry of a Sex Offender into the Community, p. 9.

8. Quindlen, So What If Law Isn't Fair to Sex Offenders? Children Come First, *Chicago Tribune,* Aug. 8, 1994, Perspective at 13.
9. "Studies show that sexually abused children often suffer greater negative psychological impact due to their parents' reaction to the crime, rather than from the crime itself." Montana, *supra* note 5, at 591.
10. Fields, We Should Lock Them Up for Life: "Megan's Law" doesn't really protect society from sexual predators. *Atlanta J. & Constitution,* Mar. 6, 1995, A8.
11. Montana, *supra* note 5, at 587.
12. Suspect Feared He Needed More Therapy, Report Says, *Record,* Aug. 6, 1994, at A7.
13. *Id.*
14. Jerusalem, *supra* note 3, at 221, n8.
15. Montana, *supra* note 5, at 591.
16. In Louisiana, paroled sex offenders whose victims were under eighteen years of age at the time of the offense "are required to notify all people within a one mile radius in a rural area and a three block area in an urban area that he is moving into the neighborhood. On a postcard, parolees must provide their name, address, and the crime of which they were convicted. The cards must then be mailed, at the parolees' own expense, to future neighbors." Jerusalem, *supra* note 3, at 241.
17. Studies show that nearly fifty percent of the sex offenders subjected to notification laws in Washington relocate to less intrusive states. Community notification laws create "a wandering nomadic tribe of sex offenders who go from town to town seeking anonymity to avoid negative repercussions when people find out they're in the community." Aun, Paroled Sex Offender an "Unwelcome" Sight, *Star Ledger,* Sept. 16, 1994, at 1, cited in Montana, *supra* note 5, at 578.
18. Montana, *supra* note 5, at 580.
19. Nearly twenty percent of Washington's convicted sex offenders have not registered. Almost seventy-five percent of the sex offenders in California have failed to register. Montana, *supra* note 5, at 588.
20. Sullivan, Whitman Approves Stringent Restrictions on Sex Criminals, *N.Y. Times,* Nov. 1, 1994, at B6, cited in Montana, *supra* note 5, at 581.
21. Megan's Law was not a carefully considered piece of legislation. The Assembly passed a community notification law within a month of Megan's death. No committee hearings were held, contrary to custom, because Assembly Speaker Chuck Haytaian called for an expedited process to deal with the emergency situation presented by sex offenders. The New Jersey Chapter of the American Civil Liberties Union criticized the Assembly for not consulting experts. The Senate did hold hearings, but it was evident that it would pass a community notification law with only token debate. Montana, *supra* note 5, at 584, n80.
22. Montana, *supra* note 5, at 577. In Passaic, Guardian Angels members demonstrated outside the home of a convicted rapist's mother even though her son was thousands of miles away. DeMarco, Flaws Surface in Megan's Law; Innocent Suffer, Urge Fine-Tuning, *Record,* Jan. 12, 1995, A1.
23. DeMarco, Innocent Man Beaten, Mistaken for Sex Offender, *Record,* Jan. 11, 1995, A1.
24. Montana, *supra* note 5, at 574.
25. Vachss, Sex Predators Can't Be Saved, *N.Y. Times,* Jan. 5, 1993, A15.
26. Goleman, Therapies Offer Hope for Sex Offenders, *N.Y. Times,* April 14, 1992, C1.
27. *Id.*
28. "The most successful candidates for treatment are men who have no other criminal record, have an established network of family and friends, hold a job and who are not so preoccupied by their sex fantasies that they think of them hours a day," says Dr. William Pithers, a psychologist who directs a sex offender program in Vermont. *Id.*
29. Vachss quotes Westley Dodd, who tortured and murdered three boys, as saying, "If I do escape, I promise you I will kill and rape again, and I will enjoy every minute of it." Vachss, *supra* note 25.
30. Glovin, Rapist's Care Under Fire; Once a Model, Avenel's Now a Muddle, *Record,* Dec. 22, 1992, A1.
31. Martone, Issue of Sex Offender Registration and Notification 2 (1994), cited in Montana, *supra* note 5, at 597.
32. Recent Legislation, *supra* note 2, at 790.

FRAME the DEBATE

Form at end of book

WiseGuide Wrap-Up

Most people believe in a proactive approach to dealing with sexual predators. However, as Steinbock points out, offenders who sexually violate children usually either live with the victim or are close friends or relatives. If "strangers" are not the primary sexual perpetrators, then public notification of sex offenders may prove ineffective in deterring these crimes. Parenting classes, victim awareness training, and other programs may offer better solutions, while protecting the rights of offenders.

R.E.A.L. Sites

This list provides a print preview of typical **Coursewise** R.E.A.L. sites. (There are over 100 such sites at the **Courselinks**™ site.) The danger in printing URLs is that web sites can change overnight. As we went to press, these sites were functional using the URLs provided. If you come across one that isn't, please let us know via email to: webmaster@coursewise.com. Use your Passport to access the most current list of R.E.A.L. sites at the **Courselinks** site.

Site name: United States Sentencing Commission
URL: http://www.ussc.gov/
Why is it R.E.A.L.? The U.S. Sentencing Commission posts a wealth of information at this site, including data on sentencing, as well as guidelines and procedures for imposing punishment.
Key topics: courts, sentencing
Try this: View the federal sentencing guidelines and policy statements.

Site name: The Legacy of Community Policing
URL: http://www.acsp.uic.edu/~ipsp/legacy/
Why is it R.E.A.L.? The Legacy of Community Policing explores the history, theories, operational challenges, and early evaluations of community policing in the United States.
Key topic: community policing
Try this: View lectures by some of the leading experts in community policing.

Site name: National Center for Victims of Crime
URL: http://www.ncvc.org/
Why is it R.E.A.L.? This is an extensive online resource for victim information and advocacy. The site has many links and much information about the organization's advocacy efforts.
Key topics: victims, crime
Try this: Examine some of the legislation that has been proposed to respond to criminal victimization.

Site name: National Center on Institutions and Alternatives
URL: http://www.ncianet.org/ncia/
Why is it R.E.A.L.? The National Center on Institutions and Alternatives has offered the criminal justice community guidance in the areas of innovative programs and services, research and information, and technical assistance.
Key topics: crime, criminal justice
Try this: Try the criminal justice test offered at this site.

Index

Note: Names and page numbers in **bold** type indicate authors and their articles; page numbers followed by *t* indicate tables; page numbers followed by *n* indicate notes.

D

E

T

U

V

W

Y

Z

Frame the Debate

Review Form

Name ______________________________ **Date** ______________

Issue ____

1. Prior to reading about and discussing this issue, my personal beliefs were:

____

____

____

____

2. Describe the credentials and/or credibility of experts cited in each of the readings for this issue.

____

____

____

____

3. Summarize the main idea presented in each of the readings for this issue.

____

____

____

____

4. Summarize the facts that support each main idea.

____

____

____

____

5. Identify any opinions expressed.

6. List any examples of bias or faulty reasoning.

7. How does this issue correlate with material presented in class and/or in your textbook?

8. Based on further consideration of this issue, my personal beliefs are now/still:

COPY ME! Copy this form as needed. This form is also available at http://www.coursewise.com
Click on STAND!